Instructor: Dave Dickey.
dickey@stat.ncsu.edu

MW01712079

Mixed Models Analyses Using the SAS® System

Course Notes

Evan
Apr. 28, 2008.

Mixed Models Analyses Using the SAS® System Course Notes was developed by Jill Tao. Additional contributions were made by John Amrhein, David Dickey, Ramon Littell, Bob Lucas, Mike Patetta, Catherine Truxillo, and Russ Wolfinger. Editing and production support was provided by the Curriculum Development and Support Department.

Mixed Models Analyses Using the SAS® System Course Notes

Book code E70292, course code AGLM, prepared date 09Nov06 AGLM_002

ISBN 978-1-59994-341-1

Table of Contents

Course Description

This course is designed for data analysts, experimental designers, and researchers with sound statistical knowledge who want to learn how to analyze linear and nonlinear mixed models using the MIXED and NLMIXED procedures, respectively. Applications in several areas are presented, such as the semiconductor, agricultural, pharmaceutical, educational, and environmental industries.

This course teaches you how to use the MIXED procedure to build a linear mixed model, accounting for different variance-covariance structures. Applications of mixed models in some basic designed experiments are discussed, including randomized complete block designs, two-way mixed models, nested mixed models, split-plot designs, and crossover designs. Hierarchical linear modeling, random coefficient regression, analysis of covariance, and repeated measures data analysis are also discussed. The concept of best linear unbiased predictor (BLUP) is introduced. Issues associated with unbalanced data, zero variance parameter estimates, and nonconvergence are addressed. In addition, the course teaches you how to use the NLMIXED procedure to analyze generalized linear mixed models.

To learn more…

sas Education

A full curriculum of general and statistical instructor-based training is available at any of the Institute's training facilities. Institute instructors can also provide on-site training.

For information on other courses in the curriculum, contact the SAS Education Division at 1-919-531-7321, or send e-mail to training@sas.com. You can also find this information on the Web at www.sas.com/training/ as well as in the Training Course Catalog.

sas Publishing

For a list of other SAS books that relate to the topics covered in this Course Notes, USA customers can contact our SAS Publishing Department at 1-800-727-3228 or send e-mail to sasbook@sas.com. Customers outside the USA, please contact your local SAS office.

Also, see the Publications Catalog on the Web at www.sas.com/pubs for a complete list of books and a convenient order form.

Prerequisites

Before attending this course, you should

- know how to create and manage SAS data sets
- have experience performing analysis of variance using the GLM procedure of SAS/STAT software
- have completed and mastered the material covered in the Statistics II: ANOVA and Regression course or completed a graduate-level course on general linear models.

Exposure to matrix algebra will enhance your understanding of the material. Some experience manipulating SAS data sets and producing graphs using SAS/GRAPH software is also recommended.

Chapter 1 Introduction to Mixed Models

1.1 Defining Mixed Models

Objectives

- Define fixed and random effects.
- Define and explain a mixed model.

3

Where Does Data Come From?

- Designed experiments
- Sample surveys
- Observational studies

6

Almost any data set is produced by one of these three sources. In designed experiments, some form of treatment is applied to experimental units and responses are observed. In sample surveys, data is collected on units according to a plan, called a *survey design*, but treatments are not applied to units. The units, typically people, already possess certain attributes such as age and gender. A value, such as annual income, is determined for each unit. In observational studies, data is collected on units that are available, rather than on units chosen according to a plan. For example, in a study to evaluate first-graders' reading skills, you collect data from several schools in a school district, including the students' ages, genders, attending schools, teachers, and the scores on some reading skill tests.

This course is concerned primarily with data from designed experiments, although the concepts can be easily extended to sample surveys and observational studies.

Fixed Effects

- All levels of interest are selected by a nonrandom process and are included in the study.
- Inferences are to be made only to those levels included in the study.

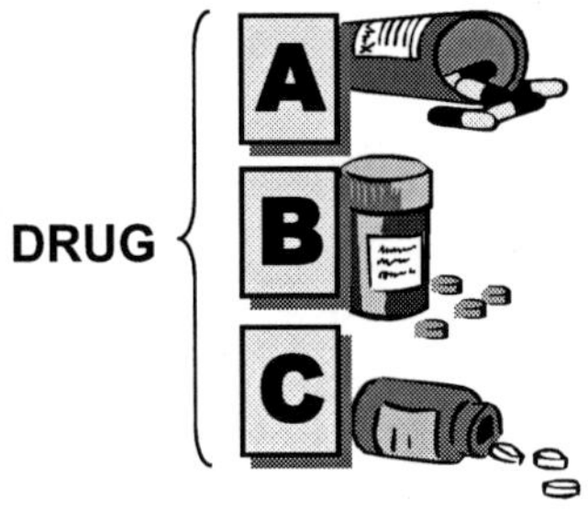

7

Fixed effects are those factors whose levels are selected by a nonrandom process or whose levels consist of the entire population of possible levels. All levels of interest are in your data set. The researcher is interested in comparing the effects of the factors on the response variable only for those levels included in the study.

For example, in a drug study, the researcher wants to compare the effect of three drugs (A, B, and C). She is only interested in the comparison of these three drugs, and she knows what they are before conducting the experiment. The variable **`drug`** is a fixed effect.

A model containing only fixed effects is called a *fixed effects model.*

Random Effects

- Levels consist of a random sample of levels from a population of possible levels.
- Inference is about the population of levels, not just the subset of levels included in the study.

CLINICS

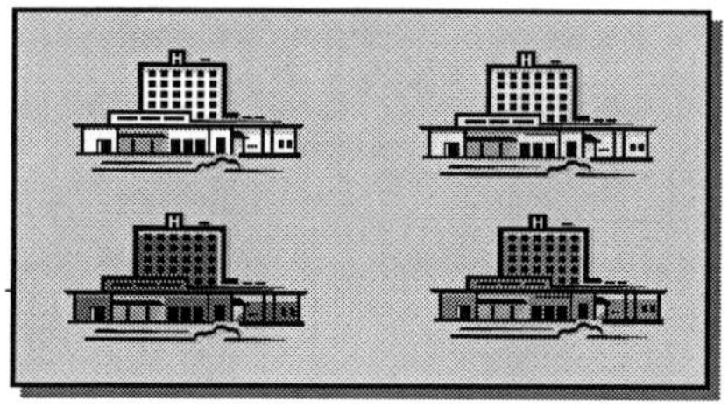

8

In some situations, a factor may have a large number of levels and the researcher/data analyst selects a subset of the levels to be included in the study. The inference from the data analysis is about the population of levels and not only the subset of levels included in the study. Effects like these are *random effects*. For example, in the same drug study, if four clinics are randomly selected from a population of clinics in a region and the researcher wants to make inference for the drug effects across the population of clinics, not only the ones included in the study, then `clinic` is a random effect.

Models in which all effects are random are called *random effects models*. Variances associated with random effects are known as *variance components*.

When deciding whether effects are fixed or random, you should ask yourself whether inferences are going to be drawn for only the levels of factors included in the experiment or across the population of possible levels.

Mixed Models

Models in which some factors are fixed effects and other factors are random effects are called *mixed models*.

CLINIC – random

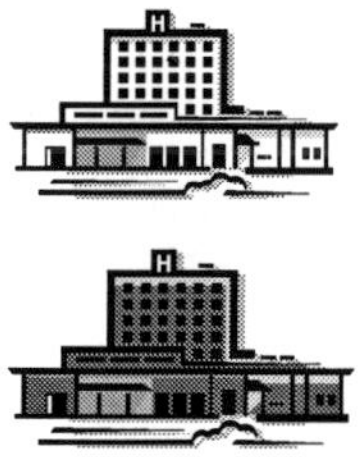

DRUG – fixed

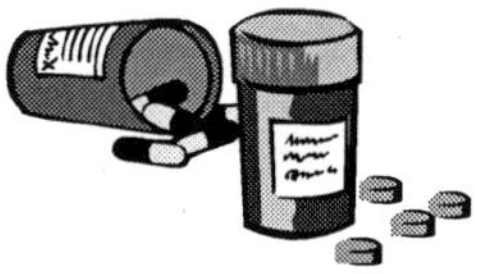

9

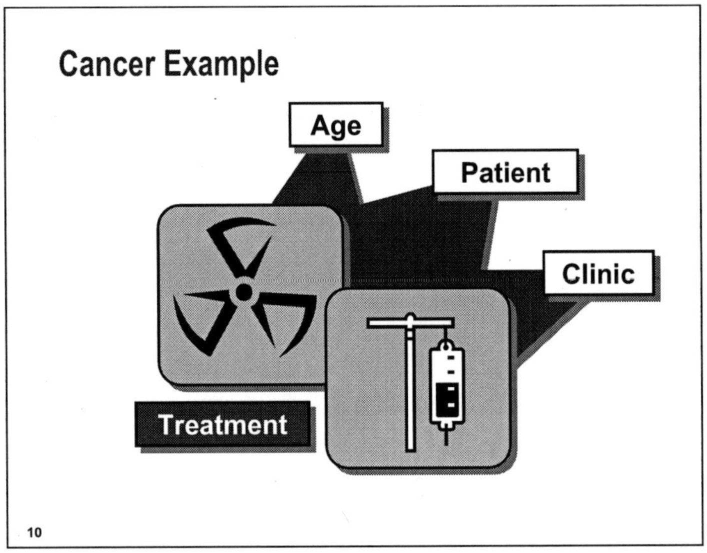

A physician studies the effect of a chemotherapy treatment and a radiotherapy treatment on a certain form of cancer. The physician also wants to determine which treatment is more effective with children. Ten adults and ten children are selected from each of five cancer treatment clinics. The reduction in the size of the tumor is measured after a two-month treatment period.

The experiment consists of the following effects:

`treatment` is a **fixed** effect (`chemotherapy` and `radiotherapy`) because the physician wants to compare only these two treatments and does not attempt to draw inference beyond these two treatments.

`age` is a **fixed** effect (`child` and `adult`).

`clinic` might be a **fixed** or a **random** effect depending on the physician's interest. If the physician is only interested in the variability associated with these five clinics, then **`clinic`** is a **fixed** effect. However, if these clinics were randomly selected from the population of clinics, and the physician wants to make inference about the population variation of clinics, then **`clinic`** is a **random** effect.

`patient` is a **random** effect because patients are a sample from a population of patients with this form of cancer.

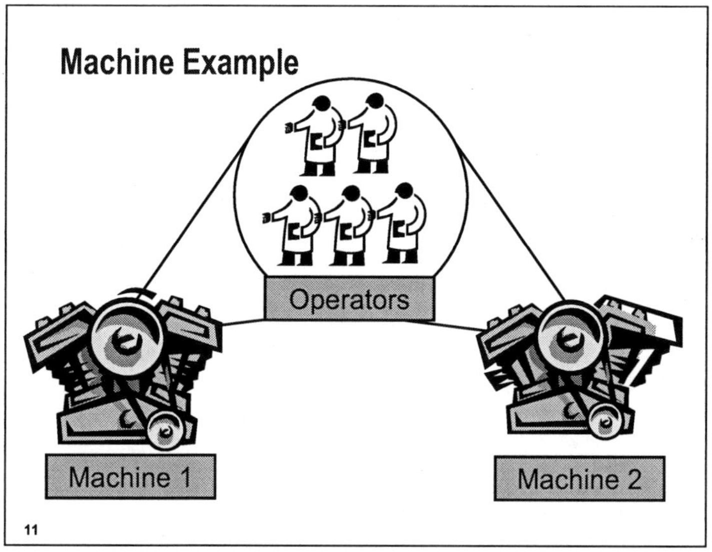

The manager of an automotive plant must replace the machines producing a certain component used in automatic transmissions. Two different machines are available. The manager wants to evaluate the productivity of the machines when operated by the plant's employees. Five employees are randomly selected from the work force to operate each machine at three time periods.

This *two-way mixed* model consists of the following effects:

`machine`	is a **fixed** effect because the manager only considers these two machines.
`operator`	is a **fixed** or **random** effect. If only these five employees operate the machine, then `operator` is a **fixed** effect. However, if these five operators are a random sample of all possible operators, then `operator` is a **random** effect.
`machine*operator`	is a **fixed** effect when `operator` is fixed and a **random** effect when `operator` is random.

This is a two-way mixed model (if `operator` is random) because each selected employee's productivity is evaluated on each machine.

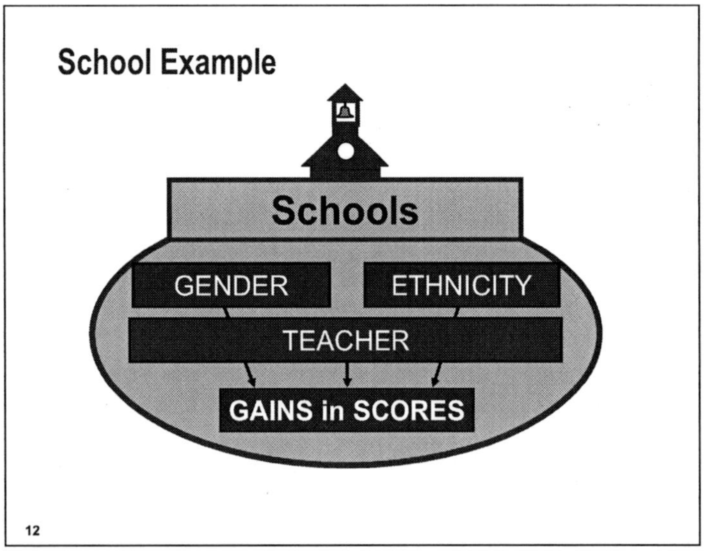

Gains in scores on a standardized test were recorded for 1,515 fourth-grade students in all schools in a district. Gain is defined as the score at the end of the year minus the score at the beginning of the year. The students' genders and ethnicities, as well as the identification numbers of the students' teachers, were also recorded. The primary objective was to evaluate and compare the schools in the gain scores. A secondary objective was to assess the effects of gender and ethnicity. This is a data set from an observational study.

The data consists of the following effects:

`school` is a **fixed** effect because only the schools included in the study are of interest

`ethnicity` is a **fixed** effect

`gender` is a **fixed** effect

`teacher` is a **random** effect because the teachers represent a sample of the population of teachers who could teach at the schools.

1.2 A Randomized Complete Block (RCB) Design

Objectives

- Define blocking effects.
- Define a randomized complete block design.

16

Blocks

- *Blocks* are groups of experimental units that are formed so that units within blocks are as homogeneous as possible.
- Common blocking factors may include land, people, batch of materials, machines, and centers.
- Blocks are almost always *random effects* in mixed model designs.

17

Blocks are designed so that an experimenter can isolate variability due to extraneous causes. These extraneous causes, or nuisance factors, may be characteristics associated with the experimental units or with the experimental setting. *Blocking* is a statistical technique designed to identify and control variation among groups of experimental units. A *blocking factor* is often referred to as a nuisance factor because it is a source of variability but usually not of research interests.

Some common blocking factors are units of test equipment or machinery, batches of raw material, people, and time.

Randomized Complete Block Design

- You randomly assign treatments to experimental units within the blocks rather than across the entire study.
- Blocking puts a restriction on randomization.

18

For example, in order to study the amount of tread wear of four brands of tires, you must mount these tires onto cars. The variable **car** can be used as a blocking factor because there will be variation from car to car where these tires can be used. You can randomly assign the four brands of tires to the four wheels on each car, rather than randomly assigning all the tires to all the wheels across all cars included in the study. This randomized complete block design usually results in more accurate results than the completely randomized design.

An even more accurate design would block on positions of the wheels as well.

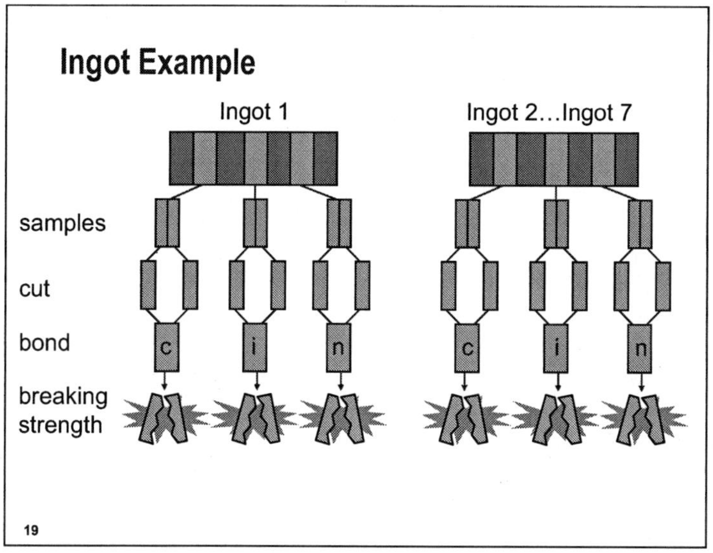

An engineer wants to test the strength of three metals used as bonding agents. Seven ingots made of a composition material are randomly selected from a population of ingots and are used for this strength test. A sample of material is taken from each ingot, and a bond is formed using one of the metals. The amount of pressure required to break the bond is then recorded. Data is stored in the SAS data set `sasuser.ingot`.

This *randomized complete block (RCB)* design consists of the following effects:

`metal` a treatment effect. This is a **fixed** effect because only three metals (copper, iron, and nickel) are used in the study, and the engineer is only interested in making inference about these three metals.

`ingots` a blocking effect. This is a **random** effect because the seven ingots are randomly selected from a population of ingots, and the inference about the treatment means is made over the entire population of ingots.

The treatments are assumed not to interact with the blocking variable.

The purpose of such an experiment is to

- estimate and compare the treatment means over the entire population of blocks
- account for the variability in the response variable due to thc blocks.

The Data

Obs	ingot	metal	pressure
1	1	nickel	67.0
2	1	iron	71.9
3	1	copper	72.2
4	2	nickel	67.5
5	2	iron	68.8
6	2	copper	66.4
7	3	nickel	76.0
8	3	iron	82.6
9	3	copper	74.5
10	4	nickel	72.7
11	4	iron	78.1
12	4	copper	67.3
13	5	nickel	73.1
14	5	iron	74.2
15	5	copper	73.2
16	6	nickel	65.8
17	6	iron	70.8
18	6	copper	68.7
19	7	nickel	75.6
20	7	iron	84.9
21	7	copper	69.0

20

Randomized Complete Block Design Model

`metal` (treatment) effects, fixed

`ingot` (block) effects, random

$$y_{ij} = \mu + \alpha_i + b_j + \varepsilon_{ij}$$

random error

$$b_j \sim N(0, \sigma_b^2)$$

$$\varepsilon_{ij} \sim N(0, \sigma^2)$$

22

y_{ij} breaking strength for the ith metal and j^{th} ingot, $i=1,...,t$ (treatments), and $j=1,...,r$ (blocks).

μ overall mean.

α_i fixed effect associated with the ith metal (treatment).

b_j random effect associated with the jth ingot (block), $b_j \sim$ i.i.d. N(0, σ_b^2). These random effects b_j's are assumed to be independently and normally distributed with mean zero and variance σ_b^2. The variance σ_b^2 is the parameter to be estimated in the mixed model for this effect.

ε_{ij} experimental error associated with samples within blocks, $\varepsilon_{ij} \sim$ i.i.d. N(0, σ^2). The random errors are assumed to follow a normal distribution with mean zero and variance σ^2. The variance σ^2 is the parameter to be estimated in the mixed model for random error.

The effects b_j and ε_{ij} are assumed to be independent random variables. Therefore,

- $E(y_{ij}) = \mu + \alpha_i$ is the mean pressure for **`metal`** i averaged across all ingots in the population.
- $var(y_{ij}) = \sigma^2 + \sigma_b^2$. The variance of an observation is the sum of the variances due to blocks (often referred to as between-block variation) and random errors (within-block variation).

This course uses Greek letters to denote fixed effects and Roman letters to denote random effects.

Hypotheses in a Mixed Model

For fixed effects: $\mathbf{H_0}$: $\alpha_i = 0$

For random effects: $\mathbf{H_0}$: $\sigma_b^2 = 0$

23

In mixed model analysis, the hypotheses about the fixed effects remain the same as those in the fixed-effects model: whether there are significant treatment effects. The hypotheses about the random effects are whether the variance components associated with the random effects equal zero. In other words, whether there are significant variations due to these random variables. Often, inferences about random effects are of little interest. The primary role of random effects is to model sources of variation so that the fixed effects can be more accurately estimated and tested.

1.3 Using the MIXED Procedure

Objectives

- Describe the estimation methods provided by PROC MIXED.
- Analyze the randomized complete block design using PROC MIXED.
- Compare PROC MIXED and PROC GLM.
- Write a CONTRAST and an ESTIMATE statement in PROC MIXED.

27

The MIXED Procedure

General form of the MIXED procedure:

PROC MIXED *options;*
  CLASS *variables;*
  MODEL *dependent=fixed-effects / options;*
  RANDOM *random-effects / options;*
  CONTRAST *'label' fixed-effect values |*
    random-effect values / options;
  ESTIMATE *'label' fixed-effect values |*
    random-effect values / options;
  LSMEANS *fixed-effects / options;*
RUN;

28

Selected MIXED procedure statements:

CLASS	names the classification variables to be used in the analysis. If the CLASS statement is used, it must appear before the MODEL statement. Classification variables can be either character or numeric.
MODEL	is a required statement that names a single dependent variable and the fixed effects. Unlike the GLM procedure, you do not specify random effects in the MODEL statement.
RANDOM	defines the random effects. The random effects can be classification or continuous, and multiple RANDOM statements are possible.
CONTRAST	tests specified hypotheses concerning fixed and/or random effects. It is patterned after the CONTRAST statement in the GLM procedure, although it has been extended to include random effects. This enables you to select an appropriate inference space.
ESTIMATE	estimates linear combinations of fixed or random effects.
LSMEANS	computes the least-squares means (LS-means) of the fixed effects. As in the GLM procedure, LS-means are *predicted population margins*; that is, they estimate the marginal means that would have been obtained over a balanced population.

Estimation Methods

The MIXED procedure provides six estimation methods for covariance parameters (specified by METHOD= option):

- REML (default)
- ML
- MIVQUE0
- Type 1
- Type 2
- Type 3.

29

Brief descriptions of each estimation method are provided below:

Maximum likelihood (ML)	iteratively searches over the parameter space for parameter values that maximize a function of the parameters related to the chance of observing the data collected. The function being maximized is called the *likelihood function*.
Restricted/residual maximum likelihood (REML)	constructs the likelihood function in two parts (one involving the fixed effects, the other free of the fixed effects), and obtains maximum likelihood estimates of the variance components from the portion of the model that is free of fixed effects.
MIVQUE0	performs minimum variance quadratic unbiased estimation of the covariance parameters. It produces method-of-moments estimates that are invariant with respect to the fixed effects. That is, the mean squares associated with the random effects are adjusted for the fixed effects.
Type 1 Type 2 Type 3	applies only to variance component models with no SUBJECT= effects and no REPEATED statement, which is discussed later. An analysis of variance table is included in the output, and the expected mean squares are used to estimate the variance components. This is a method-of-moment estimate consistent with the GLM procedure.

Many studies show that the default estimation method of the covariance parameters, REML, has many advantages over other methods. This method is recommended and is used throughout this course. A detailed discussion about the estimation methods of the covariance parameters is provided in a later chapter.

Fitting a Mixed Model Using PROC MIXED

The data set **sasuser.ingot** contains the following variables:

metal the metals used as bonding agents

ingot the ingot number

pressure the pressure to break the sample material.

Before performing an analysis of variance, you should conduct an initial data exploration. This can be accomplished, in part, by looking at a scatter plot of the data.

```
goptions reset=all;
proc gplot data=sasuser.ingot;
   plot pressure*ingot=metal /
        vaxis=axis1 haxis=axis2 vminor=0 legend=legend1;
   axis1 label=(a=90);
   axis2 offset=(2,2) minor=none;
   legend1 frame ;
   symbol1 v=circle c=red i=join l=1;
   symbol2 v=star c=blue i=join l=3;
   symbol3 v=dot c=green i=join l=5;
   title 'Pressure vs Ingot Number';
run;
title;
quit;                                          *c01s3d1.sas;
```

F12: clear output; clear log; sub;

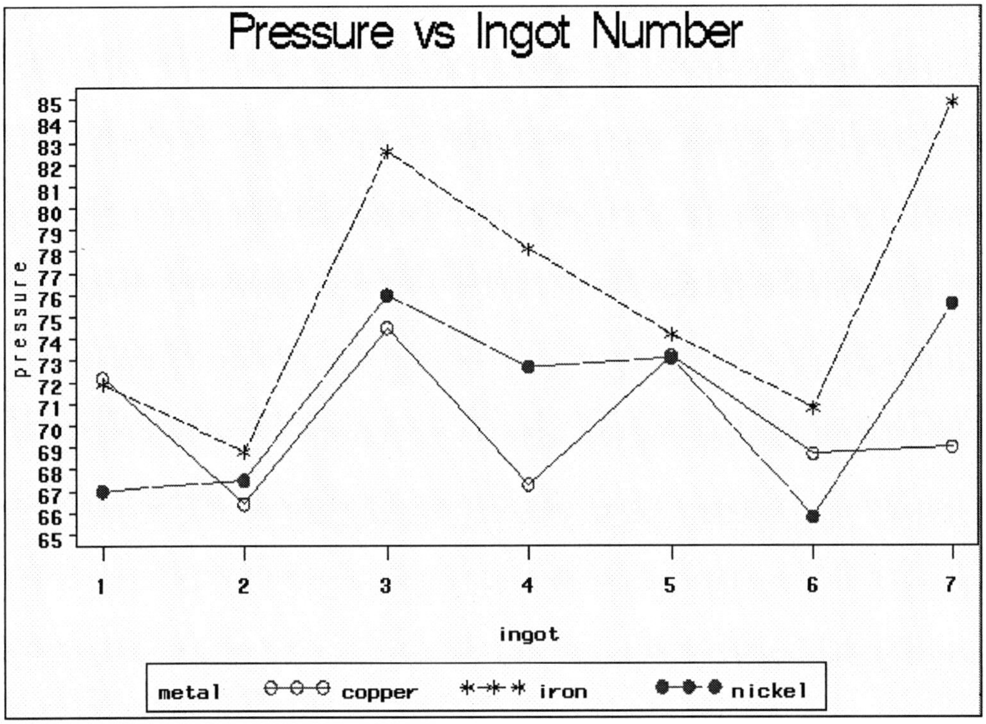

There is a substantial amount of variability among the seven blocks. Additionally, iron seems to be the strongest bonding agent in six of the seven ingots.

You can also examine the distribution of the data using a side-by-side box-and-whisker plot. For example, suppose you want to compare the pressure for the three metals. You can use the BOXPLOT procedure; however, you first must sort the data by the group variable (**metal**).

```
proc sort data=sasuser.ingot;
   by metal;
run;

goptions reset=all;
proc boxplot data=sasuser.ingot;
   plot pressure*metal / boxstyle=schematic;
run;                                             *c01s3d2.sas;
```

Selected PLOT statement option:

BOXSTYLE= specifies the style of the box-and-whisker plots displayed. If you specify BOXSTYLE=SKELETAL, the whiskers are drawn from the edges of the box to the extreme values of the group. This is the default setting. If you specify BOXSTYLE=SCHEMATIC, a whisker is drawn from the upper edge of the box to the largest value within 1.5 times the interquartile range and from the lower edge of the box to the smallest value within 1.5 times the interquartile range. Observations outside the whiskers are identified with a special symbol.

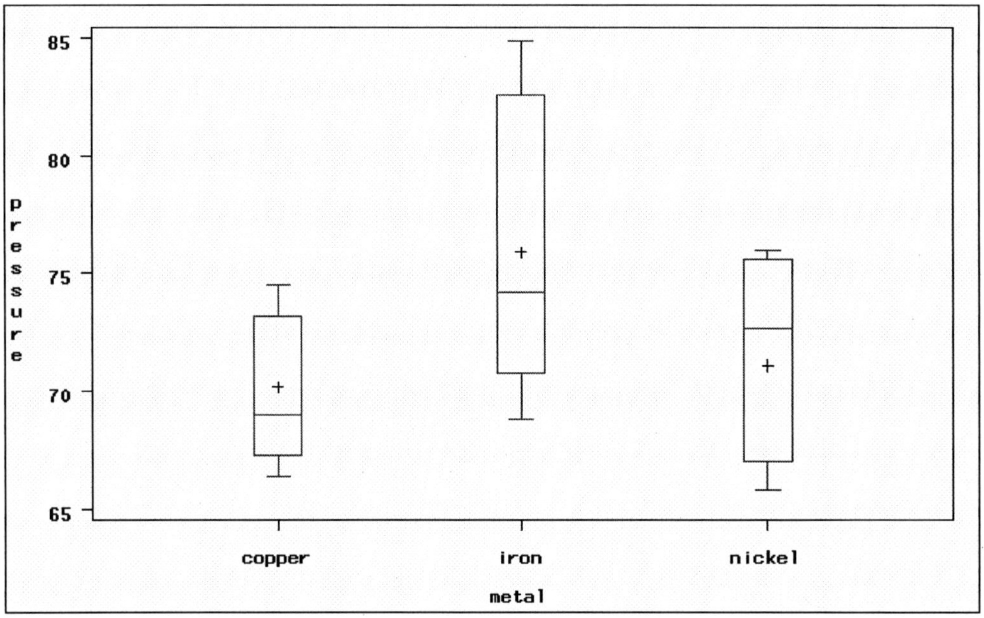

There appear to be some differences among the three treatment means. The mean for iron appears to be bigger than that for the other two metals. The variation for iron seems to be bigger as well. The variability in **pressure** for each metal is largely due to the block (**ingot**) variability.

Suppose you want to determine whether there is a significant difference in the mean breaking pressure of bonds made using the three metals. You can use the MIXED procedure to analyze the **sasuser.ingot** data, treating the block effect **ingot** as a random effect.

```
proc mixed data=sasuser.ingot covtest;
   class metal ingot;
   model pressure=metal / e3;
   random ingot;
run;                                         *c01s3d3.sas;
```

All classification variables (fixed and random effects) are listed in the CLASS statement, but only the fixed effect (for instance, **metal**) is listed in the MODEL statement. The random effect (for instance, **ingot**) is specified in the RANDOM statement.

Selected MODEL statement option:

E3 — requests that Type III **L** matrix coefficients be displayed for all specified effects. This helps you interpret the Type 3 test for the fixed effects.

Selected PROC MIXED statement option:

COVTEST — produces asymptotic standard errors and Wald *Z*-tests for the covariance parameter estimates. This test depends on large sample theory and is only asymptotically valid.

PROC MIXED Output

```
                         The Mixed Procedure

                          Model Information

     Data Set                     SASUSER.INGOT
     Dependent Variable           pressure
     Covariance Structure         Variance Components
     Estimation Method            REML
     Residual Variance Method     Profile
     Fixed Effects SE Method      Model-Based
     Degrees of Freedom Method    Containment
```

The Model Information table describes the model, some of the variables it involves, and the method used to fit it. The default covariance structure fitted by PROC MIXED is Variance Components (VC) (constant variances and zero covariance), also referred to as Independent covariance structure. Restricted/residual Maximum-Likelihood (REML) is the default variance component estimation method used by PROC MIXED.

There are four methods for handling the residual variance in the model. The *profile* method concentrates the residual variance out of the optimization problem, whereas the *fit* method retains it as a parameter in the optimization. The *factor* method keeps the residual fixed, and *none* is displayed when a residual variance is not a part of the model.

The row labeled Fixed Effects SE Method in this table describes the method used to compute the approximate standard errors for the fixed-effects parameter estimates and related functions of them. The default method is Model-Based, which can be changed to Empirical when the EMPIRICAL option in the PROC MIXED statement is used, or Prasad-Rao-Jeske-Kackar-Harville when DDFM=KR option is specified in the MODEL statement.

The row labeled Degrees of Freedom Method in this table lists the method used for estimating the denominator degrees of freedom for the fixed effect. Five possibilities for this row are Containment, Between-Within, Residual, Satterthwaite, and Kenward-Roger. Containment is the default method when the RANDOM statement is specified. You can use the DDFM= option in the MODEL statement to specify other methods.

```
                 Class Level Information

       Class    Levels    Values

       metal         3    copper iron nickel
       ingot         7    1 2 3 4 5 6 7
```

(order for contrast)

The Class Level Information table lists the levels of every variable specified in the CLASS statement. You should check this information to make sure the data is correct. You can adjust the order of the CLASS variable levels with the ORDER= option in the PROC MIXED statement.

Dimensions

Covariance Parameters	2
Columns in X	4
Columns in Z	7
Subjects	1
Max Obs Per Subject	21

The Dimensions table lists the sizes of relevant matrices. This table can be useful in determining CPU time and memory requirements.

Number of Observations

Number of Observations Read	21
Number of Observations Used	21
Number of Observations Not Used	0

The Number of Observations table shows the total number of observations in the data set and how many are used in fitting the model.

Iteration History

Iteration	Evaluations	-2 Res Log Like	Criterion
0	1	112.40987952	
1	1	107.79020201	0.00000000

Convergence criteria met.

The Iteration History table describes the optimization of the residual log likelihood function. The optimization is performed using a ridge-stabilized Newton-Raphson algorithm, and the rows of this table describe the iterations that this algorithm takes in order to minimize the objective function.

Covariance Parameter Estimates

Cov Parm	Estimate	Standard Error	Z Value	Pr Z
ingot	11.4478	8.7204	1.31	0.0946
Residual	10.3716	4.2342	2.45	0.0072

The variance component estimates are

$\hat{\sigma}_b^2 = 11.4478$ and $\hat{\sigma}^2 = 10.3716$.

The COVTEST option in the PROC MIXED statement produces the asymptotic standard errors and Wald *Z*-tests for the covariance parameter estimates. The standard errors are based on large sample theory and can be misleading for small samples. Other options and approaches of making inferences about the covariance parameter estimates are discussed later in the course.

Fit Statistics

-2 Res Log Likelihood	107.8
AIC (smaller is better)	111.8
AICC (smaller is better)	112.6
BIC (smaller is better)	111.7

The Fit Statistics table provides information for goodness of model fit. All three information criteria consider both the fitness of the model and the model complexity. The model with more parameters receives a larger penalty. Bayesian Information Criterion (BIC) tends to produce a larger penalty than both Akaike Information Criterion (AIC) and finite-sample corrected Akaike Information Criterion (AICC). The detailed formula for the computations of these information criteria can be found in the SAS online documentation. For all three information criteria, smaller values indicate a better model.

Type 3 Coefficients for metal

Effect	metal	Row1	Row2
Intercept			
metal	copper	1	
metal	iron		1
metal	nickel	-1	-1

The Type 3 Coefficients for **metal** prints the Type 3 **L** matrix that is used for the test for the **metal** effect. In this example, $\mathbf{L} = \begin{bmatrix} 0 & 1 & 0 & -1 \\ 0 & 0 & 1 & -1 \end{bmatrix}$.

Type 3 Tests of Fixed Effects

Effect	Num DF	Den DF	F Value	Pr > F
metal	2	12	6.36	0.0131

The Type 3 Tests of Fixed Effects table contains the F-test for **metal** (F=6.36), with a p-value of 0.0131. Therefore, you conclude that there is a difference between the mean breaking pressures for **metal** across all ingots at a 5% significance level.

PROC MIXED does not compute the sums of squares as PROC GLM does; therefore, you do not see Sums of Squares in the Test of Fixed Effects table. The F statistic for the fixed effect is computed as $F = \dfrac{\hat{\beta}'L'[L(X'\hat{V}^{-1}X)^{-}L']^{-}L\hat{\beta}}{rank(L)}$, where

$\hat{\beta}$ is the vector of the fixed-effect estimates

L is the coefficient matrix discussed earlier

X is the design matrix for the fixed effects

$\hat{\text{V}}$ is the estimated covariance matrix for an observation using REML method.

This statistic accounts for all variance components in the model as indicated by $\hat{V}$ in the equation.

Are You Familiar with the GLM Procedure?

- The GLM procedure is a fixed-effects procedure.
- PROC GLM is not recommended for mixed model analysis.

32

PROC MIXED versus PROC GLM

- They are very similar in syntax.
- PROC GLM uses the ordinary least squares (OLS) method to make inferences about fixed effects. Therefore, the inferences are based on a fixed-effects-only model, even when you specify a RANDOM statement.
- PROC MIXED uses the generalized least squares (GLS) method to make inferences about fixed effects. Therefore, the inferences directly incorporate the variance-covariance structure that you specify.
- PROC GLM computes analysis of variance to assess variations. PROC MIXED uses the maximum-likelihood approach to estimate the variance components. (REML is the default.)

33

The generalized least squares (GLS) method accounts for the variance-covariance structure modeled by the MIXED procedure. Theoretically, the GLS method is superior to the ordinary least squares (OLS) method for fixed effects inferences.

Although REML is the default method for estimating the variance parameters in PROC MIXED, you can use the method-of-moments techniques to estimate the variance components by specifying the METHOD= option in the PROC MIXED statement.

The GLM proc is a fixed-effects procedure, so you should use the MIXED procedure to analyze mi

CONTRAST and ESTIMATE Statements

H_0: $L'\beta = 0$

CONTRAST *'label' effect values / options;*
ESTIMATE *'label' effect values / options;*
} PROC GLM

H_0: $L'\phi = 0$

CONTRAST *'label' fixed-effect values |*
random-effect values / options;
ESTIMATE *'label' fixed-effect values |*
random-effect values / options;
} PROC MIXED

34

The CONTRAST and ESTIMATE statements in the MIXED procedure are patterned after the CONTRAST and ESTIMATE statements in the GLM procedure, although it has been extended to include random effects. In this section, you are only concerned with the fixed effects when writing a CONTRAST or ESTIMATE statement. In this case the two procedures have identical syntax.

CONTRAST enables you to perform custom hypothesis tests by specifying an **L** vector (for example, coefficients of metal effect α: (a_C, a_I, a_N)) for testing the hypothesis $\mathbf{L}'\beta = 0$ (for example, ($a_C\mu_C + a_I\mu_I + a_N\mu_N = 0$)). There is no limit to the number of CONTRAST statements you can specify, but they must appear after the MODEL statement.

ESTIMATE enables you to estimate linear functions of the parameters by multiplying the vector **L** by the parameter estimate vector **b** resulting in **L'b** (for example, $a_0\mu + a_C\alpha_C + a_I\alpha_I + a_N\alpha_N$). There is no limit to the number of ESTIMATE statements that you can specify, but they must appear after the MODEL statement.

In the CONTRAST and ESTIMATE statements,

label identifies the contrast (or estimate) on the output. A label is required for every contrast (or estimate) specified. Labels must be enclosed in quotes.

effect identifies an effect that appears in the MODEL statement, or the INTERCEPT effect. The INTERCEPT effect can be used when an intercept is fitted in the model. You do not need to include all effects that are in the MODEL statement.

values are constants that are elements of the **L** vector associated with the effect.

CONTRAST versus ESTIMATE Statements

- They are similar in syntax.
- For a single comparison, the ESTIMATE statement provides the estimate of the difference, as well as the significance of the difference; the CONTRAST statement only provides the significance of the difference.
- For two or more simultaneous comparisons, only the CONTRAST statement can be used.
- In some situations, the ESTIMATE statement requires the DIVISOR= option, whereas the CONTRAST statement does not.
- You can write CONTRAST and/or ESTIMATE statements to reproduce any hypothesis tests produced by default.

35

CONTRAST and ESTIMATE statements are similar in syntax, except that

- you can perform more-than-one-degree-of-freedom contrasts using the CONTRAST statement. Simply separate the different contrasts by commas (,). The ESTIMATE statement can only be used for one-degree-of-freedom contrasts. The ESTIMATE statement provides the estimate of the difference, as well as the significance test of the difference, whereas the CONTRAST statement only provides the significance test of the difference.
- the DIVISOR= option is provided in the ESTIMATE statement but not in the CONTRAST statement. This is because the CONTRAST statement is used for hypothesis testing. You can multiply the fractional coefficients by the common denominator without changing the test. The ESTIMATE statement is used for estimating the difference. When multiplying the fractional coefficients by the common denominator, you multiply the difference as well. The DIVISOR= option in the ESTIMATE statement divides the difference by the common denominator so that the quantity of the difference remains unchanged. It is useful when some of the coefficients are fractions.

Writing Contrasts

1. Write the general linear model for your design.
2. Write the hypothesis of interest in terms of cell means.
3. Rewrite the hypothesis as a linear combination of model parameters.
4. Compute the coefficients for the CONTRAST statement.
5. Translate the results into an appropriate CONTRAST statement.

37

The process may seem to be inefficient, especially for simple models. If you follow this process, you reduce the possibility of attempting to test a combination of parameters that is not estimable. The randomized complete block design has the model form of $y_{ij} = \mu + \alpha_i + b_j + \varepsilon_{ij}$, which implies $\mu_i = \mu + \alpha_i$. This information can be used to rewrite the hypotheses in terms of the model parameters.

The hypothesis must be simplified and rewritten with zero on one side of the equation. The terms must be written in the order in which they appear in the model, with the levels of each factor in the correct order as well. The CONTRAST or ESTIMATE statement can be included in your program.

Example of Writing a Contrast

Suppose you want to know whether there is a difference between the mean breaking pressure of copper and iron bonds. The hypothesis can be written as

$$H_0 : \mu_C = \mu_I$$

or

$$H_0 : \mu_C - \mu_I = 0$$

38

Although you may be able to use the LSMEANS statement to perform the same test using the unadjusted Type I error rate, for illustration purposes, the use of the CONTRAST statement is presented to explain how to write a CONTRAST statement to perform the test of your interest.

Rewrite the Hypothesis and Compute the Coefficients

$\mu_C - \mu_I = 0$

since $E(y_{ij}) = \mu + \alpha_i = \mu_i$, then

$(\mu+\alpha_C)-(\mu+\alpha_I)+0(\mu+\alpha_N)=0$, or

$\alpha_C - \alpha_I + 0\alpha_N = 0$

Therefore, the coefficients for the metal effect are (1 –1 0).

```
contrast 'copper vs iron' metal 1 -1 0;
```

42

The subscript I is used to indicate `iron` and the subscript i is used to indicate the general level of the **`metal`** effect.

Contrasts and Estimates

In addition to the hypothesis test discussed in this section, suppose you also want to know the magnitude of the difference between the mean breaking pressure of copper and iron bonds. You must write a similar ESTIMATE statement. Also, suppose you want to estimate the average breaking pressure for the nickel bond. You can follow the process discussed in this section to produce the following linear combination: $\mu_N = \mu + 0\alpha_C + 0\alpha_I + \alpha_N$.

```
proc mixed data=sasuser.ingot;              covtest method = type3 ;
   class ingot metal;
   model pressure=metal;
   random ingot;
   contrast 'copper vs iron' metal 1 -1 0;
   estimate 'copper vs iron' metal 1 -1 0;
   estimate 'nickel mean' intercept 1 metal 0 0 1;
   lsmeans metal / diff cl alpha=0.10;
run;                                              *c01s3d4.sas;
```

The contrast and estimates are specified in the CONTRAST and ESTIMATE statements. The default order of the coefficients corresponds to the alphabetical order of the levels. You can look in the Class Level Information table to obtain this order (for this example, copper, iron, and nickel). The LSMEANS statement is used to compute the least-squares means for the fixed effect (**`metal`**).

Selected LSMEANS statement options:

DIFF — requests that differences of the LS-means be displayed.

CL — requests that *t*-type confidence limits be constructed for each of the LS-means. The confidence level is 0.95 by default; this can be changed with the ALPHA= option.

ALPHA= — requests that a *t*-type confidence interval be constructed for each of the LS-means with confidence level 1-*number*. The value of *number* must be between 0 and 1; the default is 0.05.

CONTRAST and ESTIMATE Statements Output

Estimates

Label	Estimate	Standard Error	DF	t Value	Pr > |t|
copper vs iron	-5.7143	1.7214	12	-3.32	0.0061
nickel mean	71.1000	1.7655	12	40.27	<.0001

Contrasts

Label	Num DF	Den DF	F Value	Pr > F
copper vs iron	1	12	11.02	0.0061

The first ESTIMATE statement indicates that the mean of iron is 5.7143 (units) larger than the mean breaking pressure of copper, and this difference is significantly different from zero (*p*-value=0.0061). The second ESTIMATE statement estimates the mean breaking pressure of nickel is 71.1000 units, with a standard error of 1.7655. As noted later in this chapter, this estimate of the standard error of the nickel mean is the appropriate one, because it incorporates the variance component associated with the random effect **ingot**. Therefore, the associated *p*-value is valid for the test H_0: $\mu_N = 0$.

The *F* statistic for the contrast is 11.02 with (Pr > F) = 0.0061. Therefore, you detect a difference at a 5% significance level between the mean breaking pressures of copper and iron. This is identical to the first ESTIMATE statement result.

LSMEANS Statement Output

Least Squares Means

Effect	metal	Estimate	Standard Error	DF	t Value	Pr > |t|	Alpha
metal	copper	70.1857	1.7655	12	39.75	<.0001	0.1
metal	iron	75.9000	1.7655	12	42.99	<.0001	0.1
metal	nickel	71.1000	1.7655	12	40.27	<.0001	0.1

Least Squares Means

Effect	metal	Lower	Upper
metal	copper	67.0391	73.3324
metal	iron	72.7533	79.0467
metal	nickel	67.9533	74.2467

The estimates of the breaking pressure means for three metals and their 90% confidence intervals are produced by the LSMEANS statement. Notice that the results for the nickel mean are identical to those produced by the second ESTIMATE statement. The confidence intervals are appropriate because they used the correct standard error that accounts for the block variation.

Differences of Least Squares Means

Effect	metal	_metal	Estimate	Standard Error	DF	t Value	Pr > |t|	Alpha
metal	copper	iron	-5.7143	1.7214	12	-3.32	0.0061	0.1
metal	copper	nickel	-0.9143	1.7214	12	-0.53	0.6050	0.1
metal	iron	nickel	4.8000	1.7214	12	2.79	0.0164	0.1

Differences of Least Squares Means

Effect	metal	_metal	Lower	Upper
metal	copper	iron	-8.7824	-2.6462
metal	copper	nickel	-3.9824	2.1538
metal	iron	nickel	1.7319	7.8681

The comparisons among **`metal`** means are also produced by the LSMEANS statement with the DIFF option. Notice that the results for copper versus iron are identical to those produced by the first ESTIMATE statement.

1.4 Introduction to the Theory of General Linear Mixed Models

Objectives

- Understand the basic theory about general linear models and general linear mixed models.
- Use the GLMMOD procedure to obtain the design matrix.

50

The GLM Procedure Model

Design matrix

$$y = X\beta + \varepsilon$$

Random errors

Response

Fixed effects

Assume $E[\varepsilon] = 0, Var[\varepsilon] = \sigma^2 I_n$

Therefore, $E[y] = X\beta, Var[y] = \sigma^2 I_n$

51

y	is the vector of observed response data values.
$\mathbf{X}$	is the known design matrix based on the model specification.
β	is the vector of unknown fixed-effect parameters.
ε	is the vector of random errors.

Assume that ε is a vector of independent random variables that are independently and normally distributed with a mean of 0 and a variance of σ^2. Therefore, for the general linear model,

$E(\varepsilon) = 0$ and $Var(\varepsilon) = \sigma^2 I_n$, where I_n is a $n \times n$ identity matrix $\begin{bmatrix} 1 & & 0 \\ & 1 & \\ & & \ddots & \\ 0 & & & 1 \end{bmatrix}_{n \times n}$.

Then it follows that $E(y) = \mathbf{X}\beta$ and $Var(y) = \sigma^2 I_n$, where I_n is a n×n identity matrix.

PROC GLM always models all effects as fixed, even when the RANDOM statement is used. The RANDOM statement is used to produce expected mean squares.

The MIXED Procedure Model

Random effects

$$y = \mathbf{X}\beta + \mathbf{Z}\gamma + \varepsilon$$

Design matrix for random effects

No longer required to be independent and homogeneous

Assume $\gamma \sim N(0, \mathbf{G})$ and $\varepsilon \sim N(0, \mathbf{R})$

$\Rightarrow E(y) = \mathbf{X}\beta, \quad Var(y) = \mathbf{ZGZ'} + \mathbf{R} = \mathbf{V}$

52

constant

$Var(Z\gamma + \varepsilon)$

$= E(Z\gamma+\varepsilon)(Z\gamma+\varepsilon)'$

$= ZGZ' + R$

y	is the vector of observed response data values.
$\mathbf{X}$	is the known design matrix for the fixed effects resulting from the MODEL statement in PROC MIXED.
β	is the vector of unknown fixed-effect parameters.
$\mathbf{Z}$	is the known design matrix for the random effects resulting from the RANDOM statement in PROC MIXED.
γ	is the vector of unknown random effects parameters.
ε	is the vector of random errors.

Assume that γ and ε are independently and normally distributed with

$$E\begin{bmatrix}\gamma \\ \varepsilon\end{bmatrix} = 0 \text{ and } Var\begin{bmatrix}\gamma \\ \varepsilon\end{bmatrix} = \begin{bmatrix}\mathrm{G} & 0 \\ 0 & \mathrm{R}\end{bmatrix}.$$

In the **sasuser.ingot** data set example, $\mathrm{G} = \sigma_b^2 I_7$ and $\mathrm{R} = \sigma^2 I_{21}$. PROC MIXED enables you to specify various covariance structures for both the **G** and **R** matrices. The default is the Variance Component (or simple) structure as used in the **ingot** example.

It follows that for the observed response variable **y**, you have $E(y) = \mathbf{X}\beta$ and $Var(y) = \mathbf{ZGZ'} + \mathbf{R} = \mathbf{V}$.

The mixed model extends the general linear model by allowing a more general specification of the covariance matrix of **y**. The mixed model allows for random factors in the model and for random elements of errors ε to be correlated. The general linear model is a special case of the mixed model with $\mathbf{Z} = 0$ (which means $Z\gamma$ disappears from the model) and $\mathrm{R} = \sigma^2 I_n$.

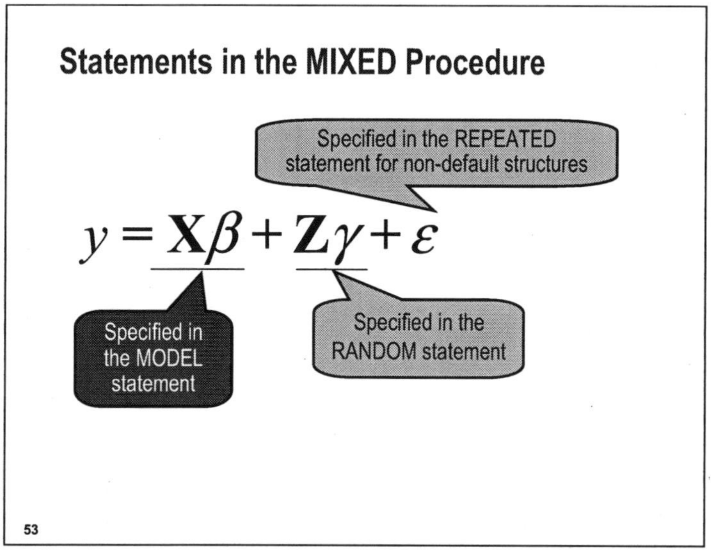

In the MIXED procedure, you use the MODEL statement to specify the fixed effects, the RANDOM statement to specify the random effects, and the REPEATED statement to specify the variance-covariance structure of the errors that is not the default $\sigma^2 I_n$. You should be careful when specifying both RANDOM and REPEATED statements in PROC MIXED. In some cases, one statement (for example, the REPEATED statement) with the specified variance-covariance structure captures all the variations in your data and the other statement (for example, the RANDOM statement) is not needed.

Linear Mixed Model Assumptions

- Random effects and residuals are normally distributed with mean zero and covariance matrices **G** and **R**, respectively.
- Random effects and residuals are independent of each other.
- The means (expected values) of the responses are linearly related to the predictor variables (linear in terms of fixed-effects parameters).

54

Because normal data can be modeled entirely in terms of its means and variances/covariances, the two sets of parameters in a mixed linear model actually specify the complete probability distribution of the data. The parameters of the mean model are referred to as *fixed-effects paramete*
the variance-covariance model are referred to as *covariance parameters*.

Define the Mixed Model—Ingot Example

$$y = \mathbf{X}\beta + \mathbf{Z}\gamma + \varepsilon$$

$$y_{21\times1} = \begin{bmatrix} y_{11} \\ y_{12} \\ \vdots \\ y_{17} \\ y_{21} \\ \vdots \\ y_{37} \end{bmatrix} \quad \beta_{4\times1} = \begin{bmatrix} \mu \\ \alpha_1 \\ \alpha_2 \\ \alpha_3 \end{bmatrix} \quad \gamma_{7\times1} = \begin{bmatrix} b_1 \\ b_2 \\ b_3 \\ b_4 \\ b_5 \\ b_6 \\ b_7 \end{bmatrix} \quad \varepsilon_{21\times1} = \begin{bmatrix} \varepsilon_{11} \\ \varepsilon_{12} \\ \vdots \\ \varepsilon_{17} \\ \varepsilon_{21} \\ \vdots \\ \varepsilon_{37} \end{bmatrix}$$

continued...

55

There are a total of 21 observations because 3×7=21 observations are taken, four fixed effect parameters (overall mean plus 3 metals), 7 random effect parameters (7 blocks), and 21 random errors corresponding to each of the observations.

Define the Mixed Model—Ingot Example

$$\mathbf{X}_{21\times4} = \begin{bmatrix} 1_7 & 1_7 & 0_7 & 0_7 \\ 1_7 & 0_7 & 1_7 & 0_7 \\ 1_7 & 0_7 & 0_7 & 1_7 \end{bmatrix} \quad \mathbf{Z}_{21\times7} = \begin{bmatrix} 1 & 0 & \dots & 0 \\ 0 & 1 & \dots & 0 \\ \dots & \dots & \dots & \dots \\ 0 & 0 & \dots & 1 \\ \vdots & \vdots & \vdots & \vdots \\ 1 & 0 & \dots & 0 \\ 0 & 1 & \dots & 0 \\ \dots & \dots & \dots & \dots \\ 0 & 0 & 0 & 1 \end{bmatrix} = \begin{bmatrix} \mathbf{I}_7 \\ \mathbf{I}_7 \\ \mathbf{I}_7 \end{bmatrix}$$

56

The design matrices for the fixed effects (**X**) and the random effects (**Z**) are constructed based on the model specifications and your data. The subscript *7* represents 7 identical rows.

Covariance Matrices—Ingot Example

$$\mathbf{G}_{7\times7} = \sigma_b^2\mathbf{I}_7$$

$$\mathbf{R}_{21\times21} = \sigma^2\mathbf{I}_{21}$$

$$\mathbf{V}_{21\times21} = Var(y) = \mathbf{ZGZ'} + \mathbf{R} \Rightarrow$$

$$\begin{cases} Var(y_{ij}) = \sigma_b^2 + \sigma^2 \\ Cov(y_{ij}, y_{kl}) = \begin{cases} \sigma_b^2 & i \neq k \text{ and } j = l \\ 0 & \text{otherwise} \end{cases} \end{cases}$$

59

The random effect vector γ has a multivariate normal distribution with mean vector 0 and variance-covariance matrix $\mathbf{G} = \sigma_b^2\mathbf{I}_7$.

The random error vector ε has a multivariate normal distribution with mean 0 and variance-covariance matrix $\mathbf{R} = \sigma^2\mathbf{I}_{21}$.

Therefore, the variance-covariance matrix of y is $Var(y) = \mathbf{ZGZ'} + \mathbf{R} = \mathbf{V}$.

✎ **G** denotes the covariance matrix for the random effects, **R** denotes the covariance matrix for random errors, and **V** denotes the covariance matrix for the observations.

Details

$$\mathbf{G} = \sigma_b^2\mathbf{I}_7 = \begin{bmatrix} \sigma_b^2 & 0 & \cdots & 0 \\ 0 & \sigma_b^2 & \cdots & 0 \\ \vdots & \vdots & \ddots & \vdots \\ 0 & 0 & 0 & \sigma_b^2 \end{bmatrix}_{7\times7}, \quad \mathbf{R} = \sigma^2\mathbf{I}_{21} = \begin{bmatrix} \sigma^2 & 0 & \cdots & 0 \\ 0 & \sigma^2 & \cdots & 0 \\ \vdots & \vdots & \ddots & \vdots \\ 0 & 0 & 0 & \sigma^2 \end{bmatrix}_{21\times21}, \text{ and}$$

$$\mathbf{V} = \left[\begin{array}{ccccccccccc}
\sigma_b^2+\sigma^2 & 0 & 0\;0\;0\;0 & 0 & \sigma_b^2 & 0 & 0\;0\;0\;0\;0 & \sigma_b^2 & 0 & 0\;0\;0\;0 & 0 \\
0 & \sigma_b^2+\sigma^2 & 0\;0\;0\;0 & 0 & 0 & \sigma_b^2 & 0\;0\;0\;0\;0 & 0 & \sigma_b^2 & 0\;0\;0\;0 & 0 \\
\vdots & & \ddots & & & & \ddots & & & \ddots & \\
0 & 0 & 0\;0\;0\;0 & \sigma_b^2+\sigma^2 & 0 & 0 & 0\;0\;0\;0\;\sigma_b^2 & 0 & 0 & 0\;0\;0\;0 & \sigma_b^2 \\
\vdots & \vdots & \vdots \quad \vdots & & \ddots & & & & \vdots & \vdots \quad \vdots & \\
\vdots & \vdots & \vdots \quad \vdots & & & & \ddots & & \vdots & \vdots \quad \vdots & \\
\sigma_b^2 & 0 & 0\;0\;0\;0 & 0 & \sigma_b^2 & 0 & 0\;0\;0\;0\;0 & \sigma_b^2+\sigma^2 & 0 & 0\;0\;0\;0 & 0 \\
0 & \sigma_b^2 & 0\;0\;0\;0 & 0 & 0 & \sigma_b^2 & 0\;0\;0\;0\;0 & 0 & \sigma_b^2+\sigma^2 & 0\;0\;0\;0 & 0 \\
\vdots & & \ddots & & & & \ddots & & & \ddots & \\
0 & 0 & 0\;0\;0\;0 & \sigma_b^2 & 0 & 0 & 0\;0\;0\;0\;\sigma_b^2 & 0 & 0 & 0\;0\;0\;0 & \sigma_b^2+\sigma^2
\end{array}\right]_{21\times21}$$

The GLMMOD Procedure

General form of the GLMMOD procedure:

```
PROC GLMMOD options;
    CLASS variables;
    MODEL dependents=independents / options;
RUN;
```

60

The GLMMOD procedure constructs the design matrix for a general linear model; it essentially constitutes the model-building front end for the GLM procedure.

Selected GLMMOD procedure statements:

CLASS	names the classification variables to be used in the analysis. If you specify the CLASS statement, it must appear before the MODEL statement.
MODEL	names the dependent variables and independent effects.

The GLMMOD procedure can be used in conjunction with other SAS/STAT software regression procedures or with SAS/IML software to obtain specialized analyses for general linear models that you cannot obtain with the GLM procedure. This procedure can help you understand the general linear model theory by explicitly printing the design matrices **X** and **Z**.

Obtaining the Design Matrix Using PROC GLMMOD

Given the model and your data, you can write the design matrices by hand. Alternatively, you can use PROC GLMMOD to obtain the design matrices for models that are not too complex.

```
proc glmmod data=sasuser.ingot;
   class metal ingot;
   model pressure=metal ingot;
run;                                         *c01s4d1.sas;
```

PROC GLMMOD does not provide a RANDOM statement where you can specify the random effects. For mixed models, you must specify both the fixed and random effects in the MODEL statement and from the output determine which part of the design matrix corresponds to the design matrix **X** and which part corresponds to the design matrix **Z**.

PROC GLMMOD Output

```
                    The GLMMOD Procedure

                  Class Level Information

         Class          Levels    Values

         metal               3    copper iron nickel

         ingot               7    1 2 3 4 5 6 7


           Number of Observations Read          21
           Number of Observations Used          21
```

Parameter Definitions

Column Number	Name of Associated Effect	CLASS Variable Values metal	ingot
1	Intercept		
2	metal	copper	
3	metal	iron	
4	metal	nickel	
5	ingot		1
6	ingot		2
7	ingot		3
8	ingot		4
9	ingot		5
10	ingot		6
11	ingot		7

The Parameter Definitions table contains the information regarding the association between model effects and design matrix columns. Column numbers 1 through 4 correspond to the fixed effect (**metal**), and the associated β vector is [Intercept, metal1, metal2, metal3] or [μ α_1 α_2 α_3]. Column numbers 5 through 11 correspond to the random effect (**ingot**), and the associated γ vector is [ingot1, ingot2, ingot3, ingot4, ingot5, ingot6, ingot7] or [γ_1 γ_2 γ_3 γ_4 γ_5 γ_6 γ_7].

✎ You can use the OUTPARM= option in PROC GLMMOD to save this table as a SAS data set.

```
                    The GLMMOD Procedure

                       Design Points

Observation                               Column Number
  Number        pressure    1   2   3   4   5   6   7   8   9   10   11

     1            72.2      1   1   0   0   1   0   0   0   0   0    0
     2            66.4      1   1   0   0   0   1   0   0   0   0    0
     3            74.5      1   1   0   0   0   0   1   0   0   0    0
     4            67.3      1   1   0   0   0   0   0   1   0   0    0
     5            73.2      1   1   0   0   0   0   0   0   1   0    0
     6            68.7      1   1   0   0   0   0   0   0   0   1    0
     7            69.0      1   1   0   0   0   0   0   0   0   0    1
     8            71.9      1   0   1   0   1   0   0   0   0   0    0
     9            68.8      1   0   1   0   0   1   0   0   0   0    0
    10            82.6      1   0   1   0   0   0   1   0   0   0    0
    11            78.1      1   0   1   0   0   0   0   1   0   0    0
    12            74.2      1   0   1   0   0   0   0   0   1   0    0
    13            70.8      1   0   1   0   0   0   0   0   0   1    0
    14            84.9      1   0   1   0   0   0   0   0   0   0    1
    15            67.0      1   0   0   1   1   0   0   0   0   0    0
    16            67.5      1   0   0   1   0   1   0   0   0   0    0
    17            76.0      1   0   0   1   0   0   1   0   0   0    0
    18            72.7      1   0   0   1   0   0   0   1   0   0    0
    19            73.1      1   0   0   1   0   0   0   0   1   0    0
    20            65.8      1   0   0   1   0   0   0   0   0   1    0
    21            75.6      1   0   0   1   0   0   0   0   0   0    1
```

The Design Points table contains the columns of the design matrix. The pressure column is the y vector. The first 4 columns constitute the design matrix **X** for the fixed effects β, and the columns 5 through 11 are the design matrix **Z** for the random effects γ. This output also illustrates that an over-parameterized model was fit to your data. The columns are not linearly independent.

In addition to the ODS OUTPUT statement, you can use the OUTDESIGN= option in PROC GLMMOD to save this table as a SAS data set.

This procedure is not only useful in helping you understand design matrices, but it is also a tool for building a regression model with many dummy variables, especially when some of them have many levels.

1.5 Chapter Summary

Almost any data is produced by designed experiments, sample surveys, or observational studies. In building statistical models to analyze your data, you frequently must identify fixed effects and random effects.

Fixed effects are those factors whose levels are selected by a nonrandom process or whose levels consist of the entire population of possible levels. Factors are fixed if all levels of interest are included in the data set.

Random effects are those factors whose levels represent a random sample of levels from a population of possible levels. Inference is to be made about a set of levels larger than those included in the data set. Variances associated with random effects are known as variance components.

Models in which some factors are fixed effects and other factors are random effects are called mixed models.

One of the simplest mixed model examples is the one fit to a randomized complete block design, in which each treatment is applied to experimental units in each block and the treatments are randomly assigned to the experimental units within each block. Blocks are groups of experimental units that are formed so that units within blocks are as homogeneous as possible. Blocks are almost always random effects.

The MIXED procedure should be used for analyzing mixed models. The GLM procedure was developed for fixed-effects models; therefore, it is not suitable for mixed model analyses.

You can use the GLMMOD procedure to obtain the design matrix for a general linear model.

General form of the MIXED procedure:

PROC MIXED *options*;
    CLASS *variables*;
    MODEL *dependent=fixed-effects / options*;
    RANDOM *random-effects / options*;
    CONTRAST *'label' fixed-effect values |*
            random-effect values / options;
    ESTIMATE *'label' fixed-effect values |*
            random-effect values / options;
    LSMEANS *fixed-effects / options*;
RUN;

General form of the GLM procedure:

> **PROC GLM** *options*;
> **CLASS** *variables*;
> **MODEL** *dependents=independents / options*;
> **MEANS** *effects / options*;
> **LSMEANS** *effects / options*;
> **CONTRAST** *'label' effect values / options*;
> **ESTIMATE** *'label' effect values / options*;
> **RANDOM** *effects / options*;
> **RUN**;

General form of the GLMMOD procedure:

> **PROC GLMMOD** *options;*
> **CLASS** *variables;*
> **MODEL** *dependents=independents / options;*
> **RUN**;

Chapter 2 Examples of Mixed Models in Some Designed Experiments

2.1 Two-Way Mixed Models

Objectives

- Recognize a two-way mixed model design.
- Analyze two-way mixed models using the MIXED procedure.

3

Grass Example

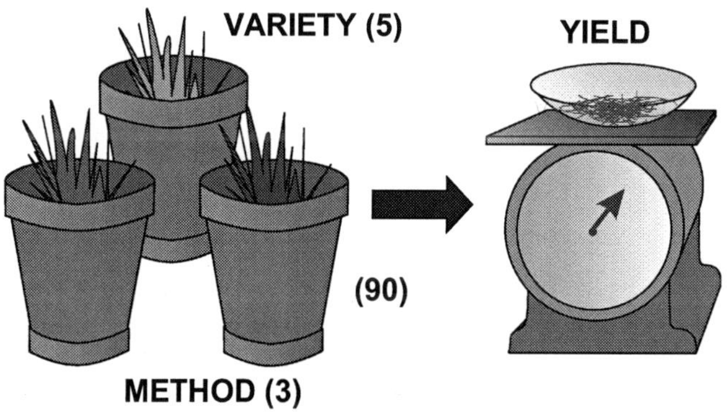

4

Three seed growth methods are applied to seeds from each of five varieties of turf grass. Six pots are planted with seeds from each method-by-variety combination. The 90 pots are randomly placed in a uniform growth chamber, and dry matter yields are measured from clippings at the end of four weeks.

This is an example of a completely randomized experiment with a factorial arrangement of treatments. The fifteen treatments are the combinations of levels of the two factors, **`variety`** (five levels) and **`method`** (three levels). Assume that the five varieties were randomly chosen from a broader population of varieties. Interest is not on these particular five varieties but on the population from which they were chosen. The variable **`variety`** is considered to be a **random** effect. The variable **`method`** is considered to be a **fixed** effect because the interest is only on these three methods. The **`method*variety`** interaction is a random effect.

Because both random and fixed effects are involved, the model is defined as being mixed. The varieties are random, and the inference about method means that differences should apply across all varieties.

The Data

method	variety	yield
A	1	22.1
A	1	24.1
A	1	19.1
A	1	22.1
A	1	25.1
A	1	18.1
A	2	29.1
A	2	17.1
A	2	21.6
A	2	28.6
A	2	17.1
A	2	26.6
A	3	25.3
A	3	25.8
A	3	22.8
A	3	28.3
A	3	21.3
A	3	18.3
A	4	19.8
A	4	28.3
...	...	...

5

Data is recorded in a SAS data set **sasuser.grass**. These variables are in the data set:

method the growth method

variety the variety of turf grass

yield the amount of dried turf growth in each pot after four weeks

Define the Mixed Model

$$y_{ijk} = \mu + \alpha_i + b_j + (\alpha b)_{ij} + \varepsilon_{ijk}$$

`method` effect, fixed

`variety` effect, random

`method*variety` effect, random

$$b_j \sim N(0, \sigma_b^2), (\alpha b)_{ij} \sim N(0, \sigma_{\alpha b}^2), \varepsilon_{ijk} \sim N(0, \sigma^2)$$

therefore,

$$E(y_{ijk}) = \mu + \alpha_i$$
$$Var(y_{ijk}) = \sigma_b^2 + \sigma_{\alpha b}^2 + \sigma^2$$

7

y_{ijk} — k^{th} observation (k=1 to 6) for the ith method (i=1, 2, 3) and the jth variety (j=1 to 5)

μ — overall mean and an unknown fixed parameter

α_i — effect for the ith method and also an unknown fixed parameter

b_j — effect of the jth variety, a random effect, $b_j \sim$ i.i.d. N(0, σ_b^2)

$(\alpha b)_{ij}$ — interaction between the ith method and the jth variety, a random effect, $(\alpha b)_{ij} \sim$ i.i.d. N(0, $\sigma_{\alpha b}^2$)

ε_{ijk} — experimental error, $\varepsilon_{ijk} \sim$ i.i.d. N(0, σ^2).

The effects b_j, $(\alpha b)_{ij}$, and ε_{ijk} are assumed to be independent random variables.

Therefore,

- $E(y_{ijk}) = \mu + \alpha_i$ is the mean for method i averaged across all varieties in the population.
- $Var(y_{ijk}) = \sigma_b^2 + \sigma_{\alpha b}^2 + \sigma^2$ is the variance of an observation. The variance components are σ_b^2 (**`variety`** variance), $\sigma_{\alpha b}^2$ (**`method*variety`** variance), and σ^2 (random errors).

Plotting the Data

Before fitting the mixed model to the **sasuser.grass** data set, you may want to perform initial data explorations. You can use the GPLOT procedure of SAS/GRAPH software to examine the yield across the five varieties for the three methods.

```
proc means data=sasuser.grass nway noprint;
   class method variety;
   var yield;
   output out=meangrass mean=Yield;
run;

goptions reset=all;
proc gplot data=meangrass;
   symbol1 v=circle i=j c=red line=1;
   symbol2 v=star i=j c=blue line=2;
   symbol3 v=diamond i=j c=green line=3;
   plot Yield*variety=method;
   title 'Yield vs. Variety for Each Method';
run;
title;
quit;                                        *c02s1d1.sas;
```

The MEANS procedure was used to compute the mean yield values for each of the method and variety combinations. The NWAY option in PROC MEANS specifies that the output data set contains only statistics corresponding to the combination of all class variables, that is, every **method** and **variety** combination.

PROC GPLOT Output

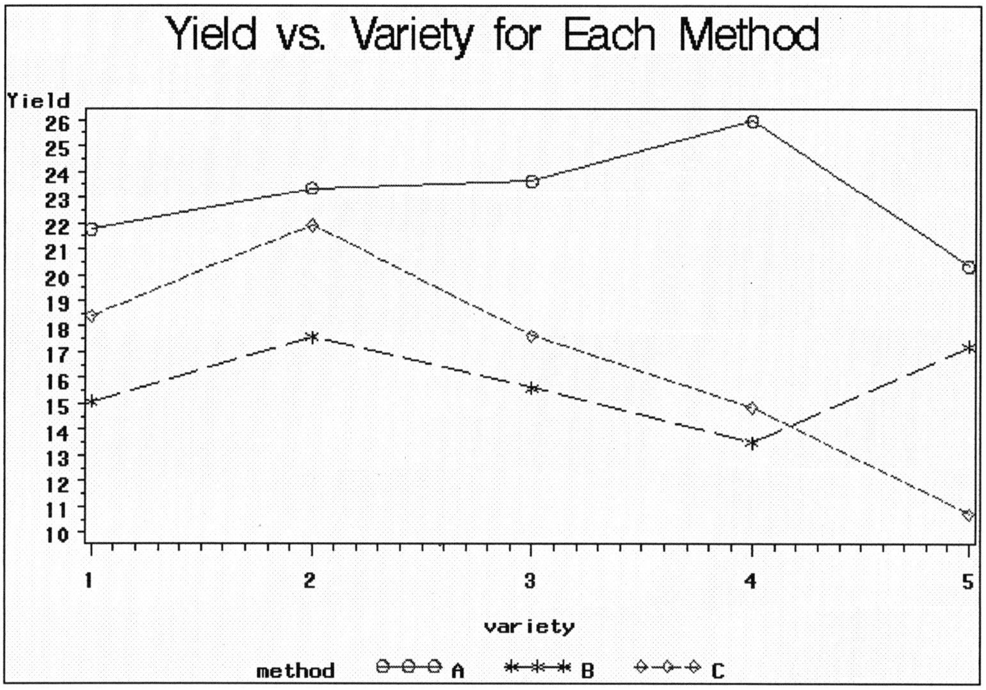

The three lines, one for each level of **`method`**, are not parallel, indicating a **`method*variety`** interaction. Method A appears to produce the largest yield for all five varieties.

Fitting the Two-Way Mixed Model

Now you can use the MIXED procedure to fit this two-way mixed model. Notice that the interaction term is a random effect as long as at least one factor involved in the interaction is random.

```
proc mixed data=sasuser.grass;
   class method variety;
   model yield=method / ddfm=kr;
   random variety method*variety;
   contrast 'A vs B and C' method 2 -1 -1;
   estimate 'A vs B and C' method 2 -1 -1 / divisor=2;
   estimate 'Method A mean' intercept 1 method 1 0 0;
run;                                          *c02s1d2.sas;
```

Selected MODEL statement option:

DDFM= specifies the method for computing the denominator degrees of freedom for the tests of fixed effects resulting from the MODEL, CONTRAST, ESTIMATE, and LSMEANS statements. Possible values are CONTAIN, BETWITHIN, SATTERTH, RESIDUAL, and KENWARDROGER/KR.

The DDFM=KENWARDROGER option performs the degrees-of-freedom calculations detailed by Kenward and Roger (1997). This approximation involves inflating the estimated variance-covariance matrix of the fixed and random effects by the method proposed by Prasad and Rao (1990) and Harville and Jeske (1992); refer also to Kackar and Harville (1984). Satterthwaite-type degrees of freedom are then computed based on this adjustment.

Studies have shown that the KENWARDROGER method of estimating the denominator degrees of freedom for the fixed effects is the most appropriate method in almost all cases. Therefore, it is a highly recommended DDFM method for your mixed model analysis. Detailed discussions on the denominator degrees of freedom estimation methods are provided later in the course.

Selected ESTIMATE statement option:

DIVISOR= specifies a value by which to divide all coefficients so that fractional coefficients can be entered as integers.

The CONTRAST statement was used to compare method A versus methods B and C. The null hypothesis is H_0: $\mu_A = \frac{1}{2}(\mu_B + \mu_C)$. The first ESTIMATE statement was used to estimate the difference in mean yield between method A and the average of methods B and C. The second ESTIMATE statement was used to compute the average yield for method A.

Partial PROC MIXED Output

```
                         The Mixed Procedure

                          Model Information

        Data Set                     SASUSER.GRASS
        Dependent Variable           yield
        Covariance Structure         Variance Components
        Estimation Method            REML
        Residual Variance Method     Profile
        Fixed Effects SE Method      Prasad-Rao-Jeske-
                                     Kackar-Harville
        Degrees of Freedom Method    Kenward-Roger

                        Class Level Information

          Class      Levels    Values

          method          3    A B C
          variety         5    1 2 3 4 5


                             Dimensions

               Covariance Parameters             3
               Columns in X                      4
               Columns in Z                     20
               Subjects                          1
               Max Obs Per Subject              90


                       Number of Observations

            Number of Observations Read             90
            Number of Observations Used             90
            Number of Observations Not Used          0
```

The Model Information, Class Level Information, Dimensions, and Number of Observations tables provide basic descriptive information about the data and model fitting.

```
                           Iteration History

      Iteration    Evaluations    -2 Res Log Like       Criterion

              0              1       528.89057283
              1              1       522.49142693      0.00000000

                      Convergence criteria met.
```

The Iteration History table summarizes the iterative process of finding the REML estimates of the parameters.

```
                Covariance Parameter
                      Estimates

           Cov Parm               Estimate

           variety                  0.4285
           method*variety           4.7715
           Residual                18.4347
```

The variance component estimates obtained by REML are

$\hat{\sigma}_b^2 = 0.4285$

$\hat{\sigma}_{\alpha b}^2 = 4.7715$

$\hat{\sigma}^2 = 18.4347$

It can be shown that the **G** matrix is a diagonal matrix of dimension 20 by 20, with 5 diagonal elements of 0.4285 and 15 diagonal elements of 4.7715. The **R** matrix is a diagonal matrix of dimension 90 by 90, with the diagonal element of 18.4347. The **V** matrix follows the pattern described below:

$$
\begin{bmatrix}
\mathbf{V}_1 & \mathbf{0} & \cdots & \mathbf{C}_1 & \mathbf{0} & \cdots & \mathbf{C}_1 & \mathbf{0} & \cdots \\
\mathbf{0} & \mathbf{V}_2 & \mathbf{0} & \cdots & \mathbf{C}_2 & \mathbf{0} & \cdots & \mathbf{C}_2 & \cdots \\
\vdots & & \ddots & & & \ddots & & & 0 \\
\mathbf{C}_1 & \mathbf{0} & \cdots & \mathbf{V}_6 & \mathbf{0} & \cdots & \mathbf{C}_6 & \mathbf{0} & \cdots \\
\mathbf{0} & \mathbf{C}_2 & & & \mathbf{V}_7 & & & \mathbf{C}_7 & \\
\vdots & & \ddots & & & \ddots & & & \ddots \\
\mathbf{C}_1 & & & \mathbf{C}_6 & & & \mathbf{V}_{11} & & \\
\mathbf{0} & \mathbf{C}_2 & & & \ddots & & & \ddots & \\
\vdots & & \ddots & & & \mathbf{C}_{10} & & & \mathbf{V}_{15}
\end{bmatrix}_{90\times 90}
$$

where $\mathbf{V}_1 = \mathbf{V}_2 = \ldots = \mathbf{V}_{15}$

$$
= \begin{bmatrix}
\sigma^2+\sigma_b^2+\sigma_{\alpha b}^2 & \sigma_b^2+\sigma_{\alpha b}^2 & \sigma_b^2+\sigma_{\alpha b}^2 & \sigma_b^2+\sigma_{\alpha b}^2 & \sigma_b^2+\sigma_{\alpha b}^2 & \sigma_b^2+\sigma_{\alpha b}^2 \\
\sigma_b^2+\sigma_{\alpha b}^2 & \sigma^2+\sigma_b^2+\sigma_{\alpha b}^2 & \sigma_b^2+\sigma_{\alpha b}^2 & \sigma_b^2+\sigma_{\alpha b}^2 & \sigma_b^2+\sigma_{\alpha b}^2 & \sigma_b^2+\sigma_{\alpha b}^2 \\
\sigma_b^2+\sigma_{\alpha b}^2 & \sigma_b^2+\sigma_{\alpha b}^2 & \sigma^2+\sigma_b^2+\sigma_{\alpha b}^2 & \sigma_b^2+\sigma_{\alpha b}^2 & \sigma_b^2+\sigma_{\alpha b}^2 & \sigma_b^2+\sigma_{\alpha b}^2 \\
\sigma_b^2+\sigma_{\alpha b}^2 & \sigma_b^2+\sigma_{\alpha b}^2 & \sigma_b^2+\sigma_{\alpha b}^2 & \sigma^2+\sigma_b^2+\sigma_{\alpha b}^2 & \sigma_b^2+\sigma_{\alpha b}^2 & \sigma_b^2+\sigma_{\alpha b}^2 \\
\sigma_b^2+\sigma_{\alpha b}^2 & \sigma_b^2+\sigma_{\alpha b}^2 & \sigma_b^2+\sigma_{\alpha b}^2 & \sigma_b^2+\sigma_{\alpha b}^2 & \sigma^2+\sigma_b^2+\sigma_{\alpha b}^2 & \sigma_b^2+\sigma_{\alpha b}^2 \\
\sigma_b^2+\sigma_{\alpha b}^2 & \sigma_b^2+\sigma_{\alpha b}^2 & \sigma_b^2+\sigma_{\alpha b}^2 & \sigma_b^2+\sigma_{\alpha b}^2 & \sigma_b^2+\sigma_{\alpha b}^2 & \sigma^2+\sigma_b^2+\sigma_{\alpha b}^2
\end{bmatrix}_{6\times 6}
$$

$$\text{and } \mathbf{C}_1 = \mathbf{C}_2 = \ldots = \mathbf{C}_{10} = \begin{bmatrix} \sigma_b^2 & \sigma_b^2 & \sigma_b^2 & \sigma_b^2 & \sigma_b^2 & \sigma_b^2 \\ \sigma_b^2 & \sigma_b^2 & \sigma_b^2 & \sigma_b^2 & \sigma_b^2 & \sigma_b^2 \\ \sigma_b^2 & \sigma_b^2 & \sigma_b^2 & \sigma_b^2 & \sigma_b^2 & \sigma_b^2 \\ \sigma_b^2 & \sigma_b^2 & \sigma_b^2 & \sigma_b^2 & \sigma_b^2 & \sigma_b^2 \\ \sigma_b^2 & \sigma_b^2 & \sigma_b^2 & \sigma_b^2 & \sigma_b^2 & \sigma_b^2 \\ \sigma_b^2 & \sigma_b^2 & \sigma_b^2 & \sigma_b^2 & \sigma_b^2 & \sigma_b^2 \end{bmatrix}_{6\times 6}$$

You can use the G and V options in the RANDOM statement to request the **G** and **V** matrices from the MIXED procedure.

```
                    Fit Statistics

          -2 Res Log Likelihood           522.5
          AIC (smaller is better)         528.5
          AICC (smaller is better)        528.8
          BIC (smaller is better)         527.3
```

The Fit Statistics table provides information for goodness of model fit. All three criteria consider both the fitness of the model and the model complexity. These statistics are useful in comparing different models. Generally speaking, smaller values indicate a better model fit.

```
                 Type 3 Tests of Fixed Effects

                       Num     Den
        Effect          DF      DF    F Value    Pr > F

        method           2       8       9.84    0.0070


                           Estimates

                           Standard
Label           Estimate      Error      DF    t Value    Pr > |t|

A vs B and C      6.7583     1.5340       8       4.41      0.0023
Method A mean    23.0100     1.2863    11.9      17.89      <.0001


                           Contrasts

                         Num     Den
       Label              DF      DF    F Value    Pr > F

       A vs B and C        1       8      19.41    0.0023
```

The Type 3 test for the fixed effect shows that the F value for **`method`** produced by PROC MIXED is 9.84, with a p-value of 0.0070. The method means, averaged across all varieties, are statistically significantly different for at least one of the methods.

The estimate for A versus B and C is 6.7583, and the standard error of the estimate is 1.5340. The average yield produced by method A is 6.7583 higher than the average yield produced by B and C. The estimate for method A mean is 23.01, and the standard error is 1.2863.

The contrast for A versus B and C agrees with the result from the ESTIMATE statement.

You can use the CL option in the ESTIMATE statement to compute the confidence limits for each estimate.

```
proc mixed data=sasuser.grass;
   class method variety;
   model yield=method / ddfm=kr;
   random variety method*variety ;
   estimate 'A vs B and C' method 2 -1 -1 / divisor=2 cl
             alpha=0.01;
   estimate 'Method A mean' intercept 1 method 1 0 0;
run;                                          *c02s1d3.sas;
```

Selected ESTIMATE statement option:

CL requests that *t*-type confidence limits be constructed. The confidence level is 0.95 by default; this can be changed with the ALPHA= option.

Partial PROC MIXED Output

Estimates

Label	Estimate	Standard Error	DF	t Value	Pr > |t|	Alpha
A vs B and C	6.7583	1.5340	8	4.41	0.0023	0.01
Method A mean	23.0100	1.2863	11.9	17.89	<.0001	0.05

Estimates

Label	Lower	Upper
A vs B and C	1.6111	11.9055
Method A mean	20.2058	25.8142

Notice that the confidence limits were generated for both ESTIMATE statements although the CL option was only specified in one of the ESTIMATE statements. However, you must specify the ALPHA= option in each CONTRAST or ESTIMATE statement if you want to change the significance level.

Analyze the Two-Way Mixed Model Using the GLM Procedure (Self-Study)

If you want to use PROC GLM to analyze the same data, be certain to use the TEST option in the RANDOM statement. Otherwise, you get erroneous test results for the **`method`** effect.

```
proc glm data=sasuser.grass;
   class method variety;
   model yield=method variety method*variety;
   random variety method*variety / test;
run;                                          *c02s1d4.sas;
```

Selected RANDOM statement option:

TEST performs hypothesis tests for each effect specified in the model, using appropriate error terms as determined by the expected mean squares.

Partial PROC GLM Output

The GLM Procedure

Dependent Variable: yield

Source	DF	Sum of Squares	Mean Square	F Value	Pr > F
Model	14	1521.538222	108.681302	5.90	<.0001
Error	75	1382.600000	18.434667		
Corrected Total	89	2904.138222			

R-Square	Coeff Var	Root MSE	yield Mean
0.523921	23.20286	4.293561	18.50444

Source	DF	Type I SS	Mean Square	F Value	Pr > F
method	2	925.9228889	462.9614444	25.11	<.0001
variety	4	219.1048889	54.7762222	2.97	0.0246
method*variety	8	376.5104444	47.0638056	2.55	0.0162

Source	DF	Type III SS	Mean Square	F Value	Pr > F
method	2	925.9228889	462.9614444	25.11	<.0001
variety	4	219.1048889	54.7762222	2.97	0.0246
method*variety	8	376.5104444	47.0638056	2.55	0.0162

The test for **`method`** is **not** a valid test because it uses MS(Error) as the denominator. The correct denominator can be derived from the next output showing the Expected Mean Square, and the correct tests show thereafter.

```
                              The GLM Procedure

Source              Type III Expected Mean Square

method              Var(Error) + 6 Var(method*variety) + Q(method)

variety             Var(Error) + 6 Var(method*variety) + 18 Var(variety)

method*variety      Var(Error) + 6 Var(method*variety)
```

Using the mean squares for **method** and **method*variety** and the expected mean squares, you can obtain the variances component estimates using the method-of-moments (rather than the maximum likelihood in PROC MIXED):

- $\hat{\sigma}^2$ = MS(Error) = 18.4347
- Because

  E{MS(**variety**)} = Var(Error) + 6 Var(**method*variety**) + 18 Var(**variety**), and

  E{MS(**method*variety**)} = Var(Error) + 6 Var(**method*variety**),

  substitute the latter in the former, and you get

  E{MS(**variety**)} = E{MS(**method*variety**)} + 18 Var(**variety**), or

  $\hat{\sigma}_b^2$ = 1/18 (MS(**variety**) – MS(**method*variety**))

  = 1/18 (54.7762-47.0638) = 0.4285
- Because

  E{MS(**method*variety**)} = Var(Error)+6Var(**method*variety**),

  you get

  $\hat{\sigma}_{\alpha b}^2$ =1/6 (MS(**method*variety**) – MS(Error))

  = 1/6 (47.0638-18.4347) = 4.7715

Compared with the variance component estimates obtained from PROC MIXED, they are identical. This is generally the case for balanced data. For balanced data, the method-of-moment estimates and the REML estimates are the same, except when one of the ANOVA variance component estimates is negative, in which case the results from the two procedures differ.

From the Expected Mean Square table, you see that MS(**method*variety**) is the correct error term for testing of the **method** effect. This is confirmed by the output on the next page.

```
                         The GLM Procedure
          Tests of Hypotheses for Mixed Model Analysis of Variance

Dependent Variable: yield

 Source                      DF    Type III SS    Mean Square  F Value  Pr > F

 method                       2     925.922889     462.961444     9.84  0.0070
 variety                      4     219.104889      54.776222     1.16  0.3946

 Error                        8     376.510444      47.063806
 Error: MS(method*variety)


 Source                      DF    Type III SS    Mean Square  F Value  Pr > F

 method*variety               8     376.510444      47.063806     2.55  0.0162

 Error: MS(Error)            75    1382.600000      18.434667
```

The TEST option in the RANDOM statement produced the correct test for **method**, using MS(**method*variety**) as the appropriate error term, with an F value of 9.84 and a p-value of 0.0070.

Knowing that the correct error term for the **method** is **method*variety**, you can use the E= option in the CONTRAST statement to produce the correct hypothesis test. If you want to know whether the mean yield for method A is the same as the average yields for methods B and C, you can submit the following statements:

```
    contrast 'A vs B and C' method 2 -1 -1 /e=method*variety;
run;
quit;                                              *c02s1d5.sas;
```

Selected CONTRAST statement option:

E= specifies an error term, which must be one of the effects in the model. The procedure uses this effect as the denominator in F-tests in univariate analysis. In addition, if you use a MANOVA or REPEATED statement, the procedure uses the effect specified by the E= option as the basis of the **E** matrix. By default, the procedure uses the overall residual or error mean square (MSE) as an error term.

CONTRAST Statement Output

```
Dependent Variable: yield

                  Tests of Hypotheses Using the Type III
                  MS for method*variety as an Error Term

 Contrast                    DF    Contrast SS    Mean Square  F Value  Pr > F

 A vs B and C                 1    913.5013889    913.5013889    19.41  0.0023
```

The test has an F value of 19.41 and a p-value of 0.0023. The test results agree with the ones produced by PROC MIXED.

2.2 Nested Mixed Models

Objectives

- Define a nested mixed model.
- Analyze a nested mixed model using the MIXED procedure.

15

Semiconductor Example

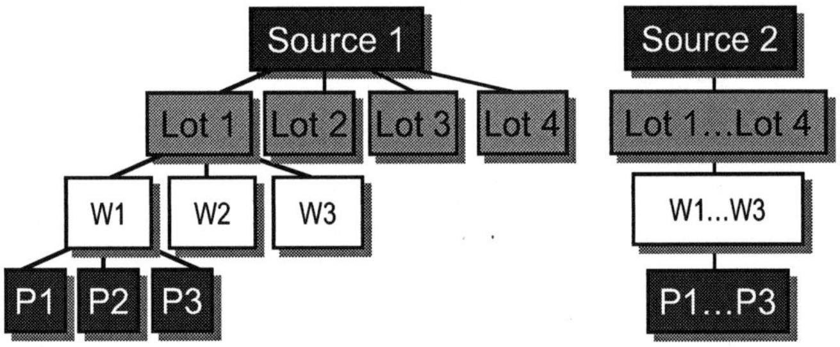

16

A study was conducted in the semiconductor industry to measure the thickness of the oxide layer on silicon wafers determined at three randomly selected positions on each wafer. The objective is to determine assignable causes for the observed variability. Eight lots of twenty-five wafers were randomly selected from the population of lots of twenty-five wafers, with four lots from one source and the other four lots from the other source. Then three wafers were randomly selected from each lot of twenty-five for the use of oxide deposition process. After the layer of oxide was deposited, the thickness of the layer was determined at three randomly selected positions on each wafer.

The Data

source	lot	wafer	position	thickness
1	1	1	1	2006
1	1	1	2	1999
1	1	1	3	2007
1	1	2	1	1980
1	1	2	2	1988
1	1	2	3	1982
1	1	3	1	2000
1	1	3	2	1998
1	1	3	3	2007
1	2	1	1	1991
1	2	1	2	1990
1	2	1	3	1988
1	2	2	1	1987
1	2	2	2	1989
1	2	2	3	1988
1	2	3	1	1985
1	2	3	2	1983
1	2	3	3	1989
...	...	...	...	...

17

The data is stored in **sasuser.thickness**. These are the variables:

thickness the thickness of the oxide layer on silicon wafers

source the source where the lots of wafers were selected

lot the lots of wafers that were selected from each source

wafer the wafers that were selected from each lot

position the positions on each wafer where the thickness measurements were taken

You can see that **source** is a fixed effect, whereas **lot**, **wafer**, and **position** are all random effects, and they have a nested or hierarchical data structure.

Hierarchical Data Structure

Nested designs have a hierarchical data structure.

- There is more than one size of experimental unit.
- A small experimental unit is nested within a larger one.

18

For example, each wafer is taken out from one lot. Thus, **`wafer`** is nested within **`lot`**. Each position is chosen from one wafer; therefore, **`position`** is nested within **`wafer`**. One way of thinking of nested versus crossed is to determine whether wafer 1, for example, always refers to the same wafer, wafer 2 always refers to the same wafer, and so on. This is clearly not the case because wafers from each lot are unique for that particular lot. Wafer 1 from lot 1 has no connection with wafer 1 from any other lot, wafer 2 from lot 1 has no connection with wafer 2 from any other lot, and so forth. Therefore, **`wafer`** is nested within **`lot`**. Similarly, **`lot`** is nested within **`source`**, and **`position`** is nested within **`wafer`**.

A Nested Mixed Model

$$y_{ijkm} = \mu + \alpha_i + l_{j(i)} + w_{k(ij)} + e_{m(ijk)}$$

source, fixed — **lot,** random — **wafer,** random — error, or **position,** random

$l_{j(i)} \sim$ *i.i.d.* N(0, σ_l^2)

$w_{k(ij)} \sim$ *i.i.d.* N(0, σ_w^2)

$e_{m(ijk)} \sim$ *i.i.d.* N(0, σ^2)

i = 1, 2 (**source**)

j = 1, 2, 3, 4 (**lot**)

k = 1, 2, 3 (**wafer**)

m = 1, 2 ,3 (**position**)

19

y_{ijkm} the thickness measurement for the mth position (m=1, 2, 3) from the kth wafer (k=1, 2, 3) of the jth lot (j=1, 2, 3, 4) from source i (i=1, 2)

μ the overall mean

α_i the effect of the ith source, a fixed effect

$l_{j(i)}$ the effect of the jth randomly selected lot from source i, ~ i.i.d. N(0, σ_l^2)

$w_{k(ij)}$ the effect of the kth randomly selected wafer from the jth lot from source i, ~ i.i.d. N(0, σ_w^2)

$e_{m(ijk)}$ the random error, that is, the effect of the mth randomly selected position from the kth wafer of the jth lot from source i, ~ i.i.d. N(0, σ^2)

This model involves both random and fixed effects; therefore, it is considered to be a mixed model. The random effects have a nested structure; therefore, this is a nested mixed model.

Fitting a Nested Mixed Model

To examine the fixed effects **source** and to estimate the variance component associated with each random effect, you can perform the following analysis using the MIXED procedure:

```
proc mixed data=sasuser.thickness cl;
   class source lot wafer;
   model thickness=source / ddfm=kr;
   random lot(source) wafer(lot source);
   *random int wafer / subject=lot(source);
run;                               *c02s2d1.sas;
```

The variable **source** was the only fixed effect; therefore, it is specified in the MODEL statement. The residual variance ($e_{m(ijk)}$) corresponds to the position-to-position variation. The variance components corresponding to **lot(source)** ($l_{j(i)}$ in the model specification) and **wafer(lot source)** ($w_{k(ij)}$ in the model specification) measure the variation in the mean thickness of the population of lots for each source, and the variability in the mean thickness of wafers within the population of lots for each source, respectively.

Selected PROC MIXED statement option:

CL requests confidence limits for the covariance parameter estimates. A Satterthwaite approximation is used to construct limits for all parameters that have a default lower boundary constraint of zero.

Satterthwaite's formula is discussed later in the course.

You can rewrite the RANDOM statement as follows:

```
   random int wafer / subject=lot(source);
```

The results will be identical. The advantage of this coding is that this is more efficient for memory. For large data sets with many levels for the random effects, using the SUBJECT= option to specify the common factor among random effects improves PROC MIXED performance significantly. The SUBJECT= option is discussed later in this course.

Partial PROC MIXED Output

Class Level Information

Class	Levels	Values
source	2	1 2
lot	4	1 2 3 4
wafer	3	1 2 3

The Class Level Information confirms the nesting structure of the model. For example, although there are three wafers, wafer 1 from lot 1 is different from wafer 1 from lot 2, and the nesting specification conveys this information.

```
                    Covariance Parameter Estimates

Cov Parm              Estimate     Alpha       Lower       Upper

lot(source)             119.89      0.05     46.1707      752.40
wafer(source*lot)      35.8657      0.05     18.7634     94.0313
Residual               12.5694      0.05      8.7411     19.6177
```

The estimate for the lot-to-lot variance (119.89) is more than three times as large as the wafer-to-wafer within-a-lot variance of 35.87, which is almost three times as large as the position-to-position within-a-wafer variance of 12.57. As a matter of fact, the lot-to-lot variation accounts for over 70% of the total variation. You might want to evaluate the cause of lot-to-lot variance to improve the consistency of the layer of oxide across population of wafers. The 95% confidence limits on the variance components with a lower bound of zero were computed based on chi-squared distribution.

You can use the G option and the V option in the RANDOM statement to print out the **G** and **V** matrices. They are arranged similarly to the ones presented in the previous section, except that the **V** matrix is a block diagonal matrix to correspond to the data structure. Basically, the observations from the same wafer within the same lot share a covariance of 155.76 (119.89+35.8657 = 155.76), and the observations from the different wafers within the same lot share a covariance of 119.89. The variance of an observation is estimated to be 119.89+35.8657+12.5694 = 168.33.

```
                    Type 3 Tests of Fixed Effects

                         Num     Den
          Effect          DF      DF    F Value    Pr > F

          source           1       6       1.53    0.2629
```

The test for the fixed effect **`source`** did not indicate a significant difference between the source means (*p*-value=0.2629).

You can obtain the method-of-moment estimates for the variance components using the MIXED procedure. This produces the identical results as PROC GLM, but it saves you from having to compute the variance parameter estimates by hand as you would have using PROC GLM.

```
proc mixed data=sasuser.thickness method=type3;
   class source lot wafer;
   model thickness=source / ddfm=kr;
   random lot(source) wafer(lot source);
run;                                         *c02s2d2.sas;
```

Selected PROC MIXED statement option:

METHOD= specifies the estimation method for the covariance parameters. Possible values for METHOD are REML, ML, MIVQUE0, TYPE1, TYPE2, and TYPE3.

The METHOD=TYPE*n* specifications apply only to variance component models with no SUBJECT= effects and no REPEATED statement. An analysis of variance table is included in the output, and the expected mean squares are used to estimate the variance components. The resulting method-of-moment variance component estimates are used in subsequent calculations, including standard errors computed from ESTIMATE and LSMEANS statements.

Partial PROC MIXED Output

```
                         Type 3 Analysis of Variance

                                              Sum of
      Source                  DF             Squares     Mean Square

      source                   1         1830.125000     1830.125000
      lot(source)              6         7195.194444     1199.199074
      wafer(source*lot)       16         1922.666667      120.166667
      Residual                48          603.333333       12.569444

                         Type 3 Analysis of Variance

Source             Expected Mean Square

source             Var(Residual) + 3 Var(wafer(source*lot))
                   + 9 Var(lot(source)) + Q(source)
lot(source)        Var(Residual) + 3 Var(wafer(source*lot))
                   + 9 Var(lot(source))
wafer(source*lot)  Var(Residual) + 3 Var(wafer(source*lot))
Residual           Var(Residual)

                         Type 3 Analysis of Variance

                                                  Error
Source             Error Term                        DF   F Value   Pr > F

source             MS(lot(source))                    6      1.53   0.2629
lot(source)        MS(wafer(source*lot))             16      9.98   0.0001
wafer(source*lot)  MS(Residual)                      48      9.56   <.0001
Residual           .                                  .       .       .

                       Covariance Parameter Estimates

                       Cov Parm                 Estimate

                       lot(source)                119.89
                       wafer(source*lot)         35.8657
                       Residual                  12.5694
```

The Type 3 Analysis of Variance table includes an ANOVA table and the expected mean squares that are used in estimating the variance components. The results are the same as those produced by PROC GLM with a TEST option in the RANDOM statement (not shown). The *F*-test on the variance component estimates tests the hypothesis of whether the variance components are zero. This test does not rely on asymptotic theory; therefore, it is an exact test. The test indicates that there is a significant lot-to-lot variation and wafer-to-wafer variation, consistent with the CL option output previously. The method-of-moment variance parameter estimates are identical to the REML estimates because you have balanced data.

The values for the Expected Mean Squares are derived mathematically by taking the expectations of the mean squares. Detailed information about the computations of the expected mean squares can be found in Montgomery (1997).

2.3 Split-Plot Designs

Objectives

- Define a split-plot design.
- Write the model for a split-plot design.
- Analyze a split-plot design using the MIXED procedure.

29

A Split-Plot Type of Design

- There are two factors: A and B.
- Factor A is applied to the large experimental units (whole unit).
- The large experimental unit (whole unit) is divided into smaller experimental units (sub-units).
- Factor B is applied to the smaller experimental units (sub-units).
- Each whole unit is a complete replicate of all the levels of factor B.
- The whole unit design may be a CRD, RCBD, or LS design.

30

Split-plot experiments are often used out of necessity. Sometimes a factor, or factorial combination, must be applied to relatively large experimental units, whereas other factors are more appropriately applied to subunits. Split-plot experiments are also used for convenience. It is often easier to apply different factors to different sized units. They may also be used to increase the precision of the estimated effect of the factor applied to the sub-units.

While the split-plot design has an agricultural heritage, with the whole-plots usually being large areas of land and the subplots being smaller areas of land within the large areas, the design is useful in many scientific and industrial experiments as well. Some books refer to it as split-unit design to convey this information.

Advantages of Split-Plot Designs

A split-plot design

- provides greater power for testing the sub-unit treatment factor and the interaction
- allows for different sized experimental units in the same experiment
- allows for including a second factor at very little cost
- involves repeated measures on the same experimental unit (whole unit) in the design.

31

Because the subunit variance is generally smaller than whole unit variance, the subunit treatment factor and the interaction are generally tested with greater sensitivity.

A split-plot design allows for experiments with a factor requiring relatively large amounts of experimental material (whole units) along with a factor requiring relatively little experimental material (subunit) in the same experiment.

If an experiment is designed to study one factor, a second factor may be included at very little cost.

The split-plot design can be considered as a design for experiments involving repeated measures (from the subunits) on the same experimental unit (whole unit)

Disadvantages of Split-Plot Designs

- Analysis is complicated by the presence of two experimental error variances, which leads to several different standard errors for comparisons.
- High variance and few replications of whole units frequently lead to poor sensitivity on the whole-unit factor.

32

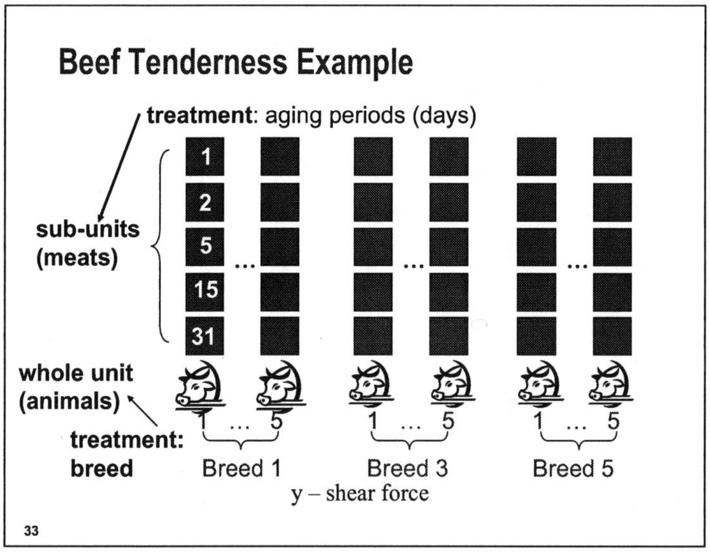

An experiment was conducted to investigate the effects of the breed and aging time on the tenderness of beef. Three breeds (1, 3, and 5) of beef cattle were included in the experiments. Five animals were randomly selected from each breed and were assigned an identification number (id). Five cuts of meat (steaks) were obtained from each animal, and each of the meats was randomly assigned to each of the five aging periods (1, 2, 5, 15, and 31). A measure of the tenderness, shear force, was obtained for each steak at the end of the aging period. *Shear force* is a standard laboratory measure of pressure required to cut meat.

In this experiment, the whole unit is the animal, and they were selected from a completely randomized design. The *treatment* applied to the whole unit is the breed. The subunit is the steak, and the treatment applied to the subunit is the aging periods. The breeds and aging periods are both fixed effects. The whole unit (animals) is a random effect. The subunit (steaks) is also a random effect and the variation among them corresponds to the residual variance components.

The Data

breed	id	age	force
1	1	1	5.79
1	1	2	5.22
1	1	5	3.80
1	1	15	3.45
1	1	31	3.27
1	2	1	5.21
1	2	2	3.94
1	2	5	3.69
1	2	15	3.36
1	2	31	2.56
1	3	1	4.61
1	3	2	3.16
1	3	5	3.30
1	3	15	2.90
1	3	31	2.85
1	4	1	8.47
1	4	2	5.31
1	4	5	4.18
1	4	15	4.33
1	4	31	4.50
...	...	...	...

34

The data is stored in the SAS data set **sasuser.beef**. These are the variables included in the data set:

breed the breeds of beef cattle

id the identification number for each animal selected from each breed

age the aging periods

force shear force, a measure of tenderness

Model for the Split-Plot Design

$$y_{ijk} = \mu + \alpha_i + \beta_j + (\alpha\beta)_{ij} + w_{k(i)} + e_{ijk}$$

breed effect, fixed

aging effect, fixed

animal effect, **id(breed)**, random

i = 1, 2, 3 (breed)
j = 1 to 5 (aging period)
k = 1 to 5 (animal)

$$w_{k(i)} \sim N(0, \sigma_w^2)$$
$$e_{ijk} \sim N(0, \sigma^2)$$

35

y_{ijk} the tenderness measurement for the steak from the ith breed, k^{th} animal, and the jth aging period.

μ the overall mean.

α_i the effect of the ith breed. This is a fixed effect.

β_j the effect of the jth aging period. This is a fixed effect.

$(\alpha\beta)_{ij}$ the effect of the breed*aging period interaction. This is a fixed effect.

$w_{k(i)}$ the whole-unit error effect, or the random effect of the kth animal from the ith breed, assumed i.i.d. $N(0, \sigma_w^2)$.

e_{ijk} the subunit error effect, assumed i.i.d. $N(0, \sigma^2)$.

As you can see, the random effect is the whole-unit error effect due to the kth animal from the ith breed. In terms of the variables in the data set, it is the **id(breed)** effect.

If the variable **id** has unique values for each animal across all breeds, you could specify **id** instead of **id(breed)** as the random effect. The results would be the same regardless of which specification you use. Note that this is true for some denominator degrees of freedom method, such as DDFM=KR or DDFM=SATTERTH, but it is not true for the default DDFM=CONTAIN, which is syntactic dependent. For the containment method, you would want to specify **id(breed)** as the random effect regardless of whether **id** has unique values or not.

Fitting a Split-Plot Type of Design

You can analyze the beef tenderness data using the MIXED procedure as follows:

```
proc print data=sasuser.beef;
run;

proc mixed data=sasuser.beef cl;
   class breed id age;
   model force=breed age breed*age / ddfm=kr;
   random id(breed);
   lsmeans age / diff adjust=tukey;
run;                                        *c02s3d1.sas;
```

The variables **breed**, **age**, and the **breed*age** interaction are fixed effects. The **id(breed)** term corresponds to the whole-unit effect; therefore, it is a random effect. The residual variance corresponds to the subunit variance. The LSMEANS statement was used to compute the LSMEANS for each value of **age**. The DIFF and ADJUST=TUKEY options compare the difference among **age** and report the Tukey-adjusted *p*-values for pairwise comparisons.

Partial PROC PRINT Output

Obs	breed	id	age	force
1	1	1	1	5.79
2	1	1	2	5.22
3	1	1	5	3.80
4	1	1	15	3.45
5	1	1	31	3.27
6	1	2	1	5.21
7	1	2	2	3.94
8	1	2	5	3.69
9	1	2	15	3.36
10	1	2	31	2.56
11	1	3	1	4.61
12	1	3	2	3.16
13	1	3	5	3.30
14	1	3	15	2.90
15	1	3	31	2.85
16	1	4	1	8.47
17	1	4	2	5.31
18	1	4	5	4.18
19	1	4	15	4.33
20	1	4	31	4.50
21	1	5	1	6.80
22	1	5	2	8.09
23	1	5	5	6.79
24	1	5	15	3.31
25	1	5	31	4.02
26	3	1	1	5.14
27	3	1	2	8.66
28	3	1	5	9.29
29	3	1	15	7.22
30	3	1	31	6.05
31	3	2	1	6.06
32	3	2	2	4.88
33	3	2	5	4.31
34	3	2	15	3.10
35	3	2	31	2.35
36	3	3	1	5.89
37	3	3	2	5.13
38	3	3	5	3.26
39	3	3	15	3.39
40	3	3	31	2.48
41	3	4	1	4.83
42	3	4	2	4.69
43	3	4	5	4.11
44	3	4	15	2.77
45	3	4	31	3.39
46	3	5	1	6.04
47	3	5	2	6.00
48	3	5	5	3.75
49	3	5	15	4.39
50	3	5	31	2.92
51	5	1	1	6.60
...	...	...	...	...

Partial PROC MIXED Output

Covariance Parameter Estimates

Cov Parm	Estimate	Alpha	Lower	Upper
id(breed)	1.1689	0.05	0.5530	3.8958
Residual	0.8895	0.05	0.6186	1.3884

The variance component associated with the whole unit (beef cattle within each breed) is 1.1689 and the variance component associated with the subunit (steaks from each animal) is 0.8895. The 95% confidence limits of these variance component estimates are provided by the CL option, and they are (0.5530, 3.8958) for $\hat{\sigma}_w^2$ and (0.6186, 1.3884) for $\hat{\sigma}^2$.

The CL option is generally preferred over the COVTEST option for making inferences about the covariance parameter estimates, especially when the number of levels for random effects is not large.

Type 3 Tests of Fixed Effects

Effect	Num DF	Den DF	F Value	Pr > F
breed	2	12	2.68	0.1089
age	4	48	21.65	<.0001
breed*age	8	48	0.94	0.4908

The tests for fixed effects indicate a nonsignificant **breed*age** interaction (*p*-value=0.4908). The effect of **age** seems to be significant (*p*-value<0.0001).

Least Squares Means

Effect	age	Estimate	Standard Error	DF	t Value	Pr > |t|
age	1	6.4247	0.3704	26.2	17.34	<.0001
age	2	5.9353	0.3704	26.2	16.02	<.0001
age	5	5.3987	0.3704	26.2	14.57	<.0001
age	15	4.1993	0.3704	26.2	11.34	<.0001
age	31	3.7613	0.3704	26.2	10.15	<.0001

The mean tenderness for each value of **age**, as well as the standard error and the *p*-value, is computed. The null hypothesis for the test is that the average value of shear force is zero for each age, which may not be practically meaningful.

It seems that as the aging period increases, the value for shear force decreases. You may want to analyze the data treating the variable **age** as a continuous variable.

Differences of Least Squares Means

Effect	age	_age	Estimate	Standard Error	DF	t Value	Pr > |t|	Adjustment	Adj P
age	1	2	0.4893	0.3444	48	1.42	0.1618	Tukey-Kramer	0.6175
age	1	5	1.0260	0.3444	48	2.98	0.0045	Tukey-Kramer	0.0349
age	1	15	2.2253	0.3444	48	6.46	<.0001	Tukey-Kramer	<.0001
age	1	31	2.6633	0.3444	48	7.73	<.0001	Tukey-Kramer	<.0001
age	2	5	0.5367	0.3444	48	1.56	0.1257	Tukey-Kramer	0.5308
age	2	15	1.7360	0.3444	48	5.04	<.0001	Tukey-Kramer	<.0001
age	2	31	2.1740	0.3444	48	6.31	<.0001	Tukey-Kramer	<.0001
age	5	15	1.1993	0.3444	48	3.48	0.0011	Tukey-Kramer	0.0090
age	5	31	1.6373	0.3444	48	4.75	<.0001	Tukey-Kramer	0.0002
age	15	31	0.4380	0.3444	48	1.27	0.2096	Tukey-Kramer	0.7094

It appears that aging periods 15 and 31 are both significantly different from other aging periods (1, 2, and 5), and they are not different from each other.

2.4 Incomplete Block Designs (Self-Study)

Objectives

- Define an incomplete block design.
- Recognize issues associated with incomplete block designs and how the MIXED procedure handles them.

43

Incomplete Block Designs

Incomplete block designs are designs in which only a subset of treatments are applied in each block. Two types of the incomplete block designs are

- *balanced* incomplete block designs (BIBD)
- *partially balanced* incomplete block designs (PBIBD).

44

In certain experiments using randomized block designs, you may not be able to run all the treatment combinations in each block. Situations like this usually occur because of shortages of experimental apparatus or facilities or the physical size of the block. For example, in an agricultural experiment, the researcher wants to examine seven varieties of a plant on the yields. The plots in each block can only accommodate a total of five varieties of the plants, which means the researcher cannot plant all seven varieties in the same block. This is an incomplete block design. The treatments that go into each block should be selected in order to provide the most information relative to the objectives of the experiment.

Two types of incomplete block designs are the balanced incomplete block design (BIBD) and the partially balanced incomplete block design (PBIBD).

An Example of a BIB Design

BLOCK	TREATMENTS
I	1, 2, 3
II	1, 2, 4
III	1, 3, 4
IV	2, 3, 4

45

The balanced incomplete block design does not mean *balanced* in the more common sense of the word, in which each treatment appears the same number of times in each block. In a balanced incomplete block design, the arrangement of the treatments in the blocks follows certain properties.

For example, consider an experiment with four treatments (1, 2, 3, and 4) and blocks of size three. This is an incomplete block design, because the number of treatments is greater than the block size. Assigning the treatments to the blocks as shown above results in a balanced incomplete block design because

- all blocks contain the same number of experimental units (3)
- all treatments occur the same number of times across all blocks (3)
- no treatment appears more than once in the same block
- all pairs of treatments appear in the same block the same number of times (2).

A partially balanced incomplete block design (PBIBD) differs from the balanced incomplete block design (BIBD) in the last bullet, where in a PBIBD, the number of times two treatments occur together in the same block may differ for different pairs of treatments. Refer to John (1971) for more information.

Issues Associated with Incomplete Block Designs

- Traditional procedures (for example, the GLM procedure) only account for intra-block variations.
- You can compute the inter-block variation and combine the intra- and inter-block variations by hand.
- The MIXED procedure does it for you.

46

In an incomplete block design, the treatment effect should be adjusted for blocks. The analyses of BIBD and PBIBD data are often referred to as *intra-block* analyses in most statistics textbooks, because treatments are compared on the basis of differences computed within blocks. The GLM procedure performs this type of analysis. Because PROC GLM essentially treats **block** as a fixed effect, it captures only part of the information. The MIXED procedure, however, combines intra- and inter-block information by treating **block** as a random effect.

The model for an incomplete block design is the same as that for an RCBD, and so is the SAS program using the MIXED procedure. You will analyze a PBIBD using PROC MIXED as one of your exercises.

2.5 Crossover Designs

Objectives

- Recognize a crossover design.
- Analyze a crossover design using the MIXED procedure.

48

Heart Rate Example

Subject	1	2	3	4	5	6	... 24
Visit 1	a	p	c	a	c	p	...
Visit 2	p	c	a	c	p	a	...
Visit 3	c	a	p	p	a	c	...
Sequence	A	B	C	D	E	F	

p=placebo c=control a=test drug

changehr – change in heart rate

49

A pharmaceutical company conducted a clinical trial to assess the effects of three treatments on the heart rate of patients. The treatments were placebo (p), control (c), and the test drug (a). Each patient in the study received the three treatments in a random order during a time period that was separated from the others so that one treatment did not influence the heart rate measurement obtained after administering the other treatment (in other words, to rule out carry-over effect). Each period was a visit to the clinic. The sequences of administering the treatments were A(a p c), B(p c a), C(c a p), D(a c p), E(c p a), and F(p a c). The drugs were assigned to twenty-four patients in a three-period crossover design, with four patients for each sequence. The change in heart rate at one hour following the treatment was measured.

The Data

patient	sequence	visit	drug	changehr
201	B	2	p	-8
201	B	3	c	12
201	B	4	a	4
202	E	2	c	10
202	E	3	p	-10
202	E	4	a	-8
203	F	2	p	-2
203	F	3	a	-10
203	F	4	c	-4
204	D	2	a	0
204	D	3	c	20
204	D	4	p	-16
205	C	2	c	-8
205	C	3	a	-32
205	C	4	p	-12
206	B	2	p	-6
206	B	3	c	8
206	B	4	a	14
207	A	2	a	-32
207	A	3	p	2
...	...	...	...	...

50

The data is stored in a SAS data set **sasuser.heart**. Here are selected variables in the data set:

patient patient (subject) ID

sequence the sequence the drugs were administered to each patient

visit the visit to the clinic

drug the drugs under investigation

changehr the change in the heart rate between one hour following the treatment and the baseline measurement.

The data set contains two other variables, **hr1h** and **basehr**. The baseline heart rate could be used as a covariate and **hr1h** could be used as the dependent variable. Because the analysis of covariance is discussed later in this chapter, use the change in the heart rate as the dependent variable for your model.

Model for the Heart Rate Example

$$y_{ijkm} = \mu + \alpha_i + \beta_j + \gamma_k + p_m + \varepsilon_{ijkm}$$

patients, random

drug, fixed

visit, fixed

sequence, fixed

i = 1, 2, 3 (drugs)

j = 1, 2, 3 (visits)

k = 1 to 6 (sequences)

m = 1 to 24 (patients)

51

y_{ijkm} the change in the heart rate for the mth patient assigned to the ith drug in the jth period using the kth sequence

μ the overall mean

α_i the effect of the ith drug, a fixed effect

β_j the effect of the jth visit, a fixed effect

γ_k the effect of the kth sequence, a fixed effect

p_m the effect of the mth patient, assumed i.i.d. N(0, σ_p^2), thus a random effect

ε_{ijkm} random error, assumed i.i.d. N(0, σ^2).

Assume p_m and ε_{ijkm} are independently and normally distributed random variables.

Fitting a Crossover Model

Questions asked in a crossover design are whether there is a treatment effect and what is the variability due to the random selection of the patients. You can analyze the data using the following program:

```
proc print data=sasuser.heart;
   var patient sequence visit drug changehr;
run;

proc mixed data=sasuser.heart;
   class patient sequence visit drug;
   model changehr=sequence visit drug / ddfm=kr;
   random patient;
   lsmeans drug / diff=control('p') adjust=dunnett;
run;                                        *c02s5d1.sas;
```

Selected LSMEANS statement options:

DIFF=<*difftype*> requests that differences of the least squares means be displayed. The optional *difftype* specifies which differences to produce, with possible values being ALL, CONTROL, CONTROLL, and CONTROLU. The *difftype* ALL requests all pairwise differences, and it is the default. The *difftype* CONTROL requests the differences with a control, which, by default, is the first level of each of the specified LSMEANS effects. To specify which levels of the effects are the controls, list the quoted formatted values in parentheses after the keyword CONTROL.

ADJUST= requests a multiple comparison adjustment for the *p*-values and confidence limits for the differences of least squares means. DUNNETT adjustment is useful when you make comparisons against the control.

The variables **`sequence`**, **`visit`**, and **`drug`** are all fixed effects. However, **`patient`** is considered to be a random effect because the patients were randomly selected from a population of patients.

Partial PROC PRINT Output

Obs	patient	sequence	visit	drug	changehr
1	201	B	2	p	-8
2	201	B	3	c	12
3	201	B	4	a	4
4	202	E	2	c	10
5	202	E	3	p	-10
6	202	E	4	a	-8
7	203	F	2	p	-2
8	203	F	3	a	-10
9	203	F	4	c	-4
10	204	D	2	a	0
11	204	D	3	c	20
12	204	D	4	p	-16
13	205	C	2	c	-8
14	205	C	3	a	-32
15	205	C	4	p	-12
16	206	B	2	p	-6
17	206	B	3	c	8
18	206	B	4	a	14
19	207	A	2	a	-32
20	207	A	3	p	2
21	207	A	4	c	-6
22	208	A	2	a	-4
23	208	A	3	p	-4
24	208	A	4	c	-12

Partial PROC MIXED Output

Class Level Information

Class	Levels	Values
patient	24	201 202 203 204 205 206 207 208 209 210 211 212 214 215 216 217 218 219 220 221 222 223 224 232
sequence	6	A B C D E F
visit	3	2 3 4
drug	3	a c p

Covariance Parameter Estimates

Cov Parm	Estimate
patient	3.1409
Residual	90.5404

The variance component associated with **`patient`** is 3.1409, and the residual variance component is 90.5404.

Type 3 Tests of Fixed Effects

Effect	Num DF	Den DF	F Value	Pr > F
sequence	5	18	0.82	0.5497
visit	2	44	1.27	0.2897
drug	2	44	1.57	0.2197

None of the fixed effects is significant; **sequence**, **visit**, and **drug** do not seem to have significant effects on the changes in the heart rate.

Least Squares Means

Effect	drug	Estimate	Standard Error	DF	t Value	Pr > |t|
drug	a	-6.6667	1.9757	60.7	-3.37	0.0013
drug	c	-2.5833	1.9757	60.7	-1.31	0.1960
drug	p	-6.9167	1.9757	60.7	-3.50	0.0009

Presuming an alpha level of 0.05, drug a and drug p seem to have a significant effect on the changes in heart rate relative to the baseline measurements. Drug c does not appear to have a significant effect on the changes in heart rate.

Differences of Least Squares Means

Effect	drug	_drug	Estimate	Standard Error	DF	t Value	Pr > |t|	Adjustment	Adj P
drug	a	p	0.2500	2.7468	44	0.09	0.9279	Dunnett-Hsu	0.9939
drug	c	p	4.3333	2.7468	44	1.58	0.1218	Dunnett-Hsu	0.2101

Either the test drug (a) or the control drug (c) showed a significant difference in the changes in heart rate from the placebo (p).

If a comparison between drugs a and c is also needed, you can use the DIFF=ALL ADJUST=TUKEY option in the LSMEANS statement.

2.6 Chapter Summary

Mixed models can be applied to a wide variety of situations, including, but not limited to, some basic designed experiments such as randomized complete block designs, two-way mixed models, split-plot designs, nested mixed models, incomplete block designs, and crossover designs.

Specifying random effects allows you to characterize the distribution of the random effects by estimating the variance associated with random effects. This variance estimate, also referred to as variance component, estimates the variance in the observed data due to the random effects, or equivalently, the covariance/correlations of the observations within the same level of the random effect.

Chapter 3 Examples of Mixed Models with Covariates

3.1 Mixed Models with Covariates

Objectives

- Perform an analysis of covariance using the MIXED procedure.
- Interpret the parameter estimates from an analysis of covariance.
- Compute adjusted means for the CLASS variable using the LSMEANS statement in an analysis of covariance.

3

Analysis of Covariance

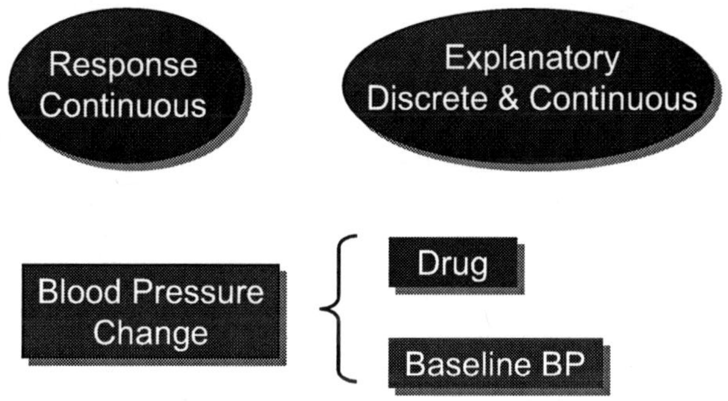

4

Analysis of covariance refers to an analysis where the response variable is continuous and the independent variables include one or more continuous variables in addition to classification variable(s). The goal of the analysis is often to examine the treatment effects accounting for the variability associated with the continuous variables, called *covariates*. A more global view of analysis of covariance describes it as a methodology to compare a series of regression models.

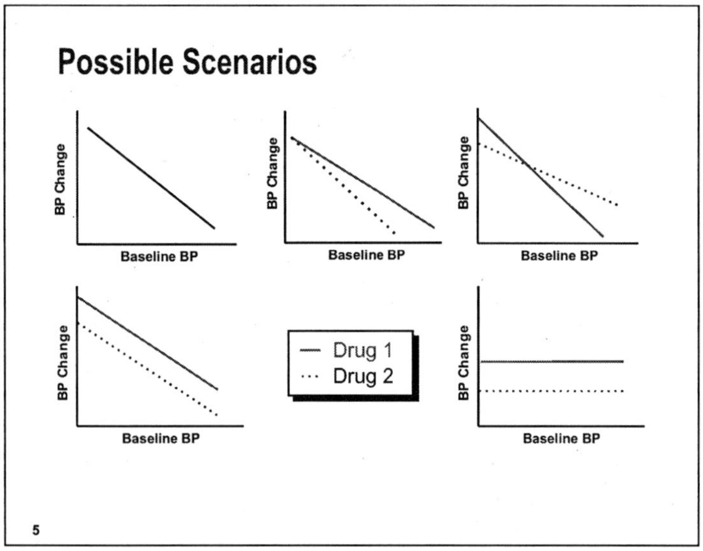

Suppose two drugs were evaluated for the effect of reducing blood pressure. Changes in blood pressure after administering one of the two drugs as well as a baseline blood pressure were measured for each subject. The relationship between the response variable and the treatment and covariate can be one of the following possible scenarios:

- the slopes and intercepts for the treatments are the same
- the slopes are different, but the intercepts are the same
- the slopes and intercepts are different
- the intercepts are different, but the slopes are the same
- the intercepts are different, but all slopes are zero (a special case of the previous scenario).

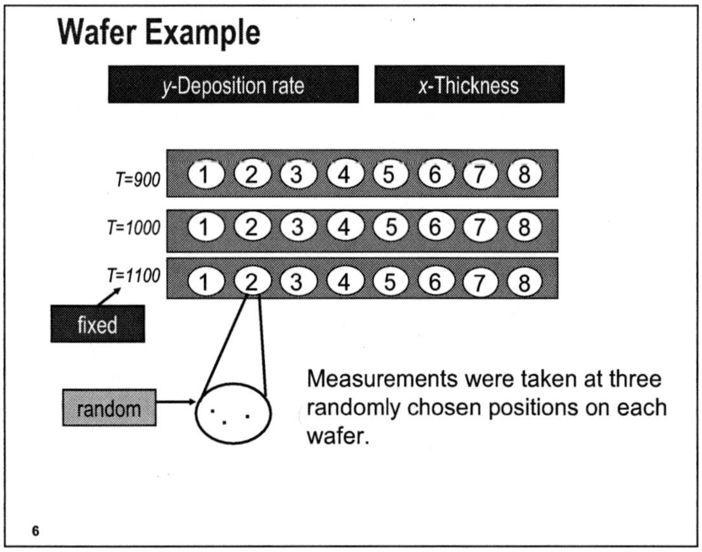

The data set **`sasuser.wafer4`** was obtained from the semiconductor industry. The experiment was designed to study the effect of temperature on the deposition rate of a layer of polysilicon in the fabrication of wafers. It was thought that the wafer thickness before the deposition process was applied might have an effect on the deposition rate. Therefore, the average thickness of each wafer (**`thick`**) was determined and used as a possible covariate.

A random sample of 24 wafers was collected and used in the experiment. Wafers were randomly assigned to one of the three levels of temperature (900°F, 1000°F, and 1100°F). As a result, each level of temperature had eight wafers assigned. The amount of deposited material at three randomly chosen sites from each wafer was measured.

The Data

temp	wafer	site	deposit	thick
900	1	1	291	1919
900	1	2	295	1919
900	1	3	294	1919
900	2	1	318	2113
900	2	2	315	2113
900	2	3	315	2113
900	3	1	306	1841
900	3	2	302	1841
900	3	3	305	1841
900	4	1	342	2170
900	4	2	341	2170
900	4	3	336	2170
900	5	1	318	2019
900	5	2	323	2019
900	5	3	323	2019
900	6	1	307	1872
900	6	2	308	1872
900	6	3	308	1872
900	7	1	295	1862
900	7	2	297	1862
...	...	...	...	...

7

These are the variables in the data sets **`sasuser.wafer4`**:

`temp` temperature (900°F, 1000°F, and 1100°F)

`wafer` wafers randomly selected and assigned to one of the three temperatures

`site` sites on each wafer where the response measurements were taken (1, 2, and 3)

`deposit` the amount of deposited material at each site

`thick` the average thickness of each wafer before the deposition process

Plotting the Data

First use the GPLOT procedure to plot the data.

```
goptions reset=all;
proc gplot data=sasuser.wafer4;
   plot deposit*thick=temp / regeqn;
   symbol1 v=star i=r c=black l=1;
   symbol2 v=circle i=r c=red l=3;
   symbol3 v=diamond i=r c=blue l=5;
run;
quit;                    *c03s1d1.sas;
```

Selected PLOT statement option:

REGEQN displays the regression equation specified in the I= option of the SYMBOL statement in the lower-left corner of the plot.

Selected SYMBOL statement option:

I=R specifies that the interpolation method of the data points is a regression equation. The default is a linear regression. You can use I=RQ or I=RC to request quadratic or cubic regression equations.

PROC GPLOT Output

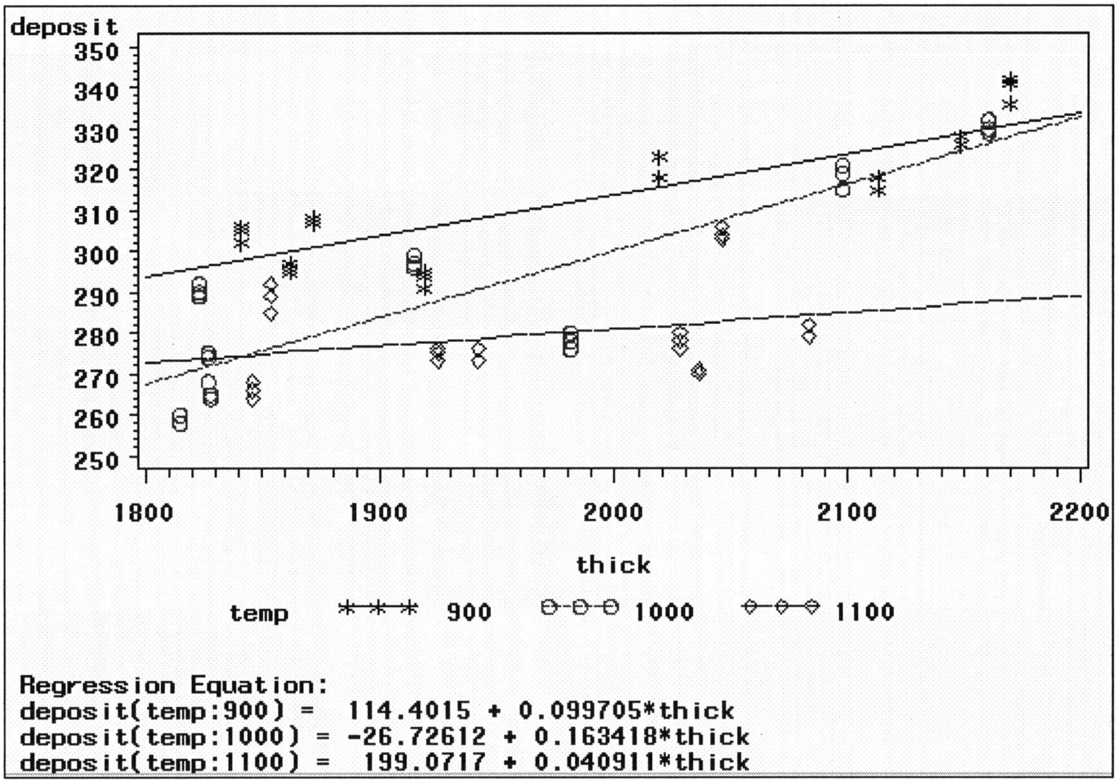

It appears that there is a positive relationship between the deposition rate and the thickness of the wafers across all three temperatures. On average, the deposition rate at 900°F seems to be higher than the deposition rate at other temperatures within the range of the data. The slopes do not seem to be the same across three temperatures.

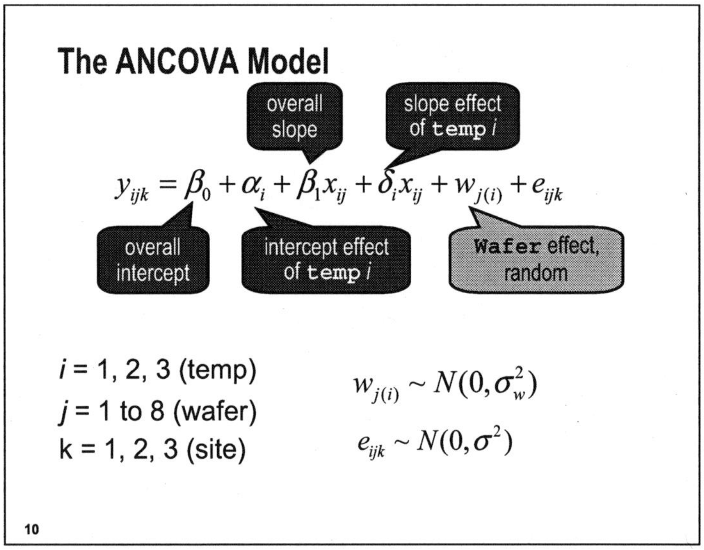

y_{ijk} the deposition rate for the kth site from the jth wafer assigned to the ith temperature.

β_0 the overall intercept.

α_i the coefficient for the ith temperature effect of the intercept.

β_1 the overall slope.

δ_i the coefficient for the ith temperature effect of the slope.

x_{ij} the covariate **thick** measured on the jth wafer assigned to the ith temperature.

$w_{j(i)}$ the wafer effect, $w_{j(i)} \sim$ i.i.d. N(0, σ_w^2). This random effect is identified by **wafer** nested within **temp**.

e_{ijk} the site effect, $e_{ijk} \sim$ i.i.d. N(0, σ^2). This term corresponds to the random error.

Fitting an ANCOVA Model

To implement the model discussed above in the MIXED procedure, you specify **temp** for the term α_i, **thick** for the term β_1, and **thick*temp** for the term δ_i.

```
proc mixed data=sasuser.wafer4;
   class temp wafer;
   model deposit=temp thick thick*temp / ddfm=kr solution;
   random wafer(temp) ;
run;                                          *c03s1d2.sas;
```

Selected MODEL statement option:

SOLUTION requests that a solution for the fixed-effects parameters be produced.

Partial PROC MIXED Output

Class Level Information

Class	Levels	Values
temp	3	900 1000 1100
wafer	8	1 2 3 4 5 6 7 8

The variable **thick** is a continuous variable, so it is not listed in this table.

Covariance Parameter Estimates

Cov Parm	Estimate
wafer(temp)	132.54
Residual	4.1944

The estimated wafer-to-wafer variance is 132.54 and the residual variance (the site-to-site variance) is 4.1944.

Solution for Fixed Effects

Effect	temp	Estimate	Standard Error	DF	t Value	Pr > |t|
Intercept		199.07	94.8320	18	2.10	0.0502
temp	900	-84.6703	114.31	18	-0.74	0.4684
temp	1000	-225.80	113.35	18	-1.99	0.0618
temp	1100	0	.	.	.	.
thick		0.04091	0.04809	18	0.85	0.4061
thick*temp	900	0.05879	0.05774	18	1.02	0.3221
thick*temp	1000	0.1225	0.05781	18	2.12	0.0483
thick*temp	1100	0	.	.	.	.

The SOLUTION option produces the estimates for the fixed effect parameters. Because this is an over-parameterized model, which means more parameters need to be estimated (8) than there are independent pieces of information for (6), PROC MIXED (and many other SAS procedures) sets the estimate of the last level of factors **temp** and **thick*temp** at zero. Therefore,

- the Intercept term corresponds to the intercept for the last level of the group variable, in this case **temp** 1100°F. The estimated intercept coefficient for **temp** 1100°F is 199.07.
- the estimate for **temp** 900°F corresponds to $\alpha_1 - \alpha_3$. It is the difference between the intercept coefficients (effects) for **temp** 900°F and **temp** 1100°F. The non-significant *p*-value indicates that these two intercept coefficients are not different from each other. The coefficient for **temp** 900°F intercept is 199.07–84.6703 = 114.40.
- the estimate for **temp** 1000°F corresponds to $\alpha_2 - \alpha_3$. It is the difference between the intercept coefficients (effects) for **temp** 1000°F and **temp** 1100°F. The marginally significant *p*-value indicates that these two intercept coefficients may be different from each other. The coefficient for **temp** 1000°F intercept is 199.07–225.80 = –26.73.
- the estimate for **thick** corresponds to the slope for the last level of the group variable, in this case **temp** 1100°F. The estimated slope for **temp** 1100°F is 0.04091.
- the estimate for **thick*temp** 900°F corresponds to the difference between the slope coefficients for **temp** 900°F and **temp** 1100°F. The nonsignificant *p*-value indicates that these two slope coefficients are not different from each other. The slope for **temp** 900°F is 0.04091+0.05879 = 0.0997.
- the estimate for **thick*temp** 1000°F corresponds to the difference between the slope coefficients for **temp** 1000°F and **temp** 1100°F. The significant *p*-value indicates that these two slope coefficients are different from each other. The slope for **temp** 1000°F is 0.04091+0.1225 = 0.1634.

The three regression lines are the following:

For **temp** 900°F, **deposit** = (199.07–84.6703) + (0.04091+0.05879) * **thick**
= 114.40 + 0.0997 * **thick**.

For **temp** 1000°F, **deposit** = (199.07–225.80) + (0.04091+0.1225) * **thick**
= –26.73 + 0.1634 * **thick**.

For **temp** 1100°F, **deposit** = 199.07 + 0.0409 * **thick**.

The equations are consistent with the PROC GPLOT output. Note that with the presence of random effects, PROC MIXED solutions may not always be consistent with the PROC GPLOT output. You obtain consistent estimates for this example because you have balanced data.

Type 3 Tests of Fixed Effects

Effect	Num DF	Den DF	F Value	Pr > F
temp	2	18	2.38	0.1209
thick	1	18	21.18	0.0002
thick*temp	2	18	2.44	0.1155

The test for **thick*temp** corresponds to the differential effects of **thick** at different levels of **temp**. In other words, it tests whether the slopes are equal across all three levels of temperatures. The nonsignificant *p*-value (0.1155) indicates that slopes are not significantly different from each other at α=0.05. There may not be enough evidence to warrant an unequal slope model.

However, from the Solutions for Fixed Effects table, you found a significant difference in the slopes between temperatures 1000°F and 1100°F. Some statisticians feel that if the overall F-test is non-significant then you may not examine the individual tests. Others feel that the individual test may be more powerful than the overall test in some situations and that you also need to examine the graph.

You may decide to keep the unequal slope model, given the graph and the Solutions results. On the other hand, if you decide that the evidence to support an unequal slope model is not enough (p-value=0.1155), you may want to take out the **thick*temp** interaction term and fit a common slope model.

```
proc mixed data=sasuser.wafer4;
   class temp wafer;
   model deposit=temp thick / solution ddfm=kr;
   random wafer(temp) ;
run;                                          *c03s1d3.sas;
```

Partial PROC MIXED Output

Covariance Parameter Estimates

Cov Parm	Estimate
wafer(temp)	151.82
Residual	4.1944

The covariance parameter estimate for **wafer(temp)** is 151.82. This is different from the estimates from the previous model (132.54). You specified a different mean model and that will likely change the parameter estimates for the fixed effects as well.

Solution for Fixed Effects

Effect	temp	Estimate	Standard Error	DF	t Value	Pr > |t|
Intercept		53.0989	43.3872	20	1.22	0.2352
temp	900	30.7988	6.2097	20	4.96	<.0001
temp	1000	13.6520	6.2477	20	2.19	0.0410
temp	1100	0	.	.	.	.
thick		0.1150	0.02191	20	5.25	<.0001

The three regression lines are the following:

For **temp** 900°F, **deposit** = (30.7988 + 53.0989) + 0.1150 * **thick**
= 83.8977 + 0.1150 * **thick**.

For **temp** 1000°F, **deposit** = (13.6520 + 53.0989) + 0.1150 * **thick**
= 66.7509+ 0.1150 * **thick**.

For **temp** 1100°F, **deposit** = 53.0989 + 0.1150 * **thick**.

Type 3 Tests of Fixed Effects

Effect	Num DF	Den DF	F Value	Pr > F
temp	2	20	12.33	0.0003
thick	1	20	27.55	<.0001

The tests for the fixed effects suggest that the common slope (indicated by **thick**) significantly differs from zero (p-value < 0.0001).

The intercept estimate for each temperature can also be obtained by specifying ESTIMATE statements in PROC MIXED. For example, the following code produces the intercept coefficient for each temperature:

```
proc mixed data=sasuser.wafer4;
   class temp wafer;
   model deposit=temp thick / ddfm=kr;
   random wafer(temp) ;
   estimate 'Intercept for temp 900' intercept 1 temp 1 0 0;
   estimate 'Intercept for temp 1000' intercept 1 temp 0 1 0;
   estimate 'Intercept for temp 1100' intercept 1 temp 0 0 1;
run;
```

Related Output

Estimates

Label	Estimate	Standard Error	DF	t Value	Pr > |t|
Intercept for temp 900	83.8977	43.8914	20	1.91	0.0704
Intercept for temp 1000	66.7510	42.5371	20	1.57	0.1323
Intercept for temp 1100	53.0989	43.3872	20	1.22	0.2352

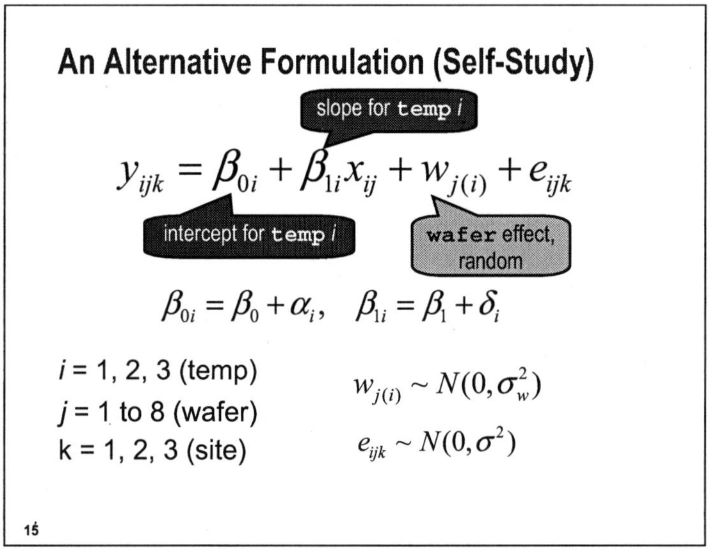

An alternative formulation of an analysis of covariance model is given.

β_{0i} the intercept coefficient for temperature i. This term corresponds to $\beta_0+\alpha_i$ in the previous model specification.

β_{1i} the slope coefficient for temperature i. This term corresponds to $\beta_1+\delta_i$ in the previous model specification.

This formulation provides the direct estimates of the intercept and slope coefficients. The test for H_0: $\beta_{1i} = 0$, however, tests for whether all slopes for different levels of temperature are equal to zero. To test whether all slopes are equal to each other, you need to write the CONTRAST statement in PROC MIXED.

Fitting the ANCOVA Model Using an Alternative Formulation (Self-Study)

To fit the model using PROC MIXED, you need to suppress the overall intercept that is fit by default. You specify **temp** for the term β_{0i} and **thick*temp** for the term β_{1i}. Notice that with the overall intercept and overall slope left out of the model, the same term **temp** has different meanings compared with that in the previous model specification. Similarly, the same term **thick*temp** has different meanings as well. For example, the test for **thick*temp** is now for the hypothesis that all slope coefficients for different temperatures equal to zero.

```
proc mixed data=sasuser.wafer4;
   class temp wafer;
   model deposit=temp thick*temp / noint ddfm=kr solution;
   random wafer(temp);
   contrast 'slopes are all equal' thick*temp 1 -1 0,
                                   thick*temp 1 0 -1;
run;                                   *c03s1d4.sas;
```

Selected MODEL statement option:

NOINT requests that no intercept be included in the model.

Without the overall intercept (NOINT option) and overall slope (would be fit by **thick**), the MODEL statement fits separate intercepts and separate slopes for each **temp**. The estimates for these intercepts and slopes are provided by the SOLUTION option. The RANDOM statement specifies the variance components associated with **wafer** nested within **temp**. The site-to-site variance is modeled by the residual variance. The CONTRAST statement was used to test whether the unequal slope model is necessary.

Partial PROC MIXED Output

Covariance Parameter Estimates

Cov Parm	Estimate
wafer(temp)	132.54
Residual	4.1944

The covariance parameter estimates are the same as those from the first model fit in this section. These two models are identical except that a different parameterization is used in this model specification.

Solution for Fixed Effects

Effect	temp	Estimate	Standard Error	DF	t Value	Pr > |t|
temp	900	114.40	63.8315	18	1.79	0.0899
temp	1000	-26.7261	62.0942	18	-0.43	0.6720
temp	1100	199.07	94.8320	18	2.10	0.0502
thick*temp	900	0.09970	0.03196	18	3.12	0.0059
thick*temp	1000	0.1634	0.03209	18	5.09	<.0001
thick*temp	1100	0.04091	0.04809	18	0.85	0.4061

The solution for the fixed effects provides estimates for the intercepts and slopes directly. For a temperature of 900°F, the intercept is 114.40 and the slope is 0.0997. For a temperature of 1000°F, the intercept is –26.7261 and the slope is 0.1634. The slopes are both significantly different from zero, as indicated by their *p*-values. Similarly, for a temperature of 1100°F, the intercept is 199.07 and the slope is 0.04091. The slopes and intercepts are identical to the ones you obtained earlier using different parameterizations.

Type 3 Tests of Fixed Effects

Effect	Num DF	Den DF	F Value	Pr > F
temp	3	18	2.60	0.0838
thick*temp	3	18	12.13	0.0001

The significant *p*-value for **thick*temp** indicates that not all slopes are equal to zero.

Contrasts

Label	Num DF	Den DF	F Value	Pr > F
slopes are all equal	2	18	2.44	0.1155

The *p*-value of 0.1155 for this test indicates that there is not enough evidence to reject the null hypothesis that the slopes are all equal for different temperatures. You may want to fit an equal slope model to the data.

You have seen the equal slope model as discussed previously. Using the alternative formulation to fit the same model, you need to specify the NOINT option in the MODEL statement. This allows you to obtain the intercept coefficients for different temperatures directly.

```
proc mixed data=sasuser.wafer4;
   class temp wafer;
   model deposit=temp thick / noint ddfm=kr solution;
   random wafer(temp);
run;                                          *c03s1d4.sas;
```

Partial PROC MIXED Output

Solution for Fixed Effects

Effect	temp	Estimate	Standard Error	DF	t Value	Pr > |t|
temp	900	83.8977	43.8914	20	1.91	0.0704
temp	1000	66.7510	42.5371	20	1.57	0.1323
temp	1100	53.0989	43.3872	20	1.22	0.2352
thick		0.1150	0.02191	20	5.25	<.0001

The intercept coefficients for each temperature are provided in this table. Because the NOINT option suppresses the overall intercept, your model is not overparameterized. Therefore, the parameter estimates are straightforward to interpret.

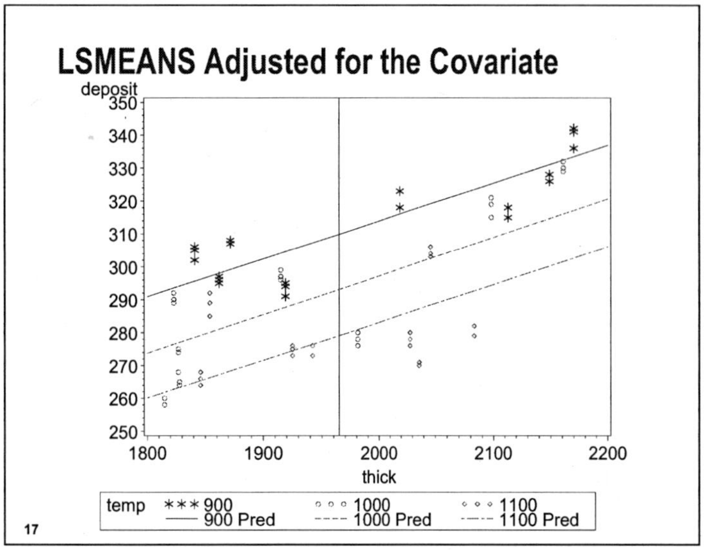

To compute the average deposition rates for temperatures 900°F, 1000°F, and 1100°F, you can use the LSMEANS statement as discussed before. The least squares means in the presence of a covariate are the adjusted treatment means—adjusted for the covariate(s). By default, the treatment means are computed for the average value of the covariate (`thick`), that is $\beta_0 + \alpha_i + \beta_1 \bar{x}_{..}$. You may specify other values of your interest for the covariate.

The adjusted treatment means are appropriate when there is no reason to believe that covariate means depend on the treatment, which is the case for this example and most other situations as well.

Computing the Least Squares Means

```
proc mixed data=sasuser.wafer4;
   class temp wafer;
   model deposit=temp thick / ddfm=kr;
   lsmeans temp / diff;
   lsmeans temp / at thick=1850 diff;
   random wafer(temp);
run;                                        *c03s1d5.sas;
```

Selected LSMEANS statement option:

AT *variable=value* enables you to modify the values of the covariates used in computing least squares means. By default, all covariate effects are set equal to their mean values for computation of standard least squares means. The AT option enables you to set the covariates to whatever values you consider interesting.

Partial PROC MIXED Output

Least Squares Means

Effect	temp	thick	Estimate	Standard Error	DF	t Value	Pr > |t|
temp	900	1964.7	309.86	4.4204	20	70.10	<.0001
temp	1000	1964.7	292.71	4.4382	20	65.95	<.0001
temp	1100	1964.7	279.06	4.3778	20	63.74	<.0001
temp	900	1850.0	296.66	5.3840	20	55.10	<.0001
temp	1000	1850.0	279.52	4.7225	20	59.19	<.0001
temp	1100	1850.0	265.87	5.1055	20	52.07	<.0001

Differences of Least Squares Means

Effect	temp	_temp	thick	Estimate	Standard Error	DF	t Value	Pr > |t|
temp	900	1000	1964.7	17.1467	6.3369	20	2.71	0.0136
temp	900	1100	1964.7	30.7988	6.2097	20	4.96	<.0001
temp	1000	1100	1964.7	13.6520	6.2477	20	2.19	0.0410
temp	900	1000	1850.0	17.1467	6.3369	20	2.71	0.0136
temp	900	1100	1850.0	30.7988	6.2097	20	4.96	<.0001
temp	1000	1100	1850.0	13.6520	6.2477	20	2.19	0.0410

At the mean value of **thick**, 1964.7, the average amount of deposit for **temp** 900°F, 1000°F, and 1100°F is 309.86, 292.71, and 279.06, respectively. At the **thick** value of 1850, the average amount of deposit for **temp** 900°F, 1000°F, and 1100°F is 296.66, 279.52, and 265.87, respectively. At any thickness level, the average amount of deposit for **temp** 900°F is 17.15 larger than that for **temp** 1000°F and 30.80 larger than that for **temp** 1100°F. These differences are significantly different from zero (*p*-value=0.0136 and <0.0001, respectively). The average amount of deposit for **temp** 1000°F is 13.65 larger than that for **temp** 1100°F, and this difference is significantly different from zero (*p*-value=0.0410, unadjusted). The same difference for different values of thickness is due to the common slope model.

3.2 Random Coefficient Models

Objectives

- Identify random coefficient models.
- Fit a random coefficient model using the MIXED procedure.

24

Random Coefficient Models

- In the analysis of covariance, the regression coefficients for the covariates are assumed to be fixed effects, that is, unknown fixed parameters estimated from data.
- In the random coefficient model, the regression coefficients for one or more covariates are assumed to be a random sample from some population of possible coefficients.

25

The basic structure of random coefficient models builds on the analysis of covariance models discussed earlier. In the analysis of covariance, the regression coefficients for the covariates are assumed to be fixed effects, that is, unknown fixed parameters that are estimated from the data. In this section, the regression coefficients for one or more covariates are assumed to be a random sample from some population of possible coefficients, hence the term *random coefficients*. Random coefficient models are sensible whenever the data arises from independent subjects or clusters, and the regression model for each subject or cluster can be assumed to be a random deviation from some population regression model.

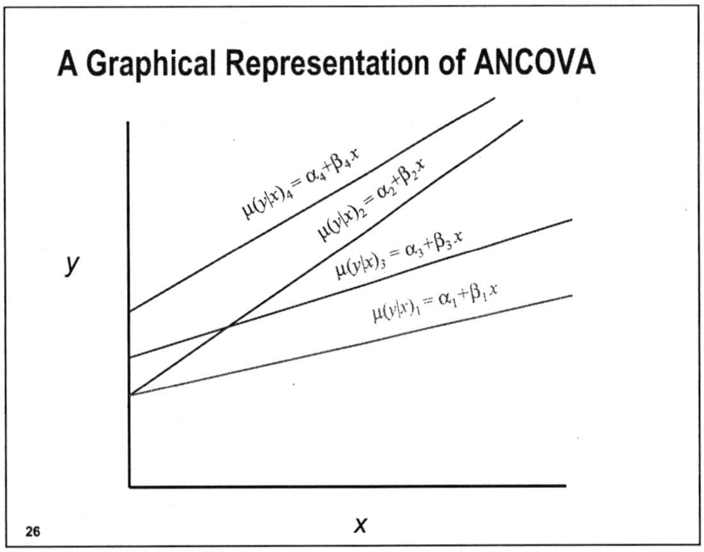

In analysis of covariance, you assume the classification variable represents all levels of interests; therefore, it is a fixed effect. The regression coefficients for each level of the classification variable represent unknown fixed parameters that are estimated from the data.

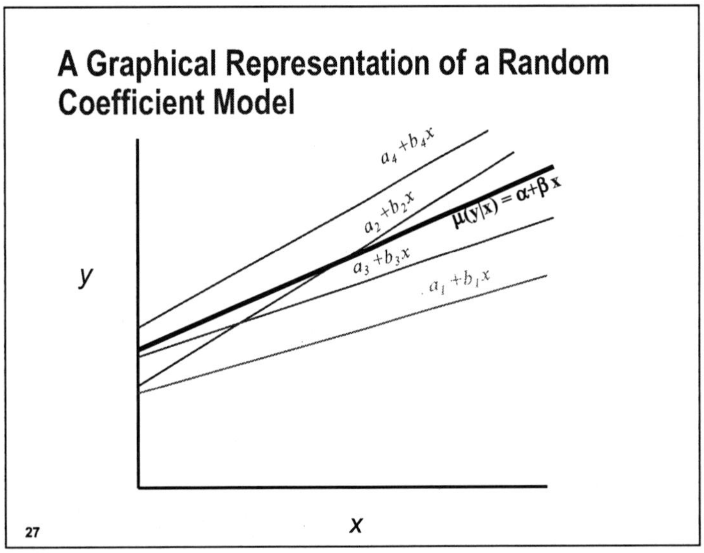

In this graph, the random regression lines for each subject deviate about the overall population regression line, $\mu(y \mid x)$. The goals of fitting a random coefficient model are (1) to estimate the variances of the intercept and the slope and any covariance between the two; and (2) to obtain the best linear unbiased predictors (BLUP) of the intercept and slope for each subject or cluster.

In this section, you only consider the standard random intercept-slope model, although the concept can be extended to more levels of hierarchy, as well as more than two random coefficients at each level.

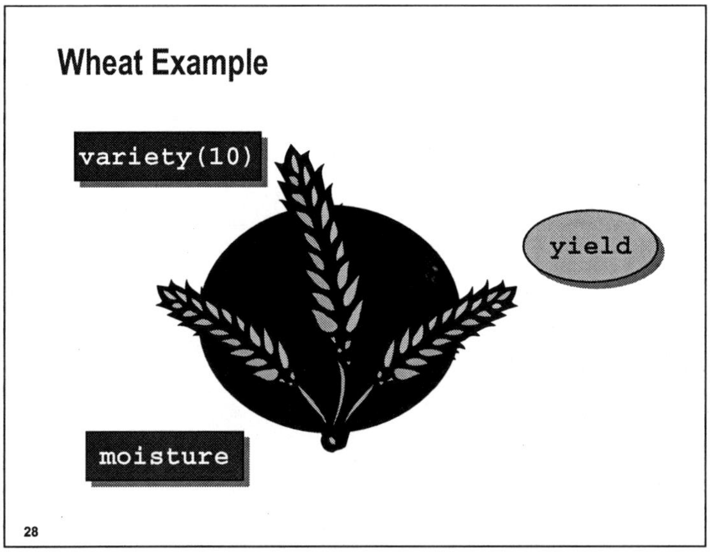

Ten varieties of wheat were randomly selected from the population of varieties of hard red winter wheat adapted to dry climate conditions. Each variety was randomly assigned to six one-acre plots of land; thus the experimental units are one-acre plots of land in a 60-acre field. It was thought that the preplant moisture content of the plots could have an influence on the germination rate and hence the eventual yield of the plots. Therefore, the amount of preplanting moisture in the top 36 inches of the soil was determined for each plot. The response variable is the yield in bushels per acre (**`yield`**), and the covariate is the measured amount of moisture (**`moist`**).

The Data

id	variety	moist	yield
1	1	10	41
2	1	57	69
3	1	32	53
4	1	52	66
5	1	47	64
6	1	48	64
7	2	30	49
8	2	21	44
9	2	20	44
10	2	26	46
11	2	44	57
12	2	19	42
13	3	50	69
14	3	40	62
15	3	23	50
16	3	58	76
17	3	21	48
18	3	30	55
19	4	22	48
...	...	...	...

29

The data set **sasuser.wheat** contains the following variables:

id the identification number for the plots

variety ten randomly selected varieties of winter wheat

moist the amount of moisture measured before planting the varieties on the plots

yield the yield of the plot in bushels per acre

Because varieties were randomly selected from the population of wheat varieties and hence a random effect, the resulting regression model for each variety represents a random sample from the model for the population of varieties. Each regression model can be expressed as deviations from the population model.

Yield versus Moisture

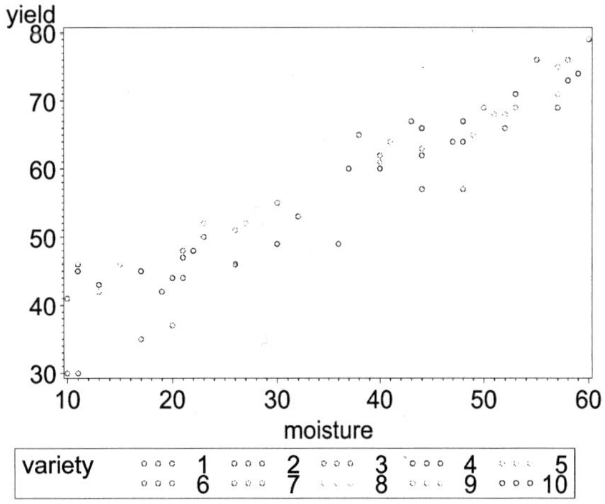

30

The **yield** increases as **moist** increases, and a linear regression model would be adequate to describe your data.

Model for the Wheat Example

slope for **variety** *i*, random

$$y_{ij} = a_i + b_i x_{ij} + e_{ij}$$

intercept for **variety** *i*, random

$$a_i \sim N(\alpha, \sigma_a^2)$$
$$b_i \sim N(\beta, \sigma_b^2)$$
$$Cov(a_i, b_i) = \sigma_{ab}$$

i = 1 to 10 (variety)

j = 1 to 6 (plot)

32

y_{ij} the yield for the ith variety in the jth plot.

x_{ij} the moisture for the ith variety in the jth plot.

a_i the intercept for the ith variety. This is a random effect because **variety** is a random effect.

b_i the slope for the ith variety. This is also a random effect because **variety** is a random effect.

e_{ij} random error, assumed to be i.i.d. with $N(0, \sigma^2)$.

For the random intercept and the random slope, assume they are normally distributed with mean α and β, respectively, and a covariance matrix of ψ, that is,

$$\begin{pmatrix} a_i \\ b_i \end{pmatrix} \sim iid\ N\left[\begin{pmatrix} \alpha \\ \beta \end{pmatrix}, \psi\right]$$

$$\psi = \begin{bmatrix} \sigma_a^2 & \sigma_{ab} \\ \sigma_{ab} & \sigma_b^2 \end{bmatrix}.$$

In Terms of a Mixed Model

$$\left.\begin{aligned} y_{ij} &= a_i + b_i x_{ij} + e_{ij} \\ a_i &= \alpha + a_i^* \\ b_i &= \beta + b_i^* \end{aligned}\right\} \qquad \begin{aligned} &a_i^* \sim N(0,\sigma_a^2) \\ &b_i^* \sim N(0,\sigma_b^2) \\ &Cov(a_i^*, b_i^*) = \sigma_{ab} \end{aligned}$$

$$y_{ij} = \alpha + \beta x_{ij} + a_i^* + b_i^* x_{ij} + e_{ij}$$

population intercept — population slope — intercept deviation — slope deviation

i = 1 to 10 (variety)

j = 1 to 6 (plot)

34

The fixed effects of the model are the intercept α and the slope β, which are expected values of the population of the intercepts and slopes of the varieties.

The variable a_i* represents the difference between the intercept α for the ith variety and the overall intercept α, and b_i* represents the difference between the slope for the ith variety and the overall slope β. Therefore, $a_i^* = a_i - \alpha$, and $b_i^* = b_i - \beta$.

Assume a_i* and b_i* are normally distributed random variables with mean 0 and the same covariance matrix ψ, that is, $\begin{pmatrix} a_i^* \\ b_i^* \end{pmatrix} \sim iid\ N\left[\begin{pmatrix} 0 \\ 0 \end{pmatrix}, \psi\right]$, and $\psi = \begin{bmatrix} \sigma_a^2 & \sigma_{ab} \\ \sigma_{ab} & \sigma_b^2 \end{bmatrix}$.

Therefore,

- $\alpha + \beta x_{ij}$ is the fixed effects part of the model
- $a_i^* + b_i^* x_{ij} + e_{ij}$ is the random effects part of the model
- $Var(y_{ij}) = \begin{bmatrix} 1 & x_{ij} \end{bmatrix} \psi \begin{bmatrix} 1 \\ x_{ij} \end{bmatrix} + \sigma^2$ is the variance for any observation.

Details

$$Var(y_{ij}) = \begin{bmatrix} 1 & x_{ij} \end{bmatrix} \begin{bmatrix} \sigma_a^2 & \sigma_{ab} \\ \sigma_{ab} & \sigma_b^2 \end{bmatrix} \begin{bmatrix} 1 \\ x_{ij} \end{bmatrix} + \sigma^2 = \begin{bmatrix} \sigma_a^2 + \sigma_{ab} x_{ij} & \sigma_{ab} + \sigma_b^2 x_{ij} \end{bmatrix} \begin{bmatrix} 1 \\ x_{ij} \end{bmatrix} + \sigma^2$$

$$= \sigma_a^2 + 2\sigma_{ab} x_{ij} + \sigma_b^2 x_{ij}^2 + \sigma^2.$$

$$Cov(y_{ij}, y_{ik}) = Cov(a_i^* + b_i^* x_{ij} + e_{ij}, a_i^* + b_i^* x_{ik} + e_{ik}) = \sigma_a^2 + \sigma_{ab} x_{ik} + \sigma_{ab} x_{ij} + \sigma_b^2 x_{ij} x_{ik}$$

A RANDOM Statement with the SUBJECT= Option

```
model yield=moist / ddfm=kr;
random int moist / type=un subject=variety;
```

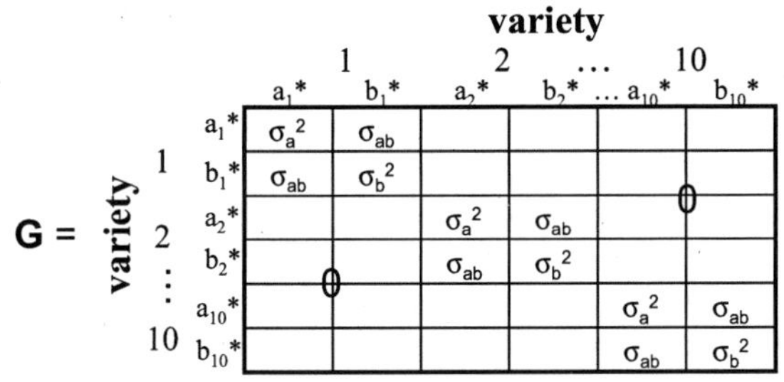

35

When you use the MIXED procedure to fit the random coefficient model to the data, you use the following MODEL and RANDOM statements in PROC MIXED:

```
model yield=moist / ddfm=kr;
random int moist / type=un subject=variety;
```

The MODEL statement specifies the fixed-effects part of the model. The intercept is included by default. The RANDOM statement specifies the random-effects part of the model. You must specify the intercept random effect explicitly. TYPE=UN in the RANDOM statement specifies the covariance structure of intercept and slope of the form $\psi = \begin{bmatrix} \sigma_a^2 & \sigma_{ab} \\ \sigma_{ab} & \sigma_b^2 \end{bmatrix}$; therefore, the estimates of the variances of the slopes (σ_b^2) and of the intercepts (σ_a^2), as well as the covariance between slopes and the intercepts (σ_{ab}) are estimated. The SUBJECT=`variety` in the RANDOM statement specifies that the intercept effect and the slope effect of one variety is independently distributed from the intercept effects and the slope effects of other varieties, but the intercept effect and the slope effect within each variety are correlated. This option produces a block-diagonal structure in **G** (the covariance matrix of the random effects) with identical blocks as shown above.

Fitting a Random Coefficient Model

When fitting a random coefficient model, it is recommended that you scale your independent variables to be between 1 and 10 if possible to improve numerical stability.

```
data wheat;
   set sasuser.wheat;
   moist10=moist/10;
run;

proc mixed data=wheat;
   class variety;
   model yield=moist10 / ddfm=kr solution outp=pred;
   random int moist10 / type=un subject=variety solution G;
   ods output SolutionF=overall;
run;

proc print data=pred;
run;

proc print data=overall;
run;                                        *c03s2d1.sas;
```

Selected MODEL statement options:

OUTP=	specifies an output data set containing predicted values and related quantities.

Selected RANDOM statement options:

TYPE=	specifies the covariance structure of **G** (the covariance matrix of the random effects). Although a variety of structures are available, most applications call for either TYPE=VC or TYPE=UN. The TYPE=VC (variance components) option is the default structure, and it models a different variance component for each random effect. The TYPE=UN (unstructured) option is useful for fitting random coefficient models.
G	requests that the estimated **G** matrix be displayed. PROC MIXED displays blanks for values that are 0. If you specify the SUBJECT= option, then the block of the **G** matrix corresponding to the first subject is displayed.
SOLUTION	requests that the solution for the random-effects parameters be produced. These estimates are the empirical best linear unbiased predictors (EBLUPs). They can be useful for comparing the random effects from different experimental units and can also be treated as residuals in performing diagnostics for your mixed model.
SUBJECT=	identifies the subjects in your mixed model. Complete independence is assumed across subjects; thus, for the RANDOM statement, the SUBJECT= option produces a block-diagonal structure in **G** (the covariance matrix for random effects) with identical blocks. The **Z** matrix (the design matrix for the random effects) is modified to accommodate this block diagonality. In fact, specifying a subject effect is equivalent to nesting all other effects in the RANDOM statement within the subject effect.

In this example, TYPE=UN in the RANDOM statement specifies the covariance structure of intercept and slope of the form $\psi = \begin{bmatrix} \sigma_a^2 & \sigma_{ab} \\ \sigma_{ab} & \sigma_b^2 \end{bmatrix}$; therefore, the estimates of the variances of the slopes (σ_b^2) and of the intercepts (σ_a^2) as well as the covariance between slopes and intercepts (σ_{ab}) will be estimated. The SUBJECT=**variety** in the RANDOM statement produces a block-diagonal structure in **G** (the covariance matrix for random effects) with identical blocks. Including INT **moist10** with SUBJECT=**variety** in the RANDOM statement generates the terms **variety** from INT and **moist10*variety** from **moist10**.

Partial PROC MIXED Output

```
                         Estimated G Matrix

        Row    Effect        variety        Col1         Col2

          1    Intercept     1           18.8947      -0.7272
          2    moist10       1           -0.7272       0.2394
```

This table shows the estimated **G** matrix for the first block (**`variety`**). The same information is also represented in the following default table.

Covariance Parameter Estimates

Cov Parm	Subject	Estimate
UN(1,1)	variety	18.8947
UN(2,1)	variety	-0.7272
UN(2,2)	variety	0.2394
Residual		0.3521

The REML estimates of the variance and covariance of the slopes and intercepts are

$\hat{\psi} = \begin{bmatrix} 18.8947 & -0.7272 \\ -0.7272 & 0.2394 \end{bmatrix}$. In other words, the intercept variance is 18.8947, the slope variance is 0.2394, and the covariance between the intercept and slope is –0.7272. The estimated residual variance is $\hat{\sigma}^2 = 0.3521$.

Fit Statistics

-2 Res Log Likelihood	181.5
AIC (smaller is better)	189.5
AICC (smaller is better)	190.3
BIC (smaller is better)	190.8

Null Model Likelihood Ratio Test

DF	Chi-Square	Pr > ChiSq
3	150.52	<.0001

The Null Model Likelihood Ratio Test provides a likelihood ratio test (LRT) to determine whether it is necessary to model the covariance structure of the data at all. The chi-square value is –2 times the log likelihood from the null model minus –2 times the log likelihood from the fitted model. The null model is the one with only the fixed effects (specified by the MODEL statement), and the covariance matrix for the errors being $\mathbf{R}=\sigma^2 I_n$, independent error terms. The DF value in the output is the difference in the number of covariance parameters between the fitted model and null model (4-1=3). The Pr > Chisq value is the upper-tail area from the chi-square distribution with 3 degrees of freedom. The *p*-value of <0.0001 indicates that the random coefficient model you fit is better than the null model.

Solution for Fixed Effects

Effect	Estimate	Standard Error	DF	t Value	Pr > |t|
Intercept	33.4339	1.3997	9.2	23.89	<.0001
moist10	6.6166	0.1683	8.66	39.32	<.0001

The Solution for Fixed Effects table provides $\hat{\alpha} = 33.4339$ and $\hat{\beta} = 6.6166$. Therefore, the expected population intercept from all varieties is 33.43 and the expected population slope from all varieties is estimated to be 6.6166. Both are significantly different from zero.

Solution for Random Effects

Effect	variety	Estimate	Std Err Pred	DF	t Value	Pr > |t|
Intercept	1	0.9578	1.5215	12.3	0.63	0.5405
moist10	1	-0.4921	0.2161	17.9	-2.28	0.0353
Intercept	2	-2.2843	1.5526	12.8	-1.47	0.1655
moist10	2	-0.6670	0.2925	24.4	-2.28	0.0316
Intercept	3	-0.4081	1.5299	12.5	-0.27	0.7940
moist10	3	0.6722	0.2298	20.1	2.93	0.0083
Intercept	4	0.6960	1.4943	11.5	0.47	0.6501
moist10	4	-0.2331	0.2483	22.3	-0.94	0.3579
Intercept	5	1.1159	1.7421	17.7	0.64	0.5300
moist10	5	-0.1990	0.2748	24	-0.72	0.4758
Intercept	6	4.6391	1.4731	11.1	3.15	0.0092
moist10	6	0.2389	0.2019	15.3	1.18	0.2547
Intercept	7	-10.7300	1.4626	10.7	-7.34	<.0001
moist10	7	0.5642	0.2285	19.9	2.47	0.0227
Intercept	8	2.4012	1.4946	11.5	1.61	0.1351
moist10	8	0.2243	0.2276	19.8	0.99	0.3363
Intercept	9	-0.1762	1.5309	12.5	-0.12	0.9102
moist10	9	0.2336	0.2293	20	1.02	0.3205
Intercept	10	3.7886	1.9211	21.4	1.97	0.0617
moist10	10	-0.3421	0.3098	24.1	-1.10	0.2804

The Solution for Random Effects table provides the predicted values for the deviation of the intercept from the population mean intercept and the deviation of the slope from the population mean slope for each variety. For example, the first variety's intercept estimate, 0.9578, is a prediction of $a_1 - \alpha$, and its slope estimate, -0.4921, is a prediction of $b_1 - \beta$. The deviations of intercepts and deviations of slopes can be used with the estimates of α and β to obtain the predicted intercept and slope for each variety.

Type 3 Tests of Fixed Effects

Effect	Num DF	Den DF	F Value	Pr > F
moist10	1	8.66	1545.93	<.0001

The test for the fixed effect **`moist10`** indicates that the population slope is significantly different from zero.

Obs	id	variety	yield	moist	moist10	Pred	Pred	DF	Alpha	Lower	Upper	Resid
1	1	1	41	10	1.0	40.5161	0.53003	45.2181	0.05	39.4487	41.5835	0.48388
2	2	1	69	57	5.7	69.3010	0.34349	43.2199	0.05	68.6084	69.9936	-0.30099
3	3	1	53	32	3.2	53.9899	0.27809	41.6972	0.05	53.4286	54.5512	-0.98989
4	4	1	66	52	5.2	66.2388	0.29446	42.0366	0.05	65.6445	66.8330	-0.23877
5	5	1	64	47	4.7	63.1766	0.25885	40.7229	0.05	62.6537	63.6994	0.82345
6	6	1	64	48	4.8	63.7890	0.26461	40.9699	0.05	63.2546	64.3234	0.21100
7	7	2	49	30	3.0	48.9983	0.25819	42.1584	0.05	48.4774	49.5193	0.00165
8	8	2	44	21	2.1	43.6437	0.28623	44.7321	0.05	43.0671	44.2203	0.35627
9	9	2	44	20	2.0	43.0488	0.30144	45.7966	0.05	42.4419	43.6556	0.95123
10	10	2	46	26	2.6	46.6185	0.24280	40.0350	0.05	46.1278	47.1092	-0.61852
11	11	2	57	44	4.4	57.3278	0.52557	48.9979	0.05	56.2716	58.3839	-0.32776
12	12	2	42	19	1.9	42.4538	0.31821	46.7050	0.05	41.8135	43.0941	-0.45381
13	13	3	69	50	5.0	69.4697	0.33297	43.9288	0.05	68.7986	70.1408	-0.46967
14	14	3	62	40	4.0	62.1809	0.24785	40.3208	0.05	61.6801	62.6817	-0.18089
15	15	3	50	23	2.3	49.7900	0.34505	44.3492	0.05	49.0947	50.4852	0.21004
16	16	3	76	58	5.8	75.3007	0.44144	45.7103	0.05	74.4120	76.1894	0.69930
17	17	3	48	21	2.1	48.3322	0.37090	44.8712	0.05	47.5851	49.0793	-0.33220
18	18	3	55	30	3.0	54.8921	0.27152	41.7963	0.05	54.3441	55.4401	0.10789
19	19	4	48	22	2.2	48.1736	0.25681	41.1551	0.05	47.6550	48.6922	-0.17359
20	20	4	60	40	4.0	59.6639	0.37298	46.2592	0.05	58.9132	60.4145	0.33613
... ...	... ...	...	...	...	...	...	...	...	...			

The OUTP= option in the MODEL statement produces an output data set that contains predicted values and related quantities. The variable **Pred** is used later to construct a plot showing predicted regression lines for each variety.

Obs	Effect	Estimate	StdErr	DF	tValue	Probt
1	Intercept	33.4339	1.3997	9.2	23.89	<.0001
2	moist10	6.6166	0.1683	8.66	39.32	<.0001

The Solution for Fixed Effects table was saved as the SAS data set **overall** by the ODS OUTPUT statement. This data set is used to construct a plot.

```
proc transpose data=overall(keep=estimate)
               out=pop(rename=(col1=alpha col2=beta));
run;

data pop(drop=alpha beta _name_);
   set pop;
   variety=0;  *identifier for 'overall';
   moist10=1;  *smallest value of moist10;
   pred=alpha+beta*moist10;
   output;
   moist10=6;  *largest value of moist10;
   pred=alpha+beta*moist10;
   output;
run;

proc format;
   value variety
   0='Population';
run;

data plot;
   set pop pred;
run;

proc gplot data=plot;
   symbol1 c=black v=none i=r l=1 w=3;
   symbol2 c=red v=none i=r l=2 w=1;
   symbol3 c=green v=none i=r l=3 w=1;
   symbol4 c=olive v=none i=r l=4 w=1;
   symbol5 c=purple v=none i=r l=8 w=1;
   symbol6 c=pink v=none i=r l=9 w=1;
   symbol7 c=brown v=none i=r l=14 w=1;
   symbol8 c=gray v=none i=r l=15 w=1;
   symbol9 c=gold v=none i=r l=20 w=1;
   symbol10 c=cyan v=none i=r l=21 w=1;
   symbol11 c=blue v=none i=r l=22 w=1;
   plot pred * Moist10=Variety;
   format variety variety.;
run;
quit;                                     *c03s2d2.sas;
```

The data set **pop** contains two predicted values from the population regression model for two values of the predictor variable **moist10**. This data set is combined with the data set **pred** for plotting.

PROC GPLOT Output

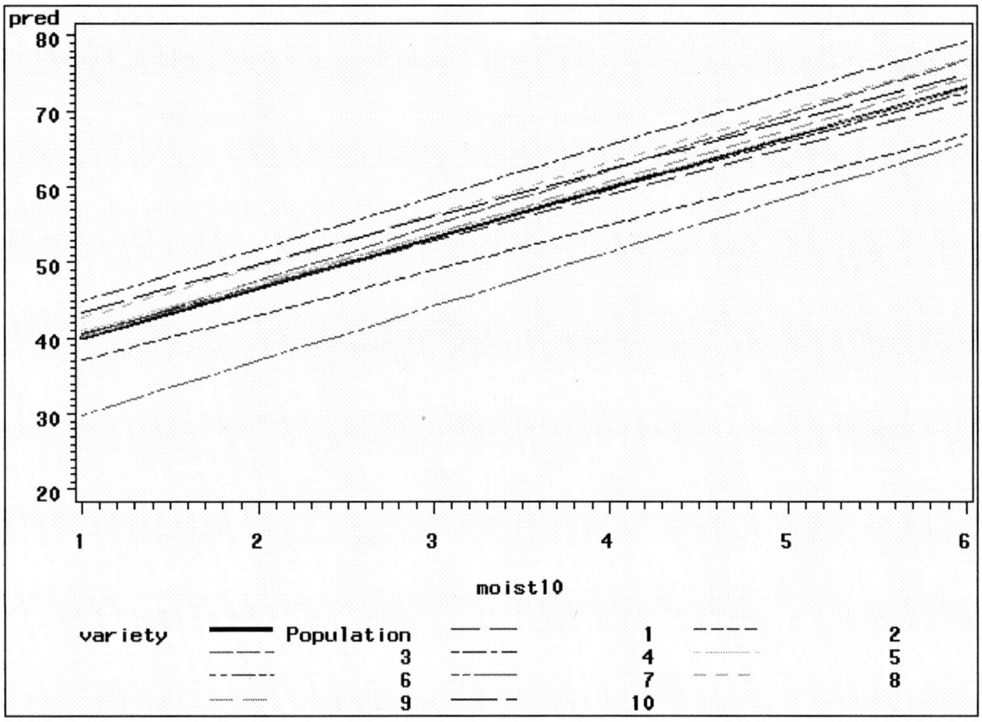

This plot shows the population regression model, as well as the predicted regression model for each variety. Random coefficient models fit subject-specific regression models that account for variations among subjects. The slope estimates are EBLUPs, which would be different from the estimates if **variety** were treated as fixed.

A RANDOM Statement with the SUBJECT= Option

```
model yield=moist / ddfm=kr;
random int moist / type=FA0(2) subject=variety;
```

G = (variety × variety)

variety		1: a_1*	1: b_1*	2: a_2*	2: b_2*	… 10: a_{10}*	10: b_{10}*
1	a_1*	λ_{11}^2	$\lambda_{11}\lambda_{21}$			0	
	b_1*	$\lambda_{21}\lambda_{11}$	$\lambda_{21}^2+\lambda_{22}^2$				
2	a_2*			λ_{11}^2	$\lambda_{11}\lambda_{21}$		
	b_2*		0	$\lambda_{21}\lambda_{11}$	$\lambda_{21}^2+\lambda_{22}^2$		
⋮ 10	a_{10}*					λ_{11}^2	$\lambda_{11}\lambda_{21}$
	b_{10}*					$\lambda_{21}\lambda_{11}$	$\lambda_{21}^2+\lambda_{22}^2$

41

Another useful covariance structure in random coefficient regression analysis is the no-diagonal factor-analytic structure with two factors, that is, FA0(2). The $(i,j)^{th}$ element of the covariance matrix of FA0(q) is given by

$$\sum_{k=1}^{\min(i,j,q)} \lambda_{ik}\lambda_{jk}\text{, where}$$

i is the row position

j is the column position

q is the number of factors

λ_{ij} is the $(i,j)^{th}$ element of the Cholesky root of the unstructured covariance matrix.

You can use this structure FA0(q) for approximating an unstructured **G** matrix in the RANDOM statement. You can also use this structure to constrain the estimate of **G** to be nonnegative definite.

Details

If **A** is positive definite of size $p \times p$, you can find an upper triangular matrix **U** such that **A=U′U**, so that **U** is a sort of square root of **A**. The elements in matrix **U** are referred to as square-root or Cholesky root of matrix **A**. For example,

$$U' = \begin{bmatrix} \lambda_{11} & 0 \\ \lambda_{21} & \lambda_{22} \end{bmatrix}, U = \begin{bmatrix} \lambda_{11} & \lambda_{21} \\ 0 & \lambda_{22} \end{bmatrix}, \quad A = U'U = \begin{bmatrix} \lambda_{11}^2 & \lambda_{11}\lambda_{21} \\ \lambda_{21}\lambda_{11} & \lambda_{21}^2 + \lambda_{22}^2 \end{bmatrix}$$

TYPE=FA0(2) versus TYPE=UN

- The two covariance structures are generally interchangeable.
- The covariance parameter estimates are different because they use different parameterizations.
- FA0(2) constrains the G matrix to be nonnegative definite, whereas TYPE=UN can occasionally result in an indefinite G matrix.
- Using FA0(2) can improve the convergence and stability in the model fitting process.

42

You can derive the covariance parameter estimates from an FA0(q) structure to a UN structure and vice versa; they use difference parameterizations. One advantage of using an FA0(2) rather than a UN in the random coefficient analysis is that the convergence and stability of the model fitting process can be improved.

Fitting a Random Coefficient Model Using TYPE=FA0(2)

Now you can submit the following program to fit a random coefficient model using the TYPE=FA0(2) covariance structure:

```
proc mixed data=wheat;
   class variety;
   model yield=moist10 / ddfm=kr solution;
   random int moist10 / type=FA0(2) subject=variety
                        G solution;
run;                                          *c03s2d3.sas;
```

Partial PROC MIXED Output

Estimated G Matrix

Row	Effect	variety	Col1	Col2
1	Intercept	1	18.8947	-0.7272
2	moist10	1	-0.7272	0.2394

The estimated G matrix is exactly the same as the one from the previous demonstration. You just reparameterized the same covariance matrix. The parameter estimates from the new parameters are displayed in the next table.

Covariance Parameter Estimates

Cov Parm	Subject	Estimate
FA(1,1)	variety	4.3468
FA(2,1)	variety	-0.1673
FA(2,2)	variety	0.4598
Residual		0.3521

The Residual variance is the same as the one produced by using TYPE=UN. The variance parameter estimates for FA(1, 1), FA(2, 1), and FA(2, 2) correspond to λ_{11}, λ_{21}, and λ_{22}, respectively, in the covariance matrix for FA0(2).

Fit Statistics

-2 Res Log Likelihood	181.5
AIC (smaller is better)	189.5
AICC (smaller is better)	190.3
BIC (smaller is better)	190.8

Null Model Likelihood Ratio Test

DF	Chi-Square	Pr > ChiSq
3	150.52	<.0001

Solution for Fixed Effects

Effect	Estimate	Standard Error	DF	t Value	Pr > |t|
Intercept	33.4339	1.3597	9.2	24.59	<.0001
moist10	6.6166	0.1538	8.66	43.02	<.0001

Solution for Random Effects

Effect	variety	Estimate	Std Err Pred	DF	t Value	Pr > |t|
Intercept	1	0.9578	1.4830	12.3	0.65	0.5302
moist10	1	-0.4921	0.2042	17.9	-2.41	0.0269
Intercept	2	-2.2843	1.5110	12.8	-1.51	0.1550
moist10	2	-0.6670	0.2802	24.4	-2.38	0.0254
Intercept	3	-0.4081	1.4910	12.5	-0.27	0.7888
moist10	3	0.6722	0.2181	20.1	3.08	0.0059
Intercept	4	0.6960	1.4546	11.5	0.48	0.6413
moist10	4	-0.2331	0.2366	22.3	-0.99	0.3352
Intercept	5	1.1159	1.7014	17.7	0.66	0.5203
moist10	5	-0.1990	0.2634	24	-0.76	0.4572
Intercept	6	4.6391	1.4343	11.1	3.23	0.0079
moist10	6	0.2389	0.1895	15.3	1.26	0.2262
Intercept	7	-10.7300	1.4231	10.7	-7.54	<.0001
moist10	7	0.5642	0.2167	19.9	2.60	0.0170
Intercept	8	2.4012	1.4554	11.5	1.65	0.1259
moist10	8	0.2243	0.2159	19.8	1.04	0.3113
Intercept	9	-0.1762	1.4920	12.5	-0.12	0.9079
moist10	9	0.2336	0.2176	20	1.07	0.2959
Intercept	10	3.7886	1.8763	21.4	2.02	0.0562
moist10	10	-0.3421	0.2979	24.1	-1.15	0.2622

Type 3 Tests of Fixed Effects

Effect	Num DF	Den DF	F Value	Pr > F
moist10	1	8.66	1850.50	<.0001

The output from PROC MIXED is almost identical to the one obtained previously by using TYPE=UN. Recall that you reparameterized the covariance structure using TYPE=FA0(2) for numerical stability.

3.3 Hierarchical Linear Models

Objectives

- Define hierarchical linear modeling.
- Analyze data from the educational field using the MIXED procedure.

48

Test Score Gains Data

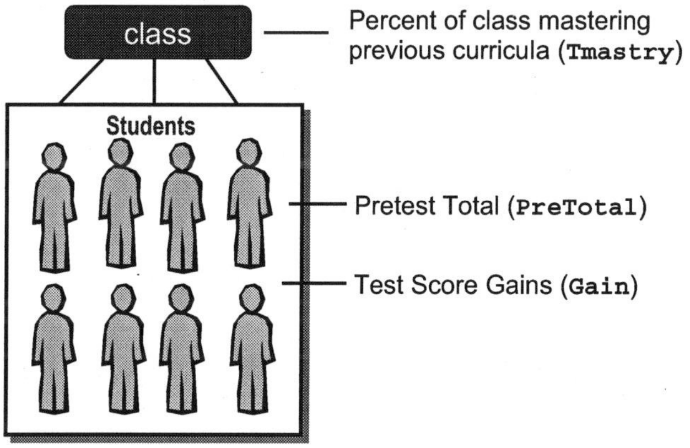

49

Data was collected for 3,111 eighth-grade students. The students' test score gains (**Gain**) on one of the mathematics achievement tests were recorded. In addition, the sum of some pretest core items (**PreTotal**) on the same students was also recorded. These students were grouped into 159 classes. A variable measuring the percent of the class with a sufficient degree of mastery of previous curricula (**Tmastry**) was recorded for each class. The data is stored in the data set **sasuser.mathscore**.

The Data

Obs	Class	Tmastry	Gain	Pre Total
1	1	50	2	20
2	1	50	-3	18
3	1	50	5	12
4	1	50	1	9
5	1	50	-3	11
6	1	50	3	12
7	1	50	-8	12
8	1	50	-6	18
9	1	50	-4	13
10	1	50	4	8
11	1	50	1	21
...	...	...	...	...
30	2	80	-2	7
31	2	80	1	13
32	2	80	-10	16
33	2	80	-4	11
34	2	80	-1	9
35	2	80	6	11
...	...	...	...	...

50

The data is stored in the data set **`sasuser.mathscore`** and these variables are included in the data:

`Gain` the test score gains on a mathematics achievement test for each student

`PreTotal` the sum of some pretest core items for each student

`Class` the class each student belongs to

`Tmastry` the percent of class mastering previous curricula.

Hierarchical Linear Modeling

- Data has a nested structure, or hierarchy of random effects.
- There may be fixed effects that are measured at each level of the experimental unit, or random effects.
- You perform multilevel analysis:
  - Fit a random coefficient model for level 1 (the smallest sized units).
  - Model the coefficients to be a function of level 2 variables.
  - Continue this pattern if you have more levels.
  - Combine models from all the levels.

51

Nested models are special cases of hierarchical linear models. In nested models, there is a hierarchy of random effects corresponding to increasingly larger units. In the semiconductor example that you saw earlier, positions were nested within wafers, wafers were nested within lots, and lots were nested within sources. The variables **`position`**, **`wafer`**, and **`lot`** were random effects, and **`source`** was a fixed effect. (The variable **`source`** could be a random effect if random samples of sources were selected from a large population of sources.) In the more general hierarchical linear models, there is also a nesting of units. In addition, there may be fixed effects (can be continuous or classification variables) that are crossed with the random effects. The hierarchical modeling comes from first developing the level I model, which is a random coefficient model for the smallest sized units. Then, the coefficients of the level I model can be modeled as a function of level 2 (the next smallest sized units) variables. This approach continues if you have more levels of experimental units. The final model is obtained by combining the models from all the levels.

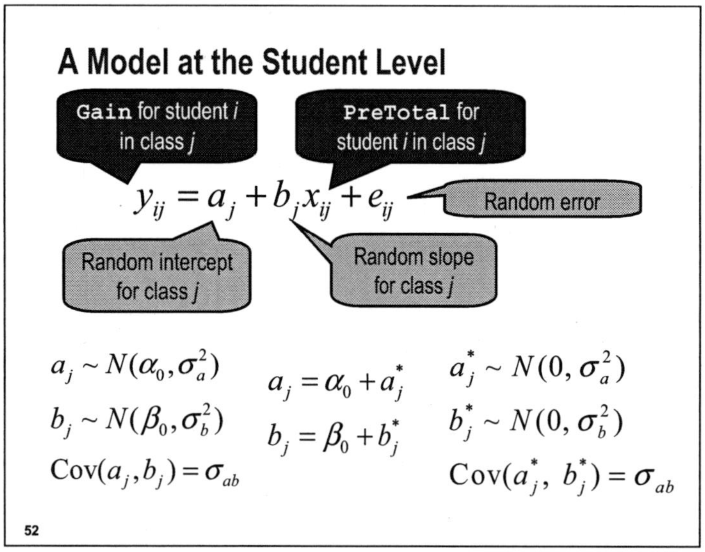

This data has a nested structure; that is, students are nested within classes. Students and classes are often considered as random effects. (In this example, the student effect is modeled by the residuals.) In addition, measurements were taken at both student and class levels. The response variable, the test score gains (**`Gain`**), was measured at the student level. The explanatory variable, the sum of some pretest scores (**`PreTotal`**), was also measured at the student level. A linear regression model may be appropriate to fit the data. Because classes are considered as random effects, a random coefficient model may be reasonable. In random coefficient models, the coefficients for each class (intercept and slope) represent a deviation from some population regression model.

Assume that the random intercept (a_j) and slope (b_j) are normally distributed with a mean of α_0 and β_0, respectively, and a covariance matrix $\psi = \begin{bmatrix} \sigma_a^2 & \sigma_{ab} \\ \sigma_{ab} & \sigma_b^2 \end{bmatrix}$. The random errors e_{ij} are assumed to be independently and identically distributed random variables with mean zero and variance σ^2.

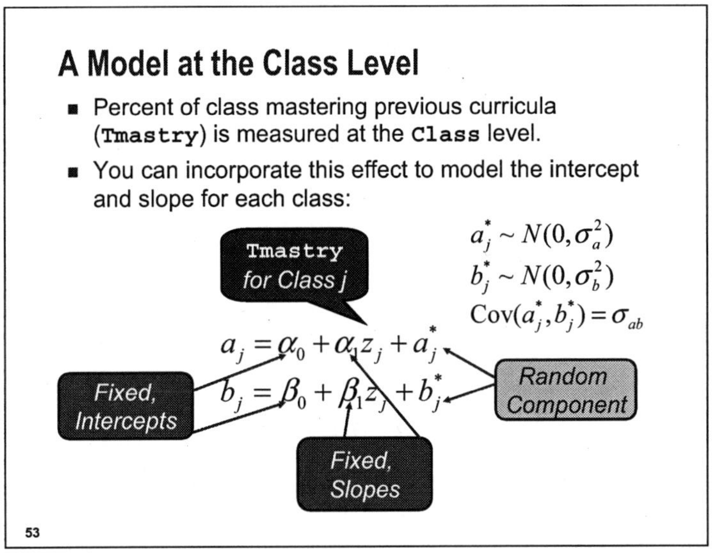

Now consider the model at the class level. The variable **Tmastry** is measured at the class level. The random coefficients for the intercept and slope can be rewritten to incorporate this effect. A reasonable model of including this class-level continuous variable is shown above. You assume that the random components a_j* and b_j* follow a normal distribution with a mean of zero and a covariance matrix ψ. Therefore, the intercept for each class follows a normal distribution with a mean of $\alpha_0+\alpha_1 z_j$ and a variance of σ_a^2, and the slope for each class follows a normal distribution with a mean of $\beta_0+\beta_1 z_j$ and a variance of σ_b^2. The covariance between the intercept and slope is σ_{ab}.

A Model of Multilevel Effects

$$y_{ij} = a_j + b_j x_{ij} + e_{ij}$$
$$a_j = \alpha_0 + \alpha_1 z_j + a_j^*$$
$$b_j = \beta_0 + \beta_1 z_j + b_j^*$$

$$y_{ij} = \alpha_0 + \alpha_1 z_j + \beta_0 x_{ij} + \beta_1 z_j x_{ij} + a_j^* + b_j^* x_{ij} + e_{ij}$$

55

Substituting the expressions for a_j and b_j into the student-level model produces the single equation involving effects at two levels (student and class levels):

$$y_{ij} = \alpha_0 + \alpha_1 z_j + \beta_0 x_{ij} + \beta_1 z_j x_{ij} + a_j^* + b_j^* x_{ij} + e_{ij}$$

α_0, α_1, β_0, and β_1 are fixed effects (or coefficients). a_j* and b_j* are random coefficients representing deviations from the population coefficients for each class. Assume that a_j* and b_j* follow a normal distribution with mean zero and covariance matrix ψ. The fixed-effects part ($\alpha_0 + \alpha_1 z_j + \beta_0 x_{ij} + \beta_1 z_j x_{ij}$) can be modeled using the MODEL statement, and the random-effects part ($a_j^* + b_j^* x_{ij}$) can be modeled using the RANDOM statement in the MIXED procedure.

Fitting a Hierarchical Linear Model

Use the MIXED procedure to fit a hierarchical linear model to your data.

```
data mathscore;
   set sasuser.mathscore;
   PreTotal10=PreTotal/10;
   Tmastry10=Tmastry/10;
run;

proc sort data=mathscore;
   by class;
run;

proc mixed data=mathscore;
   model Gain=PreTotal10 Tmastry10 PreTotal10*Tmastry10
              / s ddfm=kr;
   random Intercept PreTotal10 / subject=class type=un s;
run;                                          *c03s3d1.sas;
```

S = solution

Recall that in fitting random coefficient models, you always want to rescale your data, if appropriate, to improve the stability of the optimization process. The SORT procedure is used to sort your data by the variable **Class**.

The MODEL statement specifies the mean model effects (fixed part). An intercept is included by default. This statement corresponds to $\alpha_0 + \alpha_1 z_j + \beta_0 x_{ij} + \beta_1 z_j x_{ij}$. The DDFM=KR option requests the KENWARDROGER method of estimating the denominator degrees of freedom for the fixed effects. The S option (SOLUTION) requests that the estimates of α_0, α_1, β_0, and β_1 be printed along with their estimated standard errors and corresponding t-statistics.

The RANDOM statement with the SUBJECT= option was used to fit the random coefficient part of the model. With the SUBJECT=**Class** option, the **Intercept** (a keyword) effect corresponds to a_j*, and the **PreTotal** effect corresponds to the $b_j{*}x_{ij}$ term in the model. The SUBJECT=**Class** option is important because it instructs PROC MIXED to fit different intercepts and slopes for different classes. The TYPE=UN option specifies an unstructured covariance matrix ψ for a_j* and b_j*, that is,

$$\psi = \begin{bmatrix} \sigma_a^2 & \sigma_{ab} \\ \sigma_{ab} & \sigma_b^2 \end{bmatrix}.$$

Continuous variables are permitted as arguments to the SUBJECT= option. You must sort your data by the SUBJECT= variable first. Using a continuous variable decreases execution time for models with a large number of subjects or groups and also prevents the production of a large Class Levels Information table.

Partial PROC MIXED Output

Covariance Parameter Estimates

Cov Parm	Subject	Estimate
UN(1,1)	Class	9.0284
UN(2,1)	Class	-2.1851
UN(2,2)	Class	0.7795
Residual		21.6545

The estimated covariance parameters are $\hat{\sigma}_a^2$=9.0284, $\hat{\sigma}_b^2$=0.7795, and $\hat{\sigma}_{ab}$=–2.1851. The negative covariance between intercept and slope (-2.1851) indicates the intercept and slope are negatively correlated, that is, larger intercepts tend to have smaller slopes. Negative correlation between intercept and slope is typical.

Null Model Likelihood Ratio Test

DF	Chi-Square	Pr > ChiSq
3	246.52	<.0001

The Null Model Likelihood Ratio Test compares your model against the null model, which is the model with no random effects and independent and homogeneous residuals, in other words, $R=\sigma^2 I$. The significant result (*p*-value<0.0001) indicates that your model fits the data better than the null model.

Solution for Fixed Effects

Effect	Estimate	Standard Error	DF	t Value	Pr > |t|
Intercept	-1.4943	1.3466	151	-1.11	0.2689
PreTotal10	-1.6027	0.6605	96.3	-2.43	0.0171
Tmastry10	1.1311	0.1777	154	6.37	<.0001
PreTotal10*Tmastry10	-0.00615	0.08576	99	-0.07	0.9430

Type 3 Tests of Fixed Effects

Effect	Num DF	Den DF	F Value	Pr > F
PreTotal10	1	96.3	5.89	0.0171
Tmastry10	1	154	40.53	<.0001
PreTotal10*Tmastry10	1	99	0.01	0.9430

The Solution for Fixed Effects table and the Type 3 Tests of Fixed Effects table show consistent results. The interaction between **PreTotal10** and **Tmastry10** is not significant (*p*-value=0.9430). The marginal mean intercept is –1.49 and the marginal mean slope for **PreTotal10** is –1.60. The test for the fixed effect shows that this slope is significantly different from zero (*p*-value=0.0171). The slope for **Tmastry10** is 1.13 and is also significantly different from zero (*p*-value<0.0001).

Partial Output from the S option in the RANDOM statement

Solution for Random Effects

Effect	Subject	Estimate	Std Err Pred	DF	t Value	Pr > |t|
Intercept	1	-1.9021	1.3795	30.2	-1.38	0.1781
PreTotal10	1	0.1062	0.7421	4.15	0.14	0.8929
Intercept	2	-5.3977	1.4877	52.4	-3.63	0.0006
PreTotal10	2	0.9183	0.7333	3.79	1.25	0.2821
Intercept	3	-1.0074	1.7860	26.1	-0.56	0.5775
PreTotal10	3	0.09292	0.8035	5.26	0.12	0.9122
Intercept	4	-0.4173	2.2762	15	-0.18	0.8570
PreTotal10	4	0.3363	0.8952	4.77	0.38	0.7233
Intercept	5	1.6364	1.8483	32.5	0.89	0.3825
PreTotal10	5	-0.6782	0.8003	4.7	-0.85	0.4378
Intercept	6	0.1799	1.9919	54.1	0.09	0.9283
PreTotal10	6	-0.2033	0.7845	4.43	-0.26	0.8071
Intercept	7	-0.8639	1.7105	29.6	-0.51	0.6173
PreTotal10	7	0.02364	0.7889	4.93	0.03	0.9773
Intercept	8	-2.1874	1.5211	76.8	-1.44	0.1545
PreTotal10	8	0.2970	0.7294	4.39	0.41	0.7029
Intercept	9	2.0445	2.0049	19.1	1.02	0.3206
PreTotal10	9	-0.4623	0.8479	5.09	-0.55	0.6086
...	...	...	...	...	...	...

The solutions for the random effects show the predicted deviations from the population mean and intercept for each class. Combining information from this table with the Solution for Fixed Effects table, you can obtain the predicted equation for each class and, therefore, EBLUPs for any given values of **`PreTotal10`** and **`Tmastry10`** for each class. Alternatively, you can use the OUTP= option in the MODEL statement to obtain EBLUPs, as discussed previously.

In this example, you have continuous variables as predictors. In the hierarchical linear modeling, you can have classification variables, or both continuous and classification variables, as fixed effects or predictor variables. The same analysis strategies apply in these situations.

3.4 Chapter Summary

For mixed models with covariates, where both continuous and discrete independent variables as well as random effects are present in your data, you can use the MIXED procedure to conduct the analysis. You need to determine if the unequal slope model is necessary by examining the significance of the interaction effect. If it is not significant, you can eliminate the interaction term and fit a common slope model.

The basic structure of random coefficient models builds on the analysis of covariance models. In random coefficient models, the regression coefficients for one or more covariates are assumed to be a random sample from some population of possible coefficients. Random coefficient models are sensible when the data arises from independent subjects or clusters, and the regression model for each subject or cluster can be assumed to be a random deviation from some population regression model.

In the MIXED procedure, you use the RANDOM statement with TYPE= and SUBJECT= options to fit a random coefficient model. Two commonly used covariance structures for TYPE= option in random coefficient models are UN and FA0(2).

Here is an example program of a random coefficient model:

```
proc mixed data=sasuser.wheat;
   model yield=moist / ddfm=kr;
   random int moist / type=un subject=variety;
run;
```

The RANDOM statement specifies a block-diagonal **G** matrix for the random effects, with the identical UN structured blocks corresponding to each subject (**`variety`**).

Hierarchical linear models are usually used for data with nested structures. Additionally, there are treatment effects or independent variables measured at each (or some) of the nested subjects. Using hierarchical linear modeling, you first develop a random coefficient model for the smallest sized units (level I analysis), then you model the coefficients from the level 1 model to be a function of the level 2 variables. You continue this pattern if you have more than two levels in your data. You model the subject variance through the random coefficients, which is similar to random coefficient models.

Chapter 4 Best Linear Unbiased Prediction

4.1 Introduction to the Best Linear Unbiased Predictor

Objectives

- Discuss the roles of the random effect parameters.
- Explain the best linear unbiased predictor (BLUP) and the empirical best linear unbiased predictor (EBLUP).

3

Random Effect Parameter

$$Y = X\beta + Z\gamma + \varepsilon$$

A fixed effect parameter, β, corresponds to the negative or positive contribution of a level of a factor to the mean response.

A random effect parameter, γ, corresponds to the realized value of the random effect given the observed data.

5

In the discussions thus far in this course, the main concern is with the estimation or testing of fixed effects. The main role of random effects in the models is in determining the standard error of an estimated fixed effect or the proper form of a test statistic. In the nested model analysis, the variance parameter estimates are of interest. One of the main features distinguishing mixed model methodology from conventional linear model methods is the ability to estimate specific random effects or linear functions of random effects. For example, although the random effects were randomly selected from a larger population, you may be interested in knowing the predicted effect of one level of the random factor given the observed value of the response variable in your data.

Multicenter Clinical Trial Example

		CLINIC 1			CLINIC 2			…
Drug		1	4	3	3	1	4	
Patient		4261	4269	4270	3081	3082	3085	
Visit	1	82	86	80	80	70	80	
	2	70	84	82	70	80	60	
	3	80	90	90	70	70	70	
	4	70	82	84	60	70	90	
	5	80	70	80	60	70	70	

6

Three drugs are compared in a multicenter clinical trial for their effects on diastolic blood pressure measurements. Patients are given one of the three drugs, at random, at 1 of 26 clinics. Measurements are taken on the patients during five visits at the clinics. The visits are three weeks apart.

The actual data set contains more than 3,000 observations and is highly unbalanced. For illustration purposes, a balanced subset is selected that contains records on 78 patients at 26 clinics. Each patient receives one drug and visits the same clinic five times.

Detailed information about the data and the analysis is provided later in the chapter.

Predicting a Random Effect--BLUP

- The variable **drug** is a fixed effect; **clinic** and **patient** (or **drug*clinic**) are random effects.
- You suspect patients in some clinics may have more favorable responses than patients in other clinics.
- You want to predict the actual effect of a **clinic** based on the measurements of **diabp**.
- The prediction of a random effect or any linear combination involving random effects is a best linear unbiased prediction (BLUP).

7

In the multicenter clinical trial example, the clinics were randomly selected from a large population of clinics; therefore, **clinic** is a random effect. The variable **drug** is a fixed effect, and the **drug*clinic** interaction corresponds to the **patient** effect, and also is a random effect.

In conventional fixed-effects analysis of multicenter trials, inference focuses on the average drug effect throughout the target population. In many practical situations, you may be interested in the specific performance of treatments at a given clinic. For example, you may want to know the clinic-specific treatment mean, especially if you suspect different treatments perform better under different environmental conditions, represented by the various locations in the trial.

The prediction of the **diabp** value at a randomly selected clinic is a best linear unbiased predictor (BLUP). Any linear combinations involving random effects are also BLUPs.

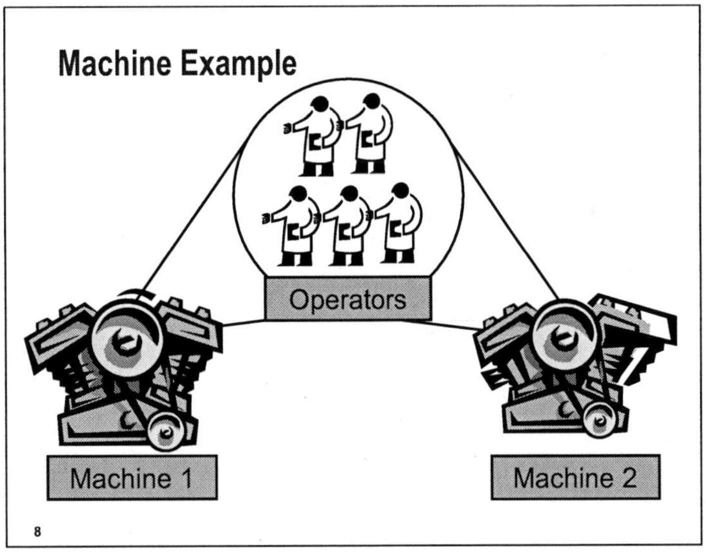

Recall the machine example presented at the beginning of this course. The manager of an automotive plant must replace the machines producing a certain component used in automatic transmissions. Two different machines are available. The manager wants to evaluate the productivity of the machines when operated by the plant's employees. Five employees are randomly selected from the work force to operate each machine, and they represent a random sample of all possible operators.

This is a two-way mixed model because each selected employee's productivity is evaluated on each machine. The variable **`machine`** is a fixed effect; **`operator`** and **`machine*operator`** are random effects.

Predicting a Random Effect--BLUP

- The variable **`machine`** is a fixed effect; **`operator`** and **`machine*operator`** are random effects.
- You may want to predict the actual effect of an **`operator`** based on the measurements of **`productivity`**.
- You may also want to know the performance of the jth **`operator`** averaged over all machines or at one specific machine.
- You can address these objectives by estimating random effects or linear combinations involving random effects--the BLUPs.

9

The analysis discussed thus far focuses on inference about fixed effects, in this case, the machine effects averaged across the population of operators. As a manager, you may also be interested in assessing the performance of various operators under your supervision. For example, you may want to predict the effect of an operator based on the observed performance: a productive operator would have a positive effect, a lousy operator would have a negative effect; you would want to know the performance of the jth operator averaged over all machines. Or, you may want to assess the performance of a given operator on a specific machine. These objectives must be addressed by estimating the corresponding linear combinations of fixed and random effects, in other words, the BLUPs.

How to Obtain the Best Linear Unbiased Prediction (BLUP)?

BLUPS can be obtained in one of the following ways:

- Computing the expected value of the random effect given the observed data using the Bayes Theorem
- Solving the mixed-model equations

An example of the BLUP for the ingot effect:

$$\hat{b}_j = \frac{\sigma_b^2}{\sigma_b^2 + \frac{1}{3}\sigma^2}(\bar{y}_{.j} - \hat{\mu})$$

11

As a special case, consider the ingot example introduced earlier in the course. It can be shown that the BLUP for the ingot effect b_j is $\hat{b}_j = \frac{\sigma_b^2}{\sigma_b^2 + \frac{1}{3}\sigma^2}(\bar{y}_{.j} - \hat{\mu})$, where $\bar{y}_{.j}$ is the average pressure value for ingot j and $\hat{\mu}$ is the grand mean. Because the factor $\frac{\sigma_b^2}{\sigma_b^2 + \frac{1}{3}\sigma^2}$ is never greater than 1, the BLUPs are often referred to as shrinkage estimator.

Details

BLUPs can be estimated using the Bayesian approach. Because the random effects are assumed to be random variables, it is most natural to estimate them using the Bayes theorem (Box and Tiao 1992). The prior distribution of a random effect is $\gamma \sim N(0, \mathbf{G})$. The conditional distribution of y given random effects γ is $y \mid \gamma \sim N(X\beta + Z\gamma, \mathbf{R})$. The posterior distribution of a random effect given the observed y, $f(\gamma \mid y)$, can be calculated using the Bayes theorem:

$$f(\gamma \mid y) = \frac{f(y \mid \gamma) f(\gamma)}{\int f(y \mid \gamma) f(\gamma) d\gamma},$$ where $f(\cdot)$ represents the probability density function.

It can be shown that the above equation is the density of a multivariate normal distribution. The prediction of the random effect γ is estimated by the mean of this posterior distribution:

$$\hat{\gamma} = E(\gamma \mid y) = \int \gamma f(\gamma \mid y) d\gamma = GZ'V^{-1}(y - X\beta).$$

Henderson (1959) has shown that BLUPs can also be obtained by solving the mixed-model equations, which is analogous to the normal equations in the fixed-effect model:

$$\begin{bmatrix} X'R^{-1}X & X'R^{-1}Z \\ Z'R^{-1}X & Z'R^{-1}Z+G^{-1} \end{bmatrix} \begin{bmatrix} \hat{\beta} \\ \hat{\gamma} \end{bmatrix} = \begin{bmatrix} X'R^{-1}Y \\ Z'R^{-1}Y \end{bmatrix}.$$

Solving these equations for $\hat{\beta}$ and $\hat{\gamma}$ yields

$\hat{\beta} = (X'V^{-1}X)^{-}X'V^{-1}y$ and

$\hat{\gamma} = GZ'V^{-1}(y - X\hat{\beta})$, where V=ZGZ′+R.

- $\hat{\beta}$ is the best linear unbiased estimator (BLUE) of the vector of the fixed effects parameters β.
- $\hat{\gamma}$ is the best linear unbiased predictor (BLUP) of the vector of random effects γ.

For a linear combination of only fixed effects (K′β), the solution of the mixed-model equations results in *best linear unbiased estimators*, or BLUEs, of K′β.

For linear combinations of random effects (M′γ), or linear combinations of fixed *and* random effects (K′β + M′γ), the solutions of the mixed-model equations result in BLUPs of M′γ or K′β + M′γ.

Properties of BLUPs

- Best: minimum variance among all linear and unbiased estimators
- Linear: linear estimator: $\hat{\gamma}$= *a*+*By*
- Unbiased: E($\hat{\gamma}$) = E(γ) = 0
- BLUPs are shrinkage estimators. For example, the predicted breaking strength for ingot *j* is the weighted average of the grand mean and the observed value.

$$\hat{y}_j = \hat{\mu} + \hat{b}_j = \hat{\mu} + \frac{\sigma_b^2}{\sigma_b^2 + \sigma^2/3}(\overline{y}_{.j} - \hat{\mu})$$

$$= \frac{\sigma^2/3}{\sigma_b^2 + \sigma^2/3}\hat{\mu} + \left(1 - \frac{\sigma^2/3}{\sigma_b^2 + \sigma^2/3}\right)\overline{y}_{.j}$$

12

A BLUP has the following properties:

- it is unbiased; that is, $E(\hat{\gamma}) = E(\gamma) = 0$.
- it is a linear estimator; that is, it is a linear combination of y: $\hat{\gamma} = a + By$, where *a* and *B* are free of the fixed effect parameters.
- it is best because it minimizes the residual error. If γ were a fixed effect, this criterion is equivalent to minimum variance.

A BLUP can be a predictor for the random effect γ or a predictor for a linear combination of the fixed (β) and random (γ) effects based on the solutions for β and γ, that is, $K'\beta + M'\gamma$.

BLUPs have a so-called shrinkage property. The predicted response for a random effect shrinks toward the overall average. In other words, they are less extreme than the observed counterparts. For example, the predicted breaking strength for ingot *j* can be interpreted as the weighted average of the grand mean and the observed value. It can be shown that the predicted pressure value for ingot *j* is

$$\hat{y}_j = \mu + \hat{b}_j = \mu + \frac{\sigma_b^2}{\sigma_b^2 + \frac{1}{3}\sigma^2}(\overline{y}_{.j} - \hat{\mu})$$

$$= \frac{\frac{1}{3}\sigma^2}{\sigma_b^2 + \frac{1}{3}\sigma^2}\hat{\mu} + \left(1 - \frac{\frac{1}{3}\sigma^2}{\sigma_b^2 + \frac{1}{3}\sigma^2}\right)\overline{y}_{.j}$$

What Is an EBLUP?

Using the estimated covariance matrices $\hat{\mathbf{G}}$ and $\hat{\mathbf{R}}$ and solving the mixed model equations yields the *empirical best linear unbiased estimator*, EBLUE $\hat{\beta}$, and the *empirical best linear unbiased predictor*, EBLUP $\hat{\gamma}$.

13

In most cases, the covariance matrices **G** (covariance matrix for random effects) and **R** (covariance matrix for random errors) are unknown. You can substitute the REML estimates of these covariance matrices ($\hat{\mathrm{G}}$ and $\hat{\mathrm{R}}$, and therefore $\hat{\mathrm{V}}$) in the mixed model equations above. The parameter estimates $\hat{\beta}$ and $\hat{\gamma}$ are then called empirical best linear unbiased estimator (EBLUE) and empirical best linear unbiased predictor (EBLUP), respectively.

4.2 Obtaining Best Linear Unbiased Predictors

Objectives

- Write the model for the multicenter clinical trial data.
- Illustrate the difference between least squares means and EBLUPs using the MIXED procedure.

17

Multicenter Clinical Trial Example

		CLINIC 1			CLINIC 2			...
Drug		1	4	3	3	1	4	
Patient		4261	4269	4270	3081	3082	3085	
Visit	1	82	86	80	80	70	80	
	2	70	84	82	70	80	60	
	3	80	90	90	70	70	70	
	4	70	82	84	60	70	90	
	5	80	70	80	60	70	70	

18

Consider the multicenter clinical trial example introduced in the last section. Three drugs are compared in a multicenter clinical trial for their effects on patients' diastolic blood pressures. Patients are given one of the three drugs, at random, at one of twenty-six clinics. Measurements are taken on the patients during five visits at the clinics. The visits are three weeks apart.

The Data

clinic	patient	visit	drug	diabp
1	4261	1	1	82
1	4261	2	1	70
1	4261	3	1	80
1	4261	4	1	70
1	4261	5	1	80
1	4269	1	4	86
1	4269	2	4	84
1	4269	3	4	90
1	4269	4	4	82
1	4269	5	4	70
1	4270	1	3	80
1	4270	2	3	82
1	4270	3	3	90
1	4270	4	3	84
1	4270	5	3	80
2	3081	1	3	80
2	3081	2	3	70
2	3081	3	3	70
2	3081	4	3	60
2	3081	5	3	60
...	...	...	...	...

19

Data is recorded in a SAS data set **sasuser.multic**. These selected variables are in the data set:

clinic	clinic identification number
patient	patient identification number
visit	visit number
drug	drug assigned to each patient
diabp	diastolic blood pressure

You try to determine whether **drug** has an effect on the response variable **diabp**. You also try to predict the **diabp** value for a specific clinic averaged across drugs.

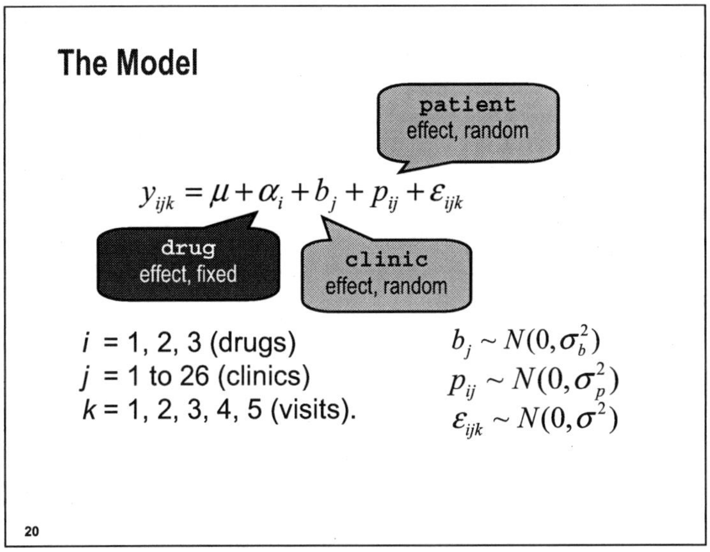

y_{ijk} observation (**diabp**) for the kth visit of a patient receiving the ith drug administered by the jth clinic.

μ the overall mean, an unknown fixed parameter.

α_i fixed effect of the ith drug.

b_j random effect of the jth clinic, $b_j \sim$ i.i.d. $N(0,\sigma_b^2)$.

p_{ij} random effect of the patient taking the ith drug at the jth clinic, $p_{ij} \sim$ i.i.d. $N(0,\sigma_p^2)$. This random effect can also be modeled using the **drug*clinic** interaction.

ε_{ijk} within-subject experimental error, $\varepsilon_{ijk} \sim$ i.i.d. $N(0,\sigma^2)$. This random effect corresponds to the variability between measurements taken on the same patients.

The random effects b_j, p_{ij}, and ε_{ijk} are assumed to be independent random variables.

Therefore,

- $E(y_{ijk}) = \mu + \alpha_i$ is the mean for the ith drug averaged across all clinics in the population
- $Var(y_{ijk}) = \sigma_b^2 + \sigma_p^2 + \sigma^2$ is the variance of an observation.

You could also analyze the data using more complex repeated measures approaches.

The CONTRAST and ESTIMATE Statements

General form of the CONTRAST and ESTIMATE statements:

CONTRAST *'label' fixed-effect values |*
random-effect values / options;

ESTIMATE *'label' fixed-effect values |*
random-effect values / options;

21

Selected ESTIMATE statement and CONTRAST statement options:

label identifies the contrast in the table. A label is required for every contrast specified. Labels can be up to 20 characters and must be enclosed in single quotes.

fixed-effect identifies an effect that appears in the MODEL statement. The keyword INTERCEPT can be used as an effect when an intercept is fitted in the model. You do not need to include all effects that are in the MODEL statement.

random-effect identifies an effect that appears in the RANDOM statement. The first random effect must follow a vertical bar (|); however, random effects do not have to be specified.

values are constants that are elements of the **L** matrix associated with the fixed (**K**) and random (**M**) effects.

The CONTRAST and ESTIMATE statements of PROC MIXED are similar to those of PROC GLM, although they are extended to include random effects. This enables you to obtain EBLUPs by specifying the appropriate random effects and the corresponding coefficients. This also enables you to select an appropriate inference space.

Computing EBLUPs

To obtain an EBLUP for clinic 1, you can submit the following program:

```
proc mixed data=sasuser.multic;
   class drug clinic patient;
   model diabp=drug / ddfm=kr;
   random clinic patient;
   estimate 'clinic 1 EBLUP' intercept 1 | clinic 1;
   *estimate 'clinic 1 EBLUP' intercept 1
             drug 0.333333 0.333333 0.333333 | clinic 1;  *same;
run;                               *c04s2d1.sas;
```

The ESTIMATE statement is used to obtain the EBLUP for clinic 1. Two ESTIMATE statements should produce identical results. Generally speaking, in an ESTIMATE statement in PROC MIXED, the coefficients for the higher-ordered terms are assigned automatically as equal shares of the marginal coefficients for fixed effects.

Partial PROC MIXED Output

Estimates

Label	Estimate	Standard Error	DF	t Value	Pr > |t|
clinic 1 EBLUP	80.2493	3.0331	17.7	26.46	<.0001

The predicted value of **diabp** for clinic 1 averaged across those three drugs and all patients within this clinic is 80.2493. If you incorrectly specify the model as a fixed-effects model, the estimate and its standard error would be different.

Now write ESTIMATE statements to obtain EBLUPs for clinic 1 through clinic 10.

```
proc mixed data=sasuser.multic;
   class drug clinic patient;
   model diabp=drug / ddfm=kr;
   random clinic patient / solution;
   estimate 'clinic 1' intercept 1|clinic 1;
   estimate 'clinic 2' intercept 1|clinic 0 1;
   estimate 'clinic 3' intercept 1|clinic 0 0 1;
   estimate 'clinic 4' intercept 1|clinic 0 0 0 1;
   estimate 'clinic 5' intercept 1|clinic 0 0 0 0 1;
   estimate 'clinic 6' intercept 1|clinic 0 0 0 0 0 1;
   estimate 'clinic 7' intercept 1|clinic 0 0 0 0 0 0 1;
   estimate 'clinic 8' intercept 1|clinic 0 0 0 0 0 0 0 1;
   estimate 'clinic 9' intercept 1|clinic 0 0 0 0 0 0 0 0 1;
   estimate 'clinic 10' intercept 1|clinic 0 0 0 0 0 0 0 0 0 1;
   ods output estimates=eblup;
run;
title;                                     *c04s2d2.sas;
```

The SOLUTION option in the RANDOM statement requests the predicted values (EBLUPs) for the random effects **`clinic`** and **`patient`**. The ten ESTIMATE statements are used to obtain the predicted responses ($\hat{\mu}+\hat{b}_j$), or EBLUPs, for the first ten clinics. Recall that the vertical bar (|) separates the fixed effects from the random effects.

Partial PROC MIXED Output

```
                    Covariance Parameter
                          Estimates

                    Cov Parm      Estimate

                    clinic         12.1253
                    patient        37.5042
                    Residual       46.9962
```

The variance component estimates are as follows:

- clinic variance: $\hat{\sigma}_b^2$=12.1253
- patient variance: $\hat{\sigma}_p^2 = 37.5042$
- within-patient variance, or the random error: $\hat{\sigma}^2 = 46.9962$.

Partial SOLUTION Output

Solution for Random Effects

Effect	clinic	patient	Estimate	Std Err Pred	DF	t Value	Pr > |t|
clinic	1		0.3237	3.0108	13.1	0.11	0.9160
clinic	2		-3.7531	3.0108	13.1	-1.25	0.2343
clinic	3		-3.8113	3.0108	13.1	-1.27	0.2275
clinic	4		0.9643	3.0108	13.1	0.32	0.7538
clinic	5		4.5751	3.0108	13.1	1.52	0.1523
clinic	6		3.8180	3.0108	13.1	1.27	0.2267
clinic	7		0.4693	3.0108	13.1	0.16	0.8785
clinic	8		2.7988	3.0108	13.1	0.93	0.3693
clinic	9		-1.2197	3.0108	13.1	-0.41	0.6919
clinic	10		-2.9960	3.0108	13.1	-1.00	0.3377
clinic	11		2.4203	3.0108	13.1	0.80	0.4358
clinic	12		-0.2587	3.0108	13.1	-0.09	0.9328
clinic	13		-2.5883	3.0108	13.1	-0.86	0.4054
clinic	14		-1.9476	3.0108	13.1	-0.65	0.5288
clinic	15		-2.2388	3.0108	13.1	-0.74	0.4702
clinic	16		1.3429	3.0108	13.1	0.45	0.6628
clinic	17		-0.1131	3.0108	13.1	-0.04	0.9706
clinic	18		0.5566	3.0108	13.1	0.18	0.8561
clinic	19		-1.6273	3.0108	13.1	-0.54	0.5979
clinic	20		-0.4626	3.0108	13.1	-0.15	0.8802
clinic	21		-0.1714	3.0108	13.1	-0.06	0.9555
clinic	22		-0.3170	3.0108	13.1	-0.11	0.9177
clinic	23		1.9835	3.0108	13.1	0.66	0.5214
clinic	24		0.3237	3.0108	13.1	0.11	0.9160
clinic	25		-1.8894	3.0108	13.1	-0.63	0.5410
clinic	26		3.8180	3.0108	13.1	1.27	0.2267
...	...		...	...	...	...	...

The Solution for Random Effects table lists EBLUPs for the random effect parameter (b_j) for **clinic** and the random effect parameter for **patient** (not shown).

The EBLUPs can be useful for comparing the random effects from different clinics and patients. They can also be treated as residuals in performing diagnostics for your mixed model. The values displayed in the Std Err Pred column are not the standard errors of $\hat{\gamma}$ displayed in the Estimate column; rather, they are the standard errors of the predictions $\hat{\gamma}_i - \gamma_i$, where $\hat{\gamma}_i$ is the ith EBLUP and γ_i is the ith random-effect parameter.

Type 3 Tests of Fixed Effects

Effect	Num DF	Den DF	F Value	Pr > F
drug	2	50	0.69	0.5056

The test indicates that there is no statistical evidence that there is a drug effect on the diastolic blood pressure. Therefore, you expect that the mean blood pressure of a patient simply corresponds to the overall mean ($\hat{\mu}$=79.9256).

The MIXED procedure does not display the overall mean response. You could estimate the overall mean by fitting a mean model (a model without the fixed effect **drug**) with a SOLUTION option in the MODEL statement.

ESTIMATE Statement Output

Estimates

Label	Estimate	Standard Error	DF	t Value	Pr > |t|
clinic 1	80.2493	3.0331	17.7	26.46	<.0001
clinic 2	76.1726	3.0331	17.7	25.11	<.0001
clinic 3	76.1143	3.0331	17.7	25.09	<.0001
clinic 4	80.8899	3.0331	17.7	26.67	<.0001
clinic 5	84.5008	3.0331	17.7	27.86	<.0001
clinic 6	83.7437	3.0331	17.7	27.61	<.0001
clinic 7	80.3949	3.0331	17.7	26.51	<.0001
clinic 8	82.7245	3.0331	17.7	27.27	<.0001
clinic 9	78.7060	3.0331	17.7	25.95	<.0001
clinic 10	76.9297	3.0331	17.7	25.36	<.0001

The values produced by the ESTIMATE statements correspond to predictions of these clinic responses. For example, the EBLUP for clinic 5 is 84.5008, and the EBLUP for clinic 3 is 76.1143.

How do these EBLUPS compare to the least squares means for **clinic**? This question will be answered next.

Comparing EBLUPS and Least Squares Means

Treating `clinic` as a Fixed Effect

First, analyze the multicenter clinical trial data treating **`clinic`** as a fixed effect, using the MIXED procedure. Also compute the least squares means for **`clinic`**.

```
proc mixed data=sasuser.multic;
   class drug clinic patient;
   model diabp=drug clinic / ddfm=kr;
   random patient;
   lsmeans clinic;
   ods output lsmeans=clinicmeans;
   title 'treating clinic as a fixed effect';
run;                                          *c04s2d3.sas;
```

The LSMEANS statement requests the least squares means for each level of **`clinic`**. The ODS statement saves the least squares means table to a SAS data set **`clinicmeans`**.

Partial PROC MIXED Output

```
                treating clinic as a fixed effect

                      Covariance Parameter
                            Estimates

                      Cov Parm      Estimate

                      patient        37.5042
                      Residual       46.9962
```

The variance component estimates for **`patient`**, $\hat{\sigma}_p^2$, and for within-patient visit, $\hat{\sigma}^2$, are the same as when **`clinic`** was treated as random. This is because the data is balanced. There is no variance component estimate for **`clinic`** because you specified this effect as fixed in the model.

```
                treating clinic as a fixed effect

                   Type 3 Tests of Fixed Effects

                        Num      Den
         Effect          DF       DF     F Value     Pr > F

         drug             2       50        0.69     0.5056
         clinic          25       50        1.78     0.0421
```

The test indicates that there is no statistical evidence that there is a drug effect on the diastolic blood pressure. This is identical to the results when **`clinic`** was treated as random because of the balanced data. The clinics seem to have a significant effect on the diastolic blood pressure.

treating clinic as a fixed effect

Least Squares Means

<table>
<tr><th>Effect</th><th>clinic</th><th>Estimate</th><th>Standard Error</th><th>DF</th><th>t Value</th><th>Pr > |t|</th></tr>
<tr><td>clinic</td><td>1</td><td>80.6667</td><td>3.9540</td><td>50</td><td>20.40</td><td><.0001</td></tr>
<tr><td>clinic</td><td>2</td><td>71.3333</td><td>3.9540</td><td>50</td><td>18.04</td><td><.0001</td></tr>
<tr><td>clinic</td><td>3</td><td>71.2000</td><td>3.9540</td><td>50</td><td>18.01</td><td><.0001</td></tr>
<tr><td>clinic</td><td>4</td><td>82.1333</td><td>3.9540</td><td>50</td><td>20.77</td><td><.0001</td></tr>
<tr><td>clinic</td><td>5</td><td>90.4000</td><td>3.9540</td><td>50</td><td>22.86</td><td><.0001</td></tr>
<tr><td>clinic</td><td>6</td><td>88.6667</td><td>3.9540</td><td>50</td><td>22.42</td><td><.0001</td></tr>
<tr><td>clinic</td><td>7</td><td>81.0000</td><td>3.9540</td><td>50</td><td>20.49</td><td><.0001</td></tr>
<tr><td>clinic</td><td>8</td><td>86.3333</td><td>3.9540</td><td>50</td><td>21.83</td><td><.0001</td></tr>
<tr><td>clinic</td><td>9</td><td>77.1333</td><td>3.9540</td><td>50</td><td>19.51</td><td><.0001</td></tr>
<tr><td>clinic</td><td>10</td><td>73.0667</td><td>3.9540</td><td>50</td><td>18.48</td><td><.0001</td></tr>
<tr><td>clinic</td><td>11</td><td>85.4667</td><td>3.9540</td><td>50</td><td>21.61</td><td><.0001</td></tr>
<tr><td>clinic</td><td>12</td><td>79.3333</td><td>3.9540</td><td>50</td><td>20.06</td><td><.0001</td></tr>
<tr><td>clinic</td><td>13</td><td>74.0000</td><td>3.9540</td><td>50</td><td>18.72</td><td><.0001</td></tr>
<tr><td>clinic</td><td>14</td><td>75.4667</td><td>3.9540</td><td>50</td><td>19.09</td><td><.0001</td></tr>
<tr><td>clinic</td><td>15</td><td>74.8000</td><td>3.9540</td><td>50</td><td>18.92</td><td><.0001</td></tr>
<tr><td>clinic</td><td>16</td><td>83.0000</td><td>3.9540</td><td>50</td><td>20.99</td><td><.0001</td></tr>
<tr><td>clinic</td><td>17</td><td>79.6667</td><td>3.9540</td><td>50</td><td>20.15</td><td><.0001</td></tr>
<tr><td>clinic</td><td>18</td><td>81.2000</td><td>3.9540</td><td>50</td><td>20.54</td><td><.0001</td></tr>
<tr><td>clinic</td><td>19</td><td>76.2000</td><td>3.9540</td><td>50</td><td>19.27</td><td><.0001</td></tr>
<tr><td>clinic</td><td>20</td><td>78.8667</td><td>3.9540</td><td>50</td><td>19.95</td><td><.0001</td></tr>
<tr><td>clinic</td><td>21</td><td>79.5333</td><td>3.9540</td><td>50</td><td>20.11</td><td><.0001</td></tr>
<tr><td>clinic</td><td>22</td><td>79.2000</td><td>3.9540</td><td>50</td><td>20.03</td><td><.0001</td></tr>
<tr><td>clinic</td><td>23</td><td>84.4667</td><td>3.9540</td><td>50</td><td>21.36</td><td><.0001</td></tr>
<tr><td>clinic</td><td>24</td><td>80.6667</td><td>3.9540</td><td>50</td><td>20.40</td><td><.0001</td></tr>
<tr><td>clinic</td><td>25</td><td>75.6000</td><td>3.9540</td><td>50</td><td>19.12</td><td><.0001</td></tr>
<tr><td>clinic</td><td>26</td><td>88.6667</td><td>3.9540</td><td>50</td><td>22.42</td><td><.0001</td></tr>
</table>

The least squares means of the diastolic blood pressure for each of the 26 clinics are provided in this table. For example, the least squares means for

- clinic 5 is 90.40, which is larger than the EBLUP for clinic 5 (84.5008).
- clinic 3 is 71.2, which is smaller than the EBLUP for clinic 3 (76.1143).

The standard errors are different as well. Some clinics have a mean that is much larger than others whereas some have a mean that is much smaller. This could occur because

- some clinics have an actual effect when administering the drugs that increase or decrease blood pressure.
- some clinics were unlucky in having patients who have high or low diastolic blood pressure measurements. The idea of obtaining BLUPs (or EBLUPs) is to remove the effect of luck. You see that the EBLUPs for these two clinics are not as extreme as their least square means. The prediction of the clinic responses is obtained by adjusting the "luck" element associated with clinics and shrinking the least squares means toward the overall mean.

To better understand the concept of shrinkage towards the mean, examine the least squares means and EBLUPs of the first ten clinics graphically.

Recall that two ODS statements were used in the previous programs to create two SAS data sets (**clinicmeans** and **eblup**), and each contains the least squares means and EBLUPs for **clinic**, respectively. The following program makes use of these two data sets to illustrate the concept of shrinkage towards the overall mean.

```
data clinicmeans(rename=(estimate=lsmean));
   set clinicmeans(keep=clinic estimate);
run;

data eblup(drop=label rename=(estimate=eblup));
   set eblup(keep=label estimate);
   clinic=input(substr(label, 8), 2.);
run;

proc sort data=clinicmeans;
   by clinic;
run;

proc sort data=eblup;
   by clinic;
run;

data lsmblup;
   merge clinicmeans eblup;
   by clinic;
run;

proc transpose data=lsmblup
     out=plotblup(rename=(col1=value _name_=type));
   var lsmean eblup;
   by clinic;
   where lsmean ne . and eblup ne .;
run;

proc print data=plotblup;
run;                                          *c04s2d4.sas;
```

The DATA steps and the SORT procedures were used to assist in creating the data set **plotblup** that will be used for plotting. The data set **plotblup** was created by the TRANSPOSE procedure. PROC TRANSPOSE creates an output data set by restructuring the values in a SAS data set, transposing selected variables into observations. More information on the TRANSPOSE procedure can be found in the SAS online documentation.

PROC PRINT Output

Obs	clinic	type	value
1	1	lsmean	80.6667
2	1	eblup	80.2493
3	2	lsmean	71.3333
4	2	eblup	76.1726
5	3	lsmean	71.2000
6	3	eblup	76.1143
7	4	lsmean	82.1333
8	4	eblup	80.8899
9	5	lsmean	90.4000
10	5	eblup	84.5008
11	6	lsmean	88.6667
12	6	eblup	83.7437
13	7	lsmean	81.0000
14	7	eblup	80.3949
15	8	lsmean	86.3333
16	8	eblup	82.7245
17	9	lsmean	77.1333
18	9	eblup	78.7060
19	10	lsmean	73.0667
20	10	eblup	76.9297

This data set will be used to create the graph.

```
proc gplot data=plotblup;
   plot value*type=clinic / vref=79.9256 haxis=axis1
                            vaxis=axis2 nolegend;
   axis1 label=none order=('lsmean' 'eblup')
         offset=(0.5,0.5)in;
   axis2  minor=none;
   format value 5.2;
   symbol i=join c=black v=none r=10
          pointlabel=(position=middle '#clinic');
   title 'Shrinkage for the Clinic Data';
run;
title;
quit;                                        *c04s2d5.sas;;
```

Selected option in the PLOT statement:

VREF= adds a vertical reference line corresponding to the overall mean (79.9256).

Selected options in the SYBMOL statement:

R= specifies the number of times that a SYMBOL definition is applied.

POINTLABEL= labels the plot points.

Selected suboptions in the POINTLABEL option in the SYMBOL statement:

POSITION= specifies the vertical placement of the label text. The default is TOP. The location of the point label is relative to the location of the corresponding data point.

"#var" specifies the variable(s) whose values will label the plot points.

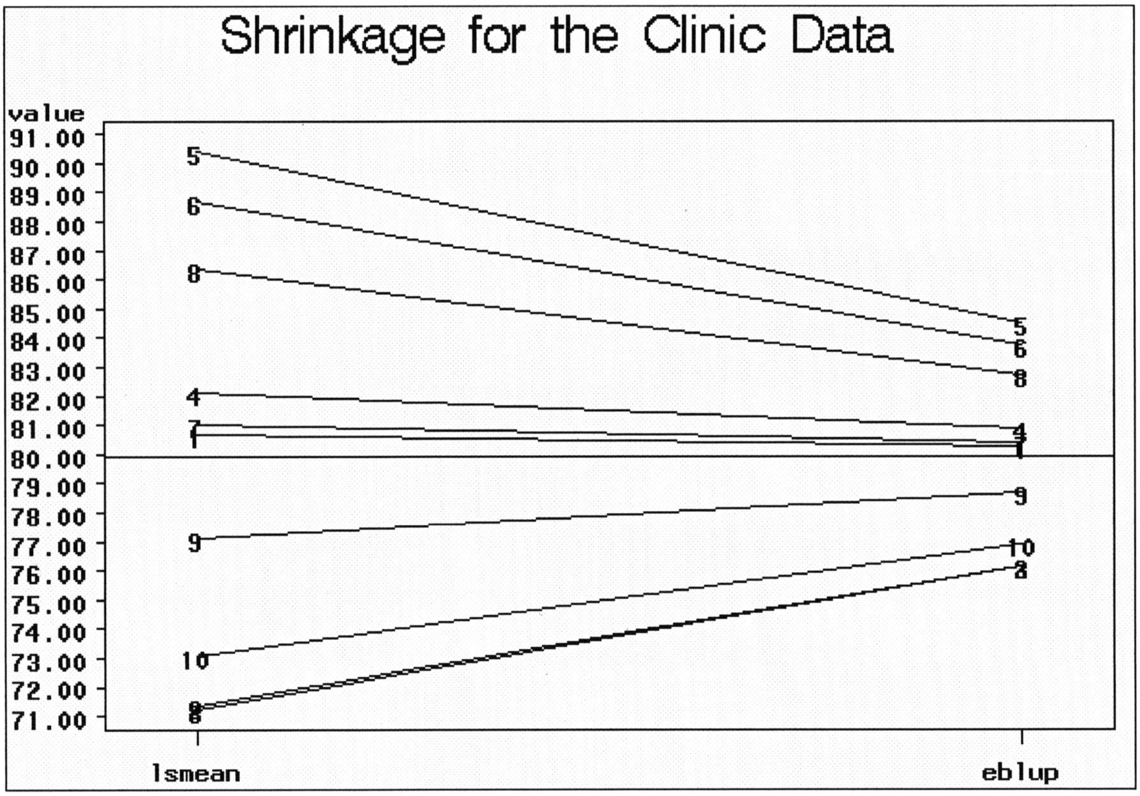

This plot illustrates that adjusting for the variability in clinics collapses the least squares means towards the overall mean. As shown on the graph, large predictions (EBLUPs) are smaller than their corresponding least squares means, and small predictions are larger than their corresponding least squares means.

Although none of the lines cross in this example, they can in other cases when the data is unbalanced or you use a more complex covariance structure.

It can be shown that the shrinkage factor for this example is $b = \dfrac{\sigma_b^2}{\sigma_b^2 + \dfrac{\sigma_p^2}{3} + \dfrac{\sigma^2}{15}} = 0.4368$. It follows that the EBLUPs for clinic *i* is $\text{EBLUPs}_i = \bar{\bar{y}} + b \times (\bar{y}_i - \hat{\mu})$. For example, the EBLUP for clinic 1 is $\text{EBLUP}_1 = 79.9256 + 0.4368\ (80.6667 - 79.9256) = 80.2493$.

4.3 Inference Space (Self-Study)

Objectives

- List different inference spaces in mixed models.
- Make inferences about the fixed effect over different inference spaces.

29

Inference Space

The inference space is determined by your choice of the coefficients associated with the random effects (M).

- If M=0, your inferences apply to the entire population from which the random effects are sampled. This is known as the *broad inference space*.
- If M represents averages over the appropriate random effects, your inferences apply only to the observed levels of the random effects. This is known as the *narrow inference space.*
- If M represents averages of some random effects and it is set to zero pertaining to other random effects, your inferences apply only to observed levels of some of the random effects. This is known as the *intermediate inference space*.

30

For a mixed model, you can test hypotheses of the form H_0: $L'\phi = 0$, where

L' is the vector of contrast coefficients for the fixed and random effects (K' M')

ϕ' is the vector of fixed and random parameters (β' γ').

The inference space is determined by your choice of the coefficients associated with the random effects (M).

The **broad** inference space (M=0) is used by PROC MIXED by default. Your inferences about the linear combination of fixed effects apply to the entire population from which the random effects are sampled. In the multicenter clinical trial example, your inferences about the drug effects apply to the population of clinics and the population of patients within a clinic in the broad inference space.

The **narrow** inference space is used by PROC GLM. It essentially treats clinics and patients within a clinic as fixed effects. In the multicenter clinical trial example, your inferences about the drug effects apply only to the specific clinics and patients within a clinic included in the study in the narrow inference space.

In the **intermediate** inference space, your inferences about the linear combination of the fixed effects apply only to observed levels of some of the random effects. In the multicenter clinical trial example, your inferences about the drug effects apply to the specific clinics included in the study and the population of patients within a clinic in the intermediate inference space.

Writing an ESTIMATE Statement (Narrow Inference Space)

Estimate **drug** 1 mean ($\mu_{1\cdot}$) in narrow inference space.

$$\mu_{1\cdot} = \frac{1}{26}(\mu_{11} + \mu_{12} + \mu_{13} + \cdots + \mu_{126})$$

$$E(y_{ijk}) = \mu_{ij} = \mu + \alpha_i + b_j + (\alpha b)_{ij}$$

$$\mu_{1\cdot} = \frac{1}{26}[26\mu + 26\alpha_1 + b_1 + b_2 + \cdots + b_{26} + (\alpha b)_{11} + (\alpha b)_{12} + \cdots + (\alpha b)_{126}]$$

$$= \mu + \alpha_1 + \frac{1}{26}[b_1 + b_2 + \cdots + b_{26} + (\alpha b)_{11} + (\alpha b)_{12} + \cdots + (\alpha b)_{126}]$$

33

Follow the steps as discussed previously for writing a CONTRAST or ESTIMATE statement. You obtain the coefficients for estimating the drug 1 mean as follows:

- Intercept (μ): 1
- `drug` (α): 1 0 0
- `clinic` (b): 1/26 1/26 1/26 1/26 1/26 1/26 1/26 1/26 1/26 1/26 1/26 1/26 1/26
  1/26 1/26 1/26 1/26 1/26 1/26 1/26 1/26 1/26 1/26 1/26 1/26 1/26
- `drug*clinic` (αb):
  1/26 1/26 1/26 1/26 1/26 1/26 1/26 1/26 1/26 1/26 1/26 1/26 1/26
  1/26 1/26 1/26 1/26 1/26 1/26 1/26 1/26 1/26 1/26 1/26 1/26 1/26
  0 0 0 0 0 0 0 0 0 0 0 0 0 0 0 0 0 0 0 0 0 0 0 0 0 0
  0 0 0 0 0 0 0 0 0 0 0 0 0 0 0 0 0 0 0 0 0 0 0 0 0 0;

You do not need to specify the trailing zeroes in a CONTRAST or ESTIMATE statement.

The **`drug*clinic`** term rather than the **`patient`** term is used here for convenience.

Writing an ESTIMATE Statement (Another Approach)

```
class drug clinic;
```

drug	clinic 1	2	...	25	26	sum
1						1
3						0
4						0
sum						

35 ...

There is another approach you can use to write a CONTRAST or an ESTIMATE statement. It works well for a two-way model. For a more complicated model, the approach introduced earlier may work better.

First, lay out a two-way table. You are interested in estimating the drug 1 mean, so the coefficients for **drug** are 1 for drug 1, 0s for drug 3 and drug 4.

Writing an ESTIMATE Statement (Another Approach)

```
class drug clinic;
```


drug	clinic 1	2	...	25	26	sum
1	1/26	1/26	...	1/26	1/26	1
3	0	0	...	0	0	0
4	0	0	...	0	0	0
sum						

36 ...

Then you equally distribute the coefficients on the marginal cells to the table cells of the same row.

Writing an ESTIMATE Statement (Another Approach)

```
class drug clinic;
```

drug	clinic 1	2	...	25	26	sum
1	1/26	1/26	...	1/26	1/26	1
3	0	0	...	0	0	0
4	0	0	...	0	0	0
sum	1/26	1/26	...	1/26	1/26	1

37 ...

Finally, you obtain the marginal coefficients in the last row by summing up the coefficients in the corresponding columns.

Now you have obtained the coefficients for the ESTIMATE statement. The values in the marginal row and column (labeled sum) are the coefficients for the main effects; the values in the body of the table are the coefficients for the interaction term, or the patient effect. The grand total corresponds to the coefficient for the intercept.

Inference Space

Suppose you want to examine the mean **diabp** of drug 1 over the narrow, intermediate, and broad inference spaces.

```
proc mixed data=sasuser.multic;
   class drug clinic;
   model diabp=drug / ddfm=kr;
   random clinic drug*clinic;
   estimate 'drug 1 mean narrow' intercept 26 drug 26 0 0
         | clinic 1 1 1 1 1 1 1 1 1 1 1 1 1 1 1 1 1 1 1
                  1 1 1 1 1 1 1
           drug*clinic 1 1 1 1 1 1 1 1 1 1 1 1 1 1 1 1 1
                       1 1 1 1 1 1 1 1 1 / divisor=26;
   estimate 'drug 1 mean intermediate' intercept 26
            drug 26 0 0 | clinic 1 1 1 1 1 1 1 1 1 1 1 1
            1 1 1 1 1 1 1 1 1 1 1 1 1 1 / divisor=26;
   estimate 'drug 1 mean broad' intercept 1 drug 1 0 0;
run;                                          *c04s2d6.sas;
```

Selected ESTIMATE statement option:

DIVISOR= specifies a value by which to divide all coefficients so that fractional coefficients can be entered as integer numerators.

Partial PROC MIXED Output

Estimates

Label	Estimate	Standard Error	DF	t Value	Pr > |t|
drug 1 mean narrow	78.6538	0.6013	312	130.82	<.0001
drug 1 mean intermediate	78.6538	1.3431	50	58.56	<.0001
drug 1 mean broad	78.6538	1.5068	69.2	52.20	<.0001

The parameter estimates produced by all three ESTIMATE statements are the same, but the standard errors are not. The standard error increases as the inference space gets broader.

In this example, you reach the same conclusions about the drug 1 mean regardless of the inference space. As mentioned before, in the narrow inference space, you make inferences over the observed clinics and patients in your study; in the intermediate inference space, you make inferences over the specific clinics, but the population of patients within the clinics; in the broad inference space, you make inferences over the population of clinics and patients.

The first two ESTIMATE statements produced EBLUPs, and the last ESTIMATE statement produced an EBLUE because only fixed effects were involved in the estimation.

4.4 Chapter Summary

The best linear unbiased predictor (BLUP) of the random effect is the expected value of the random variable(s) given the observed data. This is obtained by using the Bayes theorem, or by solving the mixed model equations for the random effect γ as implemented by PROC MIXED. The solutions to the mixed model equations for the fixed effect β yield best linear unbiased estimators (BLUEs). Solving the mixed model equations using the estimated covariance matrices, $\hat{G}$ and $\hat{R}$, yields the empirical best linear unbiased predictor (EBLUP) for the random effect γ and the empirical best linear unbiased estimator (EBLUE) for the fixed effect β.

A BLUP has the following properties:

- it is unbiased; that is, $E(\hat{\gamma}) = E(\gamma) = 0$.
- it is a linear estimator; that is, it is a linear combination of y: $\hat{\gamma} = a + By$, where a and B are free of the fixed effect parameters.
- it is best because it minimizes the residual error. If γ were a fixed effect, this criterion is equivalent to minimum variance.

BLUPs have a so-called shrinkage property. They shrink toward the overall average. In other words, they are less extreme than the observed counterparts. They can be interpreted as the weighted average of the grand mean and the observed value.

You use the SOLUTION option in the RANDOM statement and/or the ESTIMATE statement to obtain EBLUPs.

Chapter 5 Repeated Measures Data Analysis

5.1 Introduction to Repeated Measures Analysis

Objectives

- Explain the terminology of repeated measures analysis.
- Summarize and plot repeated measures data.
- Discuss basic issues in repeated measures analysis.
- List the disadvantages of the traditional approaches.
- List the advantages of the mixed model approach.

3

Repeated Measures Data

- *Repeated measures* refers to multiple measurements on the same experimental unit (or subject).
- The analysis of repeated measures data accounts for the presence of correlation between the observations obtained on the same subject and for possible nonconstant variances.

4

Usually, repeated measures are made over time, but they can be over space as well. A common example is to apply the treatments to experimental units in a completely randomized design. Then measurements are taken at each of several times. The basic objectives for repeated measures data are essentially those of any factorial experiment, that is, to examine interaction between factors and to assess either simple or main effects of the factors. The distinguishing feature of a repeated measures model is in the variance and covariance structure of the errors; that is, the independent and homogeneous error variances are no longer valid assumptions. The analysis of repeated measures data accounts for correlations between the observations obtained on the same subject and also some possible heterogeneous variances among observations obtained on the same subject.

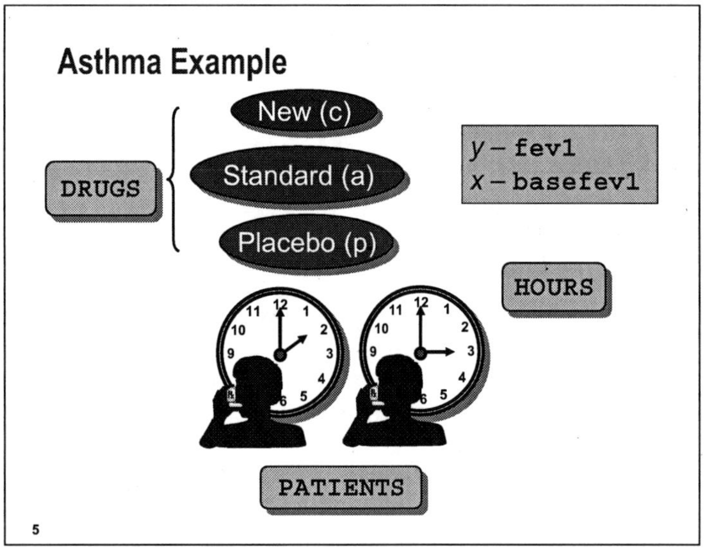

A pharmaceutical company wants to examine the effects of three drugs on the respiratory ability of asthma patients. The three drugs are labeled a, c, and p. Drug a is a standard drug used to treat asthma. Drug c is a potential competitor that was developed by the pharmaceutical company. Drug p is a placebo.

Each of the three drugs is randomly assigned to 24 patients. A total of 72 patients are included in the study. The assigned drug is administered to each patient. Then a standard measure of respiratory ability called **fev1** (forced exhaled volume in one second) is measured hourly for eight hours following treatment. Also, a baseline **fev1** is measured immediately before administering the drugs.

The data is stored in two SAS data sets, **sasuser.fev1mult** and **sasuser.fev1uni**. The **sasuser.fev1mult** data set is in a multivariate arrangement and is used to illustrate the multivariate analysis of contrasts using the REPEATED statement in the GLM procedure. The **sasuser.fev1uni** data set contains the **fev1** data in a univariate arrangement, and is used to illustrate the univariate ANOVA and mixed model approaches to the analysis of repeated measures data.

Producing the Profile Plots for the Three Drugs

These variables are in **sasuser.fev1mult**:

patient	patient identification number
basefev1	baseline **fev1** measurement taken before the administering the treatment
fev11h	**fev1** measurement one hour after administering the drug
fev12h	**fev1** measurement two hours after administering the drug
fev13h	**fev1** measurement three hours after administering the drug
fev14h	**fev1** measurement four hours after administering the drug
fev15h	**fev1** measurement five hours after administering the drug
fev16h	**fev1** measurement six hours after administering the drug
fev17h	**fev1** measurement seven hours after administering the drug
fev18h	**fev1** measurement eight hours after administering the drug
drug	drug administered (a, c, or p).

These variables are in **sasuser.fev1uni**:

patient	patient identification number
basefev1	baseline **fev1** measurement taken before administering the treatment
drug	the drug administrated (a, c, or p) to a patient.
hour	number of hours the measurement was taken after administering the drug
fev1	**fev1** measurement.

```
proc print data=sasuser.fev1mult;
proc print data=sasuser.fev1uni;
run;
```

These two PROC PRINT statements create listing outputs for the two data sets **sasuser.fev1mult** and **sasuser.fev1uni**.

Partial PROC PRINT Output for **sasuser.fev1mult** (a multivariate data structure)

Obs	patient	basefev1	fev11h	fev12h	fev13h	fev14h	fev15h	fev16h	fev17h	fev18h	drug
1	201	2.46	2.68	2.76	2.50	2.30	2.14	2.40	2.33	2.20	a
2	202	3.50	3.95	3.65	2.93	2.53	3.04	3.37	3.14	2.62	a
3	203	1.96	2.28	2.34	2.29	2.43	2.06	2.18	2.28	2.29	a
4	204	3.44	4.08	3.87	3.79	3.30	3.80	3.24	2.98	2.91	a
5	205	2.80	4.09	3.90	3.54	3.35	3.15	3.23	3.46	3.27	a
6	206	2.36	3.79	3.97	3.78	3.69	3.31	2.83	2.72	3.00	a
7	207	1.77	3.82	3.44	3.46	3.02	2.98	3.10	2.79	2.88	a
8	208	2.64	3.67	3.47	3.19	2.19	2.85	2.68	2.60	2.73	a
9	209	2.30	4.12	3.71	3.57	3.49	3.64	3.38	2.28	3.72	a
10	210	2.27	2.77	2.77	2.75	2.75	2.71	2.75	2.52	2.60	a
11	211	2.44	3.77	3.73	3.67	3.56	3.59	3.35	3.32	3.18	a
12	212	2.04	2.00	1.91	1.88	2.09	2.08	1.98	1.70	1.40	a
13	214	2.77	3.36	3.42	3.28	3.30	3.31	2.99	3.01	3.08	a
14	215	2.96	4.31	4.02	3.38	3.31	3.46	3.49	3.38	3.35	a
15	216	3.11	3.88	3.92	3.71	3.59	3.57	3.48	3.42	3.63	a
16	217	1.47	1.97	1.90	1.45	1.45	1.24	1.24	1.17	1.27	a

Partial PROC PRINT Output for **sasuser.fev1uni** (a univariate data structure)

Obs	patient	basefev1	drug	hour	fev1
1	201	2.46	a	1	2.68
2	201	2.46	a	2	2.76
3	201	2.46	a	3	2.50
4	201	2.46	a	4	2.30
5	201	2.46	a	5	2.14
6	201	2.46	a	6	2.40
7	201	2.46	a	7	2.33
8	201	2.46	a	8	2.20
9	202	3.50	a	1	3.95
10	202	3.50	a	2	3.65
11	202	3.50	a	3	2.93
12	202	3.50	a	4	2.53
13	202	3.50	a	5	3.04
14	202	3.50	a	6	3.37
15	202	3.50	a	7	3.14
16	202	3.50	a	8	2.62
17	203	1.96	a	1	2.28
18	203	1.96	a	2	2.34
19	203	1.96	a	3	2.29
20	203	1.96	a	4	2.43
21	203	1.96	a	5	2.06
22	203	1.96	a	6	2.18
23	203	1.96	a	7	2.28
24	203	1.96	a	8	2.29

You can submit the following program to produce the group profile plot for the three drugs. A *group profile plot* is a plot of the mean responses for different treatments versus the time. This type of plot can assist you in visualizing whether the treatments and/or the time have a significant effect on the mean response variable.

```
proc means data=sasuser.fev1uni nway noprint;
   var fev1;
   class drug hour;
   output out=profile mean=avgfev1;
run;

goptions reset=all;
proc gplot data=profile;
   plot avgfev1*hour=drug / haxis=0 to 9 by 1 hminor=0;
   symbol1 v=star c=red i=join l=1;
   symbol2 v=circle c=blue i=join l=3;
   symbol3 v=diamond c=green i=join l=8;
   title 'Average FEV1 vs. Hour by Drug';
run;
title;
quit;                                        *c05s1d1.sas;
```

Selected PROC MEANS statement option:

NWAY specifies that the output data set contains only statistics for the observations with the highest _TYPE_ and _WAY_ values. When you specify class variables, this corresponds to the combination of all class variables.

PROC GPLOT Output

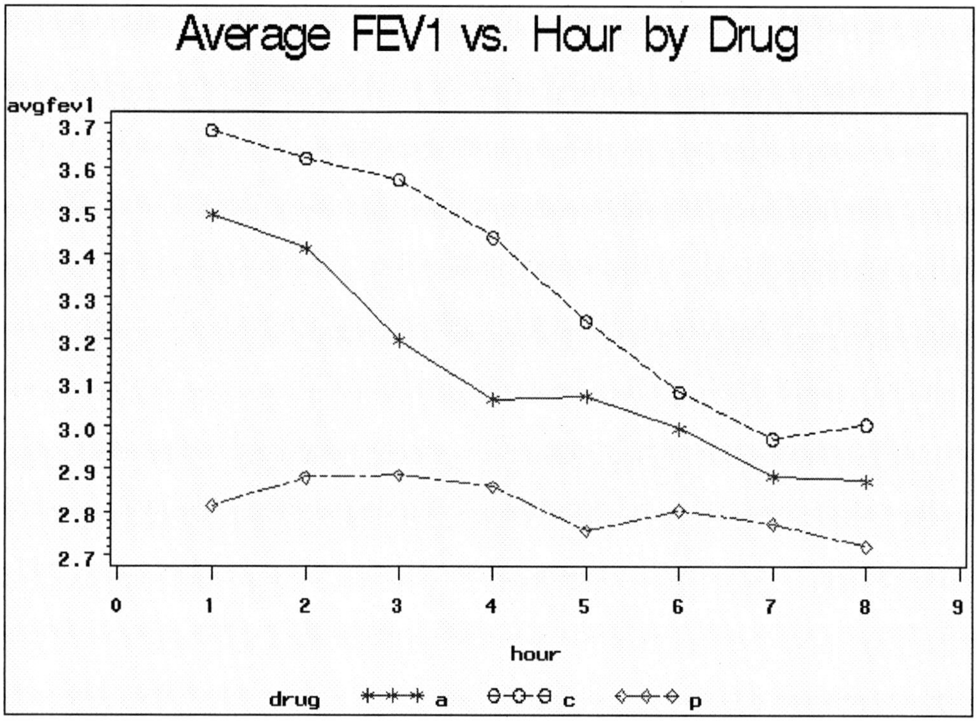

The plot shows that the average **`fev1`** measurements of the patients differ across three drugs. There appears to be a time effect for at least drugs a and c.

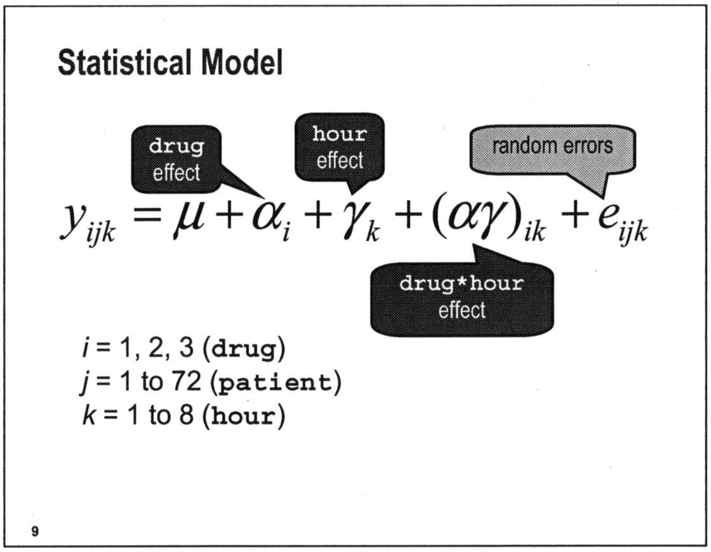

y_{ijk} the **fev1** measurement at the kth hour on the jth patient assigned to the ith drug

μ overall mean and an unknown fixed effect

α_i the fixed effect of the ith drug

γ_k the fixed effect of the kth hour

$(\alpha\gamma)_{ik}$ the fixed effect of the interaction between the ith drug and the kth hour

e_{ijk} the random error associated with the jth patient assigned to the ith drug at hour k.

Therefore, $\mu + \alpha_i + \gamma_k + (\alpha\gamma)_{ik}$ is the mean **fev1** for drug i at hour k, containing effects for **drug**, **hour**, and **drug*hour** interaction.

This model does not contain the covariate, **basefev1**, because it is difficult to implement the analysis of covariance in the repeated measures data using the ANOVA approaches discussed in the next two sections. The mixed-models approach makes the analysis of covariance easy to implement in the repeated measures data and therefore is shown in that section.

Basic Issues in Repeated Measures Data

The random errors, e_{ijk}, are not independent.

- Measures taken on the same subject tend to be more similar than measures taken on different subjects.
- Measures made close in time on the same subject tend to be more highly correlated than measures made far apart in time.

10

In the asthma example, although drugs were randomly assigned to patients, the levels of the repeated measures factor, **`hour`**, was not randomly assigned to patients. Therefore, it is not reasonable to assume the random errors e_{ijk} are independent. There are often two aspects of the covariance structure in the errors. First, two **`fev1`** measures on the same subject are more likely to be closer to each other than two measures on the different subjects. They are positively correlated simply because they possess common effects from that same subject. This is basically the phenomenon of measures on the same whole-plot unit in a split-plot type of experiment. Second, two **`fev1`** measures made close in time on the same subject are likely to be more highly correlated than two measures made far apart in time. This distinguishes repeated measures covariance from split-plot covariance structure. In a split-plot experiment, levels of sub-plot treatment are randomly assigned to sub-plot units within whole-plot units, resulting in equal correlation between all pairs of measurements in the same whole-plot unit:

General Methods in Repeated Measures Analysis

The Modern Approach

- Mixed model methodology in a two-stage approach using the MIXED procedure

Traditional Approaches

- Univariate ANOVA using the GLM procedure
- Multivariate ANOVA, or analysis of contrasts, using PROC GLM

11

The general approach discussed in this chapter is the two-stage approach using mixed models methodology. The first stage attempts to estimate the covariance structure. The second stage substitutes the covariance estimates into the mixed model and uses generalized least squares (GLS) methodology to assess treatment and time effects. This approach is appealing because it directly addresses the covariance structure and attempts to accommodate it in the statistical model. However, assessing and estimating the covariance structure is not a trivial task.

Two more traditional methods are the univariate ANOVA and the multivariate ANOVA using the GLM procedure. The univariate ANOVA approach basically treats repeated measures data as split-plot data; that is, the experimental units to which treatments are assigned are considered as the whole-plot units, and the experimental units at a particular time are considered as the sub-plot units. Thus, this approach accommodates the first aspect of repeated measures covariance (between-subject variation) but not the second (measures close in time are more highly correlated than measures far apart in time). This approach is sometimes referred to as a split-plot in time ANOVA.

The multivariate ANOVA, or analysis of contrasts, computes one or more linear combinations of data on each of the subjects and then analyzes the linear combination as data. One example of the linear combination is the contrast between levels of the factor (often **`time`**) and a reference level. This method avoids the covariance problem in repeated measures data and, therefore, is not an optimal method.

This chapter focuses on the mixed model approach. The two traditional methods are provided in Appendix B for your reference.

Limitations of the Univariate ANOVA

- This method assumes equal correlations between repeated measures regardless of their proximity in time.
- PROC GLM is a fixed-effects procedure and therefore cannot directly accommodate random effects.

13

Univariate ANOVA for repeated measures data is also referred to as split-plot in time ANOVA analysis. It assumes that differences between each pair of measures have equal variances. This condition, also called the Huynh-Feldt (H-F) condition, is a necessary condition for univariate ANOVA to be valid. The more commonly used covariance structure, the *compound symmetry* (CS) structure, assumes that the covariances of the repeated measures of the same subject obey the following conditions: measures at each time have equal variances and the correlations between any two measures are the same. This CS covariance structure is a special case of the H-F condition. While the H-F condition is mathematically more general than CS, it is often not more general from a practical point of view.

However, the equal correlation assumption is frequently unrealistic for repeated measures data. Measurements close in time are often more highly correlated than measurements far apart in time. In this case, the inference from the univariate ANOVA analysis for repeated measures data may not be valid.

Limitations of the Multivariate ANOVA

Multivariate ANOVA

- requires balanced data with the same time points for all subjects
- does not directly accommodate the covariance structure in repeated measures; therefore, it may be less powerful.

14

Multivariate ANOVA requires balanced data with the same time points for all subjects. The number of repeated measures on each subject is the same, and measurements occur at the same time points for all subjects. It uses the complete case analysis, which means if one repeated measure is missing for a subject, all the data for this subject will be eliminated from the analysis. For unbalanced data, this may result in data that is not feasible for a meaningful analysis. Additionally, if repeated measures are not obtained at the same time points across all subjects, as occurs in most observational studies, the complete case requirement probably results in less data or even no data at all that is available for the analysis.

Multivariate ANOVA, or the analysis of contrasts, is a device for avoiding the covariance problem in repeated measures analysis. The method does not directly accommodate the covariance structure. It is actually based on an unstructured within-subject variance-covariance matrix, whose parameter estimates are obtained by the method of moments. A simpler covariance structure would probably be sufficient to characterize the repeated measures data. In this case, you sacrifice power and efficiency for the fixed effects tests. Multivariate ANOVA is not an optimal method.

Advantages of Mixed Model Analyses

- Mixed model analyses enable a flexible approach to modeling covariance structures.
- Mixed model analyses handle unbalanced data with unequally spaced time points within and across subjects.
- The generalized least squares (GLS) method is generally superior to the ordinary least squares (OLS) method, assuming an appropriate covariance structure.
- The presence of missing data does not pose the major problems for analysis that can occur with a traditional analysis.

15

The univariate ANOVA ignores time-dependent correlations and, therefore, risks underestimating the standard errors of mean comparisons at different times, resulting in an excessive Type I error rate. The Greenhouse-Geiser and Huynh-Feldt adjustments attempt to account for within-subject correlations, but these corrections are often inadequate.

The multivariate ANOVA essentially assumes an unstructured covariance matrix, which is far more general than most repeated measures data requires. Thus this approach wastes a great deal of information and results in a less powerful test.

The mixed model procedure allows a flexible approach to modeling covariance structure, resulting in a parsimonious covariance model that adequately accounts for within-subject correlations and, therefore, is superior to other approaches. Additionally, the MIXED procedure uses the generalized least squares (GLS) to estimate and test fixed effects. Assuming a reasonable covariance structure was specified, this method accounts for all the covariance parameters you modeled for your data. Therefore, it is superior to the method used by PROC GLM, ordinary least squares (OLS).

PROC MIXED provides a variety of modeling techniques to handle unequally spaced time points within each subject and/or subjects that are observed at different sets of time points.

In the presence of missing repeated measures for a subject, the MIXED procedure does not exclude this subject from the analysis; instead it uses all the available data. This method (likelihood-based ignorable analysis) leads to a valid analysis when the missing data can be assumed missing at random (MAR). For more information about missing data, MAR and MCAR (missing completely at random), refer to Little and Rubin (1987).

5.2 Mixed Model Analyses of Repeated Measures Data

Objectives

- List the four-step procedure for mixed model analyses, especially how to choose the appropriate covariance structures for repeated measures.
- Analyze repeated measures data using the MIXED procedure.

18

Four-Step Procedure for Mixed Model Analyses

1. Model the mean structure, usually by specification of the fixed effects.
2. Specify the covariance structures for between-subject and within-subject effects.
3. Fit the mean model, accounting for the covariance structure using GLS. This step may include making the mean model more parsimonious.
4. Make statistical inferences based on the results of Step 3. This step may also include making the mean model more parsimonious.

19

As recommended by Littell, Pendergast, and Natajan (2000), you generally follow the four steps stated above when using PROC MIXED to analyze repeated measures data. Another excellent reference is Verbeke and Molenberghs (2000).

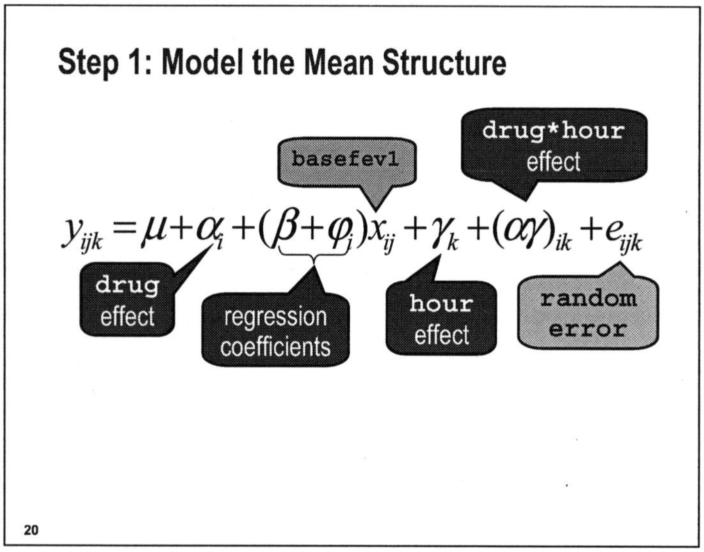

y_{ijk} the **fev1** measurement at the kth hour on the jth patient assigned to the ith drug

μ overall mean and an unknown fixed effect

α_i the fixed intercept effect of the ith drug

β the overall regression coefficient (slope) for the covariate

φ_i the slope effect for the ith drug

x_{ij} the **basefev1** measurements for the jth patient taking the ith drug

γ_k the fixed effect of the kth hour

$(\alpha\gamma)_{ik}$ the fixed effect of the interaction between the ith drug and the kth hour

e_{ijk} the random error associated with the jth patient assigned to the ith drug at hour k.

Notice that compared with the model specified previously, a covariate, **basefev1**, was added to the model. You generally want to specify a fairly complete mean model at this step. You may be able to reduce the mean model later. By accounting for the baseline measurements in the model, you can get a more accurate assessment of treatment effects. Using the GLM procedure, however, it is difficult and awkward, if not impossible, to implement the analysis of covariance in the repeated measures data, because the covariate is often measured on the larger units, for example, subjects or whole-plot units. This analysis of covariance in the repeated measures data is easy to implement in the MIXED procedure.

Therefore, the mean model is $E(y_{ijk}) = \mu + \alpha_i + (\beta + \varphi_i)x_{ij} + \gamma_k + (\alpha\gamma)_{ik}$.

Step 2: Specify the Covariance Structure

What is the covariance structure for the within-subject measurements **R**?

- The repeated measures are assumed to be correlated within subjects and independent across subjects.
- The SUBJECT= option in the REPEATED statement in the MIXED procedure defines a block diagonal matrix **R**.
- The TYPE= option in the REPEATED statement specifies the covariance structure in each block.

21

The covariance for the within-subject measurements can be complex for repeated measures data. In general, you assume that the repeated measures within a subject are correlated and the repeated measures between subjects are independent. Therefore, the variance-covariance matrix for e_{ijk}, denoted by **R**, is a block diagonal matrix, with one block per subject. You do this by using the REPEATED statement with a SUBJECT= option in the MIXED procedure to identify the blocks and a TYPE= option in the REPEATED statement to specify the covariance structure in each block.

Block Diagonal Covariance Matrix

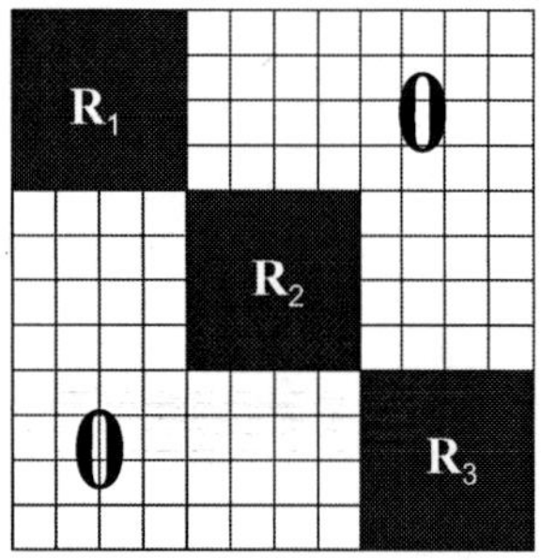

23

This slide illustrates a simple example of a block diagonal covariance matrix. There are four repeated measures on each of the three subjects, so you have a total of 12 observations and, therefore, a 12×12 covariance matrix. Each block corresponds to the covariance structure for each subject. In PROC MIXED, V_1, V_2, and V_3 must have the same structure but can have different parameter estimates (use the GROUP= option). In this matrix, the observations within each block (subject) can take on a variety of covariance structures while the observations outside of the blocks are assumed to be independent. In other words, the subjects are still assumed to be independent of each other and the measurements within each subject can be interdependent.

Covariance Matrix in Each Block — Variance Component (VC) (Default)

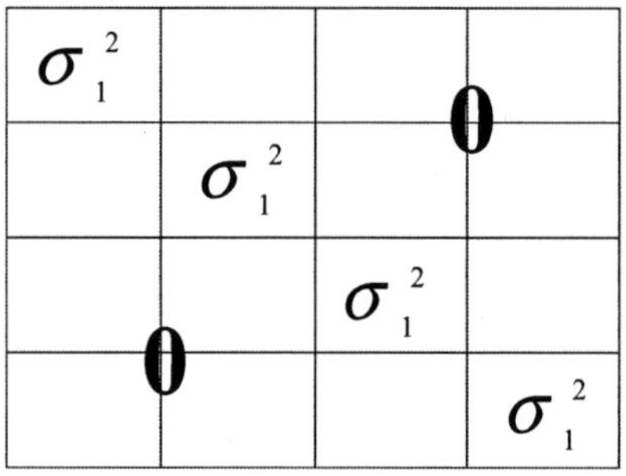

24

The simplest covariance structure in each block is the default variance component (VC) or simple structure. This is an independent and equal variance structure, where the within-subject error correlation is zero. This is usually not a reasonable structure for repeated measures data because the repeated measures within a subject are often correlated.

Covariance Matrix in Each Block — Unstructured Covariance

σ_1^2	σ_{12}	σ_{13}	σ_{14}
	σ_2^2	σ_{23}	σ_{24}
		σ_3^2	σ_{34}
			σ_4^2

25

The most complex covariance structure is unstructured, where observations for each pair of times have their own unique correlation. This is essentially what multivariate ANOVA assumes, and many times it is more complicated than is necessary.

Covariance Matrix in Each Block — Compound Symmetry

σ^2

1.0	ρ	ρ	ρ
	1.0	ρ	ρ
		1.0	ρ
			1.0

=

$\sigma_b^2+\sigma_e^2$	σ_b^2	σ_b^2	σ_b^2
	$\sigma_b^2+\sigma_e^2$	σ_b^2	σ_b^2
		$\sigma_b^2+\sigma_e^2$	σ_b^2
			$\sigma_b^2+\sigma_e^2$

26

compound symmetry

The simplest correlation model is compound symmetry (CS), also referred to as exchangeable correlation structure. It assumes that correlation is constant regardless of the distance between time points. It may not be a valid assumption for observations collected over time, but may be reasonable in situations where the repeated measurements are not obtained over time. The univariate ANOVA analysis performed previously is equivalent to assuming a CS structure in error terms for the ij^{th} subject. Recall you had $\text{var}(y_{ijk})=\sigma_b^2+\sigma_e^2$ and $\text{cov}(y_{ijk}, y_{ijl})=\sigma_b^2$ for $k \neq l$, which is identical to the CS model with

$$\sigma^2=\sigma_b^2+\sigma_e^2 \text{ and } \rho=\frac{\sigma_b^2}{\sigma_b^2+\sigma_e^2}.$$

The MIXED procedure provides the estimate of the covariance parameter σ_b^2 rather than the correlation ρ.

The V Matrix Defined by the Univariate ANOVA Approach

```
random patient(drug);
```

$$G = \begin{bmatrix} \sigma_p^2 & & & \\ & \sigma_p^2 & & \\ & & \ddots & \\ & & & \sigma_p^2 \end{bmatrix} \qquad R = \begin{bmatrix} \sigma_e^2 & & & \\ & \sigma_e^2 & & \\ & & \ddots & \\ & & & \sigma_e^2 \end{bmatrix}$$

$$V = ZGZ' + R = \begin{bmatrix} \sigma_p^2+\sigma_e^2 & \sigma_p^2 & \sigma_p^2 & \sigma_p^2 \\ & \sigma_p^2+\sigma_e^2 & \sigma_p^2 & \sigma_p^2 \\ & & \ddots & \sigma_p^2 \\ & & & \sigma_p^2+\sigma_e^2 \end{bmatrix} \text{(for one patient)}$$

28

Covariance Matrix in Each Block — First-order Autoregressive AR(1)

σ^2

1.0	ρ	ρ^2	ρ^3
	1.0	ρ	ρ^2
		1.0	ρ
			1.0

29

The AR(1) model assumes the correlation between adjacent observations is ρ, regardless of whether the pair of the observations is the first and second, second and third, third and fourth, and so on. It also assumes that the correlation for any pairs of observations two units apart (for example, first and third, second and fourth) is ρ^2. In general, observations d units apart have correlation ρ^d. So, the correlation between observations is a function of their distance in time. This appears to be a reasonable assumption in repeated measures.

AR(1) structure does not model unequally spaced time points, in which case you probably want to consider one of the spatial covariance structures.

Covariance Matrix in Each Block — Toeplitz

$$\sigma^2 \begin{bmatrix} 1.0 & \rho_1 & \rho_2 & \rho_3 \\ & 1.0 & \rho_1 & \rho_2 \\ & & 1.0 & \rho_1 \\ & & & 1.0 \end{bmatrix}$$

30

Toeplitz covariance structure is similar to AR(1), but is more general. While it assumes that observations separated by a common distance (*d*) share the same correlation, the correlation is not a power function of ρ anymore (ρ^d); instead, it can be any value between 0 and 1. Toeplitz does not model unequal spacing either.

The MIXED procedure does not provide the estimates for the correlation parameters ρ_1, ρ_2, and so on; instead it produces the covariance estimates σ_1, σ_2, and so on, which are equal to $\sigma^2\rho_1$, $\sigma^2\rho_2$, and so on. You can use the RCORR option to obtain the correlation estimates.

Account for Unequal Spacing?

	Time points are		
TYPE=	Equally spaced, same across subjects	Unequally spaced, same across subjects	Different across subjects
VC	n/a	n/a	n/a
UN	Yes	Yes	No
CS	Yes	Yes	Yes
AR(1)	Yes	No	No
TOEP	Yes	No	No

31

Covariance Matrix in Each Block — Spatial Power

σ^2

1.0	$\rho^{\lvert t_1-t_2 \rvert}$	$\rho^{\lvert t_1-t_3 \rvert}$	$\rho^{\lvert t_1-t_4 \rvert}$
	1.0	$\rho^{\lvert t_2-t_3 \rvert}$	$\rho^{\lvert t_2-t_4 \rvert}$
		1.0	$\rho^{\lvert t_3-t_4 \rvert}$
			1.0

32

Spatial covariance structures allow for unequal spacing of the repeated measures. These structures are mainly used in geostatistical models and are discussed in detail later in the course. Because repeated measures data can be viewed as a spatial process in one dimension, the spatial covariance structures are very useful for modeling repeated measures data, especially when the time points are unequally spaced and the correlations decline as a function of time difference.

The spatial power structure provides a direct generalization of the AR(1) structure for equally spaced data.

Covariance Matrix in Each Block — Spatial Exponential

σ^2

1.0	$e^{-\frac{d_{12}}{\rho}}$	$e^{-\frac{d_{13}}{\rho}}$	$e^{-\frac{d_{14}}{\rho}}$
	1.0	$e^{-\frac{d_{23}}{\rho}}$	$e^{-\frac{d_{24}}{\rho}}$
		1.0	$e^{-\frac{d_{34}}{\rho}}$
			1.0

33

Spatial exponential is another spatial covariance structure provided in PROC MIXED. The parameters are σ^2 and ρ. The value d_{ij} is computed as the distance in time between time *i* and time *j*. The values of the time points are incorporated into the computations of the covariance. The structure is useful for modeling correlations for repeated measures obtained at unequally spaced time points.

Many other covariance structures are provided in the MIXED procedure. For example, ARH(1) and TOEPH each allows for unequal variances over time. A complete listing of the covariance structures available in the MIXED procedure can be found in the SAS online documentation.

Account for Unequal Spacing?

TYPE=	Time points are: Equally spaced, same across subjects	Unequally spaced, same across subjects	Different across subjects
VC	n/a	n/a	n/a
UN	Yes	Yes	No
CS	Yes	Yes	Yes
AR(1)	Yes	No	No
TOEP	Yes	No	No
Spatial	**Yes**	**Yes**	**Yes**

34

Selecting an Appropriate Covariance Model

- If you ignore important correlations by using a model that is too simple, you risk increasing the Type I error rates for your fixed effects tests.
- If your model is too complex, you sacrifice power and efficiency for your fixed effects tests.

36

Specifying the appropriate model for within-subject correlation is essential for drawing accurate and powerful conclusions. Guerin and Stroup (2000) documented the effects of various covariance modeling decisions using the MIXED procedure for repeated measures data. It shows that inference in repeated measures analysis can be severely compromised by blatantly poor choices of covariance models. Although you usually do not know the true covariance structure, you must specify the covariance model that is approximately correct to obtain a valid analysis result.

How to Select a Covariance Model

- Use your subject matter knowledge and information from the data collection process and previous relevant studies.
- Use graphical tools to examine the patterns of correlations over time.
- Use information criteria to compare relative fit of various covariance structures.
- Use likelihood ratio tests to compare nested variance structures.

37

Before using statistical tools to select a covariance structure, you should first rule out covariance structures that clearly make no sense given your data. For example, the independent correlation structure may not be appropriate for repeated measures data when the time points are only hours apart. Also, AR(1) or TOEP models are generally inappropriate if the time points are not equally spaced. Your subject-matter knowledge and information from previous studies are important resources to help you select the most appropriate covariance structure.

Empirically you may consider using one or more of the following useful statistical tools to select the appropriate covariance model.

1. Graphical tools help visualize patterns of correlation between observations at different times.
2. Information criteria provided by PROC MIXED compare models using competing covariance structures.
3. Likelihood ratio tests compare nested variance structures, that is, one variance structure is a special case of the other variance structure.

Visualizing the Correlation Structure

The simplest graph to examine the correlation structure is a plot of correlation versus distance in time. First, you must use the MIXED procedure to fit the model:

```
proc mixed data=sasuser.fev1uni;
   class drug patient hour;
   model fev1=drug basefev1 drug*basefev1 hour drug*hour / ddfm=kr;
   repeated hour / type=un subject=patient(drug) r rcorr;
   ods output covparms=cov rcorr=corr;
run;                                              *c05s2d1.sas;
```

The MODEL statement specifies the mean model as discussed previously. The variable **basefev1** is used as a covariate. The REPEATED statement specifies the covariance structure among e_{ijk}, or the **R** matrix in mixed model theory notation.

You may drop the repeated effect (**hour**) in the REPEATED statement. Simply use the SUBJECT= option to define the blocks of **R** and the TYPE= option to define their covariance structure. In this case, the repeated measures data must be similarly ordered for each subject, and you must indicate all missing response variables with periods in the input data set unless they all fall at the end of a subject's repeated response profile. These requirements are necessary in order to inform PROC MIXED of the proper location of the observed repeated responses.

Selected REPEATED statement options:

TYPE= specifies the covariance structure of the **R** matrix. With the SUBJECT= option defining blocks, this TYPE= option specifies the covariance structure for each block. You used the unstructured type to help explore the covariance structure in your data.

SUBJECT= identifies the subjects in your mixed model. Complete independence is assumed across subjects; therefore, the SUBJECT= option produces a block-diagonal structure in **R** with identical blocks. Both discrete and continuous variables are permitted as arguments to the SUBJECT= option.

R requests that blocks of the estimated **R** matrix be displayed. The first block determined by the SUBJECT= effect is the default displayed block.

RCORR produces the correlation matrix corresponding to blocks of the estimated **R** matrix.

The ODS OUTPUT statement creates two SAS data sets, **cov** and **corr**, from two tables generated by PROC MIXED, **covparms** and **rcorr**, respectively.

Selected PROC MIXED Output

Estimated R Matrix for patient(drug) 201 a

Row	Col1	Col2	Col3	Col4	Col5	Col6	Col7	Col8
1	0.2321	0.2210	0.2162	0.2091	0.1789	0.1680	0.1328	0.1731
2	0.2210	0.2629	0.2372	0.2469	0.2226	0.1845	0.1602	0.1992
3	0.2162	0.2372	0.2586	0.2566	0.2224	0.1951	0.1729	0.2090
4	0.2091	0.2469	0.2566	0.3033	0.2434	0.2083	0.1948	0.2300
5	0.1789	0.2226	0.2224	0.2434	0.2879	0.2351	0.2069	0.2502
6	0.1680	0.1845	0.1951	0.2083	0.2351	0.2620	0.2187	0.2491
7	0.1328	0.1602	0.1729	0.1948	0.2069	0.2187	0.2748	0.2375
8	0.1731	0.1992	0.2090	0.2300	0.2502	0.2491	0.2375	0.3035

This output is produced by the R option in the REPEATED statement. It shows the covariance matrix for the first block (patient 201 drug a) and for every block because every block has identical covariance structure. The diagonal elements show the variances of repeated measures at each time point; the off-diagonal elements show the covariance of repeated measures taken at different time points. It may be easier to see the patterns of the variances and covariances from the plot produced later.

Estimated R Correlation Matrix for patient(drug) 201 a

Row	Col1	Col2	Col3	Col4	Col5	Col6	Col7	Col8
1	1.0000	0.8947	0.8828	0.7884	0.6921	0.6814	0.5260	0.6524
2	0.8947	1.0000	0.9098	0.8742	0.8092	0.7028	0.5959	0.7051
3	0.8828	0.9098	1.0000	0.9163	0.8153	0.7496	0.6487	0.7459
4	0.7884	0.8742	0.9163	1.0000	0.8239	0.7389	0.6747	0.7582
5	0.6921	0.8092	0.8153	0.8239	1.0000	0.8562	0.7358	0.8465
6	0.6814	0.7028	0.7496	0.7389	0.8562	1.0000	0.8152	0.8833
7	0.5260	0.5959	0.6487	0.6747	0.7358	0.8152	1.0000	0.8224
8	0.6524	0.7051	0.7459	0.7582	0.8465	0.8833	0.8224	1.0000

This output is produced by the RCORR option in the REPEATED statement. It shows the correlation matrix for the first block (patient 201 drug a) and for every block because every block has identical correlation structure. The diagonal elements are always equal to one; the off-diagonal elements show the correlation of repeated measures taken at different time points. This table was saved as a SAS data set **corr** by the ODS statement and will be used for producing one of the graphs later.

Covariance Parameter Estimates

Cov Parm	Subject	Estimate
UN(1,1)	patient(drug)	0.2321
UN(2,1)	patient(drug)	0.2210
UN(2,2)	patient(drug)	0.2629
UN(3,1)	patient(drug)	0.2162
UN(3,2)	patient(drug)	0.2372
UN(3,3)	patient(drug)	0.2586
UN(4,1)	patient(drug)	0.2091
UN(4,2)	patient(drug)	0.2469
UN(4,3)	patient(drug)	0.2566
UN(4,4)	patient(drug)	0.3033
UN(5,1)	patient(drug)	0.1789
UN(5,2)	patient(drug)	0.2226
UN(5,3)	patient(drug)	0.2224
UN(5,4)	patient(drug)	0.2434
UN(5,5)	patient(drug)	0.2879
UN(6,1)	patient(drug)	0.1680
UN(6,2)	patient(drug)	0.1845
UN(6,3)	patient(drug)	0.1951
UN(6,4)	patient(drug)	0.2083
UN(6,5)	patient(drug)	0.2351
UN(6,6)	patient(drug)	0.2620
UN(7,1)	patient(drug)	0.1328
UN(7,2)	patient(drug)	0.1602
UN(7,3)	patient(drug)	0.1729
UN(7,4)	patient(drug)	0.1948
UN(7,5)	patient(drug)	0.2069
UN(7,6)	patient(drug)	0.2187
UN(7,7)	patient(drug)	0.2748
UN(8,1)	patient(drug)	0.1731
UN(8,2)	patient(drug)	0.1992
UN(8,3)	patient(drug)	0.2090
UN(8,4)	patient(drug)	0.2300
UN(8,5)	patient(drug)	0.2502
UN(8,6)	patient(drug)	0.2491
UN(8,7)	patient(drug)	0.2375
UN(8,8)	patient(drug)	0.3035

These are the REML estimates of the variance-covariance matrix in each block (subject). The values are identical to those shown in the R matrix produced by the R option in the REPEATED statement; the only difference is the arrangement of the matrix elements. Notice that an 8×8 unstructured covariance matrix has 8+7+6+…+1=36 parameters that must be estimated. This table was saved as a SAS data set **cov** by the ODS statement and will be used for producing the graph later to examine the pattern of the covariance estimates.

```
data times;
   do time1=1 to 8;
      do time2=1 to time1;
          distance=time1-time2;
          output;
      end;
   end;
run;

data covplot;
   merge times cov;
run;

proc print;
run;

goptions reset=all;
proc gplot data=covplot;
   label distance='Distance in Hour';
   plot estimate*distance=time1 / nolegend
        haxis=axis1 vaxis=axis2;
   axis1 order=(0 to 7) offset=(2,2) minor=none;
   axis2 order=(0 to 0.4 by 0.05);
   symbol1 v='1' c=cyan i=j l=1;
   symbol2 v='2' c=blue i=j l=3;
   symbol3 v='3' c=green i=j l=4;
   symbol4 v='4' c=red i=j l=8;
   symbol5 v='5' c=purple i=j l=21;
   symbol6 v='6' c=brown i=j l=23;
   symbol7 v='7' c=black i=j l=25;
   symbol8 v='8' c=gold i=j l=28;
   title 'Covariance vs. Distance in Hour';
run;
title;
quit;                                           *c05s2d2.sas;
```

The data set **times** creates time pairs and distances in hours between them corresponding to the covariance parameter estimates in the data set **cov**. The GPLOT procedure plots the covariance as a function of distance in time between repeated measures. The PLOT statement plots **estimate** versus **distance** for each value of **time1**, the later time of the pair.

PROC PRINT Output

Obs	time1	time2	distance	CovParm	Subject	Estimate
1	1	1	0	UN(1,1)	patient(drug)	0.2321
2	2	1	1	UN(2,1)	patient(drug)	0.2210
3	2	2	0	UN(2,2)	patient(drug)	0.2629
4	3	1	2	UN(3,1)	patient(drug)	0.2162
5	3	2	1	UN(3,2)	patient(drug)	0.2372
6	3	3	0	UN(3,3)	patient(drug)	0.2586
7	4	1	3	UN(4,1)	patient(drug)	0.2091
8	4	2	2	UN(4,2)	patient(drug)	0.2469
9	4	3	1	UN(4,3)	patient(drug)	0.2566
10	4	4	0	UN(4,4)	patient(drug)	0.3033
11	5	1	4	UN(5,1)	patient(drug)	0.1789
12	5	2	3	UN(5,2)	patient(drug)	0.2226
13	5	3	2	UN(5,3)	patient(drug)	0.2224
14	5	4	1	UN(5,4)	patient(drug)	0.2434
15	5	5	0	UN(5,5)	patient(drug)	0.2879
16	6	1	5	UN(6,1)	patient(drug)	0.1680
17	6	2	4	UN(6,2)	patient(drug)	0.1845
18	6	3	3	UN(6,3)	patient(drug)	0.1951
19	6	4	2	UN(6,4)	patient(drug)	0.2083
20	6	5	1	UN(6,5)	patient(drug)	0.2351
21	6	6	0	UN(6,6)	patient(drug)	0.2620
22	7	1	6	UN(7,1)	patient(drug)	0.1328
23	7	2	5	UN(7,2)	patient(drug)	0.1602
24	7	3	4	UN(7,3)	patient(drug)	0.1729
25	7	4	3	UN(7,4)	patient(drug)	0.1948
26	7	5	2	UN(7,5)	patient(drug)	0.2069
27	7	6	1	UN(7,6)	patient(drug)	0.2187
28	7	7	0	UN(7,7)	patient(drug)	0.2748
29	8	1	7	UN(8,1)	patient(drug)	0.1731
30	8	2	6	UN(8,2)	patient(drug)	0.1992
31	8	3	5	UN(8,3)	patient(drug)	0.2090
32	8	4	4	UN(8,4)	patient(drug)	0.2300
33	8	5	3	UN(8,5)	patient(drug)	0.2502
34	8	6	2	UN(8,6)	patient(drug)	0.2491
35	8	7	1	UN(8,7)	patient(drug)	0.2375
36	8	8	0	UN(8,8)	patient(drug)	0.3035

PROC GPLOT Output

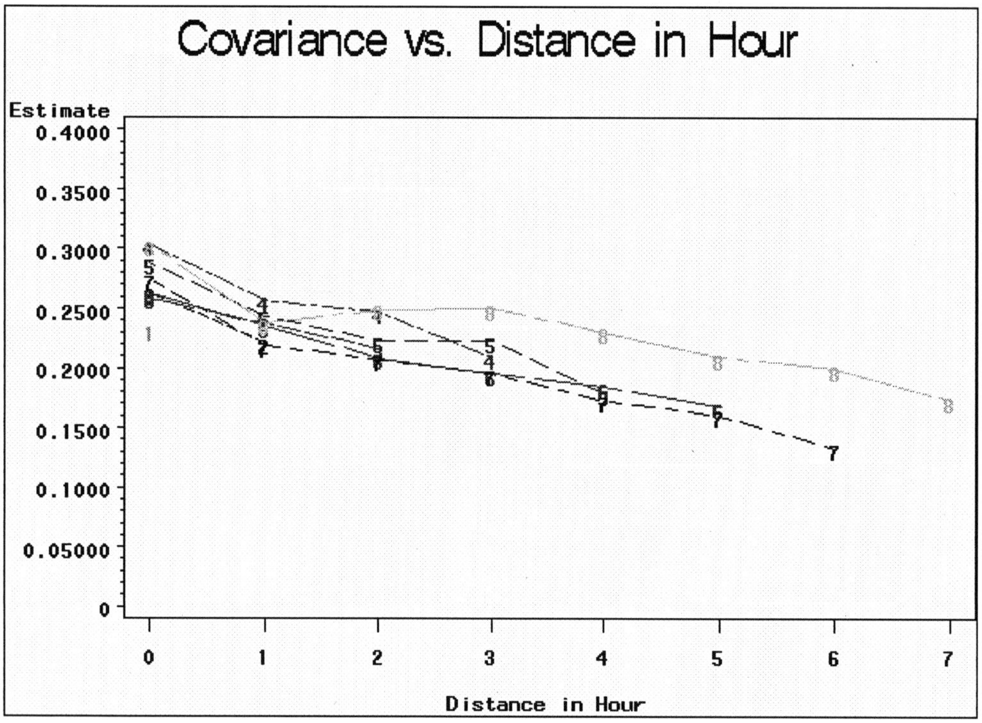

Several observations can be made from this plot:

- As the distance between pairs of observations increases, covariance tends to decrease.
- The pattern of decreasing covariance with distance is roughly the same for all reference times, indicated by the number on each line. Notice that the time is the latter time of the paired observations. For example, 8 at distance 1 plots the covariance between observations on the same subject at hours 8 and 7; 8 at distance 2 plots covariance for hours 8 and 6, and so forth. The covariance among adjacent observations (**`distance`**=1) is consistently between 0.21 and 0.26 and does not appear to depend on the value of the ending time point. The covariance at distance 2 is a little smaller and does not seem to depend on the ending time point either.
- The values plotted at **`distance`**=0 are the variances among the observations at each of the 8 hours. The values range from 0.23 to 0.31, which is not a big range at all. Additionally, there does not seem to be an increasing or decreasing trend in the variances with time. Therefore, you conclude that a model with constant variance over time is probably adequate for your data.

Based on these observations, you conclude that AR(1) or Toeplitz covariance models are probably most appropriate for the data. They are appropriate for equally spaced repeated measures. They assume constant variance over time and decreasing covariance with increasing distance in time.

You can also plot the correlation by distance in hours using the data set **corr** created by the ODS statement in the MIXED procedure. Unfortunately, the layout of the data set **corr** is not as convenient. Use PROC PRINT to obtain the listing output of this data set.

```
proc print data=corr;
run;                                              *c05s2d3.sas;
```

PROC PRINT Output

Obs	Index	Row	Col1	Col2	Col3	Col4
1	1	1	1.0000	0.8947	0.8828	0.7884
2	1	2	0.8947	1.0000	0.9098	0.8742
3	1	3	0.8828	0.9098	1.0000	0.9163
4	1	4	0.7884	0.8742	0.9163	1.0000
5	1	5	0.6921	0.8092	0.8153	0.8239
6	1	6	0.6814	0.7028	0.7496	0.7389
7	1	7	0.5260	0.5959	0.6487	0.6747
8	1	8	0.6524	0.7051	0.7459	0.7582

Obs	Col5	Col6	Col7	Col8
1	0.6921	0.6814	0.5260	0.6524
2	0.8092	0.7028	0.5959	0.7051
3	0.8153	0.7496	0.6487	0.7459
4	0.8239	0.7389	0.6747	0.7582
5	1.0000	0.8562	0.7358	0.8465
6	0.8562	1.0000	0.8152	0.8833
7	0.7358	0.8152	1.0000	0.8224
8	0.8465	0.8833	0.8224	1.0000

You want the values for the correlations to be stored in one single variable for plotting. There are different ways of creating a data set from **corr** for plotting. The one shown below is one of them.

```
%macro forplot(corrdata, dim);
   proc datasets; delete corrplot;
   run;
   %do i=1 %to %eval(&dim-1);
      data corrplot&i(rename=(col&i=corr row=time1));
         set &corrdata(keep=col&i row);
         distance=row-&i;
          time2=&i;
          if distance > 0;
      run;

      proc append base=corrplot data=corrplot&i;
      run;
   %end;
%mend;

%forplot(corr, 8);

proc print data=corrplot;
   var time1 time2 distance corr;
run;                                              *c05s2d3.sas;
```

The FORPLOT macro was used to create a SAS data set **corrplot** for the plotting. Notice that in the **corr** data set created by PROC MIXED, the lower-diagonal matrix can be thought of as the correlations between the observations at two time points, indicated by the column number and the value for row.

PROC PRINT Output

Obs	time1	time2	distance	corr
1	2	1	1	0.8947
2	3	1	2	0.8828
3	4	1	3	0.7884
4	5	1	4	0.6921
5	6	1	5	0.6814
6	7	1	6	0.5260
7	8	1	7	0.6524
8	3	2	1	0.9098
9	4	2	2	0.8742
10	5	2	3	0.8092
11	6	2	4	0.7028
12	7	2	5	0.5959
13	8	2	6	0.7051
14	4	3	1	0.9163
15	5	3	2	0.8153
16	6	3	3	0.7496
17	7	3	4	0.6487
18	8	3	5	0.7459
19	5	4	1	0.8239
20	6	4	2	0.7389
21	7	4	3	0.6747
22	8	4	4	0.7582
23	6	5	1	0.8562
24	7	5	2	0.7358
25	8	5	3	0.8465
26	7	6	1	0.8152
27	8	6	2	0.8833
28	8	7	1	0.82247

Then you can produce the plot of correlation versus distance in hours in a similar way as you did for covariance plot.

```
proc gplot data=corrplot;
   label distance='Distance in Hour';
   plot corr*distance=time1 / nolegend
        haxis=0 to 8 hminor=0 vaxis=0 to 1 by 0.1;
   symbol1 v='2' c=cyan i=j l=1;
   symbol2 v='3' c=blue i=j l=3;
   symbol3 v='4' c=green i=j l=4;
   symbol4 v='5' c=red i=j l=8;
   symbol5 v='6' c=purple i=j l=21;
   symbol6 v='7' c=brown i=j l=23;
   symbol7 v='8' c=black i=j l=25;
   title 'Correlation vs. Distance in Hour';
run;
title;
quit;                                          *c05s2d3.sas;
```

PROC GPLOT Output

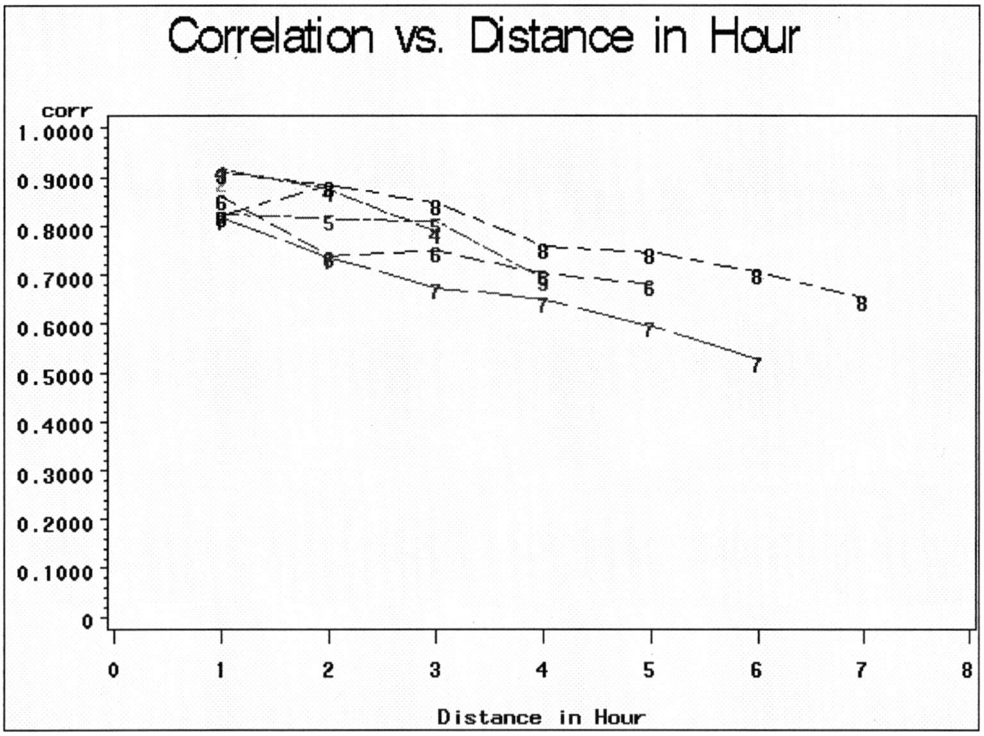

Several observations can be made about this plot:

- The correlation decreases from roughly 0.81-0.91 at distance 1 to approximately 0.65 at a larger distance. A flat correlation plot over distance would suggest compound symmetry. Now your non-flat plot for the shorter distances indicates a within-subject correlation model for which correlation is a decreasing function of distance.
- Unlike the covariance plot, you cannot use the correlation plot to diagnose possible heterogeneous variance over time because the correlation is always equal to 1 at distance 0.

Example Graphs of Correlation Structures

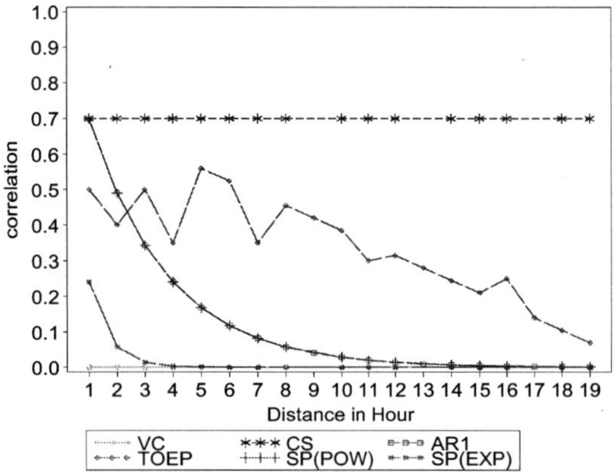

41

Note that because the correlations in the Toeplitz structure are not necessarily a function of distance in time, the pattern can be anything other than shown on the graph. One of the important features of the Toeplitz structure is that all the time pairs that are the same distance apart share the same correlation. Additionally, spatial power and the AR(1) is the same for equally spaced time points.

Information Criteria

- Akaike Information Criteria (AIC)
  - tends to favor more complex model
- Finite-sample corrected Akaike Information Criteria (AICC)
  - reduces the bias of AIC for small samples
- Schwarz's Bayesian Information Criteria (BIC)
  - tends to favor less complex model

44

You can use information criteria produced by the MIXED procedure as a tool to help you select a model with the most appropriate covariance structure. The smaller the information criteria value is, the better the model is. Theoretically, the smaller the –2 Res Log Likelihood is, the better the model is. However, you can always make this value smaller by adding parameters to the model. Information criteria attach penalties to the –2 Res Log Likelihood value; that is, the more the parameters, the bigger the penalties.

Two commonly used information criteria are Akaike's (1974) and Schwarz's (1978). Generally speaking, BIC tends to choose the less complex models than AIC. Because choosing a model that is too simple inflates Type I error rate, when Type I error control is the highest priority, you may want to choose AIC. On the other hand, if loss of power is more of a concern, BIC may be preferable (Guerin and Stroup 2000).

Starting in SAS 8.1, the MIXED procedure produces another information criterion, AICC. AICC is a finite-sample corrected Akaike Information Criterion. For small samples, it reduces the bias produced by AIC; for large samples, AICC converges to AIC. In general, AICC is preferred to AIC. For more information on information criteria, especially AICC, refer to Burnham, K.P. and Anderson, D.R. (1998).

The basic idea for repeated measures analysis is that, among plausible within-subject covariance models given a particular study, the model that minimizes AICC or BIC (your choice) is preferable. When AICC or BIC are close, the simpler model is generally preferred.

Information Criteria for Model Selection

You can compare candidate covariance models by running the MIXED procedure with various covariance structures. The resulting AICC and BIC can then be obtained and compared. From the plots you produced previously, you concluded that AR(1) or Toeplitz covariance models might be appropriate. Now you might want to compare these two models, along with the unstructured covariance model.

```
ods listing close;     ods trace on;     ods trace on / listing;
proc mixed data=sasuser.fev1uni;
   class drug patient hour;
   model fev1=drug basefev1 drug*basefev1 hour drug*hour / ddfm=kr;
   repeated hour / type=ar(1) subject=patient(drug);
   ods output FitStatistics=FitAR1(rename=(value=AR1))
              FitStatistics=FitAR1p
              Dimensions=ParmAR1(rename=(value=NumAR1));
run;
 ods trace off;
proc mixed data=sasuser.fev1uni;
   class drug patient hour;
   model fev1=drug basefev1 drug*basefev1 hour drug*hour / ddfm=kr;
   repeated hour / type=toep subject=patient(drug);
   ods output FitStatistics=FitToep(rename=(value=Toep))
              FitStatistics=FitToepp
             Dimensions=ParmToep(rename=(value=NumToep));
run;

proc mixed data=sasuser.fev1uni;
   class drug patient hour;
   model fev1=drug basefev1 drug*basefev1 hour drug*hour / ddfm=kr;
   repeated hour / type=un subject=patient(drug);
   ods output FitStatistics=FitUn(rename=(value=UN))
              FitStatistics=FitUNp
              Dimensions=ParmUN(rename=(value=NumUN));
run;

data fits;
   merge FitAR1 FitToep FitUn;
   by descr;
run;

ods listing;
proc print data=fits;
run;                                        *c05s2d4.sas;
```

The three PROC MIXED statements fit AR(1), Toeplitz, and unstructured models, respectively, to the data. The ODS OUTPUT statement inside each MIXED procedure produces SAS data sets for further processing.

PROC PRINT Output

Obs	Descr	AR1	Toep	UN
1	-2 Res Log Likelihood	276.1	229.0	150.4
2	AIC (smaller is better)	280.1	245.0	222.4
3	AICC (smaller is better)	280.1	245.3	227.6
4	BIC (smaller is better)	284.7	263.2	304.4

Based on AICC, UN is preferred over AR(1) and Toeplitz, but Toeplitz is better than AR(1) and UN based on BIC. You could use either the UN or Toeplitz model.

It may be useful to graph the information criteria.

```
data plot(drop=descr p);
   set FitAR1p (in=ar1)
       FitToepp (in=toep)
       FitUNp (in=un);
   if ar1 then structure='AR(1)';
   else if toep then structure='Toep';
   else if un then structure='UN';
   p=index(descr, '(');
   if p > 0 then FitStatistics=substr(descr, 1, p-2);
   else delete;
run;

proc gplot data=plot;
   plot value*FitStatistics=structure / haxis=axis1;
   symbol1 v=circle i=none c=red;
   symbol2 v=star i=none c=blue;
   symbol3 v=diamond i=none c=green;
   axis1 offset=(2,2);
run;
quit;                                        *c05s2d5.sas;
```

PROC GPLOT Output

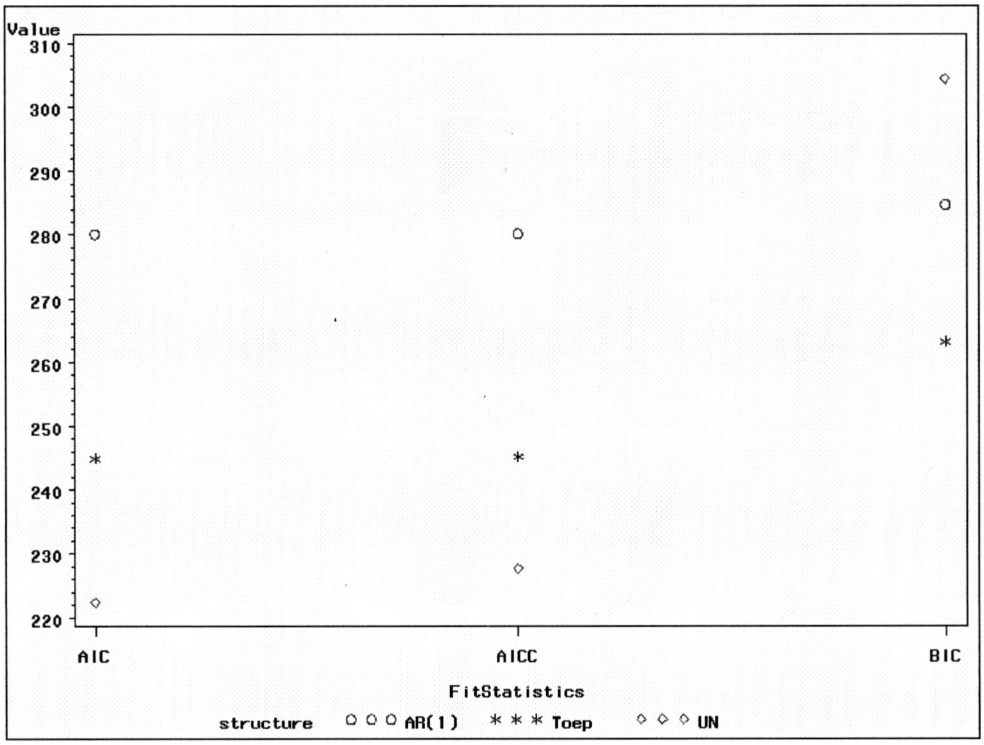

The graph provides a visual tool for comparing information criteria for different covariance structures. You reach the same conclusions as you would from the previous table showing the comparison of model fit for three covariance structures.

Construct a Likelihood Ratio Test

1. Fit two models with nested covariance structures.
2. Compute the difference of the –2 Res log likelihood values between the two models.
3. Compute the difference in the number of parameters estimated from the two models.
4. Compare the result from Step 2 with a χ^2 distribution with the degrees of freedom obtained from Step 3.

48

You can construct a likelihood ratio test to compare two different covariance structures. This test can only be applied to two nested covariance structures, that is, one structure is a special case of the other structure. For example, you can compare any covariance structures versus UN, AR(1) versus TOEP, and so forth. The null hypothesis is that the special case fits the data just as well as the more general covariance structure. It can be shown that under the null hypothesis, the –2 log of the ratio of the two likelihood functions is approximately distributed as a chi-square distribution with *r* degrees of freedom, with *r* being the difference in the number of parameters estimated from the two models. A significant *p*-value indicates the more general covariance structure is needed for your data.

This approach is conservative when the null hypothesis represented by the simpler model results from parameters being set equal to one of their boundary constraints (for example, variance component equals zero). In that case, the asymptotic distribution for the likelihood ratio statistics is often a mixture of chi-square distributions rather than the classical single chi-square distribution.

Details

One way to think about the likelihood ratio test (LRT) is with respect to maximum likelihood estimation (MLE). The LRT can be written as:

$\lambda(x) = \dfrac{L(\hat{\theta}_0 \mid x)}{L(\hat{\theta} \mid x)}$ where $\hat{\theta}$ is the MLE of θ and $\hat{\theta}_0$ is the MLE of θ under the restricted parameter space specified in the null model. If the null is specified as H_0: $\theta = \theta_0$ then the numerator is the likelihood function at $\theta = \theta_0$.

$$\begin{aligned} \log\{\lambda(x)\} &= \log\{L(\hat{\theta}_0 \mid x)\} - \log\{L(\hat{\theta} \mid x)\} \\ \Rightarrow -2\log\{\lambda(x)\} &= -2\log\{L(\hat{\theta}_0 \mid x)\} - [-2\log\{L(\hat{\theta} \mid x)\}] \\ &= -2\log(\mathit{reduced}) - [-2\log(\mathit{full})] \end{aligned}$$

It can be shown that $-2\log\{\lambda(x)\}$ follows a chi-square distribution with *r* degrees of freedom, with *r* being the difference in the number of parameters estimated from the two models.

Likelihood Ratio Tests

You can construct likelihood ratio tests to compare nested covariance structures following the four steps outlined previously.

```
data result (drop=descr);
   merge FitAR1 FitToep FitUN ParmAR1 ParmToep ParmUN;
   if _n_=1 then do;
      ChiToepUn=Toep-UN;
      dfToepUn=NumUN-NumToep;
      pToepUn=1-probchi(ChiToepUn, dfToepUn);

      ChiAR1Un=AR1-UN;
      dfAR1Un=NumUN-NumAR1;
      pAR1Un=1-probchi(ChiAR1Un, dfAR1Un);

      ChiAR1Toep=AR1-Toep;
      dfAR1Toep=NumToep-NumAR1;
      pAR1Toep=1-probchi(ChiAR1Toep, dfAR1Toep);
      output;
      stop;
   end;
run;

options nodate nonumber;
title1 'Likelihood Ratio Tests';
title2 'Toep vs UN, AR1 vs UN, and AR1 vs Toep';
proc print data=result noobs;
   var ChiToepUn dfToepUn pToepUn ChiAR1Un dfAR1Un pAR1Un
       ChiAR1Toep dfAR1Toep pAr1Toep;
run;
title;                                          *c05s2d6.sas;
```

Data sets **FitAR1**, **FitToep**, **FitUN**, **ParmAR1**, **ParmToep**, and **ParmUN** were created from the previous demonstration. In data sets **FitAR1**, **FitToep**, and **FitUN**, the first observation (_n_=1) contains –2 Res Log Likelihood values for each model. In data sets **ParmAR1**, **ParmToep**, and **ParmUN**, the first observation (_n_=1) contains the number of covariance parameters estimated by each model. These values are used to compute the chi-square statistics, the associated degrees of freedom, and thus *p*-values for the likelihood ratio tests.

PROC PRINT Output

```
                              Likelihood Ratio Tests
                      Toep vs UN, AR1 vs UN, and AR1 vs Toep

  Chi      df                    Chi      df                   Chi      df
 ToepUn ToepUn    pToepUn    AR1Un   AR1Un     pAR1Un    AR1Toep AR1Toep  pAR1Toep

78.5850    28   .000001082 125.679    34   1.9271E-12 47.0939     6     1.7922E-8
```

The variable **pToepUn** contains the *p*-value for the likelihood ratio test of comparing Toeplitz and UN covariance models. The significant *p*-value (0.000001082) indicates that the more general model, UN, is needed for your data. Similarly, the variable **pAR1Un** compares AR(1) and UN covariance models. The significant *p*-value (1.9271E-12) indicates that the UN model is needed for your data.

Different approaches can sometimes produce conflicting results. The conclusions you draw based on the likelihood ratio tests are not consistent with the conclusions based on the BIC information criterion. You might decide to choose the Toeplitz structure after you examine the graphs and the fit statistics produced earlier. However, the UN structure could also be a choice.

Likelihood ratio tests tend to favor H_0 when the degrees of freedom for the chi-squared statistics are small, and tend to reject H_0 when the degrees of freedom is large (Burnham and Anderson (1998)).

Step 3: Fit the Mean Model Accounting for the Covariance Structure

- Use the appropriate covariance structure to fit the mean model using the MIXED procedure.
- You may need to reduce the mean model.

54

After you select the covariance model, you can proceed with the analysis (in this case, the analysis of covariance) as you would in any other similar analysis. You may need to reduce the mean model to obtain a more parsimonious one based on the tests for fixed effects and/or the information criteria.

Model Development Guidelines

1. Begin with a fairly complete mean model.
2. Use REML to choose the appropriate covariance structure based on AICC or BIC.
3. Use ML to choose the appropriate mean model based on AICC or BIC.
4. Fit the final model using REML.

55

After an appropriate covariance structure is selected, model-building efforts should be directed at simplifying the mean structure of the model. Because the model should be hierarchically well formulated, the first step is to evaluate the interactions. One recommended approach is to eliminate the interactions one at a time, starting with the least significant interaction. If you use the model fit statistics such as AICC, then you must use the ML estimation method. However, after the final model is chosen, refit the model using REML because REML estimators are superior.

Another approach is to compute a likelihood ratio test that compares two models, the full model with all of the interactions and the reduced model with just a subset of terms. The difference between the –2 log likelihoods for the full and reduced models is the value of the test statistic. The likelihood ratio test comparing the full and reduced models is only valid under ML estimation.

Fit Statistics from ML and REML

- Differences in the model fit statistics under REML reflect differences in the covariance parameter estimates.
- Differences in the model fit statistics under ML reflect differences in all the parameter estimates.
- When comparing different mean models, differences under ML are a better reflection of the importance of the fixed effects than differences under REML.

56

If you reduce the mean model simply by examining *p*-values, then using the default REML method is appropriate. However, if you reduce the mean model using model fit statistics such as AICC and BIC, then the estimation method must be ML. Model fit statistics under REML are used to select the covariance structure. Fit statistics using ML reflect differences in all parameters. Specifying the same covariance model but different mean models using ML yields fit statistics that reflect the differences in the mean models.

Step 3: Fit the Mean Model Accounting for the Covariance Structure

```
proc mixed data=sasuser.fev1uni;
   class drug patient hour;
   model fev1=drug basefev1 drug*basefev1 hour drug*hour / ddfm=kr ;
   repeated hour / type=TOEP subject=patient(drug);
run;                                             *c05s2d7.sas;
```

Partial PROC MIXED Output

Covariance Parameter Estimates

Cov Parm	Subject	Estimate
TOEP(2)	patient(drug)	0.2314
TOEP(3)	patient(drug)	0.2191
TOEP(4)	patient(drug)	0.2099
TOEP(5)	patient(drug)	0.1937
TOEP(6)	patient(drug)	0.1858
TOEP(7)	patient(drug)	0.1724
TOEP(8)	patient(drug)	0.1612
Residual		0.2694

The variance is estimated by Residual with a value of 0.2694. The covariance parameter estimate for TOEP(d+1) is the covariance at distance d. The covariance decreases as the distance d increases. For example, the covariance is 0.2314 at d=1, the covariance is 0.2191 at d=2, and so on.

Null Model Likelihood Ratio Test

DF	Chi-Square	Pr > ChiSq
7	685.97	<.0001

The Null Model Likelihood Ratio Test table shows the test of comparing the model you fit with the null model, that is, independent errors with constant variance, for example, $\mathbf{R}=\sigma^2 I_n$. The significant p-value indicates that your model fits better than the null model.

Type 3 Tests of Fixed Effects

Effect	Num DF	Den DF	F Value	Pr > F
drug	2	66	0.41	0.6667
basefev1	1	65.9	74.53	<.0001
basefev1*drug	2	65.9	0.51	0.6026
hour	7	186	13.50	<.0001
drug*hour	14	249	3.73	<.0001

The Type 3 test indicates that **basefev1*drug** is not significant. This suggests the slopes are not significantly different from each other across drugs. You may want to drop the **basefev1*drug** interaction term and only fit a common slope model.

Reducing mean models can be achieved by examining the p-values for the fixed effects and removing nonsignificant (interaction) terms one at a time. Reducing mean models can also be achieved by comparing fit statistics from different models. But you need to use METHOD=ML for this purpose.

```
proc mixed data=sasuser.fev1uni method=ml;
   class drug patient hour;
   model fev1=drug basefev1 drug*basefev1 hour drug*hour / ddfm=kr;
   repeated hour / type=TOEP subject=patient(drug);
   ods output FitStatistics=FitFull(rename=(value=Full));
run;

proc mixed data=sasuser.fev1uni method=ml;
   class drug patient hour;
   model fev1=drug basefev1 hour drug*hour / ddfm=kr;
   repeated hour / type=TOEP subject=patient(drug);
   ods output FitStatistics=FitReduced
                         (rename=(value=Reduced));
run;

data fit;
   merge FitFull FitReduced;
run;

proc print data=fit;
run;                                             *c05s2d8.sas;
```

You use the METHOD=ML option in PROC MIXED to specify the maximum likelihood estimation method to be used. This is the method you should always use when comparing mean models.

✎ The REML and ML estimation methods are discussed in detail later in the course.

PROC PRINT Output

Obs	Descr	Full	Reduced
1	-2 Log Likelihood	129.7	130.8
2	AIC (smaller is better)	199.7	196.8
3	AICC (smaller is better)	204.4	201.0
4	BIC (smaller is better)	279.4	272.0

Based on all three information criteria, the reduced model appears to fit your data better than the full model.

✎ A SAS macro %COMPMIX8 can be used to compare different models. This macro is available at the following SAS Web site: http://ewe3.sas.com/techsup/download/stat.

```
proc mixed data=sasuser.fev1uni;
   class drug patient hour;
   model fev1=drug basefev1 hour drug*hour / ddfm=kr outp=pred;
   repeated hour / type=TOEP subject=patient(drug);
run;

goptions reset=all;
proc gplot data=pred;
   plot Resid*Pred;
run;
quit;                                            *c05s2d9.sas;
```

Partial PROC MIXED Output

```
                 Covariance Parameter Estimates

              Cov Parm     Subject          Estimate

              TOEP(2)      patient(drug)      0.2284
              TOEP(3)      patient(drug)      0.2162
              TOEP(4)      patient(drug)      0.2070
              TOEP(5)      patient(drug)      0.1908
              TOEP(6)      patient(drug)      0.1826
              TOEP(7)      patient(drug)      0.1691
              TOEP(8)      patient(drug)      0.1579
              Residual                        0.2664
```

The covariance parameter estimates are similar to those obtained previously.

```
                        Fit Statistics

               -2 Res Log Likelihood          227.9
               AIC (smaller is better)        243.9
               AICC (smaller is better)       244.2
               BIC (smaller is better)        262.1


                 Null Model Likelihood Ratio Test

                   DF    Chi-Square      Pr > ChiSq

                    7        689.03          <.0001
```

```
                 Type 3 Tests of Fixed Effects

                           Num     Den
            Effect          DF      DF     F Value     Pr > F

            drug             2    71.3        7.30     0.0013
            basefev1         1    67.8       75.69     <.0001
            hour             7     186       13.45     <.0001
            drug*hour       14     249        3.72     <.0001
```

The Type 3 Tests of Fixed Effects table shows that the **drug*hour** interaction is significant. You may want to make a statistical inference about **drug*hour**.

PROC GPLOT Output

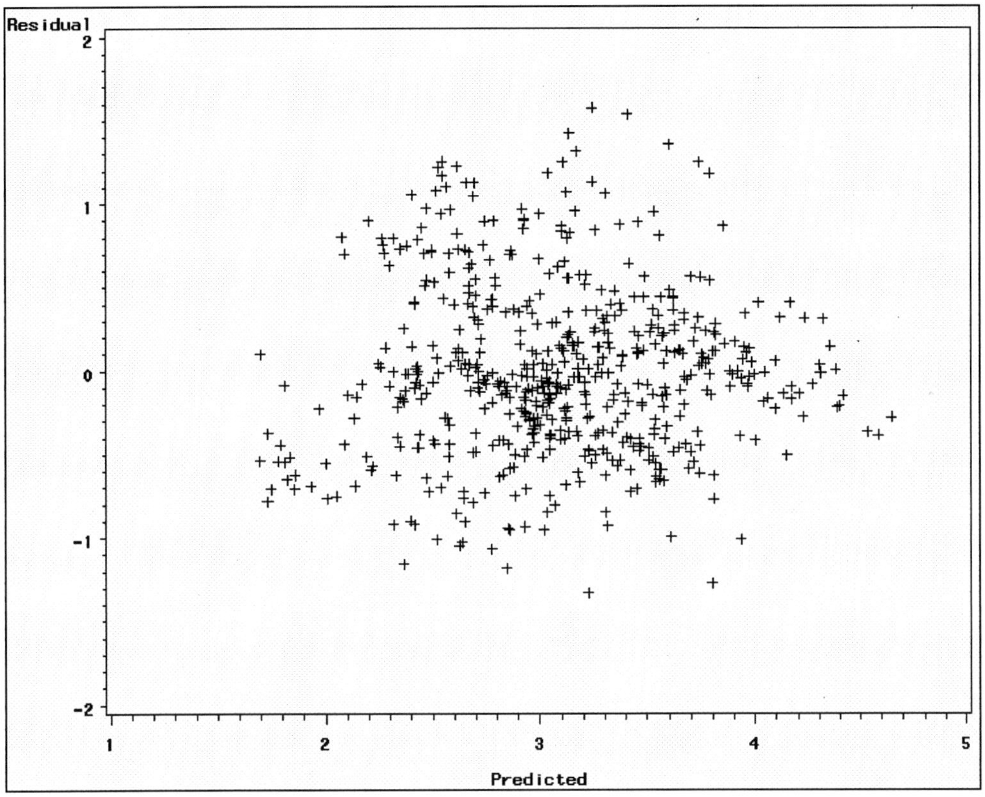

The residual plot shows fairly random scatters around zero. This plot is helpful for identifying misspecified mean models and potential outliers. It is also helpful for determining nonconstant variances. In mixed models, you can model heterogeneous variances by using one of the covariance structures that model heterogeneity in variances, such as ARH(1), CSH, power-of-the-mean model, log-linear model, or using the GROUP= option. This residual plot indicates that no misspecification of the mean model or any outliers is apparent. The variances seem to be constant as well.

Studentized residuals, one of the experimental features for PROC MIXED in SAS®9, might be preferred for residual analysis.

Step 4: Make Statistical Inferences

Based on the results of Step 3, you may want to

- compare means for **drug*hour**
- fit a regression model treating **hour** as a continuous variable.

61

Depending on the objectives of your study, you may want to compare the treatment means for **drug*hour** combinations, or you may want to use regression analysis to compare the effect of hour for the three drugs.

Comparison of Means

- Perform all pairwise comparisons.
- Test the effects of **drug** at a given **hour**.
- Define contrasts of any other meaningful comparisons.

62

These are the main types of tests for interaction terms. Different data sets and/or different objectives of the study call for different tests. The all-pairwise comparison tests may produce more tests than needed in most cases. The test of simple effects of **drug** for a given hour is probably a more meaningful test. The test of simple effects of **hour** for a given drug can be more directly addressed by the regression methods presented later in this section. Any other custom hypothesis tests can be done using the CONTRAST or ESTIMATE statement. For example, you can compare the change from hour 1 (first hour) to hour 8 (last hour) for the two treatment drugs, a and c, using an ESTIMATE statement.

Comparisons Using Regressions

You can use a regression technique to see how the **`fev1`** means change over time for different treatments.

63

Making Statistical Inference

To investigate the significant interaction term, you can submit the following program to make inferences about the **drug*hour** means:

```
ods listing exclude diffs;
ods output diffs=alldiffs;
proc mixed data=sasuser.fev1uni;
   class drug patient hour;
   model fev1=drug basefev1 hour drug*hour / ddfm=kr;
   repeated hour / type=TOEP subject=patient(drug);
   lsmeans drug*hour / slice=hour diff adjust=tukey;
   estimate '(hr1-hr8) for a vs (hr1-hr8) for c'
            drug*hour 1 0 0 0 0 0 0 -1
                     -1 0 0 0 0 0 0 1;
run;

proc print data=alldiffs;
   where drug=_drug or hour=_hour;
run;                                         *c05s2d10.sas;
```

The ODS LISTING EXCLUDE DIFFS statement prevents all pairwise comparisons (resulted from the DIFF option in LSMEANS statement) from appearing in the output window. Instead, the output will be saved to a SAS data set named **alldiffs**, as accomplished by the ODS OUTPUT statement in the next line.

Selected LSMEANS statement option:

SLICE= specifies effects by which to partition interaction LSMEANS effects. This can produce what are known as tests of simple effects.

The SLICE= option produces the tests of **drug** for each level of **hour**. Although these tests are already included in the output produced by the DIFF option, where all pairwise comparisons are made, it is easier to use the SLICE= option to perform and examine the tests of your interest. Notice that a total of 276 comparisons are made by the DIFF option.

The ESTIMATE statement compares the change from the first hour to the last hour for drugs a and c.

Partial PROC MIXED Output

Estimates

Label	Estimate	Standard Error	DF	t Value
(hr1-hr8) for a vs (hr1-hr8) for c	-0.06542	0.1345	62.3	-0.49

Estimates

Label	Pr > |t|
(hr1-hr8) for a vs (hr1-hr8) for c	0.6283

There is no evidence that the change from the first hour to the last hour is different for the two drugs (difference of –0.06542 with *p*-value=0.6283). This is consistent with what you saw in the previous plot.

Least Squares Means

Effect	drug	hour	Estimate	Standard Error	DF	t Value	Pr > |t|
drug*hour	a	1	3.4719	0.1054	109	32.95	<.0001
drug*hour	a	2	3.3952	0.1054	109	32.22	<.0001
drug*hour	a	3	3.1823	0.1054	109	30.20	<.0001
drug*hour	a	4	3.0448	0.1054	109	28.90	<.0001
drug*hour	a	5	3.0519	0.1054	109	28.96	<.0001
drug*hour	a	6	2.9777	0.1054	109	28.26	<.0001
drug*hour	a	7	2.8669	0.1054	109	27.21	<.0001
drug*hour	a	8	2.8565	0.1054	109	27.11	<.0001
drug*hour	c	1	3.6899	0.1054	109	35.02	<.0001
drug*hour	c	2	3.6253	0.1054	109	34.41	<.0001
drug*hour	c	3	3.5762	0.1054	109	33.94	<.0001
drug*hour	c	4	3.4424	0.1054	109	32.67	<.0001
drug*hour	c	5	3.2483	0.1054	109	30.83	<.0001
drug*hour	c	6	3.0841	0.1054	109	29.27	<.0001
drug*hour	c	7	2.9758	0.1054	109	28.24	<.0001
drug*hour	c	8	3.0091	0.1054	109	28.56	<.0001
drug*hour	p	1	2.8269	0.1054	109	26.83	<.0001
drug*hour	p	2	2.8928	0.1054	109	27.45	<.0001
drug*hour	p	3	2.8982	0.1054	109	27.51	<.0001
drug*hour	p	4	2.8715	0.1054	109	27.25	<.0001
drug*hour	p	5	2.7686	0.1054	109	26.28	<.0001
drug*hour	p	6	2.8157	0.1054	109	26.72	<.0001
drug*hour	p	7	2.7849	0.1054	109	26.43	<.0001
drug*hour	p	8	2.7324	0.1054	109	25.93	<.0001

The Least Squares Means table shows the mean response for every **`drug*hour`** combination. In general, the responses for drugs a and c decrease over time, whereas the response for drug p remains relatively constant.

Tests of Effect Slices

Effect	hour	Num DF	Den DF	F Value	Pr > F
drug*hour	1	2	109	18.14	<.0001
drug*hour	2	2	109	12.64	<.0001
drug*hour	3	2	109	10.44	<.0001
drug*hour	4	2	109	7.72	0.0007
drug*hour	5	2	109	5.24	0.0067
drug*hour	6	2	109	1.65	0.1976
drug*hour	7	2	109	0.83	0.4404
drug*hour	8	2	109	1.73	0.1820

The results from the SLICE= option indicate significant drug effects for hours 1 through 5, but no statistically significant differences among the three drugs for hours 6, 7, and 8.

The DIFF option can produce a large amount of output. The ODS LISTING EXCLUDE statement prevents this output from printing. The PROC PRINT step only prints those comparisons of simple effects and eliminates all other comparisons.

Obs	Effect	drug	hour	_drug	_hour	Estimate	StdErr
1	drug*hour	a	1	a	2	0.07667	0.05624
2	drug*hour	a	1	a	3	0.2896	0.06470
3	drug*hour	a	1	a	4	0.4271	0.07037
4	drug*hour	a	1	a	5	0.4200	0.07940
5	drug*hour	a	1	a	6	0.4942	0.08355
6	drug*hour	a	1	a	7	0.6050	0.09005
7	drug*hour	a	1	a	8	0.6154	0.09508
8	drug*hour	a	1	c	1	-0.2180	0.1490
16	drug*hour	a	1	p	1	0.6449	0.1490
....							
164	drug*hour	c	1	p	1	0.8630	0.1490
....							

Obs	DF	tValue	Probt	Adjustment	Adjp
1	401	1.36	0.1736	Tukey-Kramer	0.9996
2	366	4.48	<.0001	Tukey-Kramer	0.0027
3	285	6.07	<.0001	Tukey-Kramer	<.0001
4	226	5.29	<.0001	Tukey-Kramer	<.0001
5	153	5.91	<.0001	Tukey-Kramer	<.0001
6	112	6.72	<.0001	Tukey-Kramer	<.0001
7	62.3	6.47	<.0001	Tukey-Kramer	<.0001
8	109	-1.46	0.1463	Tukey-Kramer	0.9989
16	109	4.33	<.0001	Tukey-Kramer	0.0049
....					
164	109	5.79	<.0001	Tukey-Kramer	<.0001
....					

The output contains comparisons between the **fev1** means for each pair of hours holding each **drug** constant. It also contains comparisons between each pair of drugs holding **hour** constant. For drug a, the change from hour 1 to hour 2 is not significant, but the change from hour 1 to each subsequent hour is significant. Also, at hour 1, drugs a and c are not significantly different, but they are significantly different from the placebo.

Now use regression technique to investigate the significant interaction term.

Recall the graph you saw before:

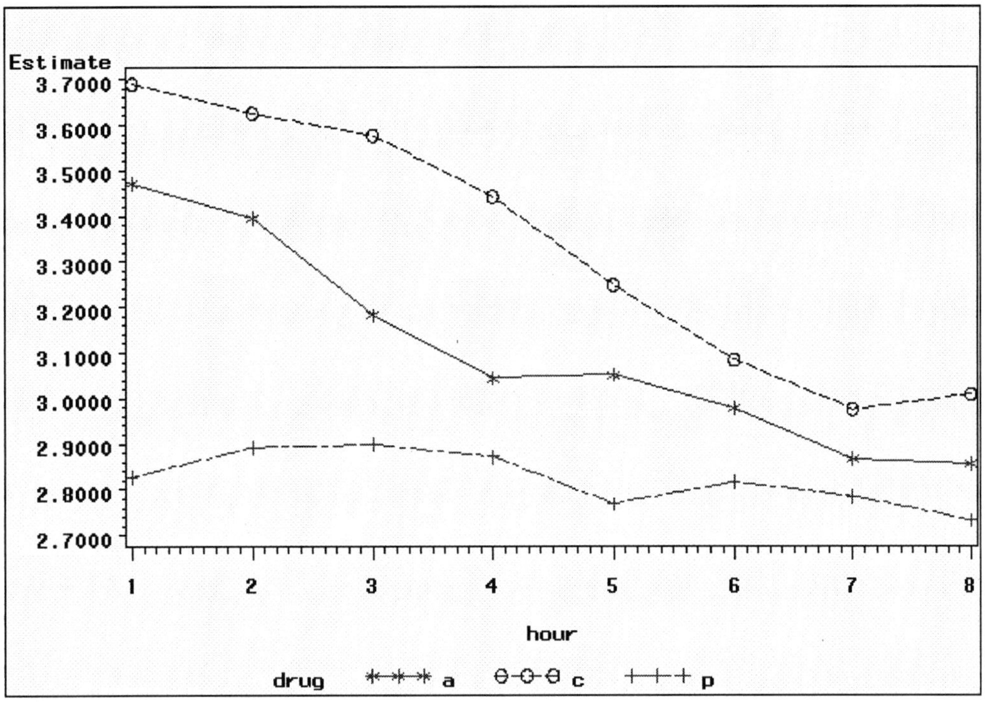

You might want to treat **hour** as a continuous variable and fit a regression model to your data. This type of analysis is sometimes referred to as a *growth curve model.*

```
proc mixed data=sasuser.fev1uni;
   class drug patient;
   model fev1=basefev1 drug hour drug*hour / ddfm=kr solution;
   repeated / type=toep subject=patient(drug);
run;                                          *c05s2d11.sas;
```

The variable **hour** is not in the CLASS statement and therefore is treated as a continuous variable in the regression model. The SOLUTION option is used to obtain the regression coefficients.

Partial PROC MIXED Output

Covariance Parameter Estimates

Cov Parm	Subject	Estimate
TOEP(2)	patient(drug)	0.2295
TOEP(3)	patient(drug)	0.2153
TOEP(4)	patient(drug)	0.2059
TOEP(5)	patient(drug)	0.1904
TOEP(6)	patient(drug)	0.1829
TOEP(7)	patient(drug)	0.1706
TOEP(8)	patient(drug)	0.1595
Residual		0.2682

The covariance parameter estimates are slightly different from previous results because you fit a different mean model.

```
                    Fit Statistics

          -2 Res Log Likelihood            196.6
          AIC (smaller is better)          212.6
          AICC (smaller is better)         212.8
          BIC (smaller is better)          230.8
```

Because a different mean model is used, you should not use this table to compare model fit to any of the previous models. Recall that if two covariance models are the same but mean models differ, you ought to use METHOD=ML to compare mean models using fit statistics.

Solution for Fixed Effects

Effect	drug	Estimate	Standard Error	DF	t Value	Pr > |t|
Intercept		0.5225	0.2911	73.8	1.80	0.0767
basefev1		0.8877	0.1021	67.8	8.69	<.0001
drug	a	0.6715	0.1569	116	4.28	<.0001
drug	c	0.9438	0.1568	116	6.02	<.0001
drug	p	0	.	.	.	.
hour		-0.01535	0.01329	66	-1.16	0.2520
hour*drug	a	-0.07532	0.01879	66	-4.01	0.0002
hour*drug	c	-0.09180	0.01879	66	-4.89	<.0001
hour*drug	p	0	.	.	.	.

Type 3 Tests of Fixed Effects

Effect	Num DF	Den DF	F Value	Pr > F
basefev1	1	67.8	75.57	<.0001
drug	2	116	19.19	<.0001
hour	1	66	85.82	<.0001
hour*drug	2	66	13.57	<.0001

The significant **hour*drug** interaction from the Type 3 tests of fixed effects indicates that an unequal slope model is necessary for this data.

Here are the models:

- drug a:
  fev1 = (0.5225+0.6715) – (0.01535+0.07532)***hour** + 0.8877***basefev1**
  = 1.1940 – 0.09067***hour** + 0.8877***basefev1**
- drug c:
  fev1 = (0.5225+0.9438) – (0.01535+0.09180)***hour** + 0.8877***basefev1**
  = 1.4663 – 0.10715***hour** + 0.8877***basefev1**
- drug p:
  fev1 = 0.5225 – 0.01535***hour** + 0.8877***basefev1**

This model is useful for making inferences or predictions for patients with known values of **basefev1**. For the purpose of making inferences or predictions for any patients, you can substitute the average **basefev1** value, 2.6493, into the above set of equations and obtain the following models:

- drug a: **fev1** = 3.5458 – 0.09067***hour**
- drug c: **fev1** = 3.8181 – 0.10715***hour**
- drug p: **fev1** = 2.8743 – 0.01535***hour**

You can write a series of ESTIMATE statements to estimate, for example, the differences between hour 1 and subsequent hours for drug a, or differences between drugs a and c at each hour, treating **hour** as a continuous variable. Refer to Littell, Pendergast, and Natarajan (2000) for more information on these ESTIMATE statements.

The best fitting model might be a polynomial model. The program and the output are provided in Appendix B.

The Regression Model

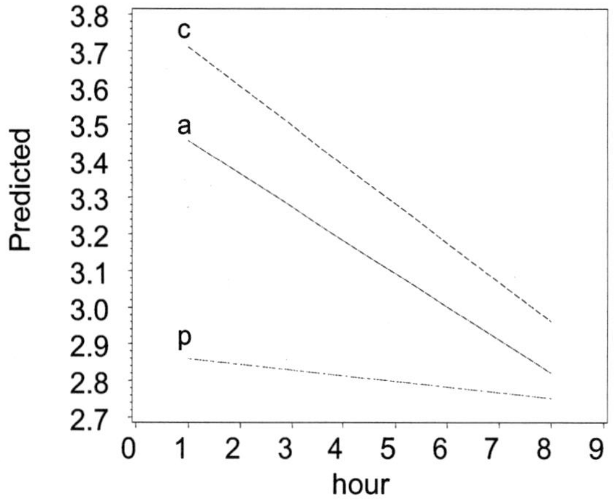

68

The regression model illustrates the significant **drug*hour** interaction. Three lines do not have the same slope for the three drugs. Regression models are also useful for making predictions for other values of **hour**.

What Else Could Have Been Done?

- Use the GROUP= option to fit a heterogeneous variance model.
- Use the RANDOM statement in addition to the REPEATED statement for an AR(1) structure to account for additional between-subject variations.
- Fit a random coefficient model.

72

The GROUP= option in a RANDOM or REPEATED statement is useful for modeling a heterogeneous variance model. All observations having the same level of the GROUP effect have the same covariance parameters. Each new level of the GROUP effect produces a new set of covariance parameters with the same structure as the original group. For example, if you suspect that repeated measures obtained from patients taking different drugs may have different variances, especially when one of the drugs is placebo, you might want to use the GROUP=**drug** option in the REPEATED statement to account for these possible heterogeneous variances.

When an AR(1) model is specified in the REPEATED statement, you may be able to use a RANDOM statement to account for additional between-subject variations that are not accounted for by the AR(1) covariance structure. In general, however, you should use caution when specifying both RANDOM and REPEATED statements in the repeated measures analysis, as variations in your data may all be accounted for by the specified covariance structures (TYPE=) in the REPEATED statement. More information is provided later in the course.

When you treat the time variable **hour** as a continuous variable, it may be interesting to fit a random coefficient model to your data, especially if you are interested in obtaining profiles (EBLUPs) for each or some of the patients included in the study.

The GROUP= Option

GROUP=**drug**

drug a patients

σ_a^2	σ_{1a}	σ_{2a}	σ_{3a}
	σ_a^2	σ_{1a}	σ_{2a}
		σ_a^2	σ_{1a}
			σ_a^2

drug c patients

σ_c^2	σ_{1c}	σ_{2c}	σ_{3c}
	σ_c^2	σ_{1c}	σ_{2c}
		σ_c^2	σ_{1c}
			σ_c^2

73

The GROUP= option defines the effect specifying heterogeneity in the covariance structure of **R**. For example, if you specify GROUP=`drug` in the REPEATED statement, all patients taking the same drug will have the same covariance parameters, patients taking different drugs are allowed to have different covariance parameters, but they all have the same covariance structure (in this example, Toeplitz). Therefore, the GROUP= option allows heterogeneity in the covariance parameters across subgroups (in this example, patients taking different drugs) of subjects.

You should exercise caution in properly defining the GROUP effect, as strange covariance patterns can result with misuse. Also, the GROUP effect can greatly increase the number of estimated covariance parameters, which may adversely affect the optimization process.

Continuous variables are permitted as arguments to the GROUP= option. Using a continuous variable decreases execution time for models with a large number of subjects or groups and also prevents the production of a large Class Levels Information table.

Random Coefficient Models

Random coefficient models

- are alternative ways to indirectly model the covariance for repeated measures data
- model the variations among the subjects in terms of regression coefficients (intercept and slopes)
- have a **G** matrix (block-diagonal) and a **R** matrix ($\sigma^2 I_n$ by default), and the resulting **V** matrix enables the correlations within subject to change over time
- are usually models of choice when data was not obtained at fixed time points and within-subject correlations cannot be modeled adequately by a specified covariance structure.

74

What Else Could Have Been Done?

```
proc mixed data=sasuser.fev1uni;
   class drug patient hour;
   model fev1=drug basefev1 drug*basefev1 hour drug*hour / ddfm=kr;
   repeated hour / type=TOEP subject=patient(drug)
                   group=drug;
   title 'Using the GROUP= Option';
run;

proc mixed data=sasuser.fev1uni;
   class drug patient hour;
   model fev1=drug basefev1 drug*basefev1 hour drug*hour / ddfm=kr;
   random patient(drug);
   repeated hour / type=AR(1) subject=patient(drug);
   title 'Using RANDOM in Addition to REPEATED';
run;

proc mixed data=sasuser.fev1uni;
   class drug patient;
   model fev1=basefev1 drug hour hour*drug / ddfm=kr ;
   random int hour / type=un subject=patient(drug) g v;
   title 'Random Coefficient Model';
run;
title;                                         *c05s2d12.sas;
```

The first MIXED procedure uses the GROUP=**drug** option in the REPEATED statement to fit a heterogeneous variance model. The resulting **R** matrix would still be a block diagonal matrix, with TOEP in each block (subject). Depending on the drug each patient took, the covariance parameter estimates are allowed to differ.

The second MIXED procedure uses a RANDOM statement in addition to the REPEATED statement to account for any additional between-subject variations. As discussed previously, you should exercise caution when specifying both RANDOM and REPEATED statements in the repeated measures analysis when the RANDOM effect is the same as the SUBJECT= effect in the REPEATED statement.

The third MIXED procedure fits a random coefficient model to your data. The G and V options in the RANDOM statement request that the estimated **G** and **V** matrices for the first subject be displayed.

Partial Output from the First MIXED Procedure

```
                    Using the GROUP= Option

                Covariance Parameter Estimates

Cov Parm     Subject          Group     Estimate

Variance     patient(drug)    drug a      0.2838
TOEP(2)      patient(drug)    drug a      0.2457
TOEP(3)      patient(drug)    drug a      0.2330
TOEP(4)      patient(drug)    drug a      0.2263
TOEP(5)      patient(drug)    drug a      0.2303
TOEP(6)      patient(drug)    drug a      0.2376
TOEP(7)      patient(drug)    drug a      0.2276
TOEP(8)      patient(drug)    drug a      0.2316
Variance     patient(drug)    drug c      0.2778
TOEP(2)      patient(drug)    drug c      0.2430
TOEP(3)      patient(drug)    drug c      0.2299
TOEP(4)      patient(drug)    drug c      0.2134
TOEP(5)      patient(drug)    drug c      0.1859
TOEP(6)      patient(drug)    drug c      0.1619
TOEP(7)      patient(drug)    drug c      0.1479
TOEP(8)      patient(drug)    drug c      0.1555
Variance     patient(drug)    drug p      0.2399
TOEP(2)      patient(drug)    drug p      0.1959
TOEP(3)      patient(drug)    drug p      0.1822
TOEP(4)      patient(drug)    drug p      0.1767
TOEP(5)      patient(drug)    drug p      0.1531
TOEP(6)      patient(drug)    drug p      0.1481
TOEP(7)      patient(drug)    drug p      0.1159
TOEP(8)      patient(drug)    drug p     0.06273
```

Now you have 24 covariance parameters that need to be estimated. Does this provide a better fit to your data?

```
                    Using the GROUP= Option

                       Fit Statistics

          -2 Res Log Likelihood          195.6
          AIC (smaller is better)        243.6
          AICC (smaller is better)       245.9
          BIC (smaller is better)        298.2
```

Compared with the model without the GROUP= option, both AICC and BIC values from this model are bigger. You conclude that the GROUP= option may not be useful for your data.

Partial Output from the Second MIXED Procedure

```
                    Using RANDOM in Addition to REPEATED

                       Covariance Parameter Estimates

                Cov Parm          Subject           Estimate

                patient(drug)                         0.1874
                AR(1)             patient(drug)       0.5400
                Residual                             0.08307
```

The additional covariance parameter estimate for **`patient(drug)`** corresponds to the between-subject variation. Is this model a better fit?

```
                    Using RANDOM in Addition to REPEATED

                              Fit Statistics

                   -2 Res Log Likelihood           248.0
                   AIC (smaller is better)         254.0
                   AICC (smaller is better)        254.0
                   BIC (smaller is better)         260.8
```

Compared with the AR(1) model without the RANDOM statement you fit previously, this model appears to be a better fit to your data. However, compared with the TOEP model, this model has a bigger AICC value but a slightly smaller BIC value. Depending on which information criteria you choose, you may choose the TOEP model or the AR(1) model with a RANDOM statement. They should give you equivalent results concerning the fixed effects in this example.

If selecting the most appropriate covariance structure is almost impossible or impractical in your situation, and you are only concerned about the inferences on the fixed effects, you may want to use the EMPIRICAL option in the PROC MIXED statement. The EMPIRICAL option computes the estimated variance-covariance matrix of the fixed-effects parameters by using the asymptotically consistent estimator. This estimator is commonly referred to as the *sandwich estimator*, and is only **asymptotically** robust to covariance structure misspecification. For practical purposes it is usually not obvious how many subjects are actually needed before the asymptotics kick in. You must include the SUBJECT= option in either a RANDOM or REPEATED statement for this option to take effect. In addition, the Satterthwaite and Kenward-Roger degrees of freedom methods are not available if you specify EMPIRICAL.

In practice, an appropriate covariance model helps to interpret the random variation in your data. Further, efficiency is gained if an appropriate covariance model can be specified. Finally, in the case of missing observations, use of the sandwich estimator only provides valid inferences for the fixed effects under strict, severe assumptions (MCAR) about the underlying missingness process. Therefore, you should always try to specify an appropriate covariance structure for your data.

Partial Output from the Third MIXED Procedure

Random Coefficient Model

Estimated G Matrix

Row	Effect	drug	patient	Col1	Col2
1	Intercept	a	201	0.2639	-0.01434
2	hour	a	201	-0.01434	0.003648

The estimated **G** matrix shows that the intercept variance among subjects is 0.2639. The slope variance among subjects is 0.003648. The covariance between the intercepts and the slopes is –0.01434.

Estimated V Matrix for patient(drug) 201 a

Row	Col1	Col2	Col3	Col4	Col5	Col6	Col7	Col8
1	0.2818	0.2282	0.2175	0.2068	0.1962	0.1855	0.1748	0.1641
2	0.2282	0.2640	0.2141	0.2071	0.2001	0.1930	0.1860	0.1789
3	0.2175	0.2141	0.2536	0.2074	0.2040	0.2006	0.1972	0.1938
4	0.2068	0.2071	0.2074	0.2505	0.2079	0.2081	0.2084	0.2086
5	0.1962	0.2001	0.2040	0.2079	0.2546	0.2157	0.2196	0.2235
6	0.1855	0.1930	0.2006	0.2081	0.2157	0.2661	0.2308	0.2383
7	0.1748	0.1860	0.1972	0.2084	0.2196	0.2308	0.2848	0.2532
8	0.1641	0.1789	0.1938	0.2086	0.2235	0.2383	0.2532	0.3109

The **V** matrix is computed as **ZGZ′+R**. It shows the variances and covariances among the repeated measures for the first subject and all other subjects as well. This is because all subjects have the same **G** matrix and the same time points (the **Z** matrix). Notice that the variances along the diagonal are not equal and the covariances off diagonals do not necessarily show a pattern. The elements in the **V** matrix are based on the variances and covariances of the random effects (the **G** matrix), along with the time values (**`hour`**) of the measurements (the **Z** matrix).

Details

$$Var(y_{ij}) = \begin{bmatrix} 1 & x_{ij} \end{bmatrix} \begin{bmatrix} \sigma_a^2 & \sigma_{ab} \\ \sigma_{ab} & \sigma_b^2 \end{bmatrix} \begin{bmatrix} 1 \\ x_{ij} \end{bmatrix} + \sigma^2 = \begin{bmatrix} \sigma_a^2 + \sigma_{ab} x_{ij} & \sigma_{ab} + \sigma_b^2 x_{ij} \end{bmatrix} \begin{bmatrix} 1 \\ x_{ij} \end{bmatrix} + \sigma^2$$

$$= \sigma_a^2 + 2\sigma_{ab} x_{ij} + \sigma_b^2 x_{ij}^2 + \sigma^2 .$$

$$Cov(y_{ij}, y_{ik}) = Cov(a_i^* + b_i^* x_{ij} + e_{ij}, a_i^* + b_i^* x_{ik} + e_{ik}) = \sigma_a^2 + \sigma_{ab} x_{ik} + \sigma_{ab} x_{ij} + \sigma_b^2 x_{ij} x_{ik}$$

where x_{ij} represents the time values (the values in the variable **`hour`** in this example).

Covariance Parameter Estimates

Cov Parm	Subject	Estimate
UN(1,1)	patient(drug)	0.2639
UN(2,1)	patient(drug)	-0.01434
UN(2,2)	patient(drug)	0.003648
Residual		0.04285

This table shows the same information as that shown by the G option.

```
                    Random Coefficient Model

                         Fit Statistics

              -2 Res Log Likelihood           219.4
              AIC (smaller is better)         227.4
              AICC (smaller is better)        227.5
              BIC (smaller is better)         236.6
```

Compared with the linear regression model with the REPEATED statement you fit in the last demonstration, this random coefficient model has similar fit statistics. Random coefficient models are useful for the purpose of obtaining EBLUPs for each subject, for example, the predicted response (**fev1**) for patient 201 (a) at hours 2.5, 4.5, and 9. They also provide the predicted slope and intercept for each patient. The techniques discussed in the random coefficient models section are useful for obtaining subject-specific regression models. You can also obtain predicted values (EBLUPs) for each subject. The EBLUPs can be used to construct the predicted profile plot for each patient.

You can also use the OUTP= option in the MODEL statement to obtain EBLUPs for each patient and then construct the predicted profile plot for each patient. To obtain predictions at hours other than those included in the data set (for example, hour 4.5), simply append to the original data set a new data set that contains values for every variable included in your model except the dependent variable (**fev1** would have missing values in this new data set). The OUTP= option will produce the predictions you want.

```
data new;
   input basefev1 drug $ hour patient;
   datalines;
   2.46 a 2.5 201
   2.46 a 4.5 201
   2.46 a 9 201
;
run;

data fev1new;
   set sasuser.fev1uni new;
run;

proc mixed data=fev1new;
   class drug patient;
   model fev1=basefev1 drug hour hour*drug / ddfm=kr outp=eblups;
   random int hour / type=un subject=patient(drug);
run;

proc print data=eblups;
   var patient drug basefev1 hour fev1 pred;
run;

proc sort data=eblups;
   by drug;
run;

proc gplot data=eblups;
   by drug;
   symbol v=none i=join l=1 c=blue r=24;
   plot pred*hour=patient / nolegend;
run;
quit;                                          *c05s2d13.sas;
```

The data set **new** contains three new observations for which you want predictions.

Partial PROC PRINT Output

Obs	patient	drug	basefev1	hour	fev1	Pred
1	201	a	2.46	1	2.68	2.69418
2	201	a	2.46	2	2.76	2.61785
3	201	a	2.46	3	2.50	2.54153
4	201	a	2.46	4	2.30	2.46520
5	201	a	2.46	5	2.14	2.38887
6	201	a	2.46	6	2.40	2.31255
7	201	a	2.46	7	2.33	2.23622
8	201	a	2.46	8	2.20	2.15990
9	202	a	3.50	1	3.95	3.57223
10	202	a	3.50	2	3.65	3.45775
11	202	a	3.50	3	2.93	3.34327
12	202	a	3.50	4	2.53	3.22879
13	202	a	3.50	5	3.04	3.11431
14	202	a	3.50	6	3.37	2.99983
15	202	a	3.50	7	3.14	2.88535
16	202	a	3.50	8	2.62	2.77087
...	...	...	...	...	...	...
577	201	a	2.46	2.5	.	2.57969
578	201	a	2.46	4.5	.	2.42704
579	201	a	2.46	9.0	.	2.08357

The EBLUP for each patient at each hour is shown in the **Pred** column. These are predicted values of **fev1** for each patient, considering the intercept and slopes for each patient randomly vary about the population regression model. The last three observations provide predicted values for patient 201 (a) at hours 2.5, 4.5, and 9. To obtain EBLUPs for other patients or at other hours, change the data set **new** accordingly.

PROC GPLOT Output

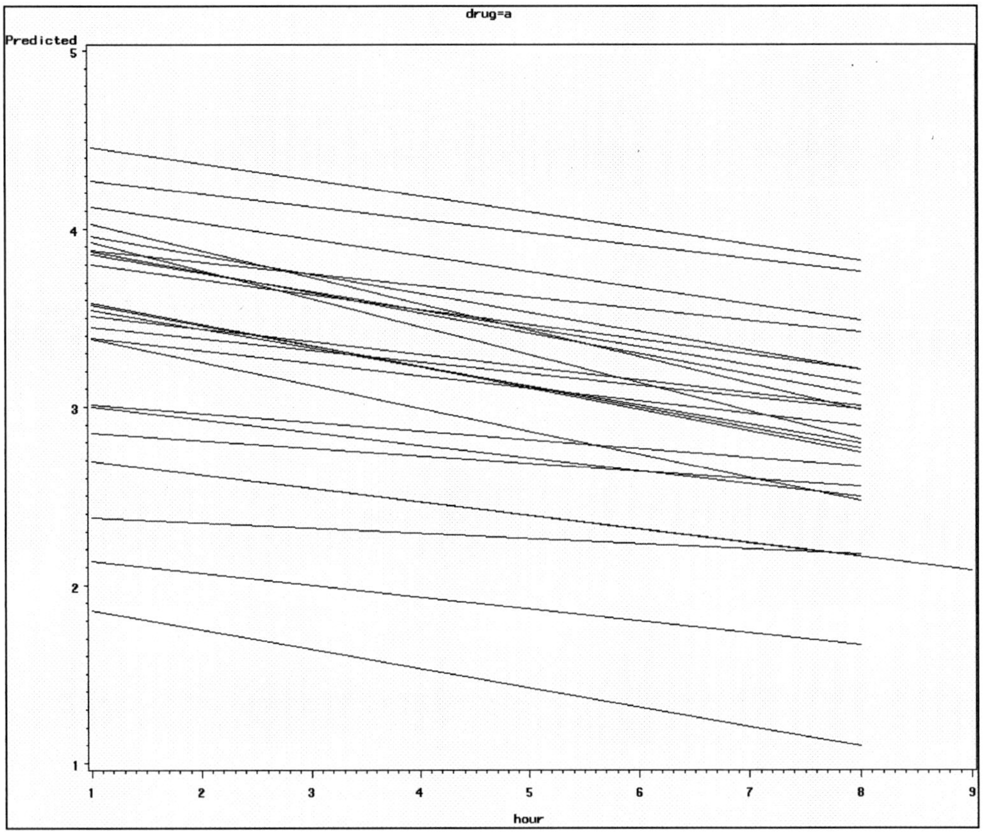

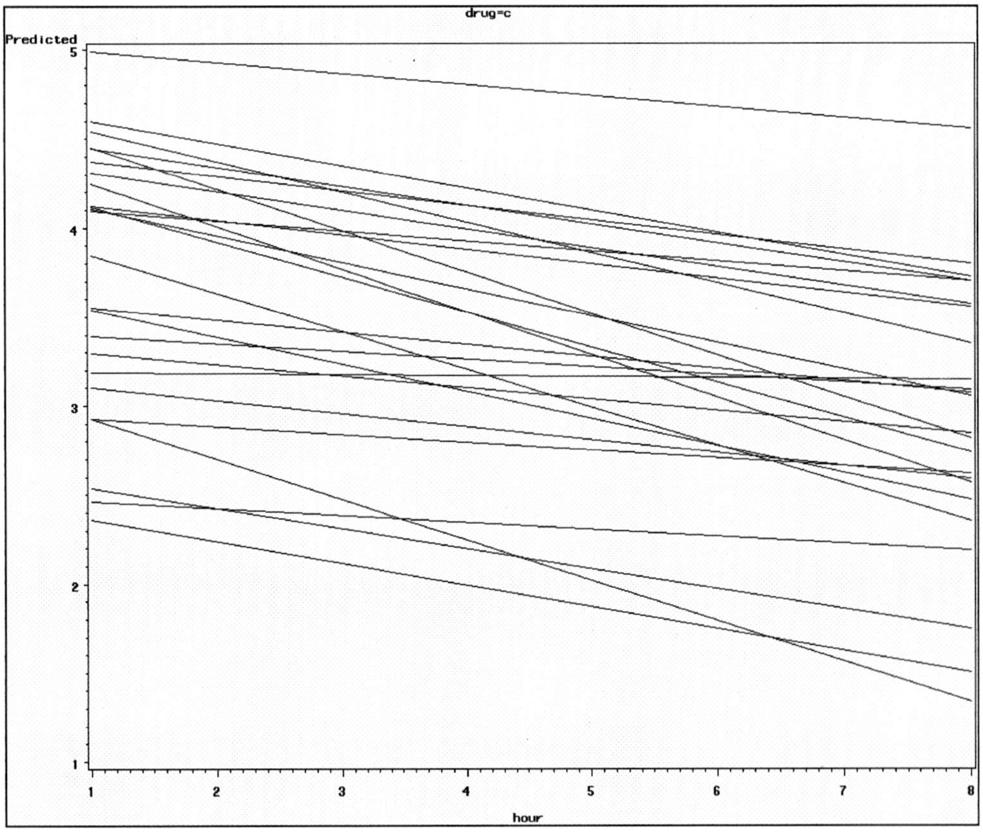

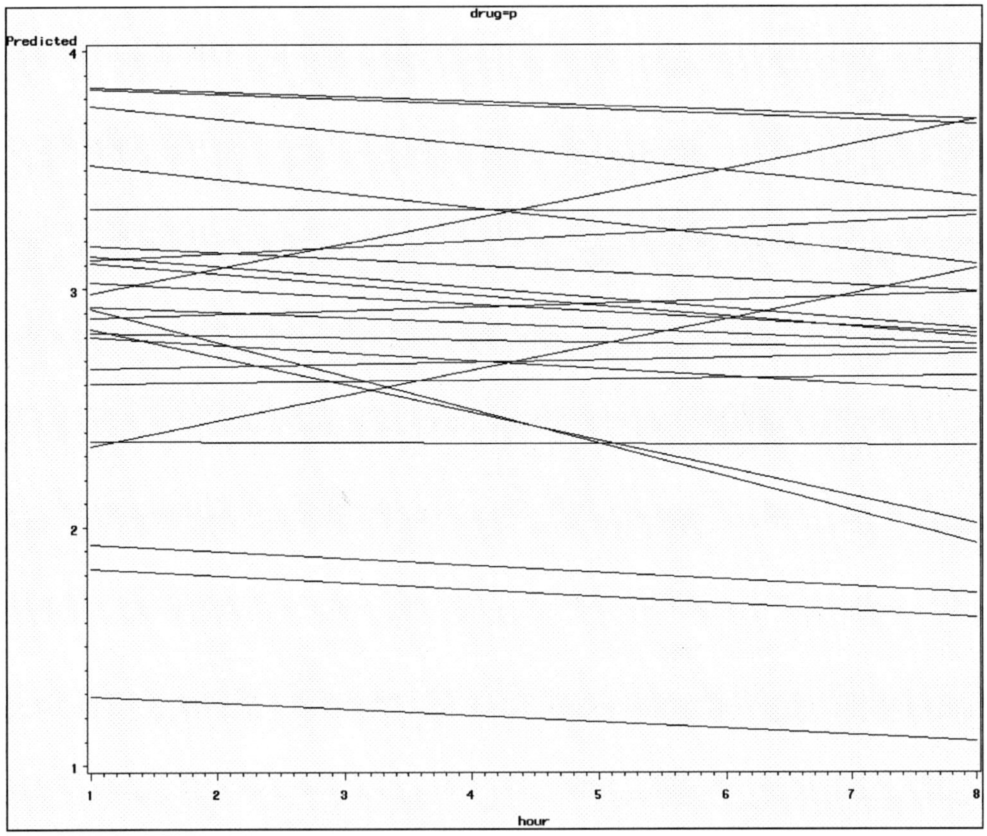

The predicted value for patient 201 (a) at hour 9 is shown on the first graph. This can be changed to obtain predictions for any other patients at other hours. Investigators can identify several interesting patients based on certain criteria and conduct further examinations on these patients.

Combining RANDOM and REPEATED Statements (Self-Study)

You may be able to specify a random coefficient model with correlated residuals, that is, use the RANDOM and REPEATED statements as shown below:

```
proc mixed data=sasuser.fev1uni;
   class drug patient;
   model fev1=basefev1 drug hour hour*drug / ddfm=kr;
   random int hour / type=un subject=patient(drug) g v;
   repeated / type=ar(1) subject=patient(drug) r;
   title 'Random Coefficient Model with Correlated '
         'Errors';
run;
title;                                          *c05s2d14.sas;
```

The RANDOM statement specifies a random coefficient model. The **G** and **V** options in the RANDOM statement ask for the G and V matrices to be displayed. The REPEATED statement specifies a correlation structure for the residuals given the random effects. It is appropriate when the residuals around the random coefficient regression model are still exhibiting some sort of serial correlations. The R option in the REPEATED statement asks for the R matrix to be displayed.

Partial PROC MIXED Output

```
                              Model Information

          Data Set                      SASUSER.FEV1UNI
          Dependent Variable            fev1
          Covariance Structures         Unstructured,
                                        Autoregressive
          Subject Effects               patient(drug),
                                        patient(drug)
          Estimation Method             REML
          Residual Variance Method      Profile
          Fixed Effects SE Method       Prasad-Rao-Jeske-
                                        Kackar-Harville
          Degrees of Freedom Method     Kenward-Roger
```

Estimated R Matrix for patient(drug) 201 a

Row	Col1	Col2	Col3	Col4	Col5	Col6	Col7	Col8
1	0.05431	0.01693	0.005277	0.001645	0.000513	0.000160	0.000050	0.000016
2	0.01693	0.05431	0.01693	0.005277	0.001645	0.000513	0.000160	0.000050
3	0.005277	0.01693	0.05431	0.01693	0.005277	0.001645	0.000513	0.000160
4	0.001645	0.005277	0.01693	0.05431	0.01693	0.005277	0.001645	0.000513
5	0.000513	0.001645	0.005277	0.01693	0.05431	0.01693	0.005277	0.001645
6	0.000160	0.000513	0.001645	0.005277	0.01693	0.05431	0.01693	0.005277
7	0.000050	0.000160	0.000513	0.001645	0.005277	0.01693	0.05431	0.01693
8	0.000016	0.000050	0.000160	0.000513	0.001645	0.005277	0.01693	0.05431

The **R** matrix is a block-diagonal variance-covariance matrix with identical blocks. The first block is shown above. It has the AR(1) structure. The estimated common variance is 0.05431. The covariance is a function of the variance and the correlation. You can use the RCORR option to display the correlation matrix.

Estimated G Matrix

Row	Effect	drug	patient	Col1	Col2
1	Intercept	a	201	0.2247	-0.00822
2	hour	a	201	-0.00822	0.002497

The **G** matrix is also a block-diagonal variance-covariance matrix with identical blocks. The blocks have the UN structure. The intercept variance among the subjects is estimated to be 0.2247, the slope variance among the subjects is estimated to be 0.0025, and covariance between the intercepts and the slopes is -0.00822.

Estimated V Matrix for patient(drug) 201 a

Row	Col1	Col2	Col3	Col4	Col5	Col6	Col7	Col8
1	0.2650	0.2219	0.2045	0.1952	0.1883	0.1822	0.1764	0.1706
2	0.2219	0.2561	0.2155	0.2006	0.1937	0.1894	0.1858	0.1824
3	0.2045	0.2155	0.2521	0.2140	0.2016	0.1972	0.1954	0.1943
4	0.1952	0.2006	0.2140	0.2531	0.2175	0.2076	0.2058	0.2064
5	0.1883	0.1937	0.2016	0.2175	0.2592	0.2260	0.2187	0.2193
6	0.1822	0.1894	0.1972	0.2076	0.2260	0.2702	0.2396	0.2347
7	0.1764	0.1858	0.1954	0.2058	0.2187	0.2396	0.2862	0.2581
8	0.1706	0.1824	0.1943	0.2064	0.2193	0.2347	0.2581	0.3072

The **V** matrix is the variance-covariance matrix for the observed data **y**. It is computed as **V=ZGZ′+R**. For this example, it is a block-diagonal matrix with identical blocks. The elements in each block are shown above.

Covariance Parameter Estimates

Cov Parm	Subject	Estimate
UN(1,1)	patient(drug)	0.2247
UN(2,1)	patient(drug)	-0.00822
UN(2,2)	patient(drug)	0.002497
AR(1)	patient(drug)	0.3117
Residual		0.05431

The estimate labeled AR(1) is the autocorrelation parameter ρ. The estimated value of 0.3117 indicates a nontrivial autocorrelation among the residuals.

Fit Statistics

-2 Res Log Likelihood	201.4
AIC (smaller is better)	211.4
AICC (smaller is better)	211.5
BIC (smaller is better)	222.8

The fit statistics indicate that this model fits your data better than the random coefficient model you fit previously assuming independent residuals. They are slightly better than the regression model you fit previously assuming a TOEP covariance structure.

Type 3 Tests of Fixed Effects

Effect	Num DF	Den DF	F Value	Pr > F
basefev1	1	68	75.58	<.0001
drug	2	67.6	19.86	<.0001
hour	1	67.8	87.76	<.0001
hour*drug	2	67.8	13.39	<.0001

All the fixed effects are significant. The significant **hour*drug** interaction indicates that an unequal slope model among different drugs is necessary for your data.

5.3 Chapter Summary

Repeated measures refer to multiple measurements on the same subject. The analysis of repeated measures data accounts for the presence of correlation between the observations obtained on the same subject and for possible nonconstant variances.

The recommended approach for repeated measures analysis is to use mixed models methodology. This approach allows for a flexible modeling of covariance structures. It also uses the generalized least squares (GLS) method, which is generally superior to the ordinary least squares (OLS) method, assuming an appropriate covariance structure.

There is a four-step procedure for mixed model analysis of repeated measures data:

1. Model the mean structure, usually by specification of the fixed effects.
2. Specify the covariance structure for between-subject and within-subject effects.
3. Fit the mean model accounting for the covariance structure. This step may include making the mean model more parsimonious.
4. Make statistical inferences based on the results of Step 3. This step may also include making the mean model more parsimonious.

Selecting an appropriate covariance model is important in repeated measures analyses. If you ignore an important correlation by using a model that is too simple, you risk increasing the Type I error rates for your fixed effects tests. If your model is too complex, you sacrifice power and efficiency.

Choosing an appropriate covariance model is not trivial. You can use graphical tools to examine the patterns of correlations over time. You can use information criteria to compare relative fit of various covariance models. You can also use likelihood ratio tests to compare nested covariance models.

The recommended general guidelines for model selections are the following:

- begin with a complete mean model
- use REML to fit different covariance models; choose one based on AICC or BIC
- use ML to fit different mean models using the selected covariance structure; choose one based on AICC and BIC
- use REML to fit the final model.

You use the REPEATED statement with TYPE= and SUBJECT= options to fit the covariance model for the repeated measures. The MIXED procedure provides a wide range of covariance models. Use the GROUP= option in the REPEATED statement to fit a heterogeneous variance model if appropriate. You can use the RANDOM statement in addition to the REPEATED statement with certain covariance structures to account for additional between-subject variations. You can also fit a random coefficient model to analyze repeated measures data.

Chapter 6 More on Linear Mixed Models

6.1 Unbalanced Data Issues

Objectives

- List issues associated with unbalanced data in linear mixed models.

3

Balanced versus Unbalanced Data

	I	II
A	6	6
B	6	6
C	6	6

	I	*II*
A	*8*	*4*
B	*6*	*7*
C	*2*	*5*

4

In balanced data, every cell (treatment combination) has an equal sample size. When the cell sizes are unequal, the data is unbalanced. In designed experiments, even when an experiment is designed for equal sample sizes in each treatment, it is often the case that something happens during the experiment to cause the sample sizes to be unequal.

Unbalanced data may be more often encountered in sample surveys or observational studies, where different numbers of observations are obtained for different survey groups or different covariate groups.

Issues Associated with Unbalanced Data

- In general, there is not a problem for one-way mean models.
- For two-way or higher mean models, the critical issue is constructing meaningful linear combinations of model parameters for hypothesis testing and estimation.
- In mixed model situations, the additional issue for unbalanced data analysis is to account for multiple sources of random variations.

5

Both ANOVA (using PROC GLM) and mixed model approaches (using PROC MIXED) result in approximate methods for unbalanced mixed model data. The mixed model methodology implemented in PROC MIXED makes the issues associated with unbalanced data a lot easier to handle than the ANOVA approach; therefore, the focus in this section is on PROC MIXED.

Using PROC MIXED for Unbalanced Data

- You need to determine which type of tests (Type I, Type II, or Type III) to use for fixed effects.
- The procedure takes into account the multiple sources of random variations for inferences about the fixed effects in unbalanced data.
- The procedure provides various methods to estimate the denominator degrees of freedom for fixed effects.

6

Different Types of Tests—Reduction Notation

Model: $y_{ijk} = \mu + \alpha_i + \beta_j + (\alpha\beta)_{ij} + \varepsilon_{ijk}$, $i = 1, 2$, $j = 1$ to 5.

```
model y = A B A*B;
```

Effects	Type I	Type II	Type III
A	$R(\alpha\|\mu)$	$R(\alpha\| \mu, \beta)$	$R(\alpha\| \mu, \beta, \alpha\beta)$
B	$R(\beta\|\mu, \alpha)$	$R(\beta\| \mu, \alpha)$	$R(\beta\| \mu, \alpha, \alpha\beta)$
A*B	$R(\alpha\beta\| \mu, \alpha, \beta)$	$R(\alpha\beta\| \mu, \alpha, \beta)$	$R(\alpha\beta\| \mu, \alpha, \beta)$
	Model-order dependent	Model-order independent	Model-order independent

7

Suppose that you have a two-way classification with factors A and B (both are fixed effects), and factor A has two levels and factor B has five levels. The different types of tests can be explained by the reduction notations shown above. For example, the Type I test for the factor A is only adjusted for the overall mean μ. The Type I test for the factor B is adjusted for the overall mean μ and the factor A effect α. The Type II test for the factor A is adjusted for everything else except for the interaction effect $\alpha\beta$, that is, μ and β. The type III test for the factor A is adjusted for everything else in the model, that is, μ, β, and $\alpha\beta$.

The Type I test depends on the order of the factors you specified in the MODEL statement. Types II and III tests are model-order independent. For models without interactions, Type II and Type III tests are identical.

Different Types of Tests—μ-Model Notation

Model: $y_{ijk} = \mu_{ij} + \varepsilon_{ijk}$, $i = 1, 2,$ $j = 1$ to 5.

where $\mu_{ij} = \mu + \alpha_i + \beta_j + (\alpha\beta)_{ij}$

H_0: $\mu_{1\bullet} = \mu_{2\bullet}$ for factor A effect

H_0: $w_{11}\mu_{11}+w_{12}\mu_{12}+\ldots+w_{15}\mu_{15} = w_{21}\mu_{21}+w_{22}\mu_{22}+\ldots+w_{25}\mu_{25}$

The different types of hypotheses assign different values to the weights:

Types	Weights for Factor A
Type I	$w_{ij} = n_{ij} / n_{i\bullet}$
Type II	Would yield minimum variance estimates in a model with no significant interaction
Type III	$w_{ij} = 1/5$

8

Another interpretation of the different types of tests is to use the μ-model notation. The hypothesis about factor A can be expressed as comparing a weighted average of the cell means for A_1 with a weighted average of the cell means for A_2, where the cell means relate to the previous model parameterizations by $E(y_{ijk}) = \mu_{ij} = \mu + \alpha_i + \beta_j + (\alpha\beta)_{ij}$. The differences between the different types of hypotheses correspond to different values assigned to the weights.

- Type I assigns weights proportional to the numbers of observations in the ij^{th} cell.
- Type II assigns weights that would yield minimum variance estimates in a model with no interaction, and therefore it yields the most power.
- Type III assigns equal weights, regardless of number of observations in each cell.

It is your decision as to which type of hypotheses to use for your tests.

Which Type to Use?

- Type I is useful for nested models, polynomial models, certain tests in analysis of covariance models, and situations where weights in the μ-model reflect the sample distributions among the factors in the population.
- Type II is useful for models with no significant interactions.
- Type III is useful for comparing main effects in the presence of interactions and situations where unequal sample sizes were not obtained by design.

9

When there is no obvious choice as to which type to use, you might want to choose the one that results in the most powerful test for the effect being tested. For more information on how to determine which type of hypothesis has the most power, refer to Littell, Stroup, and Freund (2002). Also refer to Searle (1987).

Except for situations where Type I or Type II is the obvious choice for tests of fixed effects, the default test produced by PROC MIXED (Type III) generally works well for unbalanced data.

A Multicenter Clinical Trial

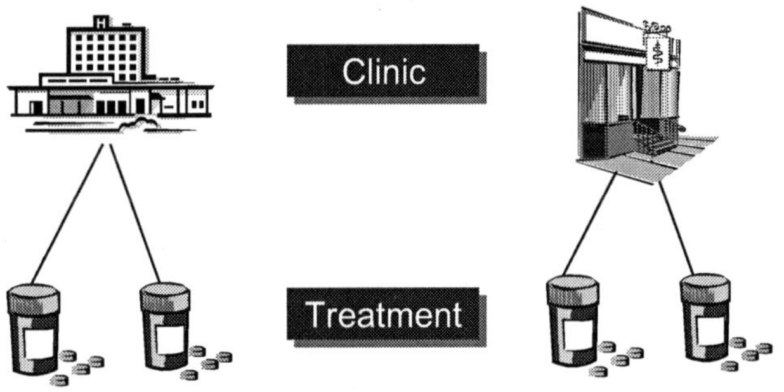

11

A pharmaceutical company compared the effects of two drugs, A and B, on a clinical measurement called *flush*. The study utilized patients in ten clinics. Multiple clinics were used in order to obtain representation of diverse patient populations. The original plan called for each drug to be randomly assigned to the same number of patients within each clinic. This was basically done, but a few patients abandoned the trial before completion, leaving unequal numbers of patients on the two drugs within some of the clinics. In addition, the availability of patients varied between the clinics, ranging from 3 to 28. Therefore, although this was a designed experiment, the realities of the situation resulted in unbalanced data.

The Data

Obs	Clinic	Trt	Patient	Flush0	Flush
1	41	B	102	77.5	72.0000
2	41	B	104	23.5	5.6250
3	41	B	105	63.5	81.8750
4	41	B	106	72.5	83.5000
5	41	B	107	58.0	75.5000
6	41	B	108	49.0	13.7500
7	41	B	109	7.5	9.3750
8	41	B	110	13.5	7.8750
9	41	B	111	13.5	6.0000
10	41	B	112	76.5	61.6000
11	41	B	113	78.5	98.1250
12	41	B	114	56.5	46.1250
13	41	B	115	61.0	24.2500
14	41	B	116	91.0	64.4000
15	41	B	117	13.5	7.3333
16	41	B	118	63.5	79.2500
17	42	A	201	50.5	70.3333
18	42	A	203	84.5	16.1429
19	42	B	202	33.5	28.3333
20	43	A	302	22.0	14.5000
...	...	...	...	...	...

12

The data is stored in **sasuser.multictr2**. These are the variables in the data set:

Clinic the clinics where the clinical trial was carried out

Trt the treatment, drug A or B

Patient patient identification

Flush0 the flush measurements obtained prior to administering the drugs

Flush the flush measurement after administering the drugs

The variable **Flush0** is available in the data set but is not used in the analysis presented in this section.

Frequency Table of `Clinic*trt`

Clinic / Frequency	Trt A	Trt B	Total
41	0	16	16
42	2	1	3
43	14	14	28
44	6	6	12
45	12	11	23
46	6	7	13
47	6	7	13
48	8	8	16
49	10	10	20
50	4	3	7
Total	68	83	151

13

The data is unbalanced. The number of observations in each **`Trt*Clinic`** combination (except for treatment A at clinic 41) ranges from 1 to 16. In addition, at clinic 41, no patients were given treatment A, resulting in an empty cell for the treatment A clinic 41 combination. (Issues with empty cells are discussed later in the section.) For the purpose of illustrating the analysis of unbalanced data without empty cells, clinic 41 is excluded from the data set. The resulting data set is stored in **`sasuser.multicenter`**.

Two-Way Mixed Model

Trt*Clinic effect, random

$$y_{ijk} = \mu + \alpha_i + b_j + (\alpha b)_{ij} + \varepsilon_{ijk}$$

Trt effect, fixed

Clinic effect, random

i = 1, 2 (**Trt**)
j = 1 to 10 (**Clinic**)
k = 1 to n_{ij} (**Patient**)

14

y_{ijk} the flush measurement taken from the kth patient at the jth clinic after taking the ith drug

μ the overall mean, a fixed effect parameter

α_i the effect of the ith drug, a fixed effect parameter

b_j the effect of the jth clinic, a random effect parameter, $b_j \sim iid\ N(0,\sigma_b^2)$

$(\alpha b)_{ij}$ the effect of the ith drug at the jth clinic, a random effect parameter, $(\alpha b)_{ij} \sim iid\ N(0,\sigma_{\alpha b}^2)$

e_{ijk} the random error, $e_{ijk} \sim iid\ N(0,\sigma^2)$.

This is a typical two-way mixed model, with **Trt** as a fixed effect and **Clinic** and **Trt*Clinic** interaction as random effects. Assuming random effects b_j, $(\alpha b)_{ij}$, and e_{ijk} are independently normally distributed variables, you have

- $E(y_{ijk}) = \mu + \alpha_i = \mu_i$, the mean **Flush** measurement for drug *i* averaged across the population of clinics.
- $Var(y_{ijk}) = \sigma_b^2 + \sigma_{ab}^2 + \sigma^2$, the variance of an observation. This variance is the sum of variance components due to **Clinic**, **Trt*Clinic**, and random errors.
- $Cov(y_{ijk}, y_{ijk'}) = \sigma_b^2 + \sigma_{ab}^2$ for $k \neq k'$, the covariance of the **Flush** measurements taken from two patients administrated the same drug at the same clinic. This covariance is the sum of the **Clinic** variance and the **Trt*Clinic** variance.
- $Cov(y_{ijk}, y_{i'jk'}) = \sigma_b^2$ for $i \neq i'$ and $k \neq k'$. The covariance of the **Flush** measurements taken from two patients administer different drugs at the same clinic. This covariance is the **Clinic** variance.

Analyze the Unbalanced Multicenter Clinical Trial Data

You use the HTYPE= option to specify different types of hypotheses provided in PROC MIXED.

```
proc mixed data=sasuser.multicenter;
   class Trt Clinic;
   model Flush=Trt / ddfm=kr htype=1,2,3;
   random Clinic Trt*Clinic;
   estimate 'TrtA-TrtB' Trt 1 -1;
run;                                           *c06s1d1.sas;
```

Partial PROC MIXED Output

```
      Covariance Parameter
            Estimates

     Cov Parm        Estimate

     Clinic                 0
     Trt*Clinic       75.3629
     Residual          447.57
```

By default, the REML estimates of the covariance parameters are constrained to be nonnegative. The zero variance parameter estimate for **Clinic** is likely a result of this constraint. You can use the NOBOUND option in a PROC MIXED statement to remove this constraint.

Issues associated with zero (or negative) variance parameter estimates are discussed later in the course.

Type 1 Tests of Fixed Effects

Effect	Num DF	Den DF	F Value	Pr > F
Trt	1	9.3	1.83	0.2075

Type 2 Tests of Fixed Effects

Effect	Num DF	Den DF	F Value	Pr > F
Trt	1	9.3	1.83	0.2075

Type 3 Tests of Fixed Effects

Effect	Num DF	Den DF	F Value	Pr > F
Trt	1	9.3	1.83	0.2075

The three types of tests of fixed effects are identical. This is because you only have one fixed effect **`Trt`**. For a one-way classification of the fixed effect, you expect that the three types of tests agree for unbalanced data. For the test of the **`Trt`** effect, you obtain an F value of 1.83 and a p-value of 0.2075. You do not have enough evidence to conclude that the treatments have significant effects on the response variable **`Flush`** across the population of clinics.

Estimates

Label	Estimate	Standard Error	DF	t Value	Pr > |t|
TrtA-TrtB	-7.8198	5.7728	9.3	-1.35	0.2075

The ESTIMATE statement from PROC MIXED provides a comparison between two treatments A and B. On average, treatment A results in a response (**`Flush`**) of 7.8198 smaller than treatment B across the population of clinics, and this difference is not statistically significantly different from zero (p-value=0.2075).

Treating `Clinic` and `Trt*Clinic` as Fixed

For the purpose of illustrating unbalanced data analysis, suppose **`Clinic`** was preselected for the study. The researchers were only interested in making inference about these clinics. Therefore, **`Clinic`** and **`Trt*Clinic`** are fixed effects.

```
proc mixed data=sasuser.multicenter;
   class Trt Clinic;
   model Flush=Trt Clinic Trt*Clinic / htype=1,2,3;
   estimate 'TrtA-TrtB' Trt 1 -1;
run;                                    *c06s1d2.sas;
```

Partial PROC MIXED Output

Type 1 Tests of Fixed Effects

Effect	Num DF	Den DF	F Value	Pr > F
Trt	1	114	2.60	0.1094
Clinic	8	114	2.00	0.0526
Trt*Clinic	8	114	2.44	0.0178

Type 2 Tests of Fixed Effects

Effect	Num DF	Den DF	F Value	Pr > F
Trt	1	114	3.16	0.0781
Clinic	8	114	2.00	0.0526
Trt*Clinic	8	114	2.44	0.0178

Type 3 Tests of Fixed Effects

Effect	Num DF	Den DF	F Value	Pr > F
Trt	1	114	4.23	0.0420
Clinic	8	114	2.03	0.0488
Trt*Clinic	8	114	2.44	0.0178

As expected, the three types of hypotheses do not agree due to the unbalanced data and the two-way classification of the fixed effects. You should select one that most precisely measures the effect you wish to test. Suppose you want to test the effect of **Trt**, and you are equally interested in each clinic, then the Type 3 tests should probably be your choice. This Type III hypothesis is a statement of equality of the drug means, averaged across the clinics, with equal weights attached to each clinic. The result (*p*-value=0.0420) suggests significant treatment effects on **Flush** averaged across those clinics included in the study.

The **Trt*Clinic** interaction is significant (*p*-value=0.0178). Depending on the situation, it may or may not be meaningful to compare the treatments averaged across clinics. In situations where you must choose one of the drugs to be used at all clinics, it is important and meaningful to compare drugs averaged over clinics.

Estimates

Label	Estimate	Standard Error	DF	t Value	Pr > |t|
TrtA-TrtB	-9.3750	4.5582	114	-2.06	0.0420

The ESTIMATE statement from PROC MIXED provides a comparison between two treatments A and B. On average, treatment A results in a response (**`Flush`**) of 9.3750 smaller than treatment B across clinics included in the study, and this difference significantly differs from zero (*p*-value=0.0420).

Issues associated with the unbalanced data analysis using PROC MIXED would remain the same if you had one or more random effects in the model.

You can use the E1, E2, and E3 options in the MODEL statement to obtain the hypothesis tests used by Type 1, Type 2, and Type 3, respectively. The output from these options shows the values for **L** for testing **L**β=0.

Data with Empty Cells

Number of observations for each **`Clinic*Trt`** combination

Clinic	Trt A	Trt B
41	0	16
42	2	1
43	14	14
...	...	...

19

The data set **`sasuser.multicenter`** has at least one observation for each cell corresponding to combinations of **`Trt`** and **`Clinic`**. As mentioned previously, in the original data set **`sasuser.multictr2`** there was another clinic (41), which had patients only for drug B. The cell for that clinic and drug A was empty. Empty cells create another layer of complications in analyzing unbalanced data.

Effects of Empty Cells in Mixed Models

CONTRAST, ESTIMATE, and LSMEANS statements may produce nonestimable linear combinations of parameters.

20

For two-way or higher mean model classifications, when you use a CONTRAST, ESTIMATE, or LSMEANS statement in PROC MIXED for data with empty cells, you may get output with missing values due to nonestimability of the linear combinations of parameters. A nonestimable linear combination of parameters can result from data with empty cells. Incorrect specifications of a CONTRAST or ESTIMATE statement can also result in a nonestimable function, but this is not a concern in this section.

Details

Because you have more unknown parameters than the number of cell means, not all linear combinations of these parameters can be estimated or tested.

A linear combination $\mathbf{L}\beta$, where **L** contains the coefficients of a linear combination and β is the vector of all parameters, is estimable if and only if

- the linear combination can be expressed as a linear combination of the cell means: $L\beta = \sum_i \sum_j c_{ij}\mu_{ij}$
- there exists a linear combination of observations $c'y = \sum_i \sum_j \sum_k c_{ijk} y_{ijk}$, such that $E(c'y) = \mathbf{L}\beta$.

The E option in CONTRAST, ESTIMATE, or LSMEANS statements provides the coefficient **L** for the linear combination $\mathbf{L}\beta$. In practice, if you can write a CONTRAST or ESTIMATE statement and get a meaningful result, the linear combination $\mathbf{L}\beta$ is estimable.

Analyze Data with Empty Cells

You run the following statements using PROC MIXED:

```
proc mixed data=sasuser.multictr2;
   class Trt Clinic ;
   model Flush=Trt / ddfm=kr htype=1,2,3;
   random Clinic Clinic*Trt;
   contrast 'TrtA-TrtB' Trt 1 -1 ;
   estimate 'TrtA-TrtB' Trt 1 -1 ;
   lsmeans Trt / diff;
run;                                  *c06s1d3.sas;
```

Partial PROC MIXED Output

Covariance Parameter Estimates

Cov Parm	Estimate
Clinic	0
Trt*Clinic	77.0369
Residual	530.50

Again, the variance parameter estimate for `Clinic` hits a boundary of zero. The issues associated with zero or negative variance parameter estimates are discussed later in the course.

Type 1 Tests of Fixed Effects

Effect	Num DF	Den DF	F Value	Pr > F
Trt	1	12.4	2.90	0.1132

Type 2 Tests of Fixed Effects

Effect	Num DF	Den DF	F Value	Pr > F
Trt	1	12.4	2.90	0.1132

Type 3 Tests of Fixed Effects

Effect	Num DF	Den DF	F Value	Pr > F
Trt	1	12.4	2.90	0.1132

The three types of hypotheses produce identical test results for unbalanced data with empty cells. Recall that your mean model involves only one factor, **Trt**. For one-way classifications of the mean model, the three tests generally agree for unbalanced data with empty cells. The result (*p*-value=0.1132) indicates nonsignificant effects of treatments on the response **Flush**. Compared with the similar analysis presented earlier in this section using the data set with no empty cells, the results change a little.

Estimates

Label	Estimate	Standard Error	DF	t Value	Pr > |t|
TrtA-TrtB	-9.9035	5.8114	12.4	-1.70	0.1132

Contrasts

Label	Num DF	Den DF	F Value	Pr > F
TrtA-TrtB	1	12.4	2.90	0.1132

Least Squares Means

Effect	Trt	Estimate	Standard Error	DF	t Value	Pr > |t|
Trt	A	22.3908	4.2569	13.4	5.26	0.0001
Trt	B	32.2943	3.9561	11.4	8.16	<.0001

Differences of Least Squares Means

Effect	Trt	_Trt	Estimate	Standard Error	DF	t Value	Pr > |t|
Trt	A	B	-9.9035	5.8114	12.4	-1.70	0.1132

The ESTIMATE, CONTRAST, and LSMEANS statements produce consistent results. The mean response **Flush** for treatment A is 9.9035 smaller than that for treatment B averaged across the population of clinics, and this difference is not significantly different from zero (*p*-value=0.1132).

Treating `Clinic` and `Trt*Clinic` as Fixed

For the purpose of illustrating the analysis of unbalanced data with empty cells, again suppose **`Clinic`** and **`Trt*Clinic`** are fixed effects. Notice that the issues associated with empty cells remain the same even if you have had one or more random effects (for example, patients).

```
proc mixed data=sasuser.multictr2;
   class Trt Clinic;
   model Flush=Trt Clinic Trt*Clinic / htype=1,2,3;
   contrast 'TrtA-TrtB' Trt 1 -1 / e;
   estimate 'TrtA-TrtB' Trt 1 -1;
   lsmeans Trt / e diff;
run;                                      *c06s1d4.sas;
```

Selected CONTRAST (or ESTIMATE) and LSMEANS statements option:

E requests that the **L** matrix coefficients for the CONTRAST, the ESTIMATE, or the LSMEANS effects are displayed.

Partial PROC MIXED Output

Type 1 Tests of Fixed Effects

Effect	Num DF	Den DF	F Value	Pr > F
Trt	1	129	5.87	0.0168
Clinic	9	129	2.29	0.0202
Trt*Clinic	8	129	2.04	0.0468

Type 2 Tests of Fixed Effects

Effect	Num DF	Den DF	F Value	Pr > F
Trt	1	129	2.64	0.1068
Clinic	9	129	2.29	0.0202
Trt*Clinic	8	129	2.04	0.0468

Type 3 Tests of Fixed Effects

Effect	Num DF	Den DF	F Value	Pr > F
Trt	1	129	3.53	0.0625
Clinic	9	129	2.18	0.0272
Trt*Clinic	8	129	2.04	0.0468

The three types of hypotheses produce inconsistent test results, especially for the **`Trt`** effect. As discussed previously, you should select one that most precisely measures the effect you want to test.

Estimates

Label	Estimate	Standard Error	DF	t Value	Pr > |t|
TrtA-TrtB	Non-est	.	.	.	.

Contrasts

Label	Num DF	Den DF	F Value	Pr > F
TrtA-TrtB	.	.	.	.

No meaningful output is given from the CONTRAST and ESTIMATE statements because the underlying linear combinations of parameters are nonestimable. The output from the E option explains why.

Coefficients for TrtA-TrtB

Effect	Trt	Clinic	Row1
Intercept			
Trt	A		1
Trt	B		-1
Clinic		41	
Clinic		42	
Clinic		43	
Clinic		44	
Clinic		45	
Clinic		46	
Clinic		47	
Clinic		48	
Clinic		49	
Clinic		50	
Trt*Clinic	A	42	0.1111
Trt*Clinic	A	43	0.1111
Trt*Clinic	A	44	0.1111
Trt*Clinic	A	45	0.1111
Trt*Clinic	A	46	0.1111
Trt*Clinic	A	47	0.1111
Trt*Clinic	A	48	0.1111
Trt*Clinic	A	49	0.1111
Trt*Clinic	A	50	0.1111
Trt*Clinic	B	41	-0.1
Trt*Clinic	B	42	-0.1
Trt*Clinic	B	43	-0.1
Trt*Clinic	B	44	-0.1
Trt*Clinic	B	45	-0.1
Trt*Clinic	B	46	-0.1
Trt*Clinic	B	47	-0.1
Trt*Clinic	B	48	-0.1
Trt*Clinic	B	49	-0.1
Trt*Clinic	B	50	-0.1

You can turn the E option output into the following two-way table:

Trt	Clinic										sum
	41	42	43	44	45	46	47	48	49	50	
A		0.1111	0.1111	0.1111	0.1111	0.1111	0.1111	0.1111	0.1111	0.1111	1
B	–0.1	–0.1	–0.1	–0.1	–0.1	–0.1	–0.1	–0.1	–0.1	–0.1	–1
sum	0	0	0	0	0	0	0	0	0	0	0

The marginal coefficient for each of the 10 clinics (0) is not equal to the sum of the corresponding cell coefficients (0.1111-0.1=0.0111≠0). When this happens, you have a nonestimable function.

```
                         Least Squares Means

                                    Standard
Effect     Trt     Estimate           Error       DF     t Value     Pr > |t|

Trt        A        Non-est               .        .           .            .
Trt        B        33.3733          3.4167      129        9.77       <.0001


                    Differences of Least Squares Means

                                         Standard
Effect    Trt    _Trt    Estimate           Error      DF    t Value    Pr > |t|

Trt       A      B        Non-est               .       .          .           .
```

The LSMEANS for drug A is nonestimable because the empty cell was for drug A. You did obtain the LSMEANS for drug B because drug B does not contain an empty cell.

Coefficients for Trt Least Squares Means

Effect	Trt	Clinic	Row1	Row2
Intercept			1	1
Trt	A		1	
Trt	B			1
Clinic		41	0.1	0.1
Clinic		42	0.1	0.1
Clinic		43	0.1	0.1
Clinic		44	0.1	0.1
Clinic		45	0.1	0.1
Clinic		46	0.1	0.1
Clinic		47	0.1	0.1
Clinic		48	0.1	0.1
Clinic		49	0.1	0.1
Clinic		50	0.1	0.1
Trt*Clinic	A	42	0.1111	
Trt*Clinic	A	43	0.1111	
Trt*Clinic	A	44	0.1111	
Trt*Clinic	A	45	0.1111	
Trt*Clinic	A	46	0.1111	
Trt*Clinic	A	47	0.1111	
Trt*Clinic	A	48	0.1111	
Trt*Clinic	A	49	0.1111	
Trt*Clinic	A	50	0.1111	
Trt*Clinic	B	41		0.1
Trt*Clinic	B	42		0.1
Trt*Clinic	B	43		0.1
Trt*Clinic	B	44		0.1
Trt*Clinic	B	45		0.1
Trt*Clinic	B	46		0.1
Trt*Clinic	B	47		0.1
Trt*Clinic	B	48		0.1
Trt*Clinic	B	49		0.1
Trt*Clinic	B	50		0.1

The E option output from the LSMEANS statement helps you understand why the LSMEANS for treatment A is nonestimable and the LSMEANS for treatment B is estimable. Follow the same steps you went through for the CONTRAST and ESTIMATE statements.

In some cases, you can approximate nonestimable least squares means by assuming that interaction terms are negligible. In this example, suppose the **`Trt*Clinic`** interaction was not significant. By dropping this term from the MODEL statement, you would be able to obtain estimable CONTRAST, ESTIMATE, and LSMEANS results.

6.2 Estimation of Covariance Parameters

Objectives

- Explain different methods of estimating covariance parameters provided in the MIXED procedure.
- Compare Maximum Likelihood (ML) and Restricted/Residual Maximum Likelihood (REML).
- Make inferences about the covariance parameters.
- Discuss issues associated with zero or negative covariance parameter estimates.

27

Estimation Methods for the Covariance Parameters

- Method of Moments:
  - MIVQUE0
  - Type 1
  - Type 2
  - Type 3
- Likelihood-based Methods:
  - ML
  - REML (default)

28

The following summarizes the estimation methods provided by PROC MIXED:

MIVQUE0	performs minimum variance quadratic unbiased estimation of the covariance parameters. It produces method-of-moments estimates that are invariant with respect to the fixed effects, that is, the mean squares associated with the random effects are adjusted for the fixed effects.
Type 1 Type 2 Type 3	applies only to variance component models with no SUBJECT= effects and no REPEATED statement. An analysis of variance table is included in the output, and the expected mean squares are used to estimate the variance components. These are method-of-moments estimates.
maximum likelihood (ML)	iteratively searches over the parameter space for parameter values that maximize a function of the parameters related to the chance of observing the data collected. The function being maximized is called the *likelihood function.*
restricted/residual maximum likelihood (REML)	constructs the likelihood function based on the residuals and obtains maximum likelihood estimates of the variance components from this restricted/residual likelihood function.

If you iterate MIVQUE0, you obtain REML. For balanced data, the REML estimates are consistent with the method-of-moments estimate (PROC GLM), as long as the estimates are not negative by PROC GLM. In many situations, the best approach is to use likelihood-based methods. PROC MIXED implements two likelihood-based methods: maximum likelihood (ML) and restricted/residual maximum likelihood (REML).

Maximum Likelihood Estimation

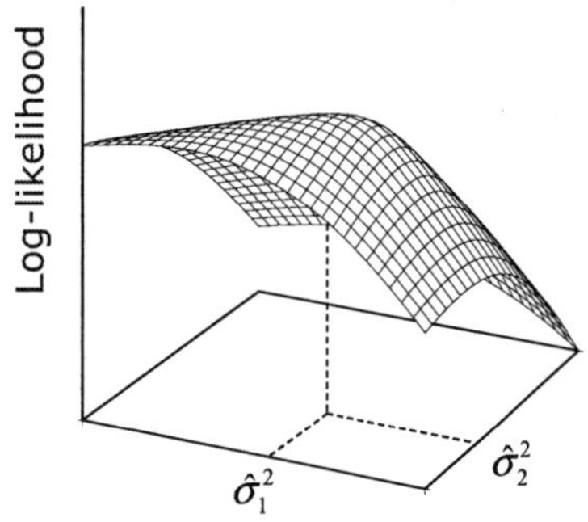

29

The maximum likelihood estimation method finds the parameter estimates that are most likely to occur given the data. The parameter estimates are derived by maximizing the likelihood function, which is a mathematical expression that describes the joint probability of obtaining the data expressed as a function of the parameter estimates.

The difference between the maximum likelihood (ML) and the restricted/residual maximum likelihood (REML) methods is the construction of the likelihood function. REML constructs the likelihood based on residuals and obtains maximum likelihood estimates of the variance components from this restricted/residual likelihood function.

Details

PROC MIXED constructs an objective function associated with ML or REML and maximizes it over all unknown parameters. The corresponding log likelihood functions are as follows:

$$ML: l(G,R) = -\frac{1}{2}\log|V| - \frac{1}{2}r'V^{-1}r - \frac{n}{2}\log 2\pi,$$

$$REML: l_R(G,R) = -\frac{1}{2}\log|V| - \frac{1}{2}\log|X'V^{-1}X| - \frac{1}{2}r'V^{-1}r - \frac{n-p}{2}\log 2\pi,$$

where $r = y - X(X'V^{-1}X)^{-}X'V^{-1}y$ and p=rank(X).

By default, PROC MIXED uses a ridge-stabilized Newton-Raphson algorithm to find the parameter estimates that minimize –2 times the log likelihood functions.

ML versus REML

- Both methods are likelihood-based and therefore are consistent, asymptotically normal, and efficient.
- Both methods require numerical optimization.
- In general, REML estimators of the variance components are unbiased; ML estimators are biased low.
- In general, REML solutions are the ANOVA estimators for balanced data.
- The fit statistics based on REML can be used to compare different covariance models based on the same mean model; the fit statistics based on ML can be used to compare different mean models based on the same covariance model.

30

By default, ML and REML constrain the parameter estimates to be nonnegative values. When none of the covariance parameter estimates hit the boundary, REML estimates are unbiased, whereas ML estimates are biased downward slightly (although the bias is generally negligible for large samples). Generally speaking, the differences between ML and REML estimation increase as the number of fixed effects in the model increases.

Geometrically, REML projects the data onto the space orthogonal to the fixed-effects design matrix, **X**. You must use the same MODEL statement in order to compare different covariance structures using the REML method. In other words, the fit statistics, for example, AICC values, from the REML method are not comparable if your fixed-effects models are different. You may use AICC values from the ML method to compare models with different fixed-effects given you have specified the same covariance model.

There seems to be a growing preference for REML over ML for obtaining covariance parameter estimates (McCulloch and Searle 2001). It is sensible for balanced data for which REML solutions are the ANOVA estimators, which are minimal variance unbiased estimators. Additionally, the REML estimators are based on taking into account the degrees of freedom for the fixed effects in the model. Therefore, they correct the downward bias produced by the ML estimators. Finally, REML is less sensitive to outliers in the data than ML is.

Estimation of Variance Components

Recall the **sasuser.multicenter** data that you analyzed in the last section. You always used the REML estimates of the covariance parameters for your analysis. Now, take a look at what you might obtain if you use other estimation methods.

```
options nodate nonumber;
proc mixed data=sasuser.multicenter method=reml;
   class Trt Clinic;
   model Flush=Trt / ddfm=kr s;
   random Clinic Trt*Clinic;
   title 'REML Method';
run;

proc mixed data=sasuser.multicenter method=ml;
   class Trt Clinic;
   model Flush=Trt / ddfm=kr s;
   random Clinic Trt*Clinic;
   title 'ML Method';
run;

proc mixed data=sasuser.multicenter method=mivque0;
   class Trt Clinic;
   model Flush=Trt / ddfm=kr s;
   random Clinic Trt*Clinic;
   title 'MIVQUE0';
run;

proc mixed data=sasuser.multicenter method=type3;
   class Trt Clinic;
   model Flush=Trt / ddfm=kr s;
   random Clinic Trt*Clinic;
   title 'Type 3';
run;
title;
quit;                                    *c06s2d1.sas;
```

Partial PROC MIXED Output

```
                              REML Method

                         The Mixed Procedure

                        Covariance Parameter
                              Estimates

                      Cov Parm        Estimate

                      Clinic                 0
                      Trt*Clinic       75.3629
                      Residual          447.57
```

```
                         Solution for Fixed Effects

                                      Standard
Effect       Trt     Estimate           Error      DF    t Value    Pr > |t|

Intercept             30.1791          4.0872       9       7.38      <.0001
Trt          A        -7.8198          5.7728     9.3      -1.35      0.2075
Trt          B              0               .       .          .           .
```

```
                       Type 3 Tests of Fixed Effects

                            Num      Den
              Effect         DF       DF    F Value    Pr > F

              Trt             1      9.3       1.83    0.2075
```

As shown in the previous section, the covariance parameter estimate for **`Clinic`** is zero by the REML method. Recall that by default, the REML method (and ML method) constrains the covariance parameter estimate to be greater than or equal to zero. There are pros and cons of this zero boundary constraint. For example, covariance parameter estimates are by definition nonnegative; this constraint is consistent with theory. On the other hand, however, by imposing this constraint, the covariance parameter estimates obtained by REML are no longer unbiased. The tests on fixed effects are affected as well.

```
                               ML Method

                         The Mixed Procedure

                        Covariance Parameter
                              Estimates

                      Cov Parm        Estimate

                      Clinic                 0
                      Trt*Clinic       48.5949
                      Residual          452.81
```

Solution for Fixed Effects

Effect	Trt	Estimate	Standard Error	DF	t Value	Pr > |t|
Intercept		29.8604	3.6724	8.8	8.13	<.0001
Trt	A	-7.3960	5.2009	9.15	-1.42	0.1882
Trt	B	0	.	.	.	.

Type 3 Tests of Fixed Effects

Effect	Num DF	Den DF	F Value	Pr > F
Trt	1	9.15	2.02	0.1882

As with the REML method, the covariance parameter estimate for **`Clinic`** is zero by the ML method. **`Trt*Clinic`** and **`Residual`** variance estimates by the ML method differ from those obtained by the REML method. The standard errors for the fixed effects are different as well.

MIVQUE0

Covariance Parameter Estimates

Cov Parm	Estimate
Clinic	0.004578
Trt*Clinic	29.0592
Residual	475.87

Solution for Fixed Effects

Effect	Trt	Estimate	Standard Error	DF	t Value	Pr > |t|
Intercept		29.5329	3.4025	11.9	8.68	<.0001
Trt	A	-6.9194	4.8314	6.11	-1.43	0.2012
Trt	B	0	.	.	.	.

Type 3 Tests of Fixed Effects

Effect	Num DF	Den DF	F Value	Pr > F
Trt	1	6.11	2.05	0.2012

The estimates provided by the MIVQUE0 method are different from both the REML and ML method results. As a matter of fact, REML uses MIVQUE0 estimates as the starting values for the iteration process. The MIVQUE0 method is provided in the MIXED procedure for backward compatibility purposes and generally is not recommended for obtaining covariance parameter estimates.

Type 3 Analysis of Variance

Source	DF	Sum of Squares	Mean Square
Trt	1	1843.572090	1843.572090
Clinic	8	7081.377266	885.172158
Trt*Clinic	8	8512.586561	1064.073320
Residual	114	49684	435.825358

Type 3 Analysis of Variance

Source	Expected Mean Square
Trt	Var(Residual) + 4.6613 Var(Trt*Clinic) + Q(Trt)
Clinic	Var(Residual) + 7.0585 Var(Trt*Clinic) + 14.117 Var(Clinic)
Trt*Clinic	Var(Residual) + 7.0585 Var(Trt*Clinic)
Residual	Var(Residual)

Type 3 Analysis of Variance

Source	Error Term	Error DF	F Value	Pr > F
Trt	0.6604 MS(Trt*Clinic) + 0.3396 MS(Residual)	11.689	2.17	0.1674
Clinic	MS(Trt*Clinic)	8	0.83	0.5995
Trt*Clinic	MS(Residual)	114	2.44	0.0178
Residual	.	.	.	.

Covariance Parameter Estimates

Cov Parm	Estimate
Clinic	-12.6728
Trt*Clinic	89.0063
Residual	435.83

Solution for Fixed Effects

Effect	Trt	Estimate	Standard Error	DF	t Value	Pr > |t|
Intercept		30.2061	4.1195	9.5	7.33	<.0001
Trt	A	-7.9297	6.0625	4.97	-1.31	0.2481
Trt	B	0	.	.	.	.

Type 3 Tests of Fixed Effects

Effect	Num DF	Den DF	F Value	Pr > F
Trt	1	4.97	1.71	0.2481

The METHOD=TYPE*n* specifications in the PROC MIXED statement apply only to variance component models with no SUBJECT= effects and no REPEATED statement. An analysis of variance table is included in the output, and the expected mean squares are used to estimate the variance components. Recall that your data is unbalanced. With unbalanced data, Type 1, Type 2, and Type 3 methods generally yield different expected mean squares and therefore different test results. If you want to give equal weights to the clinics included in the study, you choose Type 3 as your method-of-moment estimates of the covariance parameters.

The Expected Mean Squares table was traditionally used for selecting the appropriate denominator for the *F* statistic. You should select the mean square for the denominator whose expectation matches the expectation of the numerator mean square under the null hypothesis. For example, suppose you want to test the **Trt** effect, or H_0: $\alpha_i = 0$. The expected mean square for **Trt** is $\sigma^2 + 4.6613\sigma^2_{ab} + Q(Trt)$, where *Q(Trt)* is a function of $(\alpha_1 - \alpha_2)^2$. Under the null hypothesis, *Q(Trt)* would be zero, and the expected mean square for **Trt** would be $\sigma^2 + 4.6613\sigma^2_{ab}$.

Now you need another mean square with this expectation to use as the denominator for the *F* statistic. Unfortunately, none is directly available, which is almost always the case for unbalanced data or balanced data with complicated designs. A linear combination of mean squares must be used.

The next table in the output shows that the linear combination of mean squares, 0.6604*MS(**Clinic*Trt**) + 0.3396*MS(Residual), is used for the denominator of the *F* statistic. Using the information provided in the Type III Expected Mean Squares table, you can verify that the expected value of this linear combination is $\sigma^2 + 4.6613\sigma^2_{ab}$, the correct error term for testing the **Trt** effect.

The approximate degrees of freedom for this linear combination should also be estimated. Using the Satterthwaite's formula discussed later in this chapter, you obtain the approximate df = 11.69. Therefore, you have

F=MS(**Trt**) / [0.6604*MS(**Clinic*Trt**) + 0.3396*MS(Residual)]=2.17 with df=1, 11.69, and therefore a *p*-value of 0.1674.

The *F*-test is only approximate due to the complications of unbalanced data. But sometimes these approximate statistics provide the only available means of statistical inference.

One advantage of using METHOD=TYPE3 in this situation is the *F*-tests provided by this option that allow you to make inference about the covariance parameters. For example, the *F*-tests for **Clinic** and **Trt*Clinic** are for the null hypotheses H_o: $\sigma_c^2=0$ and H_o: $\sigma_{tc}^2=0$, respectively. The test statistics follow an *F* distribution. The results suggest that the **Clinic** variance is not significantly different from zero (*p*-value=0.5995), but the **Trt*Clinic** interaction variance significantly differs from zero (*p*-value=0.0178).

The ANOVA covariance parameter estimate for **Clinic** is –12.67. From the ANOVA table and the Expected Mean Squares table, you can verify that this negative value resulted from the fact that MS(**Clinic**) is less than MS(**Trt*Clinic**). Although in theory all covariance parameters should be nonnegative, you sometimes encounter negative covariance parameter estimates. This may result for several reasons. Detailed discussion on this issue is provided later in this section.

Making Inferences about Covariance Parameters

- Use the COVTEST option or the CL option in the PROC MIXED statement.
- Use the METHOD=TYPE3 option in the PROC MIXED statement and examine the *F*-test results.
- Use likelihood ratio tests. In some situations, the NOBOUND option in the PROC MIXED statement should be used.

35

You can use the COVTEST option in the PROC MIXED statement to make inferences about the covariance parameters. This option computes the Wald-Z statistics. This statistic is based on large sample theory and is only asymptotically valid.

You can also use the CL option in the PROC MIXED statement to make inferences about covariance parameters. The CL option computes the confidence limits on the covariance parameters based on a chi-squared distribution. It is also asymptotically valid.

When you do not have the REPEATED statement nor the SUBJECT= option in the RANDOM statement, you may want to use METHOD=TYPE3 in the PROC MIXED statement to request an *F*-test on the covariance parameters. For balanced data, this is the exact test. For unbalanced data, this test provides a reasonable approximation.

You can also perform likelihood ratio tests to make inferences about the covariance parameters. You must use the NOBOUND option in the PROC MIXED statement to make this a valid statistical test when one or more of the variance components hit the boundary. The *p*-value computed for the likelihood ratio test may be too conservative, because the asymptotic null distribution for the likelihood ratio test statistics for testing hypotheses regarding random effects is often a mixture of chi-squared distributions rather than the classical single chi-squared distribution (Verbeke and Molenberghs 2000).

Likelihood Ratio Test for Variance Components

You can also construct a likelihood ratio test to see whether one variance component is significantly different from zero. When one or more of the variance component estimates hit the boundary, you **must** use the NOBOUND option in the PROC MIXED statement in order for this test to be valid. For example, suppose you would like to see whether the **Trt*Clinic** variance is significantly different from zero. You can submit the following program to perform the likelihood ratio test.

```
proc mixed data=sasuser.multicenter nobound;
   class Trt Clinic;
   model Flush=Trt / ddfm=kr;
   random Clinic Trt*Clinic;
   ods output FitStatistics=FitFull (rename=(value=WithTC));
run;

proc mixed data=sasuser.multicenter nobound;
   class Trt Clinic;
   model Flush=Trt / ddfm=kr;
   random Clinic;
   ods output FitStatistics=FitReduced (rename=(value=WithoutTC));
run;

data result (drop=descr);
   merge FitFull FitReduced;
   if _n_=1 then do;
      Chi=WithoutTC - WithTC;
      pvalue=1-probchi(Chi, 1);
      output;
      stop;
   end;
run;

title 'Likelihood Ratio Tests for Trt*Clinic Variance';
proc print data=result;
run;
title;                                          *c06s2d2.sas;
```

Selected PROC MIXED statement option:

NOBOUND requests the removal of boundary constraints on covariance parameters. For example, variance components have a default lower boundary constraint of 0, and the NOBOUND option allows their estimates to be negative.

Partial Output from the First MIXED Procedure

```
             Covariance Parameter
                  Estimates

            Cov Parm        Estimate

            Clinic          -16.0628
            Trt*Clinic       93.4778
            Residual          446.87
```

The NOBOUND option uses the REML computing algorithm, except that it allows negative variance component estimates to remain negative. Therefore, the **Clinic** variance parameter is estimated to be –16.0628. This estimate and the estimates for **Trt*Clinic** and Residual variances are unbiased estimates.

```
                   Fit Statistics

     -2 Res Log Likelihood            1182.7
     AIC (smaller is better)          1188.7
     AICC (smaller is better)         1188.9
     BIC (smaller is better)          1189.3
```

Partial Output from the Second MIXED Procedure

```
             Covariance Parameter
                  Estimates

             Cov Parm     Estimate

             Clinic        26.0118
             Residual       481.10
```

```
                   Fit Statistics

     -2 Res Log Likelihood            1184.6
     AIC (smaller is better)          1188.6
     AICC (smaller is better)         1188.7
     BIC (smaller is better)          1189.0
```

PROC PRINT Output

```
     Likelihood Ratio Tests for Trt*Clinic Variance

                          Without
   Obs       WithTC            TC        Chi         pvalue

    1        1182.7        1184.6    1.83840        0.17514
```

Based on the likelihood ratio test, the **Trt*Clinic** variance is not significantly different from zero (*p*-value=0.175), which is inconsistent with the *F*-test obtained previously. The *p*-value computed for the likelihood ratio test may be too conservative, because the asymptotic null distribution for the likelihood ratio test statistics for testing hypotheses regarding random effects is often a mixture of chi-squared distributions rather than the classical single chi-squared distribution (Verbeke and Molenberghs 2000). Based on the *F*-test shown previously, you would conclude that the **Trt*Clinic** variance significantly differs from zero.

Negative Variance Component Estimates

Negative variance component estimates may arise for a variety of reasons:

- The variability in your data may be large enough to produce a negative estimate, even though the true value of the variance component is positive.
- Your data may contain outliers.
- A different model for interpreting your data may be appropriate.

39

The variance component estimates should theoretically be nonnegative because they are assumed to represent the variance of a random variable. Nevertheless, when you use METHOD=MIVQUE0 or TYPE*n*, some estimates of variance components may become negative. The REML and ML estimates are constrained to be nonnegative by default, but truncating variance component estimates at zero results in upward bias in variance component estimates. It also causes bias in affected statistics. This remains an unresolved controversy in mixed model inference.

Negative variance component estimates may arise for a variety of reasons as stated in the above slide. In particular, it may indicate an inappropriate model specification for your data. Under some statistical models for the mixed model analysis, negative estimates are an indication that observations in your data are negatively correlated (Hocking 1984). However, what to do about negative variance component estimates is another unresolved controversy in mixed model analysis.

What Can Be Done?

- Plot your data and check for extreme or unusual values.
- Respecify your model.
- Investigate significant variance components, if appropriate.

40

Statisticians and other practitioners struggle with the question of what to do with negative variance components. Some think that negative estimates should be reported as such, whereas others argue that because variance by definition cannot be negative, negative estimates have no meaning and they should be set to zero. No matter how you decide to report them, questions still remain. When the estimated variance component is negative, how do you interpret these variance components and other parameters in the model?

You might want to plot your data and check for extreme or unusual values. You might also want to consider respecifying your model. This may include specifying other alternative terms in your model, excluding the term(s) with negative variance component estimates from your model, and others. The problem with excluding the term(s) from your model is that it may produce a model that does not make sense (for example, is not hierarchically well formulated). It may also hide the true negative covariance presented in your data.

In some situations, you may want to investigate further about the significant variance component estimates. For example, because the previous F-tests indicated that the **`Trt*Clinic`** variance is significantly different from zero, whereas **`Clinic`** variance is not, you may want to see how different clinics perform differently for different drugs.

Negative Variance Component Estimates

Depending upon the estimation method you chose, the result was a zero or a negative estimate for the **Clinic** variance. You may want to drop **Clinic** from your RANDOM statement, considering the negative estimate indicates that not much variation among clinics is exhibited in your data.

```
proc mixed data=sasuser.multicenter;
   class Trt Clinic;
   model Flush=Trt / ddfm=kr;
   random Trt*Clinic;
run;                                    *c06s2d3.sas;
```

Partial PROC MIXED Output

Covariance Parameter Estimates

Cov Parm	Estimate
Trt*Clinic	75.3629
Residual	447.57

Type 3 Tests of Fixed Effects

Effect	Num DF	Den DF	F Value	Pr > F
Trt	1	9.3	1.83	0.2075

Compared with the output from the REML method with **Clinic** and **Trt*Clinic** specified in the RANDOM statement shown previously, the estimates for **Clinic(Trt)** and Residual variances remain the same. Generally speaking, dropping the zero covariance parameter from your model does not change other statistics produced by the REML method. However, it may remove the hierarchy of the model.

Recall from one of the previous demonstrations that the **Clinic*Trt** variance significantly differed from zero. It may be useful to investigate how the clinics included in the study performed differently for different drugs. You can do that by computing EBLUPs with the OUTP= option in the MODEL statement and examining the interaction graphically.

```
proc mixed data=sasuser.multicenter ;
   class Trt Clinic ;
   model Flush=Trt / ddfm=kr outp=pred;
   random Clinic Trt*Clinic;
run;

goptions reset=all;
proc gplot data=pred;
   symbol1 v=circle i=join l=1 c=red;
   symbol2 v=star i=join l=3 c=blue;
   symbol3 v=circle i=none l=1 c=red;
   symbol4 v=star i=none l=3 c=blue;
   axis1 order=(0 to 140 by 10) label=(a=90);
   axis2 offset=(2,2) minor=none;
   legend1 frame;
   plot Pred*Clinic=Trt / vaxis=axis1 haxis=axis2 legend=legend1 ;
   plot2 Flush*Clinic=Trt / vaxis=axis1 nolegend;
run;
quit;                                *c06s2d4.sas;
```

The OUTP= option in the MODEL statement specifies an output data set that contains predicted values and related quantities.

PROC GPLOT Output

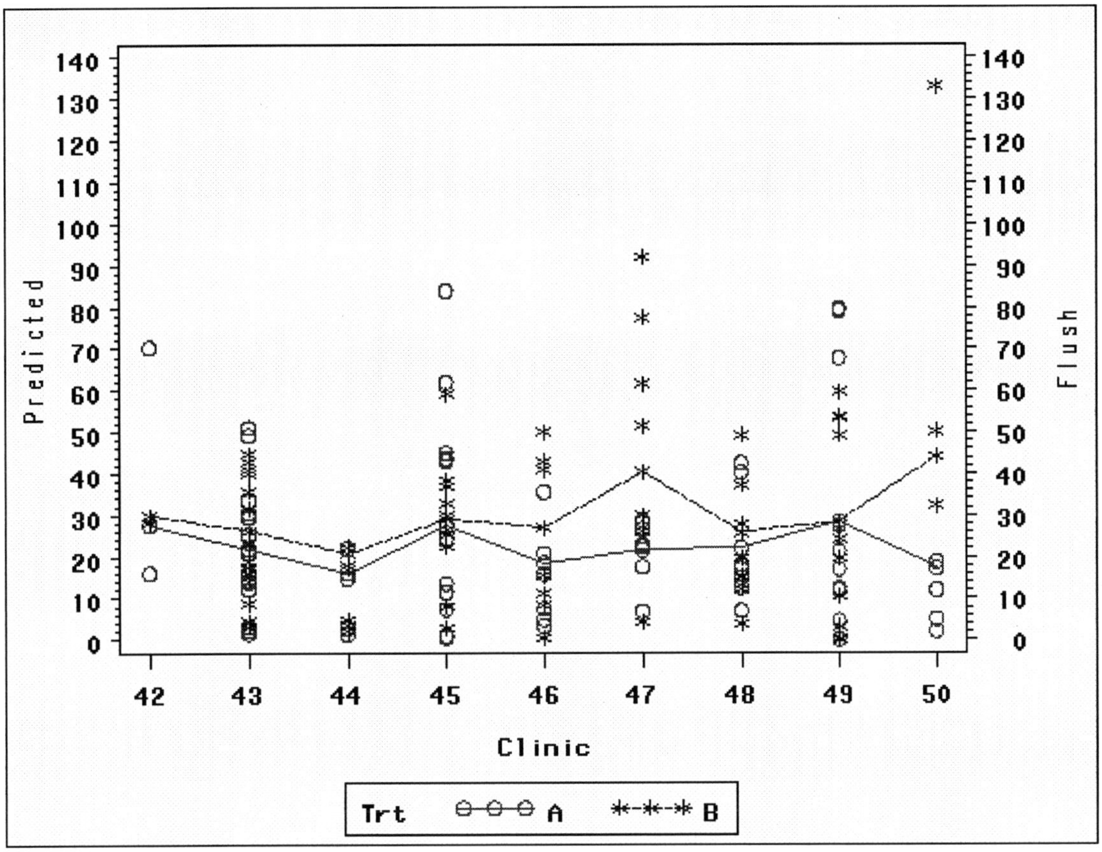

At clinics 47 and 50, taking treatment B tends to yield much higher **Flush** measurements than at other clinics. As a matter of fact, all measurements at clinic 50 have a higher **Flush** value for treatment B than that for treatment A, and one of the measurements is much higher than the rest of the values in the entire data set. As an investigator, you may want to examine these clinics more closely in order to find out the reasons behind this.

6.3 Estimated Generalized Least Squares Inference

Objectives

- Compare ordinary least squares (OLS) estimates with generalized least squares estimates (GLS).
- Explain the estimated generalized least squares (GLS) estimates.
- Discuss the inferences on estimated GLS estimates.

46

GLS versus OLS

- Ordinary least squares (OLS) estimates and standard errors are based upon the assumption that the errors are independently normally distributed with a common variance, that is, $R=\sigma^2 I_n=V$.
- Generalized least squares (GLS) estimates and standard errors are based upon the **G** and **R** matrices that can take a variety of forms.
- OLS is a special case of GLS.
- For balanced data, estimates from OLS and GLS generally agree, but the standard errors do not for mixed models.
- If the covariance structure is misspecified, sometimes OLS can perform better than GLS.

47

In general linear models, you assume all effects are fixed, and the random errors are independently normally distributed with mean of zero and a constant variance of σ^2, in other words, $\mathbf{R}=\sigma^2\mathrm{I}$. The ordinary least squares (OLS) solutions to the normal equations possess nice statistical properties such as linear, unbiased, minimum variance, and so forth. In mixed models, you assume random effects and random errors are independent of each other and follow a multivariate normal distribution with mean of zero and covariance matrices **G** and **R**, respectively. **G** and **R** can take a variety of forms, including heterogeneous variances and interdependent covariances. Likelihood-based methods are generally used for obtaining estimated **G** and **R** matrices. The solutions to the mixed model equations are generalized least squares (GLS) estimates. For balanced data, the estimates from OLS and GLS generally agree, however, the standard errors do not for mixed models. For unbalanced data, neither the estimates nor the standard errors are the same between OLS and GLS. In general, GLS estimates are superior to OLS estimates for mixed models.

The GLM procedure produces OLS estimates and standard errors; the MIXED procedure produces GLS estimates and standard errors.

Generalized Least Squares

Generalized least squares method

- takes into account the covariance matrices **G** and **R**
- requires a reasonable estimate of **G** and **R**
- produces the estimated GLS solutions when **G** or **R** is unknown.

Estimated GLS

$$\hat{\beta} = (X'\hat{V}^{-1}X)^{-}X'\hat{V}^{-1}y$$
$$\hat{\gamma} = \hat{G}Z'\hat{V}^{-1}(y - X\hat{\beta})$$

OLS

$$\hat{\beta} = (X'X)^{-}X'y$$

48

The generalized least squares (GLS) estimates take into account the covariance matrices **G** and **R**, but they also depend upon the reasonable estimates of **G** and **R** being obtained.

The MIXED procedure computes the GLS solutions for the fixed effects β. Notice that the true value of V is usually unknown. Replacing V by an estimator $\hat{V}$ yields the estimated GLS solutions.

Recall the mixed models notation $y = X\beta + Z\gamma + \varepsilon$. The variance matrix of the data is given by $V = ZGZ' + R$. The GLS solutions for β are obtained by minimizing $(y - X\beta)'V^{-1}(y - X\beta)$ for β, yielding the estimated GLS solution for β as $\hat{\beta} = (X'\hat{V}^{-1}X)^{-}X'\hat{V}^{-1}y$.

The estimated GLS solutions for the random effects γ can be obtained by $\hat{\gamma} = \hat{G}Z'\hat{V}^{-1}(y - X\hat{\beta})$.

The ordinary least squares (OLS) solutions for a fixed effect model $y = \mathbf{X}\beta + \varepsilon$ is given by $\hat{\beta} = (X'X)^{-}X'y$, which is a special case of the GLS solution with $\mathbf{V} = \sigma^2 I_n$.

See the SAS online documentation for more details.

The maximum likelihood estimator for β in the mixed model equals the generalized least squares estimator.

Properties of GLS Estimates

- If $V=\sigma^2 I_N$, the GLS solution leads to the OLS solution.
- If V is known, the GLS estimate $\hat{\beta}$ is the best linear unbiased estimator (BLUE) of β, and $\hat{\gamma}$ is the best linear unbiased predictor (BLUP) of γ.
- If V is unknown, the estimated GLS solution $\hat{\beta}$ is the empirical best linear unbiased estimator (EBLUE) of β, and $\hat{\gamma}$ is the empirical best linear unbiased predictor (EBLUP) of γ.

49

Inferences about the Fixed Effects

- The variance-covariance matrix of the GLS fixed effect estimates $\hat{\beta}_{GLS}$ is given by

$$Var(\hat{\beta}_{GLS})=(X'V^{-1}X)^{-}$$

- The variance-covariance matrix of the estimated GLS fixed effect estimates $\hat{\beta}_{EGLS}$ is given by

$$Var(\hat{\beta}_{EGLS})=(X'\hat{V}^{-1}X)^{-}$$

- The variance-covariance matrix of the OLS estimates, by comparison, is

$$Var(\hat{\beta}_{OLS})=\sigma^2(X'X)^{-}$$

50

Because **V** is usually unknown, the estimator of the variance-covariance matrix of the fixed effects is $(X'\hat{V}^{-1}X)^{-}$. This estimator is biased downward because the variability introduced by working with estimated variance components in **V**, rather than with the known variance components, is not taken into account in the approximation. PROC MIXED does not compute any inflation factors by default, but rather accounts for the downward bias by using the approximate *t*-statistic and *F* statistic. However, the DDFM=KR option in the MODEL statement does introduce an inflation factor for the estimated variance-covariance matrix of the fixed and random effects by the method proposed by Prasad and Rao (1990) and Harville and Jeske (1992), along with Satterthwaite-based degrees of freedom.

Inferences about Lβ

linear combination of β

$$H_0 : L\beta = 0$$

$$t = \frac{L\hat{\beta}}{\sqrt{L(X'\hat{V}^{-1}X)^{-}L'}}$$

design matrix of β

estimated variance

$$F = \frac{\hat{\beta}'L'[L(X'\hat{V}^{-1}X)^{-}L']^{-}L\hat{\beta}}{rank(L)}$$

51

When trying to make inference about a linear combination of the fixed effects β's, a *t*-test or *F*-test is carried out depending on the number of rows in matrix **L**. When **L** consists of a single row, the *t*-statistic shown above is well approximated by a *t*-distribution with $\hat{v}$ degrees of freedom ($\hat{v}$ must be estimated). When the rank of **L** (the number of linearly independent rows (and columns) in the matrix **L**) is greater than 1, PROC MIXED constructs the *F* statistic shown above, which has an approximate *F* distribution with rank(**L**) numerator degrees of freedom and $\hat{v}$ denominator degrees of freedom ($\hat{v}$ needs to be estimated). As you can see, both *t* and *F* statistics enable you to make inferences about your fixed effects and account for the variance-covariance model you choose.

As mentioned previously, you can use the E3 option in the MODEL statement or the E option in LSMEANS, CONTRAST, or ESTIMATE statements to obtain the matrix **L**.

Alternatively, you can use χ^2 statistics associated with the likelihood ratio test using the ML estimation (rather than REML) method to make inferences about the fixed effects.

The inferences about the random effects γ can be derived similarly. See the SAS online documentation for more details.

6.4 Degrees of Freedom Estimates

Objectives

- Discuss issues with degrees of freedom estimates.
- Explain different degrees of freedom estimation methods in the MIXED procedure.
- Use different degrees of freedom estimation methods in PROC MIXED and compare the results.

55

Issues with Degrees of Freedom Estimates

- For balanced data sets only and for a number of hypotheses, the determination of the denominator degrees of freedom is simple.
- For unbalanced data and/or more complex linear hypotheses about the fixed effects, the denominator degrees of freedom must be estimated from the data.
- The default degrees of freedom provided by the MIXED procedure might not always be appropriate.

56

If the data is balanced and if the hypothesis states that all levels of a specific fixed-effects factor are the same, the background variability that serves as the denominator in the *F*-test can be selected by looking at the expected mean squares in the ANOVA table associated with the problem under consideration. You can use the GLM procedure to obtain expected mean squares. Alternatively, if you do not have the SUBJECT= option and the REPEATED statement, you can use the TYPE3 option in the MIXED procedure to obtain the expected mean squares.

If more complex linear hypotheses of the form H_0: $\mathbf{L}\beta=0$ are tested and/or if the data is unbalanced, more complicated expressions show up as background variability used as the denominator in the appropriate *F*-test. This appropriate *F* statistic was discussed in the previous section. However, the approximate degrees of freedom must be determined as well.

PROC MIXED provides the following methods for estimating the approximate denominator degrees of freedom: containment, between-within, residual, Satterthwaite's, and KENWARDROGER. KENWARDROGER was first available in SAS 8 and is considered by many to be the most appropriate for many situations. Refer to Verbeke and Molenberghs (1997) and Guerin and Stroup (2000) for more information on degrees of freedom estimates.

Containment Method

DDFM=CONTAIN

- is the default method when you specify the RANDOM statement
- uses the degrees of freedom for the random effect syntactically containing the effect of interest.

```
model breed age breed*age;
random id(breed);
```

DDF for **breed** = DF for id(**breed**)

DDF for **age** and **breed*age** = DF for residual

57

Using the beef tenderness data as an example, **breed** is a fixed-effects factor, and you must determine the denominator degrees of freedom for testing equality of the mean response at all **breed** levels. In the containment method, the random-effects list is searched for effects that syntactically contain **breed**, for example, **id*breed** or **id(breed)**. Technically, the degrees of freedom corresponding to each of these terms is computed, and the lowest value is assigned as the denominator degrees of freedom for the appropriate *F* statistic.

If no terms in the random effects list contain the fixed effects, the residual degrees of freedom are used for the denominator degrees of freedom for the appropriate *F* statistic. The residual degrees of freedom are computed as *n-rank*(**X Z**) for the containment method, where *n* is the number of observations, and **X** and **Z** are the design matrices for the fixed effects and the random effects, respectively.

Notice that the containment method is based on a syntactical rule. If the random effect is not specified as **id(breed)**, which syntactically contains **breed**, but rather as a separate factor with its own name, the containment method no longer uses the degrees of freedom of this random effect as the denominator degrees of freedom for **breed**, although the matrix corresponding to the used specified random effect and the **id(breed)** term is exactly the same.

When the standard error of the effect of interest is a linear combination of MS rather than a single MS, the containment method does not provide the appropriate denominator degrees of freedom.

The containment method can be very computationally expensive for large **Z** matrices.

Between-Within Method

DDFM=BETWITHIN / BW

- is the default method when you specify the REPEATED statement with no RANDOM statement
- divides the residual degrees of freedom into between-subject and within-subject portions, and then determines the appropriate degrees of freedom as one of the two based on whether fixed effect changes within any subject
- is a fairly reliable, quick way to obtain DDFM for models with a REPEATED statement.

58

The default degrees of freedom for a fixed effect when you specify the REPEATED statement with no RANDOM statement are computed by dividing the residual degrees of freedom into between-subject and within-subject portions. PROC MIXED then checks whether a fixed effect changes within any subject. If so, it assigns within-subject degrees of freedom to the effect; otherwise, it assigns the between-subject degrees of freedom to the effect. If there are multiple within-subject effects containing classification variables, the within-subject degrees of freedom are partitioned into components corresponding to the subject-by-effect interactions.

One exception to the preceding method is the case when you have specified no RANDOM statements and a REPEATED statement with the TYPE=UN option. In this case, all effects are assigned the between-subject degrees of freedom to provide for better small-sample approximations to the relevant sampling distributions.

The between-within method is a fairly reliable quick way to obtain the denominator degrees of freedom for models with a REPEATED statement. DDFM=KR is likely superior in most cases.

Residual Method

DDFM=RESIDUAL

- performs all tests using the residual degrees of freedom
- typically overestimates the optimal denominator degrees of freedom
- is computationally cheap.

59

The residual degrees of freedom are computed as *n-rank(***X***)*, where *n* is the number of observations, **X** is the design matrix for the fixed effects, and rank is the number of linearly independent rows (and columns) in the matrix **X**.

This method is computationally cheap and may be appropriate when you are interested in predictions rather than inferences. For situations where the degrees of freedom are large, using RESIDUAL may provide a reasonable approximation.

Satterthwaite's Method

DDFM=SATTERTH

- provides a better approximation that usually lies between the lowest and highest values of degrees of freedom associated with variance components that contribute to the background variability
- is syntactically invariant
- is a better choice in unbalanced situations and/or when the default methods are not appropriate.

60

Satterthwaite's method is slightly more computer intensive than the default methods, but the advantages are worth it. For unbalanced data and/or when the standard error of the fixed effect of interest is a linear combination of several MS, this method provides more appropriate estimates of the denominator degrees of freedom. Additionally, unlike the containment method, Satterthwaite's method is syntactically invariant. In other words, the denominator degrees of freedom do not depend on syntactic names of the fixed or random effects.

General formulas for Satterthwaite's method are provided in the SAS online documentation.

Satterthwaite's Formula

Let MS_1, MS_2, …, MS_k be independent mean squares with degrees of freedom df_1, df_2, …, df_k, respectively.

Then the linear combination

$MS = a_1MS_1 + a_2MS_2 + \ldots + a_kMS_k$

has the approximate degrees of freedom

$$df = \frac{(MS)^2}{\frac{(a_1MS_1)^2}{df_1} + \cdots + \frac{(a_kMS_k)^2}{df_k}}$$

61

A special case of Satterthwaite's method is when the quadratic form $L(X'\hat{V}^{-1}X)^{-}L'$ can be written as a linear combination of mean squares, for instance, $a_1MS_1 + \cdots + a_kMS_k$. The estimated degrees of freedom based on Satterthwaite's formula are provided above.

An Example

Type 3 Analysis of Variance

Source	Error Term	Error DF	F Value	Pr > F
Trt	0.6604 MS(Trt*Clinic) + 0.3396 MS(Residual)	11.689	2.17	0.1674
Clinic	MS(Trt*Clinic)	8	0.83	0.5995
Trt*Clinic	MS(Residual)	114	2.44	0.0178
Residual	.	.	.	.

MS(Error) = 0.6604*MS(Trt*Clinic) + 0.3396*MS(Residual)

MS a1 MS1 a2 MS2

62

KENWARDROGER Option

DDFM=KENWARDROGER / KR

- corrects the downward bias of the variance-covariance matrix of the fixed and random effects
- computes the Satterthwaite-type degrees of freedom based on the adjusted covariance matrix
- is computationally expensive
- is considered by many to be the most appropriate method.

63

The KENWARDROGER (KR) degrees of freedom approximation seems to be the most appropriate in many situations. It involves inflating the estimated variance-covariance matrix of the fixed and random effects by the method proposed by Prasad and Rao (1990), Harville and Jeske (1992), and Kackar and Harville (1984). Satterthwaite-type degrees of freedom are then computed, based on this adjustment. By default, the observed information matrix of the covariance parameter estimates is used in the calculations.

Guerin and Stroup (2000) compared the Type I error rates for default versus KR-adjusted statistics for repeated measures analyses and concluded that unless you use the adjustment as in KR, Type I error rates tend to be highly inflated, especially for more complex covariance structures. Schaalje, McBride, and Fellingham (2001) pointed out that the complexity of the covariance structure, sample size, and imbalance affect the performance of the ddf methods. Compared with the CONTAINMENT method, the KR method works reasonably well with more complicated covariance structures when sample sizes are moderate to small and the design is reasonably balanced. However, KR does not perform perfectly in all situations. When the covariance structure is complex, such as ANTE(1) and the sample size is small, the KR method produces inflated Type I error rates.

The KENWARDROGER method uses more computer resources. It can take a long time and extensive memory for large data sets.

Estimating Degrees of Freedom

Recall the **sasuser.fev1uni** data set used in an earlier chapter. You used DDFM=KR option in the MODEL statement. You will see what happens if you choose other methods for estimating the denominator degrees of freedom. For illustration purposes, the AR(1) model with a RANDOM statement is fit to your data. Recall that this model provides a model fit just as well as the TOEP model.

```
proc mixed data=sasuser.fev1uni;
   class drug patient hour;
   model fev1=drug|hour basefev1 / ddfm=contain ;
   random patient(drug);
   repeated / type=ar(1) subject=patient(drug);
   title 'Containment Method';
run;

proc mixed data=sasuser.fev1uni;
   class drug patient hour;
   model fev1=drug|hour basefev1 / ddfm=betwithin ;
   random patient(drug);
   repeated / type=ar(1) subject=patient(drug);
   title 'Between-Within Method';
run;

proc mixed data=sasuser.fev1uni;
   class drug patient hour;
   model fev1=drug|hour basefev1 / ddfm=residual ;
   random patient(drug);
   repeated / type=ar(1) subject=patient(drug);
   title 'Residual Method';
run;

proc mixed data=sasuser.fev1uni;
   class drug patient hour;
   model fev1=drug|hour basefev1 / ddfm=satterth;
   random patient(drug);
   repeated / type=ar(1) subject=patient(drug);
   title 'Satterthwaite''s Method';
run;

proc mixed data=sasuser.fev1uni;
   class drug patient hour;
   model fev1=drug|hour basefev1 / ddfm=kr;
   random patient(drug);
   repeated / type=ar(1) subject=patient(drug);
   title 'KENWARDROGER Method';
run; title;                                    *c06s4d1.sas;
```

Partial PROC MIXED Output

Containment Method

Type 3 Tests of Fixed Effects

Effect	Num DF	Den DF	F Value	Pr > F
drug	2	68	7.28	0.0014
hour	7	483	17.10	<.0001
drug*hour	14	483	3.94	<.0001
basefev1	1	483	75.93	<.0001

The containment method shows that the denominator degrees of freedom for **drug** is 68. Because the random effect **patient(drug)** syntactically contains **drug**, the degrees of freedom of **patient(drug)** (3*(24-1)=69) is used to compute the denominator degrees of freedom for **drug**. The covariate **basefev1** takes away 1 degree of freedom from 69, resulting in 68 denominator degrees of freedom for **drug**. All other fixed effects in the model are not syntactically contained in the random effect **patient(drug)**; therefore, the residual degrees of freedom, 483 (n-rank(X Z) = 576 – (1+2+7+14+1+68) = 483), was used as the denominator degrees of freedom for each of those effects. Notice that the **basefev1** denominator degrees of freedom are the residual degrees of freedom, which are clearly wrong because there is only one **basefev1** measurement per subject.

Between-Within Method

Type 3 Tests of Fixed Effects

Effect	Num DF	Den DF	F Value	Pr > F
drug	2	68	7.28	0.0014
hour	7	483	17.10	<.0001
drug*hour	14	483	3.94	<.0001
basefev1	1	68	75.93	<.0001

The between-within method shows that the degrees of freedom for **drug** is 68. Because **drug** does not change within a subject, the between-subject degrees of freedom (3*(24-1) = 69) is used to compute the denominator degrees of freedom for **drug**. Again, the covariate **basefev1** takes away 1 degree of freedom from 69, resulting in 68 denominator degrees of freedom for **drug**. The same is true for **basefev1**. Notice that this method recognizes **basefev1** as a between-subject variable. The associated denominator degrees of freedom for **basefev1** are far more reasonable than the ones obtained by the containment method. Because **hour** and **drug*hour** do change within a subject, the within-subject degrees of freedom, 483, is used for each of these effects.

Residual Method

Type 3 Tests of Fixed Effects

Effect	Num DF	Den DF	F Value	Pr > F
drug	2	551	7.28	0.0008
hour	7	551	17.10	<.0001
drug*hour	14	551	3.94	<.0001
basefev1	1	551	75.93	<.0001

The residual method uses the residual degrees of freedom, 551 (n-rank(X) = 576 – (1+2+7+14+1) = 551), as the denominator degrees of freedom for every fixed effect in the model, and is not generally recommended for small to moderate data sets. Notice that these residual degrees of freedom are computed differently than the residual degrees of freedom for the containment method.

Satterthwaite's Method

Type 3 Tests of Fixed Effects

Effect	Num DF	Den DF	F Value	Pr > F
drug	2	68.8	7.28	0.0014
hour	7	278	17.10	<.0001
drug*hour	14	278	3.94	<.0001
basefev1	1	68	75.93	<.0001

The Satterthwaite's method produces similar denominator degrees of freedom for **drug** and identical denominator degrees of freedom for **basefev1** as did the between-within method. The degrees of freedom for **hour** and **drug*hour**, however, differ from any of the previous methods. The previous methods ignored the variance-covariance structure for the repeated measures and tended to overestimate the appropriate denominator degrees of freedom for effects involving repeated measure effect (**hour**), and therefore are not as appropriate as this method.

```
                        KENWARDROGER Method

                 Type 3 Tests of Fixed Effects

                        Num      Den
        Effect           DF       DF     F Value     Pr > F

        drug              2     68.8        7.30     0.0013
        hour              7      395       16.99     <.0001
        drug*hour        14      424        3.90     <.0001
        basefev1          1       68       76.10     <.0001
```

As mentioned before, PROC MIXED uses estimated covariance parameters in formulas that assume these quantities are known. This results in test statistics biased upward and standard errors biased downward, for all cases except independent errors models with balanced data (Kacker and Harville (1984)). The KENWARDROGER (KR) method in PROC MIXED provides a correction for standard errors and *F* statistics, as well as a generalized procedure of Satterthwaite-type to obtain degrees of freedom. This method is highly recommended, especially for repeated measure analysis. The degrees of freedom from the KR method are similar to those produced by Satterthwaite's method. The differences are the denominator degrees of freedom for **hour** and **drug*hour**, for which the KR method is based on adjusted standard errors.

Other observations about the results produced by different denominator degrees of freedom estimation methods are these:

- The *F* statistics (labeled F Value) for each effect are the same across all methods except for the KR method, which applies a bias-adjusted correction to the standard errors and the *F* statistics.
- The *p*-values for each effect are almost identical across different methods used for estimating the denominator degrees of freedom. This is true for this example, but may not always be the case.

6.5 Troubleshooting Convergence Problems

Objectives

- Explain common causes of convergence problems.
- Suggest ways of dealing with nonconvergence.
- Deal with a nonconvergence situation in the MIXED procedure.

70

Common Causes of Nonconvergence

- Two covariance parameters that are several orders of magnitude apart
- Values that are extremely large or extremely small in scale
- Infinite likelihood caused by nonpositive definite or singular **R** or **V** matrix, or not enough data to estimate the specified covariance structure
- Linear dependencies among covariance parameters, and/or confounding of mean and covariance parameters
- Over-specified or misspecified model
- Violation of model assumptions

71

When two of the covariance parameters are on a different scale, for instance, several orders of magnitude apart, the Newton-Raphson algorithm used to maximize the likelihood function sometimes does not perform well. This is because when processing jointly for the two parameters, the elements of the Hessian matrix corresponding to one of the parameters can become close to internal tolerance in the MIXED procedure. Rescaling the effects in the model so that the covariance parameters are on the same scale may be helpful.

The Hessian matrix (**H**) consists of the second derivatives of the objective function with respect to the covariance parameters.

Another need for rescaling is when you have data that is extremely large or extremely small, which can cause nonconvergence due to the internal tolerance in PROC MIXED.

When you specify a complicated variance-covariance structure in the RANDOM statement and/or the REPEATED statement but do not have enough data to estimate it, you may get an infinite likelihood and therefore be unable to obtain results from PROC MIXED. This infinite likelihood can also be caused by a nonpositive definite **R** or **V** matrix, which can be caused, for example, by duplicate values within a subject in repeated measures analysis.

A quadratic form $\mathbf{x'Ax}$ is positive definite when $\mathbf{x'Ax} > 0$ for all $\mathbf{x}$ other than $\mathbf{x} = 0$. The matrix **A** is a positive definite matrix, whose eigenvalues are all greater than zero.

Linear dependencies among the parameters and/or confounding of mean and covariance parameters can produce a nonpositive definite Hessian matrix and therefore nonconvergence. In this case, you may consider fitting another model that might be more appropriate for your situation.

If your data does not meet the normality assumptions for PROC MIXED, or you have over-specified or misspecified your model for the data, nonconvergence can occur.

Ways of Dealing with Nonconvergence

- Rescale the data to improve stability; add ITDETAILS and LOGNOTE options to obtain more information.
- Plot your data and check for extreme or unusual observations. Adjust or delete them if appropriate.
- Use the PARMS statement to input initial values. Add boundary constraints (LOWERB= and/or UPPERB=) for parameters that might be unstable. Search over a grid of parameters.
- Specify the SCORING= option to invoke the Fisher scoring estimation method.

continued...

72

When nonconvergence occurs, you may want to try one or more of the following suggested approaches.

Rescaling your data can improve algorithm numerical stability. Use ITDETAILS and LOGNOTE options in the PROC MIXED statement to obtain more information on the iteration process. The ITDETAILS option displays the parameter values at each iteration and enables the writing of notes to the SAS log pertaining to "infinite likelihood" and "singularities" during Newton-Raphson iterations. The LOGNOTE option writes periodic notes to the log describing the current status of computations.

Plot your data first to make sure no extreme or unusual observations are included in your data set. When that happens, you might consider adjusting or deleting them if appropriate.

Use the PARMS statement to specify initial values for the covariance parameters, or perform a grid search over several values of these parameters. You must specify the values in the order in which they appear in the Covariance Parameter Estimates table. The LOWERB= and UPPERB= options in the PARMS statement enable you to specify lower and upper boundary constraints on the covariance parameters, respectively. Using these options can improve the stability of the iteration process.

Specify ODS OUTPUT COVPARMS=*dataset* to save the final parameter values into *dataset*. In the new run, use the PARMSDATA=*dataset* option in the PARMS statement so that the final parameter values from the last run will be used as the starting values for the new run to improve convergence.

Use the SCORING=*number* option in the PROC MIXED statement to request a Fisher scoring algorithm to be used for the first *number* iterations. A Fisher scoring algorithm sometimes performs better than the default Newton-Raphson algorithm with respect to initial values.

Ways of Dealing with Nonconvergence

- Make sure no observations from the same subject are producing identical rows in the **R** or **V** matrix.
- Rearrange effects in the MODEL statement so that the most significant ones are first to improve stability.
- Make sure you have enough data and the parameters are not linearly dependent. Respecify the model, if necessary.
- Try fitting a simple model and then gradually increase complexity.

continued...

73

Ways of Dealing with Nonconvergence

- Tune the singularity options SINGULAR=, SINGCHOL=, and SINGRES= in the MODEL statement.
- Tune the MAXITER= and MAXFUNC= options in the PROC MIXED statement.
- Use the NOPROFILE and NOBOUND options in the PROC MIXED statement.
- Try CONVF= or CONVG=, possibly along with the ABSOLUTE option, as a convergence criterion in the PROC MIXED statement.

74

The SINGULAR= option tunes the sensitivity in sweeping. The SINGCHOL= option tunes the sensitivity in computing Cholesky roots. The SINGRES= option sets the tolerance for which the residual variance is considered to be zero. In all three options, the default is 1E4 times the machine epsilon; this product is approximately 1E-12 on most computers. You can specify a slightly larger number to tune the sensitivity measurements.

The MAXITER= option specifies the maximum number of iterations. The default is 50. The MAXFUNC= option specifies the maximum number of likelihood evaluations in the optimization process. The default is 150. You can specify these options in the PROC MIXED statement to allow for more number of iterations and/or more number of likelihood evaluations.

The NOPROFILE option includes the residual variance as part of the Newton-Raphson iterations. The NOBOUND option requests the removal of boundary constraints on covariance parameters.

By default, the convergence criterion is defined by the CONVH= option in the PROC MIXED statement. The CONVH=*number* option requests the relative Hessian convergence criterion with tolerance *number*. The default tolerance is 1E-8. You can try other convergence criteria provided by the MIXED procedure. The CONVG=*number* option requests the relative gradient convergence criterion with tolerance *number*. The CONVF=*number* option requests the relative function convergence criterion with tolerance *number*. In both options, the default tolerance is 1E-8. The ABSOLUTE option makes the convergence criterion absolute rather than relative. Information on the computations of these criteria can be found in the SAS online documentation.

If you achieve the convergence by tuning the sensitivity measures or the convergence criteria, make sure to examine the output from PROC MIXED for covariance parameter estimates and the tests for fixed effects to determine the true cause of nonconvergence, for example, an over- or misspecified model.

Example 1

```
proc mixed data=sasuser.fev1uni;
   class drug patient hour;
   model fev1=drug basefev1 drug*basefev1
              hour drug*hour / ddfm=kr;
   random patient(drug);
   repeated hour / type=cs
                   subject=patient(drug);
run;
```

75

Recall the program you fit to the **sasuser.fev1uni** data set in the previous chapter. You used the RANDOM statement in addition to the REPEATED statement with TYPE=AR(1). What happens if you specify TYPE=CS instead in the REPEATED statement?

The Log and the Output Windows

```
NOTE: Convergence criteria met but final hessian is not positive
      definite.
NOTE: Asymptotic variance matrix of covariance parameter estimates
      has been found to be singular and a generalized inverse was
      used. Covariance parameters with zero variance do not
      contribute to degrees of freedom computed by DDFM=KENWARDROGER.
```

```
Convergence criteria met but final hessian is not positive
                         definite.

              Covariance Parameter Estimates

     Cov Parm            Subject             Estimate

     patient(drug)                             0.2088
     CS                  patient(drug)              0
     Residual                                 0.06313
```

76

The Hessian matrix, **H,** is a matrix of the second partial derivative of the objective function with respect to the model parameters. The inverse of the matrix, $\mathbf{H}^{-1}$, contains information about the variance-covariance of the model parameters.

A quadratic form $\mathbf{x'Ax}$ is positive definite when $\mathbf{x'Ax} > 0$ for all $\mathbf{x}$ other than $\mathbf{x} = 0$. A positive definite matrix has eigenvalues all greater than zero.

When the Hessian matrix is found to be singular, a generalized inverse is computed by PROC MIXED. The algorithm is numerically stable but computationally expensive; it may or may not be acceptable to use the parameter estimates produced by the procedure under various situations. You may want to try different approaches to stabilize the optimization process, such as changing the scale of the data/parameters, respecifying your model, and so forth.

Example 1—What Went Wrong?

- It is an over-parameterized model.
  - The REPEATED statement fits a compound symmetry structure for the residual covariance.
  - The RANDOM statement is redundant because the resulting **V** matrix is also a compound symmetry.
  - Similar issues exist for TYPE=UN, TYPE=TOEP, and some of other structures.
  - You may want to delete the RANDOM statement, or keep it and specify serial correlations such as AR(1) for the REPEATED statement.

77

Having the REPEATED statement alone as specified in the program (TYPE=CS) produces a compound symmetry structure for the **V** matrix. With the additional RANDOM statement as specified in the program, the resulting **V** matrix is still compound symmetry (**V**=**ZGZ′**+**R**). Therefore, the RANDOM statement is redundant. This is true if the same variable (**`patient(drug)`**) is specified in both the RANDOM statement and the SUBJECT= option in the REPEATED statement. A similar issue exists for other covariance structures in the REPEATED statement that do not belong to serial correlations, such as TYPE=UN and TYPE=TOEP.

Having the RANDOM statement alone also produces a compound symmetry **V** matrix. For this example (TYPE=CS in the REPEATED statement), deleting either the RANDOM statement or the REPEATED statement would work.

Example 2

```
proc mixed data=sasuser.fev1test;
   class drug patient hour;
   model fev1=drug basefev1 hour drug*hour
            / ddfm=kr;
   repeated hour / type=TOEP
                   subject=patient(drug);
run;
```

```
NOTE: An infinite likelihood is assumed in iteration 0 because of a
      nonpositive definite estimated R matrix for patient(drug) 214 a.
```

79

The data set **`sasuser.fev1test`** is slightly different from the data set **`sasuser.fev1uni`**. The message indicates that observations for patient 214 taking drug a may need to be investigated further.

Example 2—What Went Wrong?

```
proc print data=sasuser.fev1test;
   where patient=214 and drug='a';
run;
```

obs	patient	basefev1	drug	hour	fev1
97	214	2.77	a	1	3.36
98	214	2.77	a	2	3.42
99	214	2.77	a	3	3.28
100	214	2.77	a	4	3.30
101	214	2.77	a	5	3.31
102	214	2.77	a	6	2.99
103	214	2.77	a	7	3.01
104	214	2.77	a	7	3.08

82

You cannot have multiple observations for a specific subject at a specific time point. The observation must be unique. You must make sure data mistakes like this do not exist for your data.

Example 3

When specifying TYPE=UN in the RANDOM or the REPEATED statement and the program failed to converge, try to specify TYPE=FA0(*q*) where *q* corresponds to the dimension of the UN matrix.

```
proc mixed data=sasuser.wheat;
   class variety;
   model yield=moisture / ddfm=kr;
   random int moisture / type=FA0(2)
                         subject=variety;
   parms / lowerb=.,.,0.001;
run;
```

84

The no-diagonal factor analytic structure FA0(q) is a reparameterization of the unstructured matrix, and is more numerically stable because the matrix is always at least positive semidefinite. The PARMS statement with the LOWERB= option is helpful in some cases to further improve the numerical performance of the model.

Example 4

```
proc mixed data=mydata;
   class network hospital;
   model y=network / ddfm=kr;
   random hospital;
run;
```

```
ERROR: Out of memory.
NOTE: The SAS System stopped processing this step because of
      insufficient memory.
```

86

A linear mixed model is fit to a data set **mydata**. This data arises from a nested design from a health care research institute. The response variable **y** is a composite index of customers' satisfactory to the services received. The randomly selected subjects are nested within hospitals and hospitals are nested within networks. The goal is to compare the networks accounting for correlations among the subjects from the same hospital.

Example 4—What Went Wrong?

Dimensions

Covariance Parameters	2
Columns in X	5
Columns in Z	378
Subjects	1
Max Obs Per Subject	7560

Number of Observations

Number of Observations Read	7560
Number of Observations Used	7560
Number of Observations Not Used	0

- There are 378 levels for the random effect **hospital**.
- Large **Z** matrix is resource intensive.

87

The data set only contains 7560 observations, so why was it out of memory? It is the large **Z** matrix (378 columns) that caused the problem. Large **Z** matrix requires huge computer memory in PROC MIXED computations.

Example 4—Modify Your Program

```
proc mixed data=mydata;
   class network hospital;
   model y=network / ddfm=kr;
   random int / subject=hospital;
run;
```

```
NOTE: Convergence criteria met.
NOTE: PROCEDURE MIXED used (Total process time):
      real time           0.35 seconds
      cpu time            0.33 seconds
```

89

Using the SUBJECT= option in the RANDOM statement is like factoring out the common factor among the random effects. The resulting model is identical, but specifying the SUBJECT= option is more computationally efficient.

Example 4—Other Possible Specifications

```
proc sort data=mydata;
   by hospital;
run;

proc mixed data=mydata;
   class network;
   model y=network / ddfm=kr;
   random int / subject=hospital;
run;
```

```
proc mixed data=mydata;
   class network hospital;
   model y=network / ddfm=kr;
   repeated/type=cs subject=hospital;
run;
```

90

You can further improve the computational efficiency by treating the SUBJECT= variable as a continuous variable. Make sure your data is grouped by this variable first. Alternatively, you can specify a model using the REPEATED statement with TYPE=CS structure. This statement gives rise to the same **V** matrix as the RANDOM statement. You would obtain exactly the same results. Using the REPEATED statement is more computationally efficient than using the RANDOM statement, especially when the **Z** matrix is large.

Detailed information about why these two statements produce the same **V** matrix can be found in the SAS online documentation or Littell et al. (1996).

Equivalent Marginal Models

```
random int / subject=hospital;
```

➡ $\mathbf{G} = \sigma_1^2 \mathbf{I}_m, \mathbf{R} = \sigma^2 \mathbf{I}_n$

It follows that the **V** matrix has a compound symmetry structure (**V=ZGZ'+R**).

```
repeated/type=cs subject=hospital;
```

➡ No **G** matrix. **R** is compound symmetry.

It follows that the **V** matrix has the same compound symmetry structure (**V=R**).

91

The blocks in the **V** matrix have the following form:

$$\begin{bmatrix} \sigma_1^2 + \sigma^2 & \sigma_1^2 & \cdots & \sigma_1^2 \\ & \sigma_1^2 + \sigma^2 & \cdots & \sigma_1^2 \\ & & \ddots & \vdots \\ & & & \sigma_1^2 + \sigma^2 \end{bmatrix}$$

6.6 Chapter Summary

Many issues associated with unbalanced data are not unique to the mixed models. In unbalanced data analysis, you must determine which type of test is more appropriate for your situation. In the presence of empty cells, you may encounter problems of nonestimable contrasts and estimates.

The MIXED procedure provides several methods for estimating covariance parameters: ML, REML (default), MIVQUE0, Type 1, Type 2, and Type 3. The default method (REML) is preferred in many situations.

Sometimes you can obtain negative variance component estimates. They can arise for a variety of reasons. You may need to examine your data for any potential outliers or unusual values, respecify your model, or investigate other significant variance components, if appropriate.

The MIXED procedure uses generalized least squares (GLS) to obtain estimates and standard errors of fixed effects. This method takes into account the covariance matrices **G** and **R**, but requires a reasonable estimate of **G** and **R**. In general, GLS is superior to ordinary least squares (OLS) assuming an appropriate covariance structure. The GLS estimates are EBLUEs for the fixed effects and EBLUPs for the random effects.

The MIXED procedure provides several methods for estimating the denominator degrees of freedom for fixed effects: containment, between-within, residual, Satterthwaite, and KENWARDROGER. Simulation studies have shown that the KENWARDROGER method produces appropriate estimates in many situations and therefore is highly recommended. You use DDFM=KR in the MODEL statement to specify this option.

You may encounter convergence problems in running the MIXED procedure. This may be caused by a variety of reasons such as extremely large or small values in scale; infinite likelihood caused by nonpositive definite or singular **R** or **V** matrix; not enough data; over-specified or misspecified model; violation of model assumptions, and so forth.

There are a number of ways of dealing with nonconvergence. Here are some examples:

- rescale your data
- use ITDETAILS and LOGNOTE options in the PROC MIXED statement
- plot your data and check for extreme or unusual observations
- make sure no observations from the same subject are producing identical rows in **R** or **V** matrix
- respecify your model, if necessary
- tune the singularity options using SINGULAR= in the MODEL statement.

Chapter 7 Introduction to Nonlinear Mixed Models

7.1 Introduction to Generalized Linear Mixed Models and Nonlinear Mixed Models

Objectives

- Review assumptions of linear mixed models.
- Identify situations where linear mixed model assumptions are violated.
- Define generalized linear mixed models.
- Define nonlinear mixed models.

3

Linear Mixed Models Assumptions

- Random effects and residuals are normally distributed with mean zero and covariance matrices **G** and **R**, respectively.
- Random effects and model errors are independent of each other.
- The means (expected values) of the responses are linearly related to the predictor variables (linear in terms of fixed-effects parameters).

4

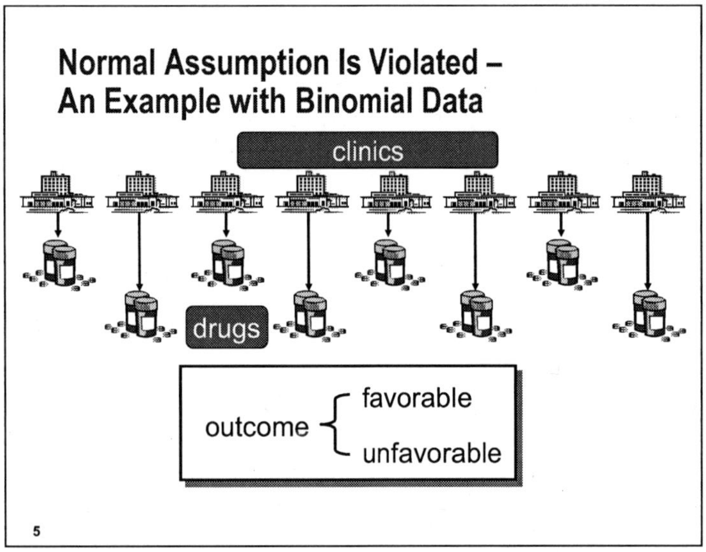

A clinical trial study involved two drug treatments and eight clinics. The eight clinics represented a sample from a larger target population. At each clinic, subjects were randomly assigned to receive one of the two treatments. Each subject was classified as having a favorable or unfavorable response to the treatment.

This is a mixed model with **`drug`** being a fixed effect and **`clinic`** being a random effect. But you have a binary response: favorable or unfavorable. Because the distribution of the response variable is binomial, the normal assumption of a linear mixed model is violated. You can actually fit a generalized linear mixed model, a special case of nonlinear mixed models, to your data.

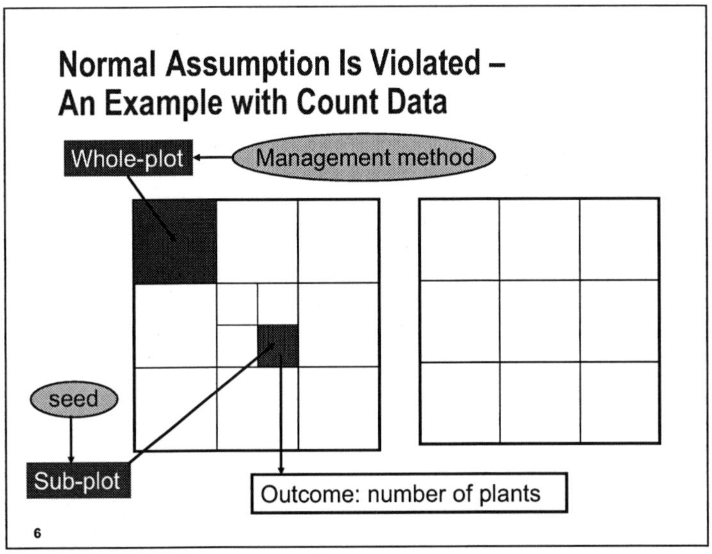

A split-plot experiment was conducted to compare various treatments for improving damaged rangeland. The whole-plot treatments were various management methods. They were applied in randomized complete blocks. The whole-plot units are plots of land of equal sizes within a block. Each whole-plot was split into four subplots, and different seed mixes were applied to the subplot units. The response variable of interest was botanical composition, measured by the number of plants of various species present in a given plot.

This is a mixed model with a typical split-plot design structure, except that the response variable is a count. Typically, counts are assumed to follow a Poisson distribution, although overdispersion problems often exist for count data. Clearly the normality assumption of a linear mixed model is violated. Again, you can fit a generalized linear mixed model, a special case of nonlinear mixed models, to this data.

Linearity Assumption Is Violated – Orange Tree Growth Example

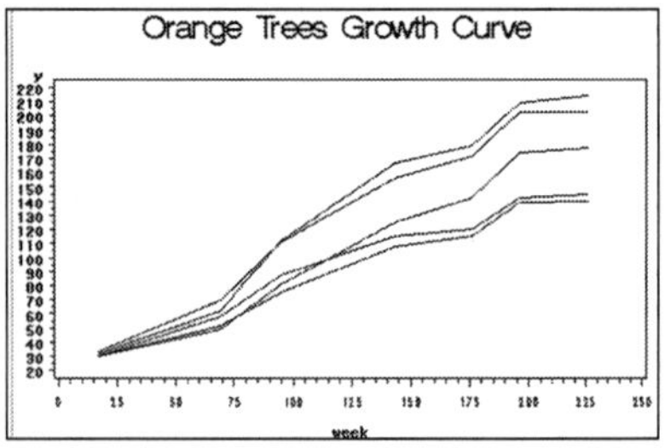

$$y_{ij} = \frac{\beta_1 + u_i}{1 + \beta_2 e^{-\beta_3 x_{ij}}} + \varepsilon_{ij}$$

7

Suppose you are a botanist studying growth patterns in five randomly selected orange trees. You record the trunk circumferences (y) of these five orange trees, measured at seven time points (in weeks), since planted (x). As an experienced botanist, you think a logistic growth model $y_{ij} = \frac{\beta_1}{1 + \beta_2 e^{-\beta_3 x_{ij}}} + \varepsilon_{ij}$ might be appropriate. In addition, you want to model the variation of the upper horizontal asymptote (the thickest a tree can get) among different trees, which is a random effect. You are dealing with a nonlinear mixed model. The linearity assumption between the expected value of y and the predictor variable x is violated in this example. They follow a logistic growth model, which is nonlinear in the parameters. You can use the NLMIXED procedure to analyze this data.

General Linear Models

$$y = X\beta + \varepsilon$$

unknown fixed effect

unknown random error

known design matrix

assume $\varepsilon \sim iid\ N(0, \sigma^2 I_n)$

therefore $E(y) = X\beta$, $Var(y) = \sigma^2 I_n$

9

In general linear models, you assume that

- errors ε_i are independently normally distributed with mean 0 and constant variance σ^2
- the expected values of the observations, $E(\mathbf{y})$, can be modeled by a linear function $\mathbf{X}\beta$.

The main functions of $\mathbf{X}\beta$ are to provide, for example, predicted $E(\mathbf{y})$ for a given $\mathbf{X}$, as in regression analysis, or comparisons among the $E(\mathbf{y})$ for various $\mathbf{X}$, as in the analysis of variance where functions of the $E(\mathbf{y})$ typically represent treatment means.

Generalized Linear Models

- The distribution of the observations can come from the exponential family of distributions:

  $$f(y) = \exp\{\frac{y\theta - b(\theta)}{a(\phi)} + c(y,\phi)\}$$

  – discrete responses: Bernoulli, Binomial, Poisson, negative Binomial, geometric
  – continuous responses: Normal, Gamma, Inverse Gaussian, Beta
- $\mathbf{X}\beta$ is fit to a function of E(y) (called link function) suggested by the distribution of the observations: $g(E(y)) = g(\mu) = \mathbf{X}\beta$.

Link function

10

In many situations, the normal error assumptions are violated, such as for the binary response variable or count data. Generalized linear models were defined by Nelder and Wedderburn (1972) and expanded upon by McCullagh and Nelder (1989).

Notice that a generalized linear model extends general linear models in two ways:

1. the distribution of the response can come from the family of exponential distributions; not necessarily normal as assumed in standard linear models.
2. the link function is introduced to fit the linear model. This link function must be monotonic, but does not have to be the identity function, as used in the standard linear models.

Details

The general form for a density or probability function of the exponential family can be expressed as

$$f(y) = \exp\{\frac{y\theta - b(\theta)}{a(\phi)} + c(y,\phi)\},$$

where θ is the natural location parameter and ϕ is the dispersion parameter.

For this family of distributions, it can be shown that the variance of y, Var(**y**), can be expressed as a function of the mean of **y** by $Var(y)=V(\mu)a(\phi)$, where $V(\mu)$ denotes the variance function, the function of the mean involved in Var(**y**), and $a(\phi)$ denotes a function of the dispersion parameter.

For example, a Bernoulli distribution has the following probability density function (pdf):

$f(y) = \pi^y(1-\pi)^{1-y}$ for $y = 0$ or 1. Rewriting this pdf yields

$$f(y) = \exp(y\ln\pi + (1-y)\ln(1-\pi))$$
$$= \exp\left(y\ln\left(\frac{\pi}{1-\pi}\right) + \ln(1-\pi)\right).$$

Comparing it with the general form of the pdf of exponential family distributions, you can see $\theta = \ln\left(\frac{\pi}{1-\pi}\right)$. This is how the canonical link function is determined.

Logit Link Function for Binary Response

$$\text{logit}(p) = \log\left(\frac{p}{1-p}\right)$$

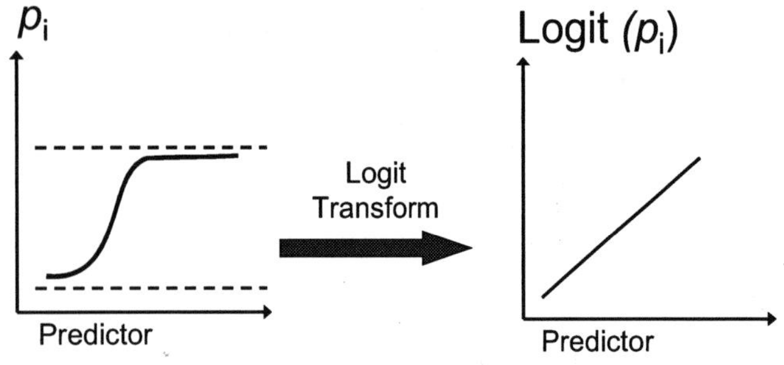

11

The *logit transformation* is the log of the *odds*, which is the ratio of the probability of the outcome to the probability of no outcome. Unlike a probability, the logit is unbounded because transforming the probability to odds removes the upper bound, whereas taking the natural logarithm of the odds removes the lower bound. The logit of the probability is assumed to be linearly related to the predictor variables (linear in its parameters.) Furthermore, the model gives estimated probabilities that are between 0 and 1.

Examples of Generalized Linear Models

Model	Distribution	Mean	Variance	Link	Inverse Link Function
linear regression	Normal	μ	σ^2	(identity) μ	identity
logistic regression	Binomial	π	$\pi(1-\pi)/n$	(logit) $\log[\pi/(1-\pi)]$	$\frac{1}{1+e^{-\text{logit}}}$
Poisson regression	Poisson	λ	λ	(log) $\log(\lambda)$	exponential

12

The link functions are monotonic functions that link the mean μ to the linear predictor η. Link functions shown above are called canonical link functions, which are obtained from the probability density function for each distribution. This is a common method of choosing the link function, but not the only way. The canonical link functions for normal, binomial, and Poisson data are identity, logit, and natural log, respectively. The variances for these three distributions are σ^2 (normal), $\pi(1-\pi)/n$ (binomial), and λ (Poisson), Other distributions from the exponential family of distributions include negative binomial, inverse Gaussian, gamma, and multinomial.

The model you fit to your data is $g(E(y))=g(\mu)=\mathbf{X}\beta$, where g is the link function that depends on the distribution of your response variable. To obtain the predicted value of $E(y)$, or μ, from the model output, you must use the inverse link function.

General Linear Mixed Models

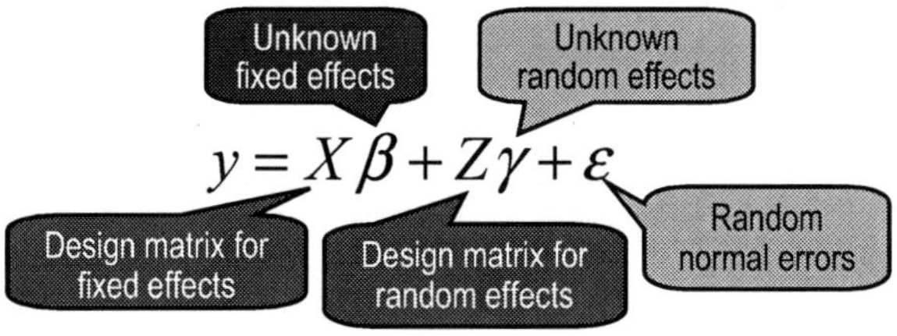

Assume $\gamma \sim \text{MVN}(0, \text{G}), \varepsilon \sim \text{MVN}(0, \text{R})$

The conditional mean and variance are

$$E(y \mid \gamma) = \mu = \text{X}\beta + Z\gamma,\ Var(y \mid \gamma) = \text{R} = \text{Var}(\varepsilon)$$

13

In general linear mixed models discussed thus far, you assume random effects and errors are independently normally distributed with a mean of zero and a variance-covariance matrix of **G** and **R**, respectively. The conditional mean of the observations given the random effects, $E(y|\gamma)$, or μ, and the conditional variance are shown above.

Generalized Linear Mixed Models

The generalized linear mixed model is

$$g(E(y \mid \gamma)) = g(\mu) = X\beta + Z\gamma$$

where $g(\mu)$ is the link function and μ is the conditional mean $E(y \mid \gamma)$.

14

In the generalized linear mixed model, you apply a link function to the conditional mean $E(y|\gamma)$. The conditional distribution of $y|\gamma$ plays the same role as the distribution of y in the fixed-effects generalized linear model. You apply the same basic strategies for fitting a generalized linear model to $E(y)$ in a fixed effect model to fitting a mixed model to conditional mean $E(y|\gamma)$.

However, to obtain the parameter estimates, you must obtain the marginal log-likelihood function, which is a challenge in fitting generalized linear mixed models (and nonlinear mixed models). The GLIMMIX procedure uses the linearization technique to approximate the model as a linear mixed model. The NLMIXED procedure uses numerical techniques to integrate out the random effects to obtain the marginal log-likelihood function, which is then maximized to obtain the parameter estimates.

Nonlinear Mixed Models

$$y_{ij} = f(x_{ij}, \beta, u_i) + e_{ij}$$

where

- f is some nonlinear function
- y_{ij} is the jth observation on the ith subject
- x_{ij} is a known vector of independent variables
- β is an unknown vector of fixed-effect parameters
- u_i is the unknown vector of random effect parameters
- e_{ij} are unknown random errors.

15

Not all data can be adequately characterized by linear models. Many applications, such as in physical sciences, pharmacokinetics, and so forth, require nonlinear models, and often with one or more random effects in the model. For example, to analyze a repeated measures data, you must fit a model that simultaneously accounts for the overall mean structure, which may be nonlinear in parameters, as well as both between- and within-subject variability. This situation calls for a nonlinear mixed model.

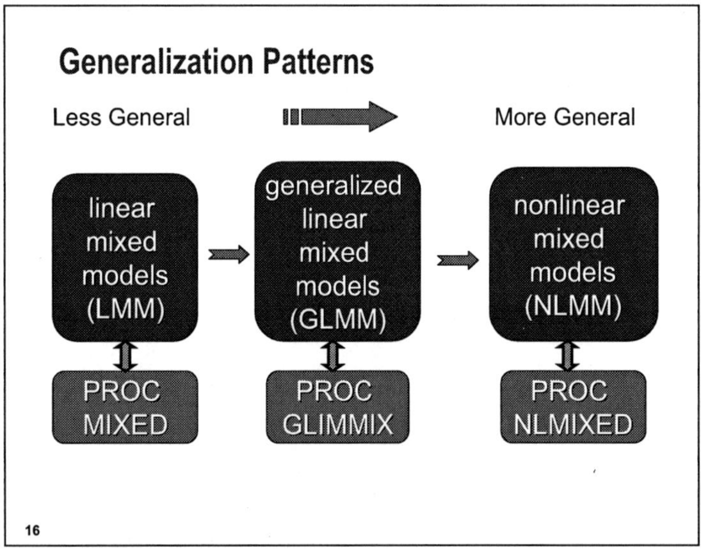

Generalized linear mixed models can be viewed as a generalization of linear mixed models and a special case of nonlinear mixed models. In generalized linear mixed models, the expected values of the responses linearly relate to the predictors through a link function. After applying the inverse link function, the expected values of the responses relate to the predictors nonlinearly, but the form of the nonlinear function is dictated by the link function. In nonlinear mixed models, the expected values of the responses can relate to the predictors through any type of nonlinear form.

Generally speaking, you use PROC MIXED to fit a linear mixed model, you use PROC GLIMMIX for generalized linear mixed models, and you use PROC NLMIXED for nonlinear mixed models.

7.2 Fitting a Generalized Linear Mixed Model Using the GLIMMIX Procedure

Objectives

- Fit a logistic regression model with random effects using the GLIMMIX procedure.

20

Drug Study Example

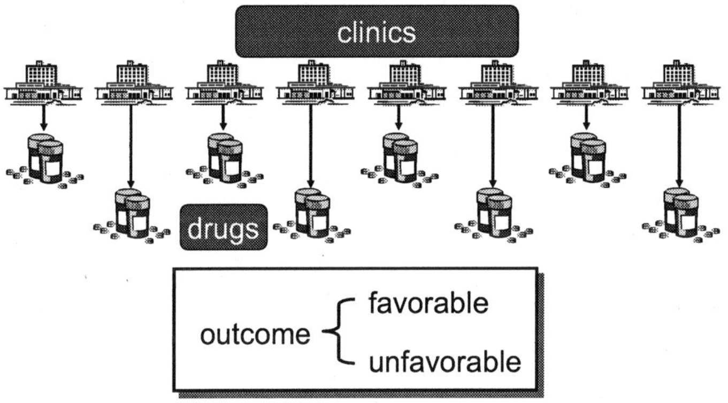

21

Consider the example introduced in the last section. A clinical trial study involved two drug treatments and eight clinics. The eight clinics represented a sample from a larger target population; therefore, `clinic` is a random effect. At each clinic i, n_{i1} subjects were randomly assigned to receive treatment 1 and n_{i2} subjects were randomly assigned to receive treatment 2. Each subject was classified as having a favorable or unfavorable response to the treatment. The objective of the study was to determine the effect of treatment on the probability of a favorable response across a population of clinics.

The Data

clinic	trt	fav	unfav	n
1	1	11	25	36
1	0	10	27	37
2	1	16	4	20
2	0	22	10	32
3	1	14	5	19
3	0	7	12	19
4	1	2	14	16
4	0	1	16	17
5	1	6	11	17
5	0	0	12	12
6	1	1	10	11
6	0	0	10	10
7	1	1	4	5
7	0	1	8	9
8	1	4	2	6
8	0	6	1	7

22

The data is stored in the SAS data set **sasuser.favorable**. These are the variables:

clinic clinic where the study was performed

trt treatment (1 = drug or 0 = control)

fav number of favorable responses

unfav number of unfavorable responses

n total number of subjects (**n**=**fav**+**unfav**)

The Model

$$fav_{ij} \mid c_i \sim Binomial(n_{ij}, p_{ij})$$

i = 1 to 8 (`clinic`)
j = 1, 2 (`trt`)

$$\eta_{ij} = \log\left(\frac{p_{ij}}{1-p_{ij}}\right) = \mu + t_j + c_i + (ct)_{ij}$$

trt effect, fixed

clinic effect, random

trt*clinic effect, random

link function logit(p_{ij})

23

fav_{ij}	the number of favorable responses for the ith clinic and the jth treatment ($i = 1,\ldots,8$ and $j = 0,1$)
c_i	the random effect of the ith clinic, assumed to be i.i.d. N(0, σ_c^2)
n_{ij}	the number of trials for the ith clinic and the jth treatment
p_{ij}	the probability of obtaining a favorable response for the ith clinic and the jth treatment
t_j	the jth treatment, an indicator variable (0 = control, 1 = drug)
μ	the overall mean
$(ct)_{ij}$	the interaction between the ith clinic and the jth treatment

The link function of p_{ij}, logit(p_{ij}) can be modeled as a linear function of the fixed and random effects.

The GLIMMIX Procedure

The GLIMMIX procedure is

- a new procedure in SAS/STAT for estimation and inference in generalized linear mixed models
- an add-on to SAS 9.1 for Windows, 64-bit UNIX, and LINUX operating systems
- available by download from support.sas.com
- available for SAS 9.2 for all platforms that are supported by SAS/STAT.

24

The GLIMMIX Procedure

General form of the GLIMMIX procedure:

```
PROC GLIMMIX options ;
    ...programming statements...;
    CLASS variables;
    MODEL response=fixed-effects / dist= link= options;
    RANDOM random-effects / options;
    RANDOM _residual_ / options;
RUN;
```

25

Selected GLIMMIX procedure statements:

CLASS names the classification variables to be used in the analysis. If the CLASS statement is used, it must appear before the MODEL statement.

MODEL names the dependent variable and the fixed effects. The fixed effects determine the X matrix of the model. In contrast to many other SAS/STAT procedures, continuous variables that are used as the response or fixed-effects in the MODEL statement can be computed through PROC GLIMMIX programming statements.

The dependent variable can be specified using either the *response* syntax or the *events/trials* syntax. The *events/trials* syntax is specific to models for binomial data. The MODEL statement is required.

RANDOM defines the random effects. The random effects can be classification or continuous, and multiple RANDOM statements are possible. The RANDOM statement defines the **Z** matrix of the mixed model, the random effects in the γ vector, the structure of **G**, and the structure of **R**.

The RANDOM _RESIDUAL_ statement indicates a residual-type (R-side) random component that defines the **R** matrix. Alternatively, you can use RANDOM *random-effects* / RESIDUAL *other-options*; to define the R-side random effects.

Selected MODEL statement options:

DIST= specifies the built-in (conditional) probability distribution of the data. If you specify the DIST= option and you do not specify a user-defined link function, a default link function is chosen. If you do not specify a distribution, the GLIMMIX procedure defaults to the normal distribution for continuous response variables and to the multinomial distribution for classification or character variables, unless the *events/trial* syntax is used in the MODEL statement. If you choose the *events/trial* syntax, the GLIMMIX procedure defaults to the binomial distribution.

LINK= specifies the link function in generalized linear mixed model.

The GLIMMIX procedure distinguishes two types of random effects. Depending on whether the variance of the random effect is contained in **G** or in **R**, these are referred to as *G-side* and *R-side* random effects. R-side effects are also named *residual* effects.

An R-side effect in the GLIMMIX procedure is equivalent to a REPEATED effect in the MIXED procedure. In the GLIMMIX procedure, all random effects are specified through the RANDOM statement.

GLMM Formulation

$$g(\mu \mid \gamma) = \mathbf{X}\beta + \mathbf{Z}\gamma$$

$Y|\gamma$ ~ exponential family

$var(\gamma) = G$

$Var(y|\gamma)=A_{\mu}^{1/2} R A_{\mu}^{1/2}$

26

Y represents the $(n \times 1)$ vector of observed data.

γ represents an $(r \times 1)$ vector of random effects.

$g(\cdot)$ represents a differentiable monotonic link function and $g^{-1}(\cdot)$ is its inverse.

X represents an $(n \times p)$ design matrix for the fixed effects with rank *k*.

Z represents an $(n \times r)$ design matrix for the random effects.

G represents the variance-covariance matrix for random effects. The random effects are assumed to be normally distributed with mean 0 and covariance matrix G. Random effects modeled through the G matrix are referred to as *G-side random effects.*

μ represents the expected value of Y.

$\mathbf{A}_{\mu}$ represents a diagonal matrix and contains the variance function of the model. The variance function expresses the variance of a response as a function of the mean.

R represents the variance-covariance matrix of the residual effects. The residual effects are referred to as the *R-side random effects*. The R matrix is, by default, the scaled identity matrix, $R=\phi I$, where ϕ is the scale parameter, and is, by definition, 1 for some distributions (for example, binary, binomial, Poisson, and exponential distribution). To specify a different R matrix, use the RANDOM statement with the _RESIDUAL_ keyword or the RESIDUAL option in the RANDOM statement.

R-side effects are also named *residual* effects. Simply put, if a random effect is an element of **G**, it is a G-side effect; otherwise, it is an R-side effect. Models without G-side effects are also known as *marginal* (or population-averaged) models. Models fit with the GLIMMIX procedure can have none, one, or more of each type of effect. An R-side effect in the GLIMMIX procedure is equivalent to a REPEATED effect in the MIXED procedure. In the GLIMMIX procedure, all random effects are specified through the RANDOM statement.

GLMM Formulation and PROC GLIMMIX

$$g(\mu \mid \gamma) = \mathbf{X}\beta + \mathbf{Z}\gamma$$

LINK= option

MODEL statement

RANDOM statement

$Y|\gamma$ ~ exponential family — DIST= option

$\mathrm{var}(\gamma) = G$ — Options in the RANDOM statement

$\mathrm{Var}(y \mid \gamma) = A_{\mu}^{1/2} R A_{\mu}^{1/2}$ — RANDOM _RESIDUAL_ statement

27

Fitting a Generalized Linear Mixed Model Using PROC GLIMMIX

```
proc glimmix data=sasuser.favorable;
   class trt clinic;
   model fav/n = trt / dist=binomial link=logit;
   random int trt / subject=clinic;
   lsmeans trt / oddsratio ilink diff;
run;                            ***c07s2d1.sas;
```

Selected PROC GLIMMIX statements:

MODEL — names the dependent variable and the fixed effects. The dependent variable can be specified using either the *response* syntax or the *events/trials* syntax. The *events/trials* syntax is specific to models for binomial data. The MODEL statement is required.

RANDOM — defines the random effects. The INTERCEPT (or INT) keyword is used in conjunction with the SUBJECT= option to block the **G** matrix for more efficient processing of the random effects.

LSMEANS — computes the least-squares means for fixed effects. Least-squares means estimate the marginal means over a balanced population. Least-squares means are constructed on the linked scale.

Selected MODEL statement options:

DIST= — specifies the built-in (conditional) probability distribution of the data. If you specify the DIST= option and you do not specify a user-defined link function, a default link function is chosen. If you do not specify a distribution, the GLIMMIX procedure defaults to the normal distribution for continuous response variables and to the multinomial distribution for classification or character variables, unless the *events/trial* syntax is used in the MODEL statement. If you choose the *events/trial* syntax, the GLIMMIX procedure defaults to the binomial distribution.

LINK= — specifies the link function in generalized linear mixed model.

Selected RANDOM statement option:

SUBJECT= — identifies the subjects in the model. Complete independence is assumed across subjects. Specifying a subject effect is equivalent to factoring out common factors in the effects specified in the RANDOM statement.

Selected options in the LSMEANS statement:

DIFF	requests that the differences of the least-squares means be displayed. The default comparison is for all pairwise differences (diff=ALL). Other types of comparisons include ANOM, CONTROL, CONTROLL, and CONTROLU. The ANOM value requests differences between each least-squares means and the average least-squares mean. The average is computed as the weighted mean of the least-squares means.
ILINK	requests that estimates and their standard errors in the Least Squares Means table are also reported on the scale of the mean (the inverse linked scale). This enables you to obtain estimates of predicted probabilities and their standard errors in logistic models, for example. If you also specify the CL option, the GLIMMIX procedure computes confidence intervals for the predicted means.
ODDSRATIO | OR	requests that differences of least-squares means are also reported in terms of the odds ratio. This option is ignored unless you are using either the LOGIT, CUMLOGIT, or GLOGIT link. If you specify the CL option, confidence intervals for the odds ratios are also computed. These intervals are adjusted for multiplicity when you specify the ADJUST= option.

PROC GLIMMIX Output

```
                         Model Information

          Data Set                         SASUSER.FAVORABLE
          Response Variable (Events)       fav
          Response Variable (Trials)       n
          Response Distribution            Binomial
          Link Function                    Logit
          Variance Function                Default
          Variance Matrix Blocked By       clinic
          Estimation Technique             Residual PL
          Degrees of Freedom Method        Containment
```

The Model Information table describes the data set, the response variables, the conditional distribution given the random effects, the link function, the variance function, the block (or the SUBJECT=) variable in the marginal covariance matrix, the estimation technique, and the degrees-of-freedom method used to estimate the denominator degrees of freedom for fixed effects. Always check the model information table to make sure that the correct distribution and link function are used.

The default estimation method for models containing random effects is RSPL (labeled as Residual PL in the Output), which is the acronym for the Residual Subject-specific Pseudo-Likelihood method. Other estimation methods include MSPL, RMPL, and MMPL. The first letter determines whether estimation is based on a residual likelihood (R) or a maximum likelihood (M). The second letter identifies the expansion locus for the linearization, which can be the vector of random effects solutions (S) or the mean of the random effects (M). You use the METHOD= option in PROC GLIMMIX to specify the estimation method.

If the model does not contain random effects, the GLIMMIX procedure estimates model parameters by residual maximum likelihood (for normally distributed data), maximum likelihood (for nonnormal data), or quasi-likelihood (for data with unknown distributions).

The default method of computing the denominator degrees of freedom for models containing G-side random effects is containment. Other methods include BETWITHIN, RESIDUAL, SATTERTH, KENWARDROGER, and NONE. Detailed information about each method is provided in the PROC GLIMMIX documentation.

```
                         Class Level Information

                    Class      Levels    Values

                    trt             2    0 1
                    clinic          8    1 2 3 4 5 6 7 8


                   Number of Observations Read          16
                   Number of Observations Used          16
                   Number of Events                    102
                   Number of Trials                    273
```

The Class Level Information table lists the levels of every variable specified in the CLASS statement. You should check this information to make sure the data is correct. You can adjust the order of the CLASS variable levels with the ORDER= option in the PROC GLIMMIX statement. Because the response is specified in the *events/trial* syntax, the total number of events and the total number of trials are also included in the Number of Observations table.

```
                               Dimensions

                    G-side Cov. Parameters           2
                    Columns in X                     3
                    Columns in Z per Subject         3
                    Subjects (Blocks in V)           8
                    Max Obs per Subject              2
```

The Dimensions table lists the size of the relevant matrices. The two G-side covariance parameters correspond to the clinic variance and trt*clinic variance. There are three columns in the **X** matrix, corresponding to an intercept and the two levels of **`trt`**. For each subject (**`clinic`**), the **Z** matrix contains three columns, one for the intercept and two for the two levels of **`trt`**.

```
                         Optimization Information

               Optimization Technique        Dual Quasi-Newton
               Parameters in Optimization    2
               Lower Boundaries              2
               Upper Boundaries              0
               Fixed Effects                 Profiled
               Starting From                 Data
```

Dual Quasi-Newton is the default optimization technique for generalized linear mixed models. Other optimization techniques can be found in the GLIMMIX procedure documentation. The two covariance parameters involved in the optimization are the **`clinic`** variance and **`trt*clinic`** variance. Both variance components have a lower boundary constraint: the variance estimates cannot be less than zero.

Iteration History

Iteration	Restarts	Subiterations	Objective Function	Change	Max Gradient
0	0	5	49.333442394	0.98121340	9.692E-6
1	0	4	50.203384936	0.22259161	0.000013
2	0	3	50.296648484	0.01554534	4.394E-6
3	0	2	50.301395017	0.00066927	4.714E-6
4	0	1	50.301576065	0.00002378	3.875E-6
5	0	0	50.301581858	0.00000000	3.843E-6

Convergence criterion (PCONV=1.11022E-8) satisfied.

The Iteration History table displays the progress of the optimization process. After five optimizations the process converged. The values for Subiterations indicate the number of iterations performed in each optimization step.

Fit Statistics

-2 Res Log Pseudo-Likelihood	50.30
Generalized Chi-Square	13.55
Gener. Chi-Square / DF	0.97

The ratio of the generalized chi-square statistic and its degrees of freedom is 0.97. This is a measure of the residual variability in the linearized pseudo-model. The smaller this value the better the model fits to the data.

Covariance Parameter Estimates

Cov Parm	Subject	Estimate	Standard Error
Intercept	clinic	2.0103	1.2716
trt	clinic	0.06057	0.2043

The Covariance Parameter Estimates table displays estimates and asymptotic standard errors for covariance parameters. The variance of the random **clinic** effect on the logit scale is estimated to be 2.0103. The variance of the random **trt*clinic** effect on the logit scale is estimated to be 0.06057, rather small compared with its standard error (0.2043) and the **clinic** variance (2.0103).

Type III Tests of Fixed Effects

Effect	Num DF	Den DF	F Value	Pr > F
trt	1	7	5.06	0.0592

The Type III Tests of Fixed Effects table indicates that **trt** is almost significant (p-value=0.0592). Different treatments seem to have a marginally significant effect on the probability of having a favorable response on the logit scale.

trt Least Squares Means

trt	Estimate	Standard Error	DF	t Value	Pr > |t|	Mean	Standard Error Mean
0	-1.1650	0.5657	7	-2.06	0.0784	0.2378	0.1025
1	-0.4164	0.5606	7	-0.74	0.4818	0.3974	0.1343

Differences of trt Least Squares Means

trt	_trt	Estimate	Standard Error	DF	t Value	Pr > |t|	Odds Ratio
0	1	-0.7485	0.3326	7	-2.25	0.0592	0.473

The Estimate column for each of the treatments is on the logit scale. The Mean column represents the probability of having a favorable response for the treatment. **Trt** 0 has a lower probability (0.24) compared with **trt** 1 (0.40).

The Differences of trt Least Squares Means table lists the comparison on the logit scale and the odds ratio as well. The odds ratio for **trt** 0 versus **trt** 1 is estimated to be 0.473. The odds of having a favorable response for **trt** 0 are 47.3% of the odds for **trt** 1. In other words, **trt** 1 is 2.11 (1/0.473 = 2.11) times the odds in terms of having favorable response compared with **trt** 0.

PROC GLIMMIX versus PROC MIXED

- PROC GLIMMX is **not** PROC MIXED with a LINK= and a DIST= option.
- PROC GLIMMIX models nonnormal data. PROC MIXED does not.
- PROC GLIMMIX allows programming statements. PROC MIXED does not.
- PROC GLIMMIX uses the RANDOM statement to model **R**-side random effects. PROC MIXED uses the REPEATED statement to model **R**-side random effects.

33

The GLIMMIX and MIXED procedures are closely related and have certain functionalities in common. However, there are important differences, such as no REPEATED statement in PROC GLIMMIX. Furthermore, MODEL, WEIGHT, and FREQ variables, as well as variables specifying RANDOM effects and SUBJECT= and GROUP= structures, do not have to be in the data set with PROC GLIMMIX. They can be computed with programming statements in the procedure.

Syntax: PROC GLIMMIX versus PROC MIXED

PROC GLIMMIX	PROC MIXED
BY	BY
CLASS	CLASS
CONTRAST	CONTRAST
ESTIMATE	ESTIMATE
FREQ	
ID	ID
LSMEANS	LSMEANS
LSMESTIMATE	
MODEL	MODEL
NLOPTIONS	
OUTPUT	
PARMS	PARMS
RANDOM	RANDOM
	REPEATED
WEIGHT	WEIGHT
<Programming Statements>	

34

The GLIMMIX and MIXED procedures are closely related to syntax although there are a few differences. Notice that both the FREQ statement and the WEIGHT statement are available in PROC GLIMMIX. The variable in the FREQ statement identifies a numeric variable that contains the frequency of occurrence for each observation. PROC GLIMMIX treats each observation as if it appears f times, where f is the value of the FREQ variable for the observation. The analysis that is produced using a FREQ statement reflects the expanded number of observations. The WEIGHT statement replaces $\mathbf{R}$ with $\mathbf{W}^{-1/2}\mathbf{R}\mathbf{W}^{-1/2}$, where $\mathbf{W}$ is a diagonal matrix containing the weights.

More detailed information about the GLIMMIX procedure can be found in the GLIMMIX documentation or the Live Web class Statistical Analysis with the GLIMMIX Procedure.

7.3 Fitting a Nonlinear Mixed Model Using the NLMIXED Procedure (Self-Study)

Objectives

- Fit a nonlinear mixed model using the NLMIXED procedure.

38

Orange Tree Growth Example

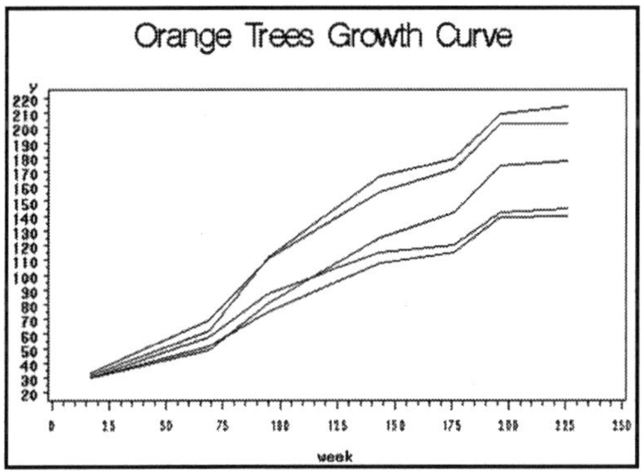

tree	week	y
1	16.86	30
1	69.14	58
1	94.86	87
......		

40

Suppose you are a botanist studying growth patterns in five randomly selected orange trees. The trunk circumferences of these five orange trees measured at seven time points (in weeks since planted) are recorded and stored in a SAS data set **`sasuser.trees`**. These are the variables in the data:

`y` the trunk circumference measurements in millimeters

`tree` trees' identification number (`1`, `2`, `3`, `4`, and `5`)

`week` the number of weeks since planting when the measurements were taken.

Orange Tree Growth Model

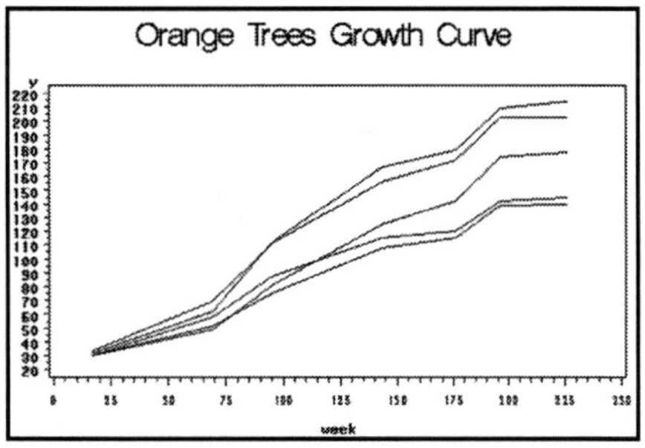

$$E[Y_{ij}] = \frac{\beta_1 + u_i}{1 + \beta_2 \exp(-\beta_3 x_{ij})}$$

$u_i \sim N(0, \sigma_u^2),\ i = 1 \text{ to } 5$

$Var[Y_{ij} \mid u_i] = \sigma^2$

β_1—upper horizontal asymptote

$\dfrac{\beta_1}{1+\beta_2}$ --y intercept

β_3—shape

41

As an experienced botanist, you think a logistic growth model $y = \dfrac{\beta_1}{1+\beta_2 e^{-\beta_3 x}} + e$ may be appropriate. In this model, β_1 estimates the upper horizontal asymptote, $\beta_1/(1+\beta_2)$ estimates the y-intercept, and β_3 indicates the shape of the curve (the bigger the value, the steeper the curve). You may also want to model the tree-to-tree variations by adding a random component to one or more of the model parameters.

The NLMIXED Procedure

General form of the NLMIXED procedure:

```
PROC NLMIXED options;
    PARMS parameters and starting values;
    programming statements;
    MODEL dependent ~ distribution;
    RANDOM random-effects ~ distribution
            SUBJECT=variable <options>;
    ESTIMATE 'label' expression;
    PREDICT expression;
RUN;
```

Programming statements enable you to code the log-likelihood function in PROC NLMIXED using DATA step statements.

42

Selected NLMIXED procedure statements:

PARMS — lists names of parameters and specifies initial values, possibly over a grid. You can specify the parameters and values either directly in a list or provide the name of a SAS data set that contains them using the DATA= option. Parameters not listed in the PARMS statement are assigned an initial value of 1.

MODEL — specifies the conditional distribution of the data given the random effects. You must specify a single dependent variable from the input data set, a tilde (~), and then a distribution with its parameters.

RANDOM — defines the random effects and their distribution. The random effects must be represented by symbols that appear in your SAS programming statements. Typically, they influence the mean value of the distribution specified in the MODEL statement. The RANDOM statement consists of a list of the random effects (usually just one or two symbols), a tilde (~), the distribution for the random effects, and then a SUBJECT= variable.

The only distribution currently available for the random effects is normal(m,v) with mean m and variance v. The SUBJECT= variable determines when new realizations of the random effects are assumed to occur. Your input data set should be clustered according to this variable.

ESTIMATE — enables you to compute an additional estimate that is a function of the parameter values.

PREDICT — enables you to construct predictions of an expression across all of the observations in the input data set.

✎ The models fit by PROC NLMIXED can be viewed as generalizations of the random coefficient models fit by the MIXED procedure. This generalization allows the random coefficients to enter the model nonlinearly, whereas in PROC MIXED they enter linearly.

Model Assumptions in PROC NLMIXED

- The conditional distribution of the data given the random effects can be normal, binary, binomial, Poisson, or of any general form.
- The means (expected values) of the responses and the predictor variables can have any nonlinear relationship.
- Random effects can enter the model nonlinearly.
- Random effects follow a normal distribution.

43

Fitting a Nonlinear Mixed Model Using the NLMIXED Procedure

First, you may want to graph the data to see how the circumferences change over time and also to obtain the initial values for the parameters:

```
goptions reset=all;
proc gplot data=sasuser.trees;
   symbol v=none c=black i=join r=5;
   axis1 value=(h=0.8) order=(0 to 250 by 25);
   axis2 order=(20 to 220 by 10);
   plot y*week=tree / nolegend haxis=axis1 vaxis=axis2;
   title 'Orange Trees Growth Curve';
run;
title;
quit;                                        *c07s3d1.sas;
```

Selected SYMBOL statement option:

R specifies the number of times that a SYMBOL definition is applied before the next SYMBOL definition is used. By default, REPEAT=1.

PROC GPLOT Output

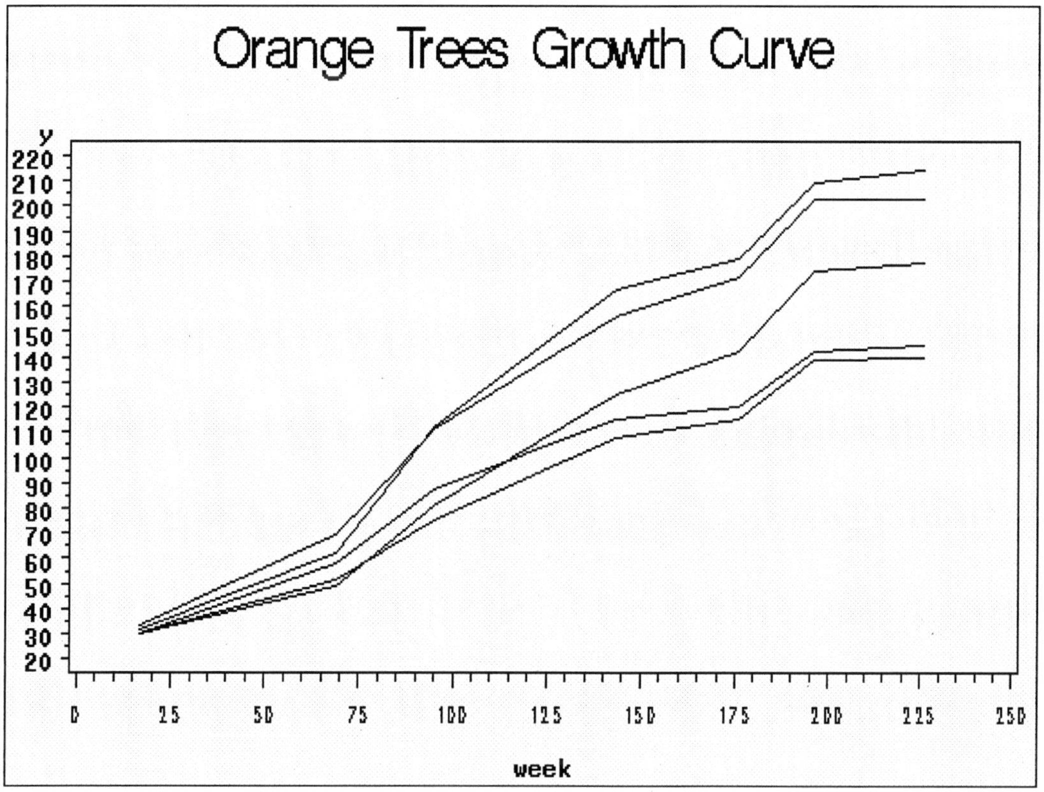

The plot shows a mild nonlinear trend along with a marked increase on variability over time. Although a higher order polynomial model with a heterogeneous variance-covariance structure may fit the data well, subject-matter knowledge suggests that a logistic growth model may be more interpretable and appropriate.

From the logistic growth model $y = \dfrac{\beta_1}{1+\beta_2 e^{-\beta_3 x}} + e$, you know that β_1 estimates the upper horizontal asymptote, $\beta_1/(1+\beta_2)$ estimates the y-intercept, and β_3 indicates the shape of the curve (the bigger the value, the steeper the curve). Based on the graph, you estimate good starting values as $\hat{\beta}_1$ =180, $\hat{\beta}_2$=8, and $\hat{\beta}_3$=0.6.

You also notice that the variations among the circumferences increase as the trees grow bigger. You may want to model the tree-to-tree variation by adding a random component to one of the model parameters. Based on the meanings of the model parameters and the plot of the data, you decide to model the variations among the trees by adding a random component to β_1, the upper horizontal asymptote.

An alternative approach of obtaining starting values for fixed effects parameters is to run the model without random effects using PROC NLIN.

The model becomes

$$y_{ij} = \frac{\beta_1 + u_i}{1+\beta_2 e^{-\beta_3 x_{ij}}} + e_{ij},$$

where

- y_{ij} is the jth observation for the ith tree.
- x_{ij} is the jth week for the ith tree.
- β_1, β_2, and β_3 are the fixed-effect parameters. β_1 estimates the upper horizontal asymptote, $\beta_1/(1+\beta_2)$ estimates the y-intercept, and β_3 indicates the shape of the curve.
- u_i is the random coefficient parameter that models the tree-to-tree random variation of the upper horizontal asymptote, in other words, the circumference that a full-grown tree approaches. This parameter is assumed to follow a normal distribution with mean 0 and variance σ_u^2.
- e_{ij} are the residual random errors and are assumed i.i.d. N(0, σ^2).

You assume that u_i and e_{ij} are independent normal random variables.

```
proc sort data=sasuser.trees;
   by tree;
run;

proc nlmixed data=sasuser.trees;
   parms b1=180 b2=8 b3=0.6 s2u=10 s2e=5;
   num=b1+u;
   den=1+b2*exp(-b3*week);
   pred=num/den;
   model y ~ normal(pred, s2e);
   random u ~ normal(0, s2u) subject=tree;
   predict pred out=preddata
run;
```

```
goptions reset=all;
proc gplot data=preddata;
   symbol1 v=none c=red i=join l=1;
   symbol2 v=none c=blue i=join l=3;
   symbol3 v=none c=green i=join l=5;
   symbol4 v=none c=purple i=join l=8;
   symbol5 v=none c=black i=join l=13;
   symbol6 v=circle c=red i=none;
   symbol7 v=star c=blue i=none;
   symbol8 v=square c=green i=none;
   symbol9 v=diamond c=purple i=none;
   symbol10 v=plus c=black i=none;
   axis2 label=(a=90);
   plot pred*week=tree / vaxis=axis2 nolegend;
   plot2 y*week=tree / noaxis nolegend;
   title1 'Predicted Orange Tree Growth Curve';
run;
title;
quit;                                        *c07s3d2.sas;
```

Your data must be grouped by the SUBJECT= variable specified in the RANDOM statement. Notice that you can use programming statements inside PROC NLMIXED to perform some calculations. Most of the programming statements that can be used in the SAS DATA step can also be used in PROC NLMIXED. For detailed information on available statements in PROC NLMIXED and their differences to DATA step programming statements, refer to the SAS®9 online documentation about PROC NLMIXED.

The MODEL statement's syntax in PROC NLMIXED differs from the MODEL statement's syntax in PROC MIXED or PROC GLIMMIX. You use the MODEL statement in PROC NLMIXED to specify the conditional distribution of the response variable.

The RANDOM statement is used to specify the random effects and their distribution (only the normal distribution is currently available). The random effects must be represented by symbols that appear in your SAS programming statements. Only one RANDOM statement is permitted, so multilevel nonlinear mixed models are not currently accommodated in PROC NLMIXED. The SUBJECT= specification is required in the RANDOM statement, and it determines when new realizations of the random effects are assumed to occur.

PROC MIXED (or PROC GLIMMIX) will internally sort the data by subjects when the subject effect is a classification effect. PROC NLMIXED will not do that. In fact, PROC NLMIXED treats the subject effect as PROC MIXED (or PROC GLIMMIX) does for continuous subject effects. Each value that is different from the previous one starts a new subject. Therefore, you must group your data by the SUBJECT= variable before running PROC NLMIXED (for example, use PROC SORT).

The PREDICT statement gives you the predicted value of p_{ij}, analogous to an EBLUP of p for a given treatment and clinic in the linear mixed model case.

Partial PROC NLMIXED Output

```
                              The NLMIXED Procedure

                                 Specifications

          Data Set                                    SASUSER.TREES
          Dependent Variable                          y
          Distribution for Dependent Variable         Normal
          Random Effects                              u
          Distribution for Random Effects             Normal
          Subject Variable                            tree
          Optimization Technique                      Dual Quasi-Newton
          Integration Method                          Adaptive Gaussian
                                                      Quadrature
```

PROC NLMIXED provides a number of estimation methods to numerically integrate a log-likelihood function (Integration Method) and to maximize the integrated likelihood (Optimization Technique). The default methods are shown in this table. More information about these integration methods and optimization techniques can be found in SAS®9 online documentation.

```
                                   Dimensions

                   Observations Used                      35
                   Observations Not Used                   0
                   Total Observations                     35
                   Subjects                                5
                   Max Obs Per Subject                     7
                   Parameters                              5
                   Quadrature Points                       1
```

The default integration method is Adaptive Gaussian Quadrature. PROC NLMIXED selects the number of quadrature points adaptively by evaluating the log-likelihood function at the starting values of the parameters until two successive evaluations have a small relative difference (defined by the QTOL= option). For this example, the number of quadrature points is 1.

```
                                 Fit Statistics

                   -2 Log Likelihood                   263.1
                   AIC (smaller is better)             273.1
                   AICC (smaller is better)            275.2
                   BIC (smaller is better)             271.2
```

The log-likelihood and fit statistics computed by PROC NLMIXED honor the distribution of the data and therefore are valid statistics for the purpose of model comparisons.

Parameter Estimates

Parameter	Estimate	Standard Error	DF	t Value	Pr > |t|	Alpha	Lower	Upper	Gradient
b1	192.05	15.6576	4	12.27	0.0003	0.05	148.58	235.53	5.584E-7
b2	8.0950	0.8566	4	9.45	0.0007	0.05	5.7167	10.4734	0.000021
b3	0.02011	0.001564	4	12.85	0.0002	0.05	0.01577	0.02445	-0.00045
s2u	1001.50	649.48	4	1.54	0.1979	0.05	-801.75	2804.75	1.627E-8
s2e	61.5059	15.8808	4	3.87	0.0179	0.05	17.4136	105.60	7.306E-7

The parameter estimates and related quantities are provided in the Parameter Estimates table. The variance of upper horizontal asymptote among trees is 1001.50, suggesting a fairly large amount of variation among the trees regarding the ultimate circumference a tree approaches.

PROC GPLOT Output

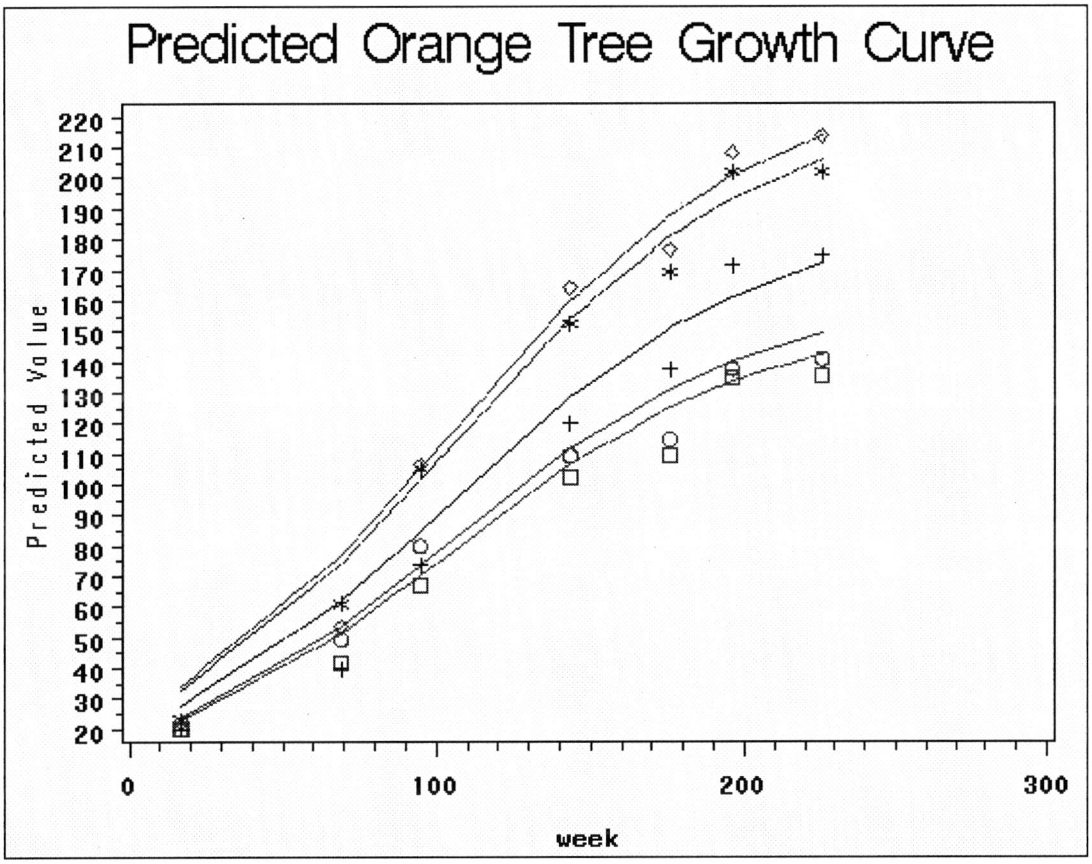

PROC NLMIXED versus PROC MIXED

- The models fit by PROC NLMIXED can be viewed as generalizations of the random coefficient models fit by PROC MIXED.
- PROC NLMIXED allows the random coefficients to enter the model nonlinearly; PROC MIXED does not.
- PROC MIXED assumes normally distributed data; PROC NLMIXED allows normal, binomial, Poisson, or any likelihood programmable with SAS statements.
- PROC MIXED performs ML or REML estimations; PROC NLMIXED only performs ML.
- PROC NLMIXED has no CLASS or REPEATED statement, only allows one RANDOM statement, and requires one SUBJECT= variable; PROC MIXED is just the opposite.

47

The models fit by PROC NLMIXED can be viewed as generalizations of the random coefficient models fit by PROC MIXED. This generalization allows the random coefficients to enter the model nonlinearly, whereas in PROC MIXED they enter linearly. PROC NLMIXED also allows data from normal, binomial, Poisson, or any other distributions whose likelihood functions can be programmed in SAS, whereas PROC MIXED only models normal data. PROC NLMIXED only implements maximum likelihood estimation, whereas PROC MIXED also performs REML estimation. PROC MIXED has a larger variety of covariance structures to choose from, and allows you to specify the CLASS statement and the REPEATED statement, as well as multiple RANDOM statements, whereas PROC NLMIXED does not offer any of these. The syntax for MODEL, RANDOM, CONTRAST, and ESTIMATE statements is different between PROC MIXED and PROC NLMIXED.

More detailed information about PROC NLMIXED, as well as the GLIMMIX and NLINMIX macros, can be obtained by taking the Live Web class Fitting Generalized Linear Mixed Models and Nonlinear Mixed Models Using the SAS System.

PROC NLMIXED versus PROC GLIMMIX

- PROC NLMIXED uses integral approximation to approximate the objective function; PROC GLIMMIX uses linearization to approximate the model.
- PROC NLMIXED does not have CLASS or RANDOM _RESIDUAL_ statements; PROC GLIMMIX can handle CLASS statements and the R-side random effects.
- PROC NLMIXED does not support more than one RANDOM statement or more than one SUBJECT= variable; PROC GLIMMIX supports multiple RANDOM statements and multiple SUBJECT= variables.
- PROC NLMIXED produces consistent results for binary outcome that has few clusters, few observations per cluster, large variance components, or success probability near 0 or 1; PROC GLIMMIX may produce biased results for these situations.

48

Please refer to Rodriguez and Goldman (1995), Goldstein and Rasbash (1996), Lin and Breslow (1996), and Breslow and Lin (1995) for more information about biased results in PROC GLIMMIX.

7.4 Chapter Summary

When model assumptions in the MIXED procedure are violated, you may be able to fit a generalized linear mixed model and/or a nonlinear mixed model to your data depending upon the situation.

Generalized linear mixed models extend general linear mixed models in two aspects: (1) the conditional distribution of the observation given random effects can come from the exponential family of distribution or of any general form; (2) a function of the conditional mean μ (called a link function) is linearly related to predictor variables, that is, $g(\mu)=g(E(y|\gamma)) = X\beta + Z\gamma$. Examples of the exponential family of distributions are binomial, Poisson, normal, negative binomial, and so on. The canonical link functions are suggested by the distribution of your data. You can use the GLIMMIX procedure to fit a generalized linear mixed model.

General form of the GLIMMIX procedure:

> **PROC GLIMMIX** *options* ;
>   *programming statements…;*
>   **CLASS** *variables*;
>   **MODEL** *response=fixed-effects* / ***dist***= ***link***= *options*;
>   **RANDOM** *random-effects / options;*
>   **RANDOM _RESIDUAL_** */ options;*
> **RUN**;

Nonlinear mixed models extend generalized linear mixed models one step further in the second aspect. In nonlinear mixed models, the expected values of the responses can relate to the predictor variables through any type of nonlinear form, not only limited to the inverse link function as in generalized linear mixed models. You use the NLMIXED procedure to fit a nonlinear mixed model.

The following is a summary of the self-study materials.

The models fit by PROC NLMIXED can be viewed as generalizations of the random coefficient models fit by PROC MIXED. This generalization allows the random coefficients to enter the model nonlinearly, whereas in PROC MIXED they enter linearly. PROC NLMIXED also allows data from normal, binomial, Poisson, or any other distributions whose likelihood functions can be programmed in SAS, whereas PROC MIXED only models normal data.

General form of the NLMIXED procedure:

> **PROC NLMIXED** *options*;
>   **PARMS** *parameters and starting values*;
>   **MODEL** *dependent ~ distribution;*
>   **RANDOM** *random-effects ~ distribution*
>   *SUBJECT=variable <options>;*
>   **ESTIMATE** *'label' expression;*
>   **PREDICT** *expression;*
>   *programming statements*;
> **RUN**;

Appendix A Exercises and Solutions

Chapter 1 Exercises

1. Analyzing a Randomized Complete Block Design Using the MIXED Procedure

An investigator wants to study the effect of three surfactants on the specific volume of bread loaves. Four flours from different sources are used as blocking factors. The data is stored in the SAS data set **`sasuser.bakery`** and these variables are included in the data set:

`flour`	the source of flour (1, 2, 3, or 4)
`surf`	the type of surfactant (1, 2, or 3)
`volume`	the volume of the bread loaf.

a. This is a randomized complete block design. **`flour`** is the blocking factor, and **`surf`** is the treatment factor of interest. Use pencil and paper to write the appropriate linear model for this design assuming that **`surf`** is a fixed effect and **`flour`** is a random effect.

b. Use the GPLOT procedure to examine **`volume`** versus **`flour`** for each level of **`surf`**. Does there seem to be any difference in the mean volumes across flours? How about across **`surf`**?

c. Use the MIXED procedure to determine whether there is a difference in the mean volumes using different surfactants. Use the LSMEANS statement with the DIFF option to determine which surfactants are different. What are the estimates of the variance components? What do you conclude about the fixed effect **`surf`**?

d. Use the CONTRAST statement in PROC MIXED to test the difference between volumes using surfactant 1 and 2. Also, estimate the difference and estimate the mean volume for surfactant 2.

Solutions to the Chapter 1 Exercises

1. Analyzing a Randomized Complete Block Design Using the MIXED Procedure

An investigator wants to study the effect of three surfactants on the specific volume of bread loaves. Four flours from different sources are used as blocking factors. The data is stored in the SAS data set **sasuser.bakery** and these variables are included in the data set:

flour the source of flour (1, 2, 3, or 4)

surf the type of surfactant (1, 2, or 3)

volume the volume of the bread loaf.

a. Write the appropriate linear model for this design assuming that **surf** is a fixed effect and **flour** is a random effect.

The model is $y_{ij} = \mu + \alpha_i + b_j + \varepsilon_{ij}$, where

μ is the overall mean

α_i is the fixed effect of the ith surfactant (i = 1, 2, or 3)

b_j is the random effect of the jth flour and is normally distributed with mean 0 and variance σ_b^2

ε_{ij} is the random error and is normally distributed with mean 0 and variance σ^2.

b. Use PROC GPLOT to examine **volume** versus **flour** for each level of **surf**.

```
goptions reset=all;
proc gplot data=sasuser.bakery;
   plot volume*flour=surf /
        vaxis=axis1 haxis=axis2 vminor=0 legend=legend1;
   axis1 label=(a=90);
   axis2 offset=(2,2) minor=none;
   legend1 frame;
   symbol1 v=circle c=red i=join l=1;
   symbol2 v=star c=blue i=join l=3;
   symbol3 v=dot c=green i=join l=5;
   title 'Volume vs Flour for Each Surfactant';
run;
title;
quit;
```

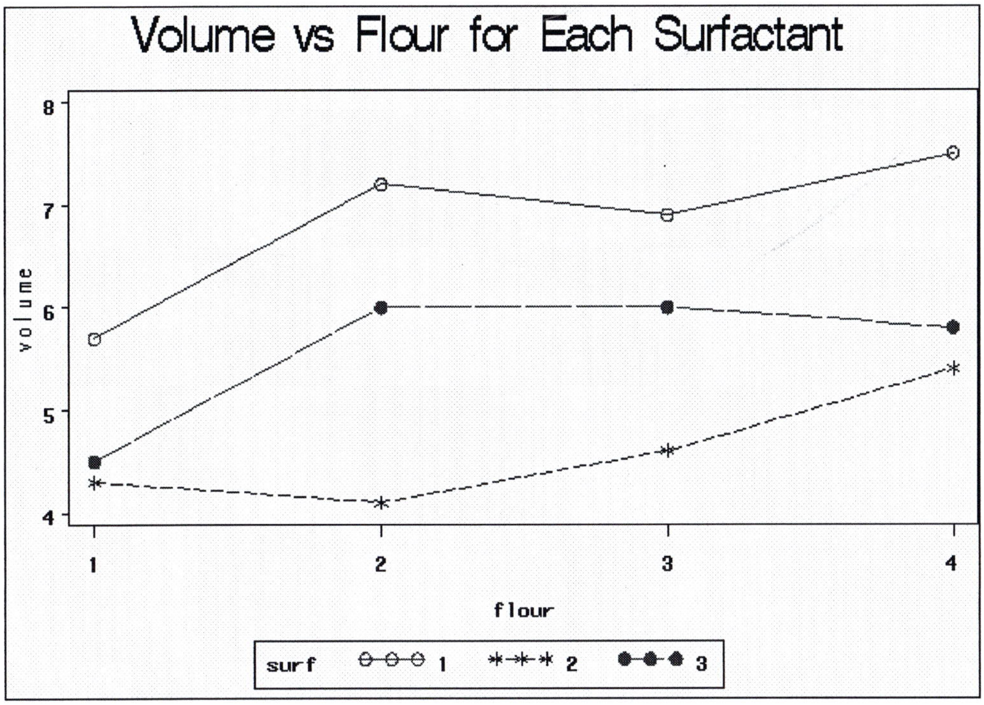

There appear to be differences between the average volumes among three surfactants: surfactant 1 appears to yield higher volume than surfactant 3, followed by surfactant 2. There also appear to be flour-to-flour variations, for example, flour 4 seems to have higher average volume than flour 1.

c. Use the MIXED procedure to determine whether there is a difference in the mean volumes using different surfactants. Use the LSMEANS statement with the DIFF option to determine which surfactants are different.

```
proc mixed data=sasuser.bakery;
   class surf flour;
   model volume=surf;
   random flour;
   lsmeans surf / diff;
run;
```

Partial PROC MIXED Output

Covariance Parameter Estimates

Cov Parm	Estimate
flour	0.2814
Residual	0.2092

Type 3 Tests of Fixed Effects

Effect	Num DF	Den DF	F Value	Pr > F
surf	2	6	23.79	0.0014

The estimates of the variance components are 0.2814 for **flour** and 0.2092 for **Residual**. The fixed effect **surf** has a significant effect on **volume** across all populations of flours of interest.

Least Squares Means

Effect	surf	Estimate	Standard Error	DF	t Value	Pr > |t|
surf	1	6.8250	0.3502	6	19.49	<.0001
surf	2	4.6000	0.3502	6	13.14	<.0001
surf	3	5.5750	0.3502	6	15.92	<.0001

Differences of Least Squares Means

Effect	surf	_surf	Estimate	Standard Error	DF	t Value	Pr > |t|
surf	1	2	2.2250	0.3234	6	6.88	0.0005
surf	1	3	1.2500	0.3234	6	3.87	0.0083
surf	2	3	-0.9750	0.3234	6	-3.01	0.0236

There appear to be significant differences between any two surfactants included in the study (surf 1 and surf 2, surf 1 and surf 3, surf 2 and surf 3). Note that the standard error for the least squares means is 0.3502; the standard error of the difference between the least squares means is 0.3234.

d. Use the CONTRAST statement in PROC MIXED to test the difference between volumes using surfactant 1 and 2. Also, estimate the difference and estimate the mean volume for surfactant 2.

```
proc mixed data=sasuser.bakery;
   class surf flour;
   model volume=surf;
   random flour;
   contrast '1 vs 2' surf 1 -1 0;
   estimate '1 vs 2' surf 1 -1 0;
   estimate 'surf 2 mean' intercept 1 surf 0 1 0;
run;
```

Partial PROC MIXED Output

Estimates

Label	Estimate	Standard Error	DF	t Value	Pr > |t|
1 vs 2	2.2250	0.3234	6	6.88	0.0005
surf 2 mean	4.6000	0.3502	6	13.14	<.0001

Contrasts

Label	Num DF	Den DF	F Value	Pr > F
1 vs 2	1	6	47.34	0.0005

The mean **volume** for surfactant 1 is 2.225 higher than that for surfactant 2, and this difference is significant. The average volume for surfactant 2 is 4.6. The standard errors are consistent with the LSMEANS results: 0.3234 for the difference between treatment means, and 0.3502 for the treatment mean.

Chapter 2 Exercises

1. **Fitting a Two-Way Mixed Model**

   A market researcher is interested in comparing the average monthly sales of three brands (A, B, and C) of washing machines at various types of stores. She wants to see whether certain brands of washing machines sell better at certain types of stores. There are three stores that she can investigate, although she wants to make inferences about the population of various types of stores. The types of stores are `depart`, `nation`, and `region` in her study. The response is **`sales`**. The 9 treatment combinations are replicated 4 times for a total of 36 observations. The data is stored in a SAS data set **`sasuser.washer`**. The variables included in the data set are **`brand`**, **`store`**, and **`sales`**.

   a. Is **`brand`** a fixed effect or a random effect? How about **`store`** and **`brand*store`**?

   b. Write the linear model for this design. What are the expected value and variance of an observation?

   c. Analyze this design using the MIXED procedure. What are the estimates of variance components? Is **`brand`** a significant factor?

   d. Add CONTRAST and ESTIMATE statements to compare the average monthly sales of brand A and brand B.

2. **Analyzing a Nested Data**

   A large school district is studying four sets of instructional materials and their relationship to test scores on a standardized test. Twenty teachers are randomly selected to use these materials in their classes. Each set of materials will be used by five teachers in classes consisting of six randomly selected students. The data is stored in a SAS data set **`sasuser.sscores`**, and include the following variables:

`material`	type of instructional material (A, B, C, or D)
`teacher`	teachers selected for the study (1 to 5 for each type of material)
`student`	student id (1 to 6 for each teacher)
`score`	score of student on standardized test.

   a. Use the PRINT procedure to print out the data set **`sasuser.sscores`**.

   b. Are the teachers nested within materials or crossed with materials? Why?

   c. Use the MIXED procedure to analyze this data, specifying **`teacher(material)`** as a random effect. Use the CL option in the PROC MIXED statement to obtain confidence limits for the variance components. What is the estimated variance component for the teacher random effect? Is **`material`** a significant factor?

   d. Use METHOD=TYPE3 option in the PROC MIXED statement to analyze this data again. Is the variance of **`teacher(material)`** significant? What is the error term for the **`material`** effect?

3. Fitting a Model for a Split-Plot Design

A fabric manufacturer wants to determine which combination of polymer and coating produces the strongest clothing fabric. The manufacturer decides to evaluate the effect of three polymers and two coatings in a split-plot design. Five lots of fabric rolls are randomly selected from the warehouse. Each polymer is applied to a fabric roll randomly selected from each lot. The rolls are then cut into two, and each coating is randomly assigned to a half roll of fabric. The simple diagram of this experiment is shown as follows:

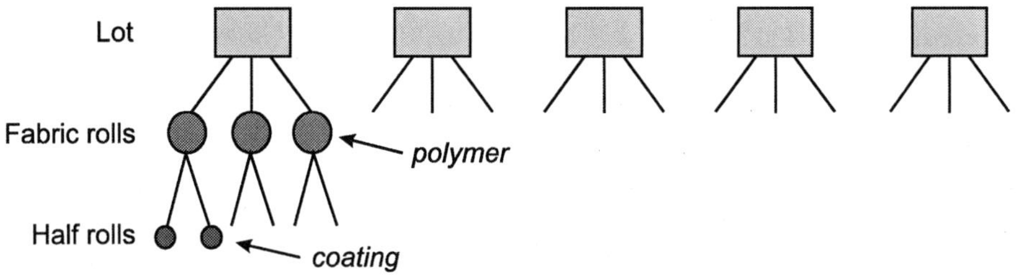

The data is stored in a SAS data set **sasuser.fibers**. These variables are in the data set:

coating	coating type
lot	lot number
polymer	polymer type
strength	strength measurement.

a. Generate an interaction plot displaying the mean strength for the six treatments (**polymer*coating** combinations). You may want to use the file **exercise_template.sas** for this exercise. The steps are outlined below.

1) Compute the treatment means using PROC MEANS with the NWAY option to produce only the six treatment means. Use an OUTPUT statement to save the means to an output data set.

2) Produce a plot of the mean **strength** versus **polymer** by **coating** using the GPLOT procedure. Use SYMBOL statements to identify each level of **coating** with colors and symbols. Use the I=JOIN option to connect the means for each level of **polymer**.

Does there appear to be a **polymer*coating** interaction?

b. What is the blocking factor? What is the whole-unit? The whole-unit treatment? What is the split-unit? The split-unit treatment?

c. Which of the effects (**lot**, **polymer**, **coating**, **lot*polymer**, and **polymer*coating**) are fixed effects? Which of them are random effects?

d. Fit a model using the MIXED procedure for this split-plot design. Use the CL option in the PROC MIXED statement to obtain 95% confidence limits for variance components. Use an LSMEANS statement to compare mean strength for different polymers.

Solutions to Chapter 2 Exercises

1. Fitting a Two-Way Mixed Model

a. The variable `brand` is a fixed effect, whereas `store` and `brand*store` are random effects.

b. $Y_{ijk} = \mu + \alpha_i + b_j + (\alpha b)_{ij} + \varepsilon_{ijk}$, where

Y_{ijk} the kth monthly sales of the ith brand of washing machine at the jth type of store

α_i fixed effect of the ith brand

b_j random effect of the jth store where $b_j \sim N(0, \sigma_b^2)$

$(\alpha b)_{ij}$ random interaction between the ith brand and the jth store where $(\alpha b)_{ij} \sim N(0, \sigma_{\alpha b}^2)$

ε_{ijk} experimental error of the kth observation for the ith brand in the jth store where $\varepsilon_{ijk} \sim N(0, \sigma^2)$.

The effects b_j, $(\alpha b)_{ij}$ and ε_{ijk} are assumed to be independent random variables.

Therefore,

- $E(Y_{ijk}) = \mu + \alpha_i$ is the mean for brand i averaged across all the stores in the population
- $Var(Y_{ijk}) = \sigma_b^2 + \sigma_{\alpha b}^2 + \sigma^2$ is the variance of an observation.

c. Analyze this design using the MIXED procedure.

```
proc mixed data=sasuser.washer;
   class brand store;
   model sales=brand / ddfm=kr;
   random store brand*store;
run;
```

Partial PROC MIXED Output

```
                 Covariance Parameter
                       Estimates

                Cov Parm        Estimate

                store             3.4931
                brand*store       339.57
                Residual          197.91
```

The estimated variance components are 3.49 for **store**, 339.57 for **brand*store** interaction, and 197.91 for **Residual**.

```
             Type 3 Tests of Fixed Effects

                      Num     Den
        Effect         DF      DF    F Value    Pr > F

        brand           2       4       2.87    0.1687
```

The variable **brand** does not appear to have a significant effect on the **sales** across all population of types of stores.

d. Add CONTRAST and ESTIMATE statements to compare the average monthly sales of brand A and brand B.

```
proc mixed data=sasuser.washer;
   class brand store;
   model sales=brand / ddfm=kr;
   random store brand*store;
   contrast 'brand A vs brand B' brand 1 -1;
   estimate 'brand A vs brand B' brand 1 -1;
run;
```

Partial PROC MIXED Output

Estimates

Label	Estimate	Standard Error	DF	t Value	Pr > |t|
brand A vs brand B	-19.5833	16.1048	4	-1.22	0.2908

Contrasts

Label	Num DF	Den DF	F Value	Pr > F
brand A vs brand B	1	4	1.48	0.2908

The average monthly sales for brand A is 19.58 lower than those for brand B, and this difference is not statistically significant (p-value=0.2908).

2. Analyzing a Nested Data

A large school district is studying four sets of instructional materials and their relationship to test scores on a standardized test. Twenty teachers are randomly selected to use these materials in their classes. Each set of materials will be used by five teachers in classes consisting of six randomly selected students. The data is stored in a SAS data set **sasuser.sscores** and include **material**, **teacher**, **student** and **score**.

a. Use the PRINT procedure to print out the data set **sasuser.sscores**.

```
proc print data=sasuser.sscores;
run;
```

Partial PROC PRINT Output

Obs	material	teacher	student	score
1	A	1	1	92
2	A	1	2	93
3	A	1	3	88
4	A	1	4	91
5	A	1	5	95
6	A	1	6	89
7	A	2	1	94
8	A	2	2	86
9	A	2	3	91
10	A	2	4	98
11	A	2	5	82
12	A	2	6	95
13	A	3	1	91
14	A	3	2	99
15	A	3	3	92
16	A	3	4	100
17	A	3	5	92
18	A	3	6	88
19	A	4	1	91
20	A	4	2	99
21	A	4	3	97
22	A	4	4	98
23	A	4	5	94
24	A	4	6	97
25	A	5	1	92
26	A	5	2	90
27	A	5	3	91
28	A	5	4	89
29	A	5	5	95
30	A	5	6	90
31	B	1	1	104
32	B	1	2	102
33	B	1	3	102
34	B	1	4	105
35	B	1	5	106
36	B	1	6	106

b. Are the teachers nested within materials or crossed with materials? Why?

Teachers are nested within materials because each teacher used only one of the four materials. If teachers and materials were crossed, the same teacher would be using all four materials.

c. Use the MIXED procedure to analyze this data, specifying **teacher(material)** as a random effect. Use the CL option in the PROC MIXED statement to obtain confidence limits for the variance components. What is the estimated variance component for the teacher random effect? Is **material** a significant factor?

```
proc mixed data=sasuser.sscores cl;
   class teacher material;
   model score=material / ddfm=kr;
   random teacher(material);
run;
```

Partial PROC MIXED Output

Covariance Parameter Estimates

Cov Parm	Estimate	Alpha	Lower	Upper
teacher(material)	34.6596	0.05	18.4470	87.5230
Residual	17.2550	0.05	13.3180	23.2478

The estimated variance for the teacher random effect is 34.66 and it is significantly different from zero.

Type 3 Tests of Fixed Effects

Effect	Num DF	Den DF	F Value	Pr > F
material	3	16	0.54	0.6647

material is not significant (p-value = 0.6647).

d. Use METHOD=TYPE3 option in the PROC MIXED statement to analyze this data again. Is the variance of **teacher(material)** significant? What is the error term for the **material** effect?

```
proc mixed data=sasuser.sscores method=type3;
   class teacher material;
   model score=material / ddfm=kr;
   random teacher(material);
run;
```

Partial PROC MIXED Output

Type 3 Analysis of Variance

Source	DF	Sum of Squares	Mean Square	Expected Mean Square
material	3	361.691667	120.563889	Var(Residual) + 6 Var(teacher(material)) + Q(material)
teacher(material)	16	3603.400000	225.212500	Var(Residual) + 6 Var(teacher(material))
Residual	100	1725.500000	17.255000	Var(Residual)

Type 3 Analysis of Variance

Source	Error Term	Error DF	F Value	Pr > F
material	MS(teacher(material))	16	0.54	0.6647
teacher(material)	MS(Residual)	100	13.05	<.0001
Residual	.	.	.	.

The **teacher(material)** variance is significantly different from zero (p-value < 0.0001). The error term for the F-test for the **material** effect is MS(teacher(material)).

Covariance Parameter Estimates

Cov Parm	Estimate
teacher(material)	34.6596
Residual	17.2550

Type 3 Tests of Fixed Effects

Effect	Num DF	Den DF	F Value	Pr > F
material	3	16	0.54	0.6647

3. Fitting a Model for a Split-Plot Design

A fabric manufacturer wants to determine which combination of polymer and coating produces the strongest clothing fabric. The manufacturer decides to evaluate the effect of three polymers and two coatings in a split-plot design. Five lots of fabric rolls are randomly selected from the warehouse. Each polymer is applied to a fabric roll randomly selected from each lot. The rolls are then cut into two, and each coating is randomly assigned to a half roll of fabric. The simple diagram of this experiment is shown as follows:

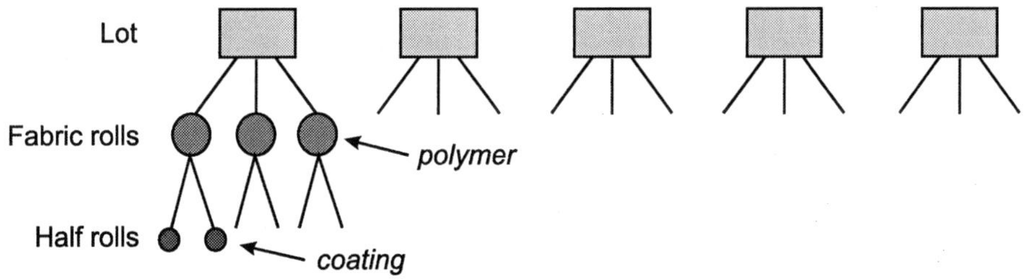

The data is stored in a SAS data set **sasuser.fibers**. The variables in the data set are **coating**, **lot**, **polymer**, and **strength**.

a. Generate an interaction plot displaying the mean strength for the six treatments (**`polymer*coating`** combinations).

```
proc means data=sasuser.fibers nway;
   class polymer coating;
   var strength;
   output out=meanout mean=meanstr;
run;

proc gplot data=meanout;
   symbol1 v=circle c=red i=join l=1;
   symbol2 v=star c=blue i=join l=2;
   plot meanstr*polymer=coating;
run;
quit;
```

PROC GPLOT Output

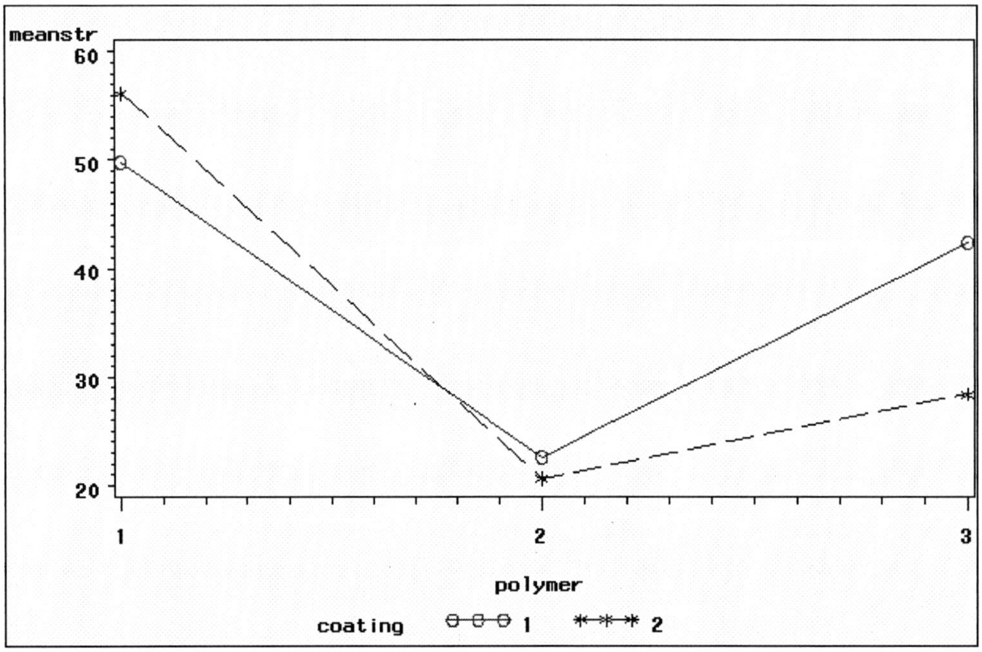

There could be a significant interaction between **`polymer`** and **`coating`** because the **`coating`** effect is not consistent across all levels of **`polymer`**.

b. The blocking factor is **`lot`**, the whole-unit is a roll, the whole-unit treatment is **`polymer`**, the split-unit is a half roll, and the split-unit treatment is **`coating`**.

c. The variable **`lot`** is a random effect, and the variables **`polymer`** and **`coating`** are fixed effects. Therefore, **`lot*polymer`** is a random effect, which for this example corresponds to the whole-plot error. The interaction term **`polymer*coating`** is a fixed effect.

d. Fit a model using the MIXED procedure for this split-plot design. Use the CL option in the PROC MIXED statement to obtain 95% confidence limits for variance components. Use an LSMEANS statement to compare mean strength for different polymers.

```
proc mixed data=sasuser.fibers cl;
   class lot polymer coating;
   model strength=polymer|coating / ddfm=kr;
   random lot lot*polymer;
   lsmeans polymer / diff;
run;
```

Partial PROC MIXED Output

Covariance Parameter Estimates

Cov Parm	Estimate	Alpha	Lower	Upper
lot	56.2958	0.05	8.2911	37548088
lot*polymer	53.5042	0.05	5.7306	7.997E14
Residual	421.30	0.05	216.64	1148.01

The covariance parameter estimates and their associated 95% confidence limits are given as shown above. The wide range of the confidence limits is probably due to the small degrees of freedom estimated using KENWARDROGER approximation.

Type 3 Tests of Fixed Effects

Effect	Num DF	Den DF	F Value	Pr > F
polymer	2	8	4.69	0.0449
coating	1	12	0.18	0.6770
polymer*coating	2	12	0.62	0.5524

There does not appear to be a significant interaction effect, nor does **`coating`** significantly affect strength. However, **`polymer`** does have a significant effect on strength (*p*-value=0.045).

Least Squares Means

Effect	polymer	Estimate	Standard Error	DF	t Value	Pr > |t|
polymer	1	53.0000	8.0056	11.3	6.62	<.0001
polymer	2	21.6000	8.0056	11.3	2.70	0.0203
polymer	3	35.4000	8.0056	11.3	4.42	0.0010

Differences of Least Squares Means

Effect	polymer	_polymer	Estimate	Standard Error	DF	t Value	Pr > |t|
polymer	1	2	31.4000	10.2792	8	3.05	0.0157
polymer	1	3	17.6000	10.2792	8	1.71	0.1252
polymer	2	3	-13.8000	10.2792	8	-1.34	0.2163

In terms of the mean strength of clothing fabrics, polymer 1 is significantly different from polymer 2.

Chapter 3 Exercises

1. Fitting an Analysis of Covariance Model with Random Effects

Recall the **sasuser.heart** data you analyzed previously in the Crossover Design section in Chapter 2.

A pharmaceutical company conducted a clinical trial to assess the effects of three treatments on the heart rate of patients. The treatments were placebo (p), control (c), and the test drug (a). Each patient in the study received the three treatments in a random order during a time period that was separated from the others, so that one treatment did not influence the heart rate measurement obtained after administering the other treatment (in other words, to rule out carry-over effect). Each period was a visit to the clinic. The sequences of administering the treatments were A(a p c), B(p c a), C(c a p), D(a c p), E(c p a), and F(p a c). The drugs were assigned to twenty-four patients in a three-period crossover design, with four patients for each sequence. The data set includes the following variables:

patient	patient (subject) ID
sequence	the sequence the drugs were administered to each patient
visit	the visit to the clinic
drug	the drugs under investigation
hr1h	the heart rate one hour after the drug was given to the patient
basehr	baseline heart rate for the patient.

a. Use the GPLOT procedure to plot **hr1h** versus **basehr** for each **drug**, **visit** and **sequence**. What do you think about the slopes?

b. Use the MIXED procedure to fit an analysis of covariance model to this data. Include two-way interactions of **basehr** and **drug**, **basehr** and **visit**, and **basehr** and **sequence**. Are they significant?

c. Remove nonsignificant interaction terms one at a time until all the interaction terms are significant. What is the variance estimate for **patient**? Does drug appear to be significant? How about the covariate **basehr**?

d. Perform all pairwise comparisons among the drugs at the average value for **basehr**. Which drugs seem to be different?

2. Fitting a Random Coefficient Model

Data is collected from 7181 high school students from 160 schools and is stored in a SAS data set **`sasuser.school`**. These selected variables are in the data set:

`student_id`	numeric code that uniquely identifies each student
`math`	continuous variable that indicates student's mathematical ability
`ses`	grand mean centered continuous variable that indicates the student's socioeconomic status
`school_id`	numeric code that identifies the school the student attends.

One of the objectives of the study is to evaluate the relationship between students' mathematical ability (**`math`**) and the students' socioeconomic status (**`ses`**), accounting for school-to-school variations.

a. Use the GPLOT procedure to produce a scatter plot of **`math`** versus **`ses`**.

b. Do you think it is reasonable to treat **`school_id`** as a random effect? Why?

c. Fit a random coefficient model to this data. Use the OUTP= option in the MODEL statement to save the predicted values. What is the estimated variance in the intercepts among the schools? What is the estimated variance in the rates of change (slopes) among the schools?

d. Use the GPLOT procedure to produce subject (school) specific plots. Use the NOLEGEND option in the PLOT statement. Use the following SYMBOL statement: **`symbol v=none i=j r=160 l=1;`**

3. Fitting a Hierarchical Linear Model

The data set **`sasuser.school`** you analyzed in the previous exercise has another variable **`school_disclim`** that is a continuous variable that measures the disciplinary climate of the school. This is a variable measured at the school level rather than the student level.

Fit a model to evaluate how **`math`** is related to **`ses`** accounting for school variance and incorporating the variable **`school_disclim`**. Use the SOLUTION option in both the MODEL statement and the RANDOM statement. What are the covariance parameter estimates and what do they correspond to? What fixed effects are significant?

4. Fitting another Hierarchical Linear Model

Data is collected for students who took a standardized exam and received scores on a quantitative scale and a qualitative scale in a school district. The students are in classes taught by teachers, and teachers teach in a particular school. In addition, the students are classified according to a socio-economic criterion with two levels (0 and 1). Data is stored in a SAS data set **`sasuser.scores`**. These variables are included in the data set:

`school`	schools in a school district
`teacher`	teachers in each school
`student`	students taught by teachers
`social`	the socio-economic criterion (0 or 1) for a student
`scale`	the scales the test scores are for (`qual` or `quan`)
`score`	the test scores.

a. Identify the data structure. Which factor is nested within teachers? Which factor is nested within schools? Are **`student`** and **`teacher`** fixed effects or random effects? Is **`school`** a fixed effect or random effect? (Hint: You have data for all schools in a school district.) Are there any fixed effects that are crossed with students, teachers, or schools?

b. Assume that schools, teachers, and students have unique identification codes. The linear model for your data is

$y_{ijksm} = \mu + \alpha_i + \beta_k + (\alpha\beta)_{ik} + \tau_m + (\alpha\tau)_{im} + (\beta\tau)_{km} + t_{jm} + e_{ijksm}$, where

- α_i, β_k, and τ_m are effects of school, socio-economic criterion, and scale, respectively
- $(\alpha\beta)_{ik}$, $(\alpha\tau)_{im}$, and $(\beta\tau)_{km}$ are associated interaction effects
- t_{jm} is the random effect for teacher j on scale m
- e_{ijksm} is the random error.

Write a linear model considering the qualitative scale separately from the quantitative scale.

c. Fit a model to your data using the MIXED procedure. Consider the scales separately using the BY statement. You must sort your data by **`scale`** first. What conclusions do you draw concerning the fixed effects?

Solutions to Chapter 3 Exercises

1. Fitting an Analysis of Covariance Model with Random Effects

Recall the **sasuser.heart** data you analyzed previously in the Crossover Design section in Chapter 2.

A pharmaceutical company conducted a clinical trial to assess the effects of three treatments on the heart rate of patients. The treatments were placebo (p), control (c), and the test drug (a). Each patient in the study received the three treatments in a random order during a time period that was separated from the others, so that one treatment did not influence the heart rate measurement obtained after administering the other treatment (in other words, to rule out carry-over effect). Each period was a visit to the clinic. The sequences of administering the treatments were A(a p c), B(p c a), C(c a p), D(a c p), E(c p a), and F(p a c). The drugs were assigned to twenty-four patients in a three-period crossover design, with four patients for each sequence. The variables included in the data set are **patient**, **sequence**, **visit**, **drug**, **hr1h**, and **basehr**.

a. Use the GPLOT procedure to plot **hr1h** versus **basehr** for each **drug**, **visit**, and **sequence**. What do you think about the slopes?

```
goptions reset=all;
proc gplot data=sasuser.heart;
   plot hr1h*basehr=drug / regeqn;
   symbol1 v=star i=r c=black l=1;
   symbol2 v=circle i=r c=red l=3;
   symbol3 v=diamond i=r c=blue l=5;
run;
quit;

proc gplot data=sasuser.heart;
   plot hr1h*basehr=visit / regeqn;
run;
quit;

proc gplot data=sasuser.heart;
   plot hr1h*basehr=sequence / regeqn;
   symbol1 v='A' i=r c=black l=1;
   symbol2 v='B' i=r c=red l=3;
   symbol3 v='C' i=r c=blue l=5;
   symbol4 v='D' i=r c=green l=8;
   symbol5 v='E' i=r c=purple l=13;
   symbol6 v='F' i=r c=orange l=15;
run;
quit;
```

PROC GPLOT Output

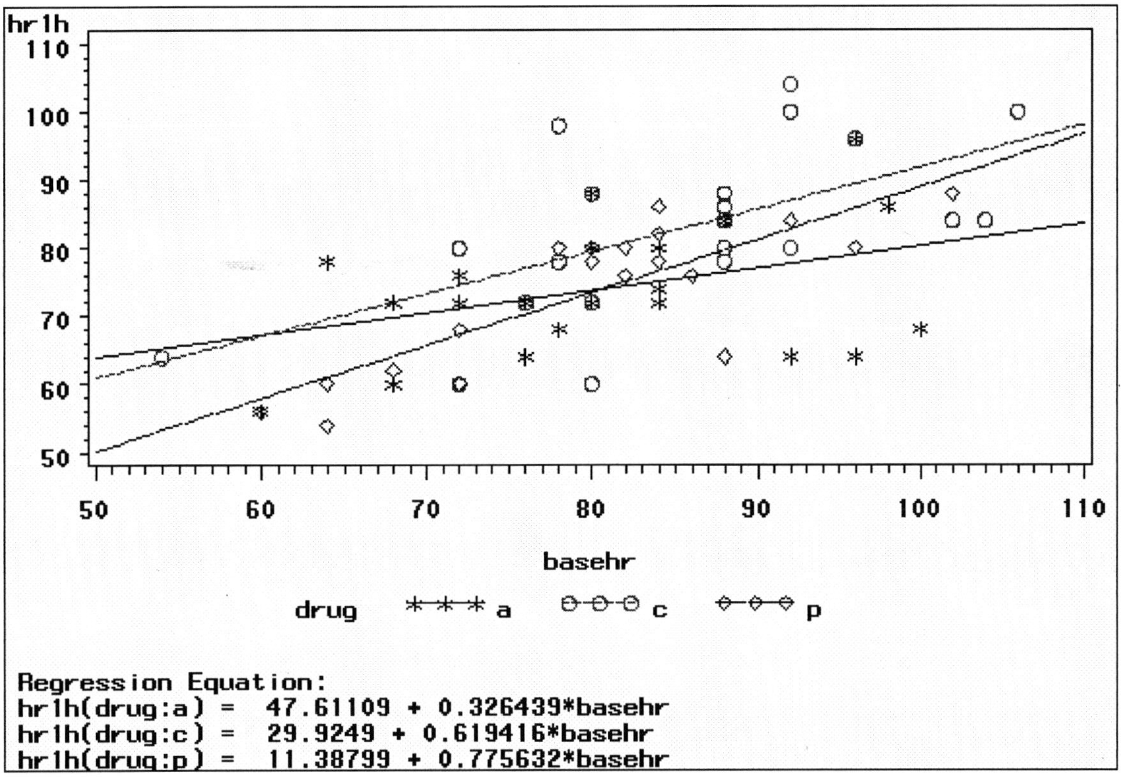

The slopes for drugs c and p are close. The slope for drug a seems to be a little different from other slopes.

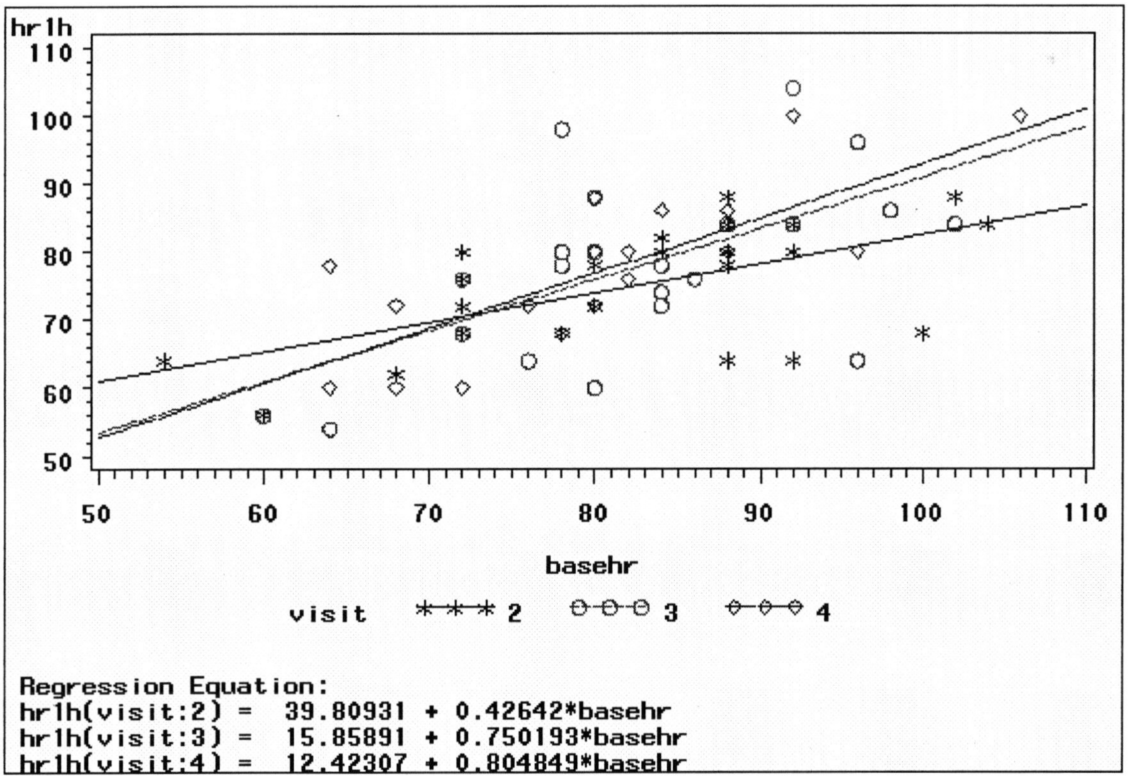

The slopes for visits 3 and 4 are close. The slope for visit 2 seems to be a little different from other slopes.

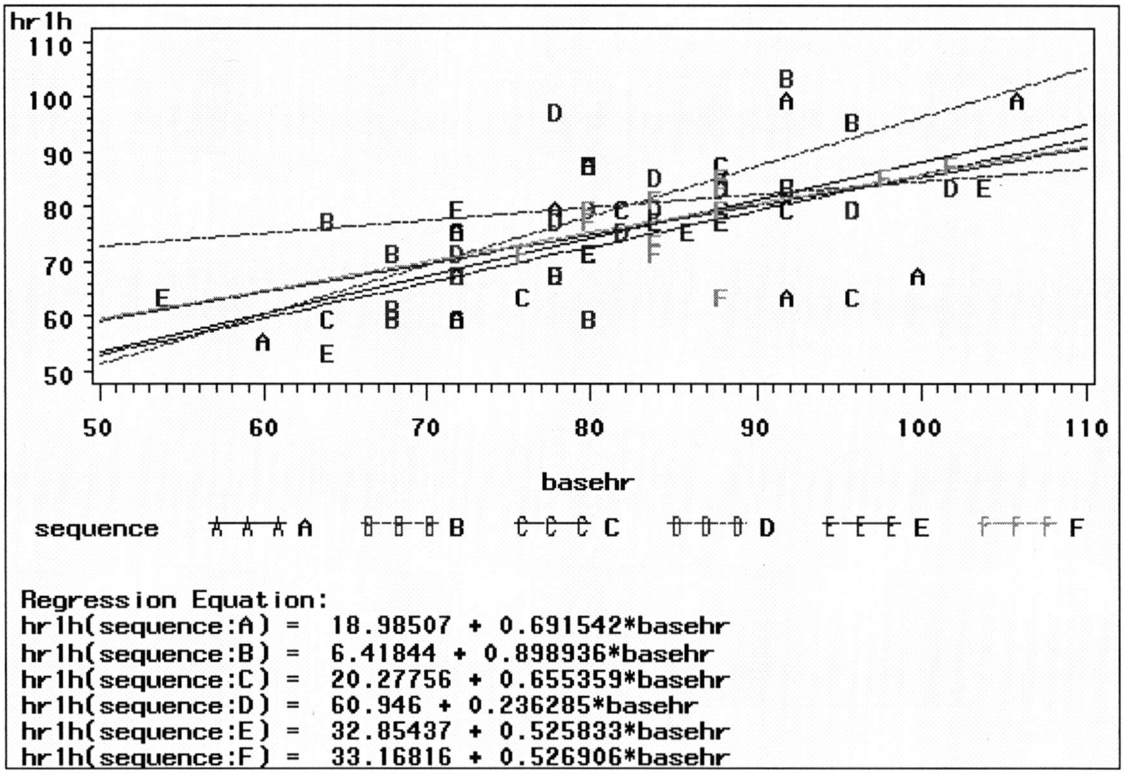

All the slopes seem to be pretty close to each other, with a possible exception of sequence D.

b. Use the MIXED procedure to fit an analysis of covariance model to this data. Include two-way interactions of **basehr** and **drug**, **basehr** and **visit**, and **basehr** and **sequence**. Are they significant?

```
proc mixed data=sasuser.heart;
   class patient sequence visit drug;
   model hr1h = sequence visit drug basehr sequence*basehr
                visit*basehr drug*basehr / solution ddfm=kr;
   random patient;
run;
```

Partial PROC MIXED Output

Covariance Parameter Estimates

Cov Parm	Estimate
patient	23.8040
Residual	52.3232

Solution for Fixed Effects

Effect	sequence	drug	visit	Estimate	Standard Error	DF	t Value	Pr > |t|
Intercept				15.1232	39.8952	48.1	0.38	0.7063
sequence	A			0.5775	40.0326	43.1	0.01	0.9886
sequence	B			-14.8528	42.0547	43.4	-0.35	0.7257
sequence	C			2.7827	40.9684	49.6	0.07	0.9461
sequence	D			55.4333	44.2541	50.8	1.25	0.2161
sequence	E			4.4092	40.6144	47.1	0.11	0.9140
sequence	F			0	.	.	.	.
visit			2	13.8202	19.5887	40.6	0.71	0.4845
visit			3	-1.1190	21.5328	43.8	-0.05	0.9588
visit			4	0	.	.	.	.
drug		a		27.5619	19.0793	43.3	1.44	0.1558
drug		c		7.3436	19.5827	39.8	0.38	0.7096
drug		p		0	.	.	.	.
basehr				0.7457	0.4618	48.6	1.61	0.1129
basehr*sequence	A			-0.01598	0.4662	43.9	-0.03	0.9728
basehr*sequence	B			0.2140	0.4915	44	0.44	0.6654
basehr*sequence	C			-0.05405	0.4733	50.2	-0.11	0.9095
basehr*sequence	D			-0.6276	0.5138	51.2	-1.22	0.2275
basehr*sequence	E			-0.06158	0.4756	48.1	-0.13	0.8975
basehr*sequence	F			0	.	.	.	.
basehr*visit			2	-0.2155	0.2375	40.6	-0.91	0.3696
basehr*visit			3	0.01169	0.2597	43.4	0.04	0.9643
basehr*visit			4	0	.	.	.	.
basehr*drug		a		-0.3480	0.2345	43.3	-1.48	0.1450
basehr*drug		c		-0.02571	0.2309	39.7	-0.11	0.9119
basehr*drug		p		0	.	.	.	.

Type 3 Tests of Fixed Effects

Effect	Num DF	Den DF	F Value	Pr > F
sequence	5	49.4	0.96	0.4531
visit	2	41	0.44	0.6474
drug	2	41.3	1.07	0.3519
basehr	1	51.8	16.39	0.0002
basehr*sequence	5	49.5	0.93	0.4691
basehr*visit	2	40.9	0.72	0.4916
basehr*drug	2	41.1	1.25	0.2964

All the interaction terms in the model seem to be nonsignificant.

c. Remove nonsignificant interaction terms one at a time until all the interaction terms are significant. What is the variance estimate for **`patient`**? Does **`drug`** appear to be significant? How about the covariate **`basehr`**?

The most nonsignificant interaction term is **`basehr*visit`**, which will be removed first.

```
proc mixed data=sasuser.heart;
   class patient sequence visit drug;
   model hr1h = sequence visit drug basehr sequence*basehr
                drug*basehr / solution ddfm=kr;
   random patient;
run;
```

Partial PROC MIXED Output

Type 3 Tests of Fixed Effects

Effect	Num DF	Den DF	F Value	Pr > F
sequence	5	51.6	0.96	0.4493
visit	2	38.8	2.29	0.1146
drug	2	42.9	1.33	0.2754
basehr	1	53.6	15.34	0.0003
basehr*sequence	5	51.7	0.93	0.4708
basehr*drug	2	42.9	1.54	0.2257

Then remove **basehr*sequence**:

```
proc mixed data=sasuser.heart;
   class patient sequence visit drug;
   model hr1h = sequence visit drug basehr
                drug*basehr / solution ddfm=kr;
   random patient;
run;
```

Partial PROC MIXED Output

Type 3 Tests of Fixed Effects

Effect	Num DF	Den DF	F Value	Pr > F
sequence	5	14.9	0.34	0.8826
visit	2	38.7	1.79	0.1808
drug	2	46.9	1.05	0.3575
basehr	1	59	21.58	<.0001
basehr*drug	2	47	1.11	0.3379

Then remove **basehr*drug**:

```
proc mixed data=sasuser.heart;
   class patient sequence visit drug;
   model hr1h = sequence visit drug basehr
                / solution ddfm=kr;
   random patient;
run;
```

Partial PROC MIXED Output

Cov Parm	Estimate
patient	28.7146
Residual	49.8710

The patient variance is estimated to be 28.71.

Type 3 Tests of Fixed Effects

Effect	Num DF	Den DF	F Value	Pr > F
sequence	5	15.1	0.43	0.8236
visit	2	40.4	1.68	0.1996
drug	2	40.9	6.52	0.0035
basehr	1	60.9	21.05	<.0001

drug and **basehr** are both significant.

d. Perform all pairwise comparisons among the drugs at the average value for **basehr**. Which drugs seem to be different?

```
proc mixed data=sasuser.heart;
   class patient sequence visit drug;
   model hr1h = sequence visit drug basehr / ddfm=kr;
   random patient;
   lsmeans drug / diff;
run;
```

Partial PROC MIXED Output

Least Squares Means

Effect	drug	Estimate	Standard Error	DF	t Value	Pr > |t|
drug	a	74.8054	1.8199	40.9	41.10	<.0001
drug	c	81.5130	1.8323	41.3	44.49	<.0001
drug	p	75.0983	1.8120	40.7	41.45	<.0001

Differences of Least Squares Means

Effect	drug	_drug	Estimate	Standard Error	DF	t Value	Pr > |t|
drug	a	c	-6.7076	2.0947	41.5	-3.20	0.0026
drug	a	p	-0.2929	2.0410	40.3	-0.14	0.8866
drug	c	p	6.4146	2.0741	41	3.09	0.0036

Drug c is different from drug a, and is also different from drug p. Drugs a and p do not seem to be different in the heart rate measurements.

2. Fitting a Random Coefficient Model

Data is collected from 7181 high school students from 160 schools and is stored in a SAS data set sasuser.school. Selected variables in the data set are **student_id**, **math**, **ses**, and **school_id**.

a. Use the GPLOT procedure to produce a scatter plot of **math** versus **ses**.

```
goptions reset=all;
proc gplot data=sasuser.school;
   plot math*ses;
   symbol v=circle;
run;
quit;
```

PROC GPLOT Output

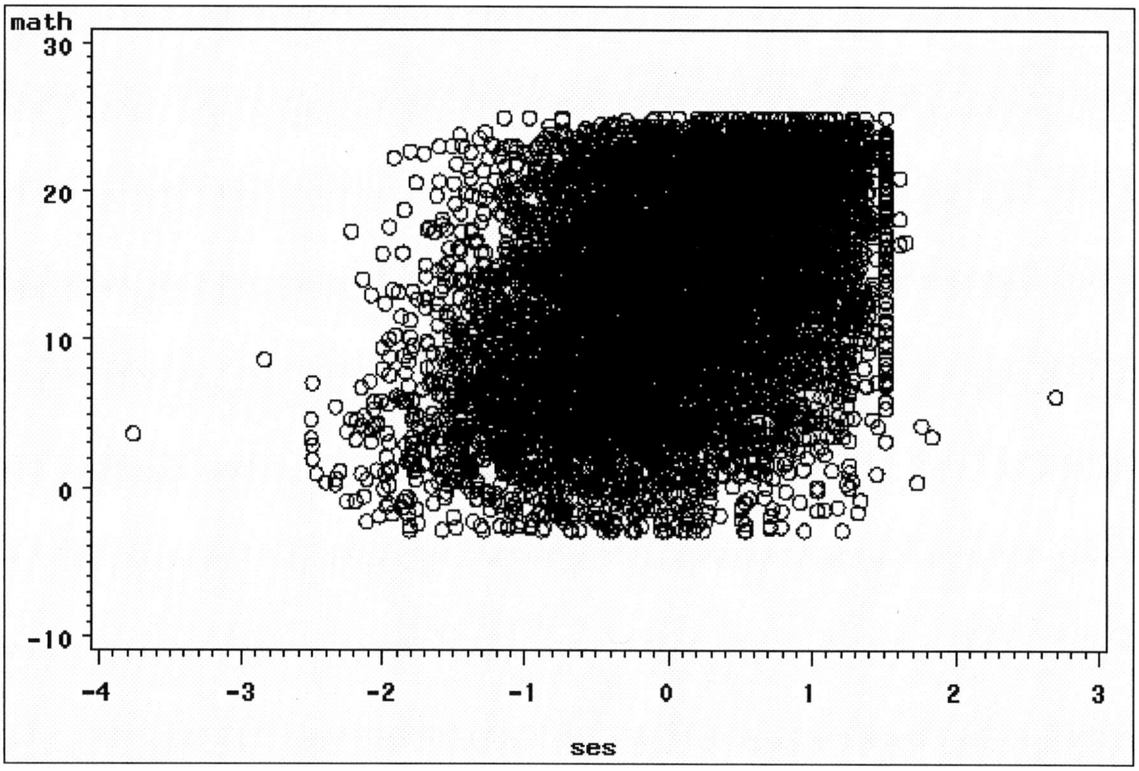

Because of the large number of data points the scatter plot does not clearly show the relationship between the math achievement and the socioeconomic status. However, the overall trend seems to be positive.

b. Do you think it is reasonable to treat **school_id** as a random effect? Why?

It may be reasonable to treat **school_id** as a random effect because students are clustered within a school. Observations within a cluster are typically correlated. One way of modeling the correlations among the observations within a cluster is to treat the cluster variable as a random effect. By treating **school_id** as a random effect, you can also estimate the school variance to evaluate school to school variability.

c. Fit a random coefficient model to this data. Use the OUTP= option in the MODEL statement to save the predicted values. What is the estimated variance in the intercepts among the schools? What is the estimated variance in the rates of change (slopes) among the schools?

```
proc mixed data=sasuser.school;
   model math=ses / ddfm=kr solution outp=pred;
   random int ses / subject=school_id type=un;
run;
```

Note that because your data is already sorted by **school_id**, you do not need to specify the subject variable **school_id** in a CLASS statement. In fact, specifying a continuous subject variable makes PROC MIXED use fewer resources and run much faster.

Partial PROC MIXED Output

Covariance Parameter Estimates

Cov Parm	Subject	Estimate
UN(1,1)	school_ID	4.8207
UN(2,1)	school_ID	-0.1509
UN(2,2)	school_ID	0.4164
Residual		36.8269

The intercept variance is estimated to be 4.82. In other words, the variance in students' math achievement among the schools when the socioeconomic status is the grand mean is 4.82. The slope variance is 0.4164. That is, the variance in the rate of change as a function of **ses** in students' math achievement among the schools is 0.4164.

Solution for Fixed Effects

Effect	Estimate	Standard Error	DF	t Value	Pr > |t|
Intercept	12.6647	0.1899	146	66.70	<.0001
ses	2.3954	0.1186	157	20.20	<.0001

The overall intercept and slope are both significant.

d. Use the GPLOT procedure to produce subject (school) specific plots. Use the NOLEGEND option in the PLOT statement. Use the following symbol statement: **symbol v=none i=j r=160 l=1;**

```
proc gplot data=pred;
   plot pred*ses = school_id / nolegend;
   symbol v=none i=join r=160 l=1;
run;
quit;
```

PROC GPLOT Output

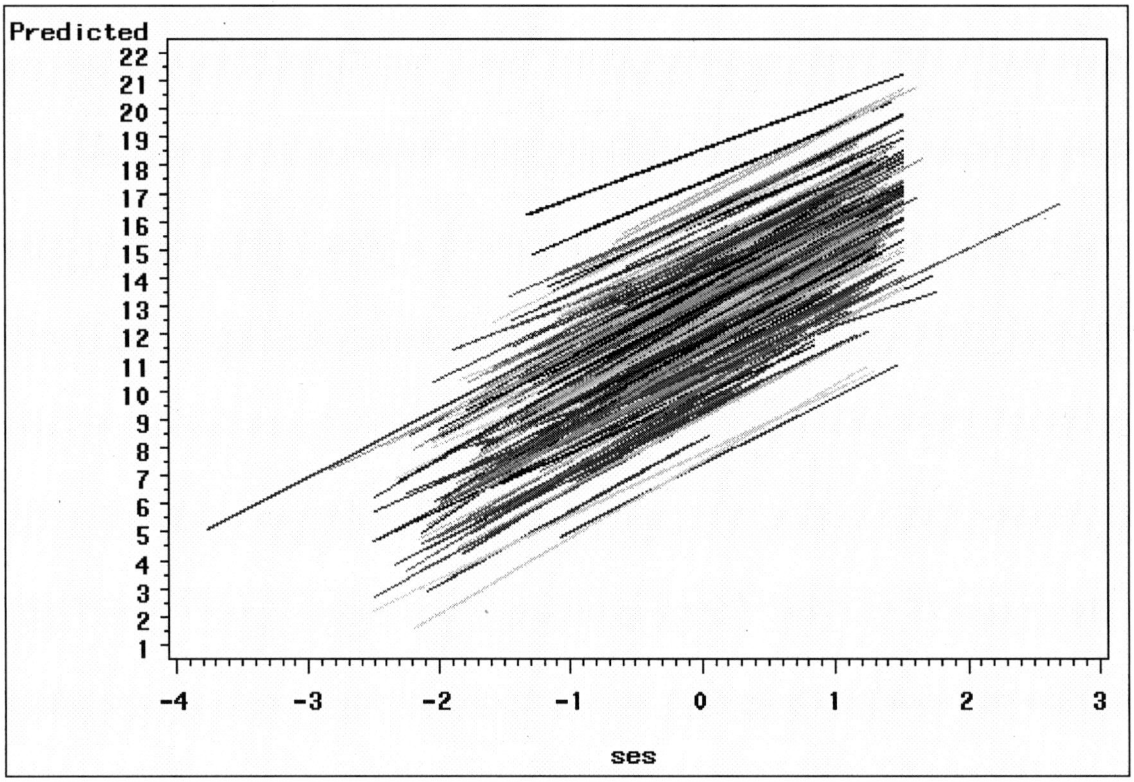

The graph shows the school-specific regression models between **math** and **ses**.

3. Fitting a Hierarchical Linear Model

The data set **sasuser.school** you analyzed in the previous exercise has another variable **school_disclim** that is a continuous variable that measures the disciplinary climate of the school. This is a variable measured at the school level rather than the student level.

Fit a model to incorporate the variable **school_disclim**. Use the SOLUTION option in both the MODEL statement and the RANDOM statement. What are the covariance parameter estimates and what do they correspond to? What fixed effects are significant?

```
proc mixed data=sasuser.school;
   model math=ses school_disclim ses*school_disclim / ddfm=kr
                                                      solution;
   random int ses / subject=school_id type=un solution;
run;
```

Partial PROC MIXED Output

Covariance Parameter Estimates

Cov Parm	Subject	Estimate
UN(1,1)	school_ID	3.7386
UN(2,1)	school_ID	0.3437
UN(2,2)	school_ID	0.1854
Residual		36.7923

The intercept variance is 3.74. In terms of students' math ability, the school-to-school variance at the grand mean socioeconomic status is 3.74. The slope variance is 0.19. The school-to-school variance in terms of the rate of change in students' math ability as a function of socioeconomic status is 0.19. The covariance of intercept and slope is 0.34. The residual variance (36.8) corresponds to the unexplained variance by the model.

Solution for Fixed Effects

Effect	Estimate	Standard Error	DF	t Value	Pr > |t|
Intercept	12.6595	0.1713	146	73.90	<.0001
ses	2.4106	0.1113	155	21.66	<.0001
school_disclim	-1.1229	0.1772	150	-6.34	<.0001
ses*school_disclim	0.5698	0.1188	179	4.80	<.0001

All the fixed effects are significant. The significant **`ses*school_disclim`** interaction indicates that the effect of socioeconomic status on students' math ability is different for schools with different disciplinary climate.

Solution for Random Effects

Effect	Subject	Estimate	Std Err Pred	DF	t Value	Pr > |t|
Intercept	1	0.1998	0.8921	518	0.22	0.8228
ses	1	-0.04574	0.4616	1.53	-0.10	0.9324
Intercept	2	0.5452	1.0326	986	0.53	0.5976
ses	2	0.08230	0.4393	1.48	0.19	0.8738
Intercept	3	-3.5989	0.8520	596	-4.22	<.0001
ses	3	-0.3434	0.4630	1.55	-0.74	0.5542
Intercept	4	1.1720	1.0987	465	1.07	0.2867
ses	4	0.09667	0.4260	1.46	0.23	0.8482
...						

The intercept and slope deviations from the population intercept and slope for each school are presented in this table.

Type 3 Tests of Fixed Effects

Effect	Num DF	Den DF	F Value	Pr > F
ses	1	155	469.02	<.0001
school_disclim	1	150	40.13	<.0001
ses*school_disclim	1	179	23.01	<.0001

4. Fitting another Hierarchical Linear Model

a. Data has a nested structure. The students are in classes taught by teachers, so students are nested within teachers. Likewise, teachers are nested within schools. Students and teachers are considered to be random factors. Schools are considered fixed factors because you have data on all schools in the district. The other fixed effects are **`social`** and **`scale`**. Because the socio-economic criterion and scales on the exam were the same for all students, teachers, and schools, the **`social`** and **`scale`** factors are crossed with students within teachers, with teachers within schools, and with schools.

b. For the scores on either qualitative or quantitative scales, the linear model is

$y_{ijks} = \mu + \alpha_i + \beta_k + (\alpha\beta)_{ik} + t_j + e_{ijks},$ where

- α_i, β_k, and $(\alpha\beta)_{ik}$ are effects of school, socio-economic criterion and the interaction between school and socio-economic criterion
- t_j is the random effect for teacher j, and e_{ijks} is the random error.

```
proc sort data=sasuser.scores out=scores;
   by scale;
run;

proc mixed data=scores;
   by scale;
   class school teacher social;
   model score=school social school*social / ddfm=kr;
   random teacher;
run;
```

Partial PROC MIXED Output

```
----------------------------- scale=qual ------------------------------

                          The Mixed Procedure

                         Covariance Parameter
                               Estimates

                         Cov Parm      Estimate

                         teacher         2.9666
                         Residual        133.32
```

```
                    Type 3 Tests of Fixed Effects

                            Num      Den
       Effect                DF       DF    F Value    Pr > F

       school                13     47.2       1.89    0.0555
       social                 1      861      23.90    <.0001
       school*social         13      856       1.94    0.0232
```

For the qualitative exam scores, you conclude that

- the **school*social** interaction effect is significant (p-value=0.0232)
- the p-values of <0.0001 for **social** effect indicates that **social** is a significant factor
- the Type 3 test for the **school** effect is marginally significant (p-value=0.0555).

```
----------------------------- scale=quan ------------------------------

                              The Mixed Procedure

                             Covariance Parameter
                                   Estimates

                             Cov Parm      Estimate

                             teacher         8.0573
                             Residual        105.23
```

```
                       Type 3 Tests of Fixed Effects

                               Num      Den
           Effect               DF       DF     F Value     Pr > F

           school               13     43.6        1.78     0.0787
           social                1      856       10.61     0.0012
           school*social        13      850        0.97     0.4813
```

For the quantitative exam scores, you conclude that

- the **school*social** interaction effect is not significant (p-value=0.4813)
- the **social** effect is significant across all schools (p-value=0.0012)
- the Type 3 tests for the **school** effect shows a marginal significant result (p-value=0.0787).

Chapter 4 Exercises

1. **Obtaining EBLUPs for Operators**

   The manager of an automotive plant must replace the machines producing a certain component used in automatic transmissions. Two different machines are available. The manager wants to evaluate the productivity of the machines when operated by the plant's employees. Three employees are selected randomly from the workforce to operate each machine at two different time periods. The three employees represent a random sample of all possible operators.

   The data is stored in a SAS data set **`sasuser.machine`**. The variables included in the data set are **`machine`**, **`operator`**, and **`productivity`**.

   a. Write the linear model for this data. What factors are fixed and what factors are random?

   b. Fit the linear mixed model using PROC MIXED. Write ESTIMATE statements to obtain EBLUPs for operators 1, 2, and 3. Use the ODS OUTPUT statement to save the EBLUPs.

   c. Write an ESTIMATE statement to obtain the EBLUP for operator 1 using machine 1. Is the result the same as the EBLUP for operator 1 in the previous exercise?

2. **Producing a Shrinkage Plot**

   Continue to work with the **`sasuser.machine`** data set you analyzed previously.

   a. Use the LSMEANS statement to obtain the LSMEANS for operators. For illustration purposes, treat **`operator`** as a fixed effect, and treat **`operator*machine`** as a random effect. Use the ODS statement to save the LSMEANS. How do the LSMEANS compare with the EBLUPS?

   b. Merge the two data sets containing EBLUPs and LSMEANS by **`operator`**. Transpose the resulting data set for plotting. Use the PRINT procedure to generate listing output for the plotting data set.

   Hint: Rename the variable **`estimate`** in both data sets before the merge. Also use the following statement in the EBLUP data set to ensure a correct merge:

   ```
   operator=input(substr(label, 16), 1.);
   ```

   c. Use PROC GPLOT to produce the shrinkage plot. In the PLOT statement, use VREF=51.4525 to produce the reference line for the grand mean. What can you tell from the graph?

3. **Obtaining EBLUPs for Teachers**

   Recall the data set **`sasuser.scores`** you analyzed as an exercise for Chapter 3.

   Now use the ESTIMATE statement to compute the average exam scores for the two scales separately (using the BY statement). Also use ESTIMATE statements with the CL option to obtain EBLUPs for the first four teachers (10664, 10665, 10667, and 10668).

4. (Self-Study) Making Inferences in Broad and Narrow Inference Spaces

Continue to work with the `sasuser.machine` data set you analyzed previously.

a. Write an ESTIMATE statement to estimate the mean productivity for machine 1 in the broad inference space. What is the standard error of the estimate? Write an ESTIMATE statement to estimate the mean productivity for machine 1 in the narrow inference space. What is the standard error of the estimate?

b. Write ESTIMATE statements to estimate the difference in mean productivity for machine 1 and machine 2 in both the broad inference space and in the narrow inference space. What inferences can you make about the difference between machine 1 and machine 2 in both cases?

Solutions to Chapter 4 Exercises

1. Obtaining EBLUPs for Operators

The manager of an automotive plant must replace the machines producing a certain component used in automatic transmissions. Two different machines are available. The manager wants to evaluate the productivity of the machines when operated by the plant's employees. Three employees are selected randomly from the workforce to operate each machine at two different time periods. The three employees represent a random sample of all possible operators.

The data is stored in a SAS data set **sasuser.machine**. The variables included in the data set are **machine**, **operator**, and **productivity**.

a. Write the linear model for this data. What factors are fixed and what factors are random?

This is a two-way mixed model. The variable **machine** is a fixed effect; **operator** and **machine*operator** are random effects.

$$Y_{ijk} = \mu + \alpha_i + b_j + (\alpha b)_{ij} + \varepsilon_{ijk}$$

where

Y_{ijk} the kth productivity measurement for the jth operator using the ith machine

μ overall mean

α_i fixed effect of the ith machine

b_j random effect of the jth operator where $b_j \sim N(0, \sigma_b^{\ 2})$

$(\alpha b)_{ij}$ random interaction between the ith machine and the jth operator where $(\alpha b)_{ij} \sim N(0, \sigma_{\alpha b}^{\ 2})$

ε_{ijk} experimental error of the kth observation for the jth operator using the ith machine where $\varepsilon_{ijk} \sim N(0, \sigma^2)$

The effects b_j, $(\alpha b)_{ij}$, and ε_{ijk} are assumed to be independent random variables.

b. Fit the linear mixed model using PROC MIXED. Write ESTIMATE statements to obtain EBLUPs for operators 1, 2, and 3. Use the ODS OUTPUT statement to save the EBLUPs.

```
proc mixed data=sasuser.machine;
   class machine operator;
   model productivity=machine / ddfm=kr;
   random operator machine*operator;
   estimate 'EBLUP-operator 1' intercept 1 | operator 1 0 0;
   estimate 'EBLUP-operator 2' intercept 1 | operator 0 1 0;
   estimate 'EBLUP-operator 3' intercept 1 | operator 0 0 1;
   ods output estimates=eblup;
run;
```

Partial PROC MIXED Output

Estimates

Label	Estimate	Standard Error	DF	t Value	Pr > |t|
EBLUP-operator 1	51.6820	0.2391	2.99	216.15	<.0001
EBLUP-operator 2	51.5376	0.2391	2.99	215.54	<.0001
EBLUP-operator 3	51.1378	0.2391	2.99	213.87	<.0001

These EBLUPs are predicted productivity for each operator regardless of which machines they operate.

c. Write an ESTIMATE statement to obtain the EBLUP for operator 1 using machine 1. Is the result the same as the EBLUP for operator 1 in the previous exercise?

```
proc mixed data=sasuser.machine;
   class machine operator;
   model productivity=machine / ddfm=kr;
   random operator machine*operator;
   estimate 'EBLUP-operator 1 machine 1'
            intercept 1 machine 1 0
          | operator 1 0 0 machine*operator 1 0 0 0 0 0;
run;
```

Partial PROC MIXED Output

Estimates

Label	Estimate	Standard Error	DF	t Value	Pr > |t|
EBLUP-operator 1 machine 1	51.2979	0.1724	7.89	297.48	<.0001

The predicted productivity for operator 1 using machine 1 is 51.2979 with a standard error of 0.1724. Compared with the last output for operator 1, the estimates are not identical but similar. The standard error of this one is smaller (0.1724 versus 0.2391) due to a narrower inference space.

2. Producing a Shrinkage Plot

Continue to work with the **sasuser.machine** data set you analyzed previously.

a. Use the LSMEANS statement to obtain the LSMEANS for operators. For illustration purposes, treat **operator** as a fixed effect and treat **operator*machine** as a random effect. Use the ODS statement to save the LSMEANS.

```
proc mixed data=sasuser.machine;
   class machine operator;
   model productivity=machine operator / ddfm=kr;
   random machine*operator;
   lsmeans operator;
   ods output lsmeans=opmeans;
run;
```

Partial PROC MIXED Output

Least Squares Means

Effect	operator	Estimate	Standard Error	DF	t Value	Pr > |t|
operator	1	51.7625	0.1940	2	266.83	<.0001
operator	2	51.5675	0.1940	2	265.82	<.0001
operator	3	51.0275	0.1940	2	263.04	<.0001

The LSMEANS are slightly different from the EBLUPS. They are more extreme than the EBLUPS.

b. Merge the two data sets containing EBLUPs and LSMEANS by **operator**. Transpose the resulting data set for plotting. Use the PRINT procedure to generate listing output for the plotting data set.

```
data opmeans(rename=(estimate=lsmean));
   set opmeans(keep=operator estimate);
run;

data eblup(drop=label rename=(estimate=eblup));
   set eblup(keep=label estimate);
   operator=input(substr(label, 16), 1.);
run;

proc sort data=opmeans;
   by operator;
run;

proc sort data=eblup;
   by operator;
run;

data lsmblup;
   merge opmeans eblup;
   by operator;
run;

proc transpose data=lsmblup
   out=plotblup(rename=(col1=value _name_=type));
   var lsmean eblup;
   by operator;
   where lsmean ne . and eblup ne .;
run;

proc print data=plotblup;
run;
```

PROC PRINT Output

```
Obs    operator    type        value

  1        1       lsmean    51.7625
  2        1       eblup     51.6820
  3        2       lsmean    51.5675
  4        2       eblup     51.5376
  5        3       lsmean    51.0275
  6        3       eblup     51.1378
```

c. Use PROC GPLOT to produce the shrinkage plot. In the PLOT statement, use VREF=51.4525 to produce the reference line for the grand mean.

```
goptions reset=all;
proc gplot data=plotblup;
   plot value*type=operator / vref=51.4525 haxis=axis1;
   axis1 label=none order=('lsmean' 'eblup')
         offset=(0.5,0.5)in;
   symbol1 i=join c=black v=star l=1;
   symbol2 i=join c=blue v=circle l=3;
   symbol3 i=join c=red v=diamond l=5;
   title1 'Shrinkage for the Operator EBLUPs';
run;
title;
quit;
```

PROC GPLOT Output

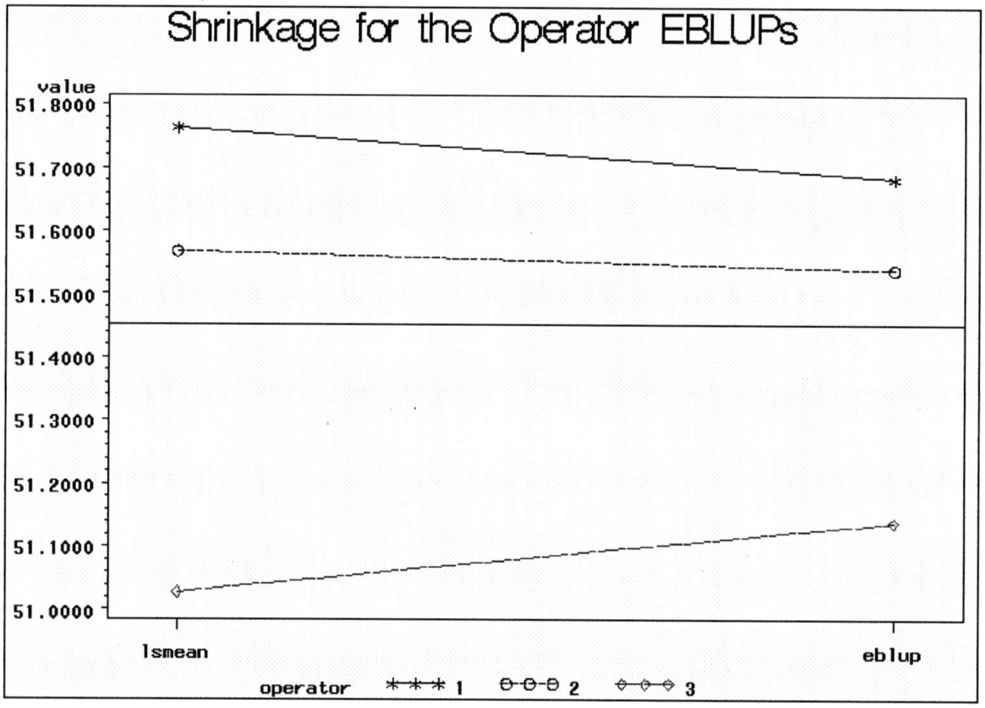

Compared with the least squares means, the EBLUPS shrink toward the overall mean of 51.4525.

3. Obtaining EBLUPs for Teachers

Recall the data set **sasuser.scores** you analyzed as an exercise for Chapter 3. Now use the ESTIMATE statement to compute the average exam scores for the two scales separately (using the BY statement). Also use ESTIMATE statements with the CL option to obtain EBLUPs for the first four teachers (10664, 10665, 10667, and 10668).

```
proc mixed data=scores;
   by scale;
   class school teacher social;
   model score=school social school*social / ddfm=kr;
   random teacher;
   estimate 'overall mean' intercept 1;
   estimate 'teacher 10664' intercept 1 | teacher 1 / cl;
   estimate 'teacher 10665' intercept 1 | teacher 0 1 / cl;
   estimate 'teacher 10667' intercept 1 | teacher 0 0 1 / cl;
   estimate 'teacher 10668' intercept 1 | teacher 0 0 0 1 / cl;
run;
```

Partial PROC MIXED Output

scale=qual

Estimates

Label	Estimate	Standard Error	DF	t Value	Pr > |t|	Alpha	Lower	Upper
overall mean	39.1751	0.7006	112	55.92	<.0001	0.05	37.7869	40.5632
teacher 10664	40.4144	1.8177	5.3	22.23	<.0001	0.05	35.8211	45.0077
teacher 10665	39.2800	1.8094	5.46	21.71	<.0001	0.05	34.7435	43.8165
teacher 10667	38.0687	1.7965	5.63	21.19	<.0001	0.05	33.6020	42.5354
teacher 10668	38.9371	1.8233	5.2	21.36	<.0001	0.05	34.3042	43.5700

For the qualitative exam, the average score is 39.1751. The predicted score for teacher 10664 is 40.4144, higher than the average score. The predicted score for teacher 10667 is 38.0687, lower than the average score. The EBLUPs for teachers can provide useful information for school administrators.

scale=quan

Estimates

Label	Estimate	Standard Error	DF	t Value	Pr > |t|	Alpha	Lower	Upper
overall mean	34.6035	0.7271	75.9	47.59	<.0001	0.05	33.1553	36.0516
teacher 10664	36.4821	2.3551	25.3	15.49	<.0001	0.05	31.6344	41.3299
teacher 10665	34.2920	2.3224	25.9	14.77	<.0001	0.05	29.5171	39.0668
teacher 10667	33.6719	2.2840	26.5	14.74	<.0001	0.05	28.9810	38.3628
teacher 10668	33.9678	2.3782	24.8	14.28	<.0001	0.05	29.0682	38.8674

For the quantitative exam, the average score is 34.6035. The predicted score for teacher 10664 is 36.4821, higher than the average score. The predicted score for teacher 10667 is 33.6719, lower than the average score. The EBLUPs for teachers can provide useful information for school administrators.

4. (Self-Study) Making Inferences in Broad and Narrow Inference Spaces

a. Write an ESTIMATE statement to estimate the mean productivity for machine 1 in the broad inference space. What is the standard error of the estimate? Write an ESTIMATE statement to estimate the mean productivity for machine 1 in the narrow inference space. What is the standard error of the estimate?

```
proc mixed data=sasuser.machine;
   class machine operator;
   model productivity=machine / ddfm=kr;
   random operator machine*operator;
   estimate 'Machine 1 broad' intercept 1 machine 1 0;
   estimate 'Machine 1 narrow'
            intercept 3 machine 3 0 | operator 1 1 1
            machine*operator 1 1 1 0 0 0 / divisor=3;
run;
```

Partial PROC MIXED Output

Covariance Parameter Estimates

Cov Parm	Estimate
operator	0.1073
machine*operator	0.05100
Residual	0.04852

Type 3 Tests of Fixed Effects

Effect	Num DF	Den DF	F Value	Pr > F
machine	1	2	20.26	0.0460

Estimates

Label	Estimate	Standard Error	DF	t Value	Pr > |t|
Machine 1 broad	50.9483	0.2467	2.97	206.50	<.0001
Machine 1 narrow	50.9483	0.08993	6	566.53	<.0001

The mean productivity for machine 1 is 50.95. The standard error for this mean is 0.2467 in the broad inference space and 0.0899 in the narrow inference space.

b. Write ESTIMATE statements to estimate the difference in mean productivity for machine 1 and machine 2 in both the broad inference space and in the narrow inference space. What inferences can you make about the difference between machine 1 and machine 2 in both cases?

```
proc mixed data=sasuser.machine;
   class machine operator;
   model productivity=machine / ddfm=kr;
   random operator machine*operator;
   estimate 'Machines 1 vs 2 broad' machine 1 -1;
   estimate 'Machines 1 vs 2 narrow' machine 3 -3
           | machine*operator 1 1 1 -1 -1 -1 / divisor=3;
run;
```

Partial PROC MIXED Output

Estimates

Label	Estimate	Standard Error	DF	t Value	Pr > |t|
Machines 1 vs 2 broad	-1.0083	0.2240	2	-4.50	0.0460
Machines 1 vs 2 narrow	-1.0083	0.1272	6	-7.93	0.0002

Machine 1 is 1.0083 less productive than machine 2. The standard error is 0.2240 with a *p*-value of 0.0460 in the broad inference space. Across the population of operators, machine 1 is significantly different from machine 2 in terms of productivity. In the narrow inference space, the standard error is 0.1272 with a *p*-value of 0.0002. For the three operators included in the experiment, machine 1 is significantly different from machine 2 in terms of productivity.

Chapter 5 Exercises

Medical researchers are interested in growth measurements for children. The growth measurements consist of dental measurements from the center of the pituitary gland to the pteryomaxillary fissure for 11 girls and 16 boys at ages 8, 10, 12, and 14 years. The subjects are individual children, and there are four repeated measures on each. Data is stored in a SAS data set `sasuser.growthuni`. The variables included in the data set are `person`, `gender`, `age`, and `growth`.

1. **Producing a Profile Plot for Repeated Measures Data**

   a. Use the MEANS procedure and the OUTPUT statement to compute the means for each age by gender combination and save them to a data set. Use the NWAY option in the PROC MEANS statement to produce only the means for the eight groups. Specify the NOPRINT option in the PROC MEANS statement to suppress the printed output.

   b. Use the GPLOT procedure to plot the means versus age for each gender. Use SYMBOL statements to join the means of each group and different symbols for each gender. What do you observe from the plot?

2. **Determining the Candidate Covariance Structures Using Graphs**

   a. Write the mean model for this data accounting for gender and age.

   b. Use the TYPE=UN option in the REPEATED statement to fit an unstructured model to your data. Specify R and RCORR options and the ODS statement to save the output to SAS data sets.

   c. Produce a plot of covariance versus distance in time for the latter time point of a pair. (Hint: See the demonstration program `c05s2d2.sas`, or use `exercise_template.sas`.) What do you observe about the covariance structure?

   d. Produce a plot of correlation versus distance in time for the latter time point of a pair. (Hint: See the demonstration program `c05s2d3.sas`, or use `exercise_template.sas`.) What do you observe about the correlations between repeated measures? Based on your observations, what covariance structure may be appropriate?

3. **Determining the Appropriate Covariance Structure**

   Fit several covariance structures to your data and compare the fit statistics. Use TYPE=UN, TYPE=AR(1), TYPE=TOEP, and TYPE=CS. Use the ODS OUTPUT statement to save the fit statistics to a data set for each model. Rename the variable `value` for each model. Merge the data sets containing fit statistics for each model and compare the results. Which model(s) appear(s) to provide the best fit?

4. **Making Statistical Inference**

   a. Based on the covariance model you selected in the previous exercise, fit the mean model to account for this covariance in the MIXED procedure. What do you observe regarding the covariance parameter estimates? Use the LSMEANS statement with the SLICE= option to compare **`gender*age`** effect. What conclusion do you draw regarding **`gender*age`** effect?

   b. .Fit a linear growth curve including **`gender`**, **`age`**, and **`gender*age`**, treating **`age`** as a continuous variable. Use the OUTP= option in the MODEL statement to obtain predicted values. Use the S option to obtain the parameter estimates. Plot the predicted values by using PLOT **`pred*age=gender`** in the GPLOT procedure. Is **`gender*age`** significant? How about **`age`**? What are the linear regression equations for boys and girls?

5. **Adding the GROUP= Option**

   Add the GROUP=**`gender`** option to the TOEP model and the CS model. Does it seem to provide a better fit?

   Redo the previous exercise with the best fitting covariance structure you find.

6. **Fitting a Random Coefficient Model**

   Fit a random coefficient model to your data. Use the RANDOM statement (INT AGE / TYPE=UN SUBJECT=PERSON.) Use the S option in both MODEL and RANDOM statements. What is the predicted growth measurement for the first person at age 13? (Hint: Append the new observation for person 1 age 13 gender F to your data set and use PROC MIXED with the OUTP= option in the MODEL statement.)

7. **(Self-Study) Fitting a Random Coefficient Model Plus an AR(1) Structure with GROUP=`gender` for the Residual Variances (the R Matrix)**

   Does this model fit your data better or worse compared with the previous random coefficient model with independent errors?

8. **(Optional) Using the REPEATED Statement to Model Multivariate Responses**

   Recall the **`sasuser.scores`** data set you analyzed previously as an exercise in Chapter 3.

   Fit a linear mixed model to this data considering the scales jointly. Use the LSMEANS statement with DIFF and CL options to compare the differences between the **`social*scale`** least squares means. What do you find?

   - Include **`scale`** and the associated two-way interactions in the mean model.
   - Use the RANDOM statement to model the **`teacher`** effect allowing the possibility that the effect of **`teacher`** depends on the **`scale`** of the exam. Some teachers are better at teaching qualitative subjects and others are better at teaching quantitative subjects. Use TYPE=CS option. (Hint: RANDOM **`scale`** / SUBJECT=**`teacher`** TYPE=CS;).
   - Use the REPEATED statement to model the **`student`** effect allowing the possibility that the effect of **`student`** depends on the **`scale`** of the exam. Some students do better in qualitative subjects and others do better in quantitative subjects. Use the TYPE=UN option. (Hint: REPEATED **`scale`** / SUBJECT=**`student`** TYPE=UN;).
   - Do not specify **`teacher`** and **`student`** in the CLASS statement, as this will slow down the procedure and produce a large amount of output for the Class Level Information table.

Solutions to Chapter 5 Exercises

1. Producing a Profile Plot for Repeated Measures Data

a. Use the MEANS procedure and the OUTPUT statement to compute the means for each age by gender combination and save them to a data set. Use the NWAY option in the PROC MEANS statement to produce only the means for the eight groups. Specify the NOPRINT option in the PROC MEANS statement to suppress the printed output.

```
proc means data=sasuser.growthuni nway noprint;
   var growth;
   class gender age;
   output out=profile mean=avggrowth;
run;
```

b. Use the GPLOT procedure to plot the means versus age for each gender. Use SYMBOL statements to join the means of each group and different symbols for each gender. What do you observe from the plot?

```
goptions reset=all;
proc gplot data=profile;
   plot avggrowth*age=gender;
   symbol1 v=star c=red i=join l=1;
   symbol2 v=circle c=blue i=join l=3;
   title 'Average Growth vs. Age by Gender';
run;
title;
quit;
```

PROC GPLOT Output

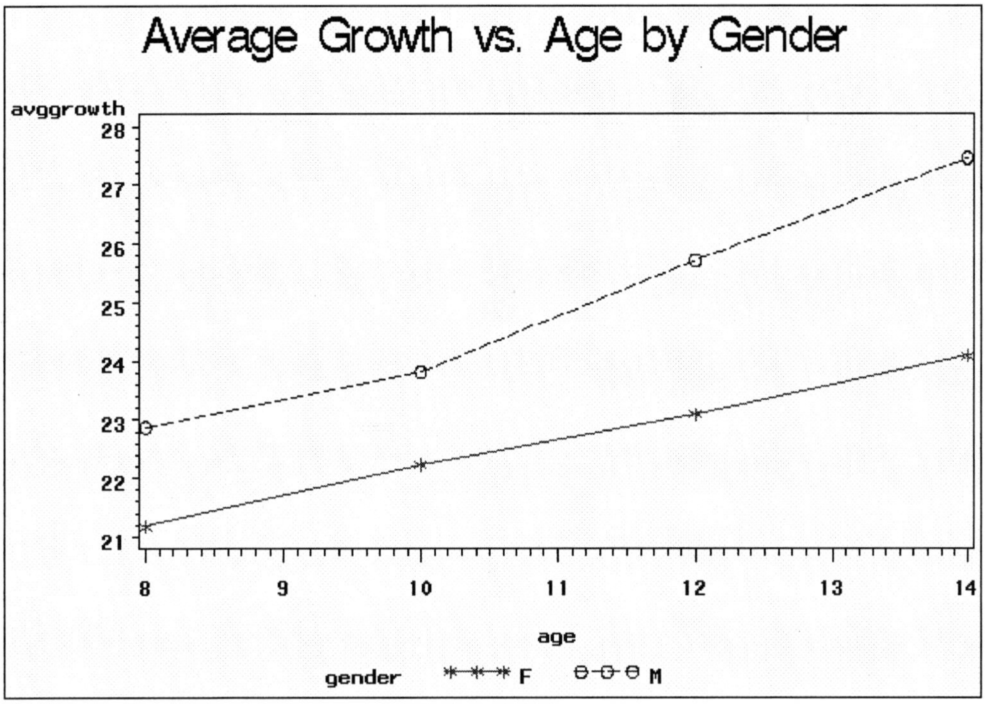

The average growth measurements for boys and girls are relatively linear. Boys appear to have bigger growth measurements than girls; boys also appear to have a slightly faster growth rate than girls starting from age 10.

2. Determining the Candidate Covariance Structures Using Graphs

a. Write the mean model for this data.

The mean model is $\mu + \alpha_i + \beta_j + (\alpha\beta)_{ij}$, where

μ	overall mean
α_i	the fixed effect of gender
β_j	the fixed effect of age
$(\alpha\beta)_{ij}$	the interaction between gender and age.

b. Use the TYPE=UN option in the REPEATED statement to fit an unstructured model to your data. Specify R and RCORR options and the ODS statement to save the output to SAS data sets.

```
proc mixed data=sasuser.growthuni;
   class gender age;
   model growth=gender age gender*age / ddfm=kr;
   repeated age / type=un subject=person r rcorr;
   ods output covparms=cov rcorr=corr;
run;
```

Partial PROC MIXED Output

Estimated R Matrix for Subject 1

Row	Col1	Col2	Col3	Col4
1	5.4155	2.7168	3.9102	2.7102
2	2.7168	4.1848	2.9272	3.3172
3	3.9102	2.9272	6.4557	4.1307
4	2.7102	3.3172	4.1307	4.9857

Estimated R Correlation Matrix for Subject 1

Row	Col1	Col2	Col3	Col4
1	1.0000	0.5707	0.6613	0.5216
2	0.5707	1.0000	0.5632	0.7262
3	0.6613	0.5632	1.0000	0.7281
4	0.5216	0.7262	0.7281	1.0000

The variances and covariances appear to be fairly constant.

c. Produce a plot of covariance versus distance in time for the latter time point of a pair.

```
data times;
   do time1=1 to 4;
      do time2=1 to time1;
         distance=time1-time2;
         output;
      end;
   end;
run;

data covplot;
   merge times cov;
run;

proc print data=covplot;
run;

goptions reset=all;
proc gplot data=covplot;
   label distance='Distance in Time';
   plot estimate*distance=time1 / nolegend
        haxis=axis1 vaxis=axis2;
   axis1 order=(0 to 3) offset=(2,2) minor=none;
   axis2 order=(0 to 7 by 1);
   symbol1 v='1' c=cyan i=j l=1;
   symbol2 v='2' c=blue i=j l=3;
   symbol3 v='3' c=green i=j l=4;
   symbol4 v='4' c=red i=j l=8;
   title 'Covariance vs. Distance in Time';
run;
title;
quit;
```

PROC GPLOT Output

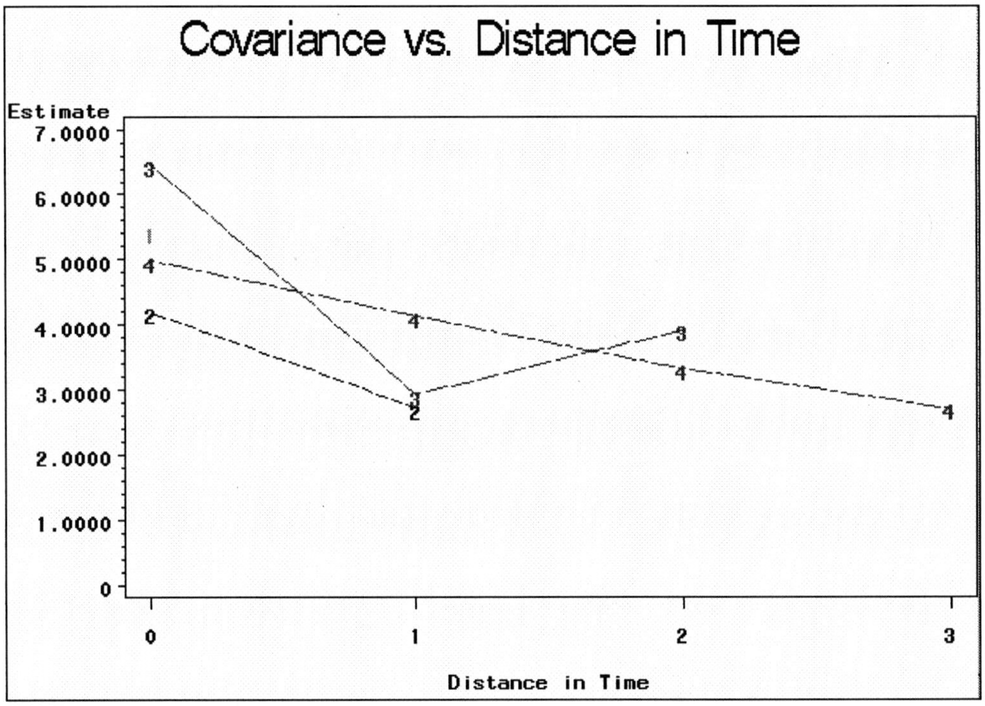

The values plotted at distance 0 are the variances among the observations at each of the four time points. They range from 4.2 to 6.5 and do not seem to be increasing or decreasing with time. The values plotted at distances 1, 2, and 3 represent the covariances between pairs 1, 2, or 3 distances apart. They appear to be fairly constant.

d. Produce a plot of correlation versus distance in time for the latter time point of a pair.

```
%macro forplot(corrdata, dim);
   proc datasets; delete corrplot;
   run;
   %do i=1 %to %eval(&dim-1);
       data corrplot&i(rename=(col&i=corr row=time1));
       set &corrdata(keep=col&i row);
       distance=row-&i;
       time2=&i;
       if distance > 0;
       run;

       proc append base=corrplot data=corrplot&i;
       run;
   %end;
%mend;

%forplot(corr, 4);

proc print data=corrplot;
run;

proc gplot data=corrplot;
   label distance='Distance in Time';
   plot corr*distance=time1 / nolegend
        haxis=0 to 3 hminor=0 vaxis=0 to 1 by 0.1;
   symbol1 v='2' c=red i=j l=1;
   symbol2 v='3' c=blue i=j l=3;
   symbol3 v='4' c=green i=j l=4;
   title 'Correlation vs. Distance in time';
run;
title;
quit;
```

PROC GPLOT Output

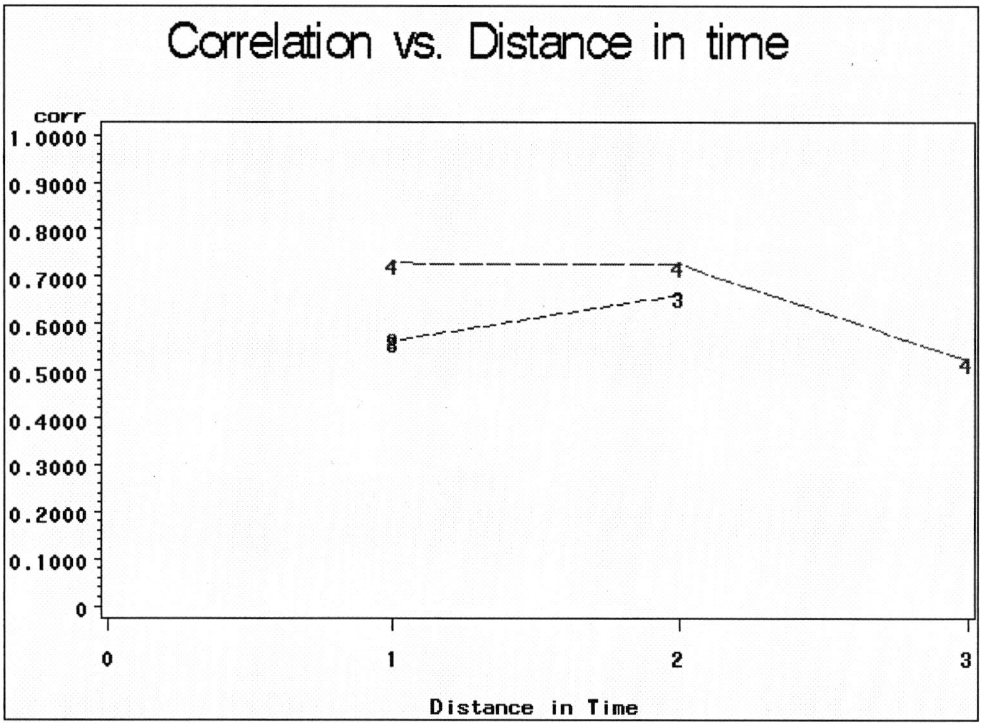

The correlations between pairs of observations at distances 1, 2, and 3 apart in time appear to be fairly constant.

Based on your observations, you suspect a compound symmetry (CS) covariance structure may be appropriate.

3. Determining the Appropriate Covariance Structure

Fit several covariance structures to your data and compare the fit statistics. Use TYPE=UN, TYPE=AR(1), TYPE=TOEP, and TYPE=CS. Use the ODS OUTPUT statement to save the fit statistics to a data set for each model. Rename the variable `value` for each model. Merge the data sets containing fit statistics for each model and compare the results. Which model(s) appear(s) to provide the best fit?

```
ods listing close;
proc mixed data=sasuser.growthuni;
   class gender age person;
   model growth=gender age gender*age / ddfm=kr;
   repeated age / type=un subject=person;
   ods output FitStatistics=FitUn(rename=(value=UN));
run;

proc mixed data=sasuser.growthuni;
   class gender age person;
   model growth=gender age gender*age / ddfm=kr;
   repeated age / type=ar(1) subject=person ;
   ods output FitStatistics=FitAR1(rename=(value=AR1));
run;
```

```
proc mixed data=sasuser.growthuni;
   class gender age person;
   model growth=gender age gender*age / ddfm=kr;
   repeated age / type=toep subject=person;
   ods output FitStatistics=FitToep(rename=(value=Toep));
run;

proc mixed data=sasuser.growthuni;
   class gender age person;
   model growth=gender age gender*age / ddfm=kr;
   repeated age / type=cs subject=person;
   ods output FitStatistics=FitCS(rename=(value=CS));
run;

data fits;
   merge FitUN FitAR1 FitToep FitCS;
   by descr;
run;

ods listing;
proc print data=fits;
run;
```

PROC PRINT Output

Obs	Descr	UN	AR1	Toep	CS
1	-2 Res Log Likelihood	414.0	434.5	418.9	423.4
2	AIC (smaller is better)	434.0	438.5	426.9	427.4
3	AICC (smaller is better)	436.5	438.7	427.4	427.5
4	BIC (smaller is better)	447.0	441.1	432.1	430.0

The CS model and TOEP model seem to provide similar fits to your data.

4. Making Statistical Inference

a. Based on the covariance model you selected in the previous exercise, fit the mean model to account for this covariance in the MIXED procedure. What do you observe regarding the covariance parameter estimates? Use the LSMEANS statement with the SLICE= option to compare **gender*age** effect. What conclusion do you draw regarding **gender*age** effect?

If you chose the CS model, here are the program and the output:

```
proc mixed data=sasuser.growthuni;
   class gender age person;
   model growth = gender age gender*age / ddfm=kr;
   repeated age / type=cs subject=person ;
   lsmeans gender*age / slice=gender slice=age;
run;
```

Partial PROC MIXED Output

Covariance Parameter Estimates

Cov Parm	Subject	Estimate
CS	person	3.2854
Residual		1.9750

The covariance of the growth measurements between any pair of the repeated measures for a given subject is estimated to be 3.29. The residual variance is estimated to be 1.98.

Type 3 Tests of Fixed Effects

Effect	Num DF	Den DF	F Value	Pr > F
gender	1	25	9.29	0.0054
age	3	75	35.35	<.0001
gender*age	3	75	2.36	0.0781

The **gender*age** interaction has a p-value of 0.078, which is marginally significant.

Least Squares Means

Effect	gender	age	Estimate	Standard Error	DF	t Value	Pr > |t|
gender*age	F	8	21.1818	0.6915	46.1	30.63	<.0001
gender*age	F	10	22.2273	0.6915	46.1	32.14	<.0001
gender*age	F	12	23.0909	0.6915	46.1	33.39	<.0001
gender*age	F	14	24.0909	0.6915	46.1	34.84	<.0001
gender*age	M	8	22.8750	0.5734	46.1	39.89	<.0001
gender*age	M	10	23.8125	0.5734	46.1	41.53	<.0001
gender*age	M	12	25.7187	0.5734	46.1	44.85	<.0001
gender*age	M	14	27.4687	0.5734	46.1	47.91	<.0001

Tests of Effect Slices

Effect	gender	age	Num DF	Den DF	F Value	Pr > F
gender*age	F		3	75	8.55	<.0001
gender*age	M		3	75	33.84	<.0001
gender*age		8	1	46.1	3.55	0.0658
gender*age		10	1	46.1	3.11	0.0843
gender*age		12	1	46.1	8.56	0.0053
gender*age		14	1	46.1	14.14	0.0005

The output from the SLICE=**gender** option in the LSMEANS statement suggests that **age** is a significant factor for both boys and girls. The output from the SLICE=**age** option indicates that at ages 12 and 14, the growth measurements between boys and girls are significantly different (*p*-values are 0.0053 and 0.0005, respectively). At ages 8 and 10, the differences in growth measurements between boys and girls are marginally significant (*p*-values are 0.066 and 0.084, respectively).

If you chose the TOEP model, here are the program and output.

```
proc mixed data=sasuser.growthuni;
   class gender age person;
   model growth = gender age gender*age / ddfm=kr;
   repeated age / type=toep subject=person ;
   lsmeans gender*age / slice=gender slice=age;
run;
```

Partial PROC MIXED Output

Covariance Parameter Estimates

Cov Parm	Subject	Estimate
TOEP(2)	person	3.3325
TOEP(3)	person	3.7210
TOEP(4)	person	2.4870
Residual		5.3195

Type 3 Tests of Fixed Effects

Effect	Num DF	Den DF	F Value	Pr > F
gender	1	25.3	9.19	0.0055
age	3	40.5	29.03	<.0001
gender*age	3	40.5	2.27	0.0953

Least Squares Means

Effect	gender	age	Estimate	Standard Error	DF	t Value	Pr > |t|
gender*age	F	8	21.1818	0.6954	45.8	30.46	<.0001
gender*age	F	10	22.2273	0.6954	45.8	31.96	<.0001
gender*age	F	12	23.0909	0.6954	45.8	33.20	<.0001
gender*age	F	14	24.0909	0.6954	45.8	34.64	<.0001
gender*age	M	8	22.8750	0.5766	45.8	39.67	<.0001
gender*age	M	10	23.8125	0.5766	45.8	41.30	<.0001
gender*age	M	12	25.7188	0.5766	45.8	44.60	<.0001
gender*age	M	14	27.4688	0.5766	45.8	47.64	<.0001

Tests of Effect Slices

Effect	gender	age	Num DF	Den DF	F Value	Pr > F
gender*age	F		3	40.5	6.77	0.0008
gender*age	M		3	40.5	28.56	<.0001
gender*age		8	1	45.8	3.51	0.0673
gender*age		10	1	45.8	3.08	0.0860
gender*age		12	1	45.8	8.46	0.0056
gender*age		14	1	45.8	13.98	0.0005

The results are very similar to the CS model.

b. Fit a linear growth curve including **gender**, **age**, and **gender*age**, treating **age** as a continuous variable. Use the OUTP= option in the MODEL statement to obtain predicted values. Use the S option to obtain the parameter estimates. Plot the predicted values by using PLOT **pred*age=gender** in the GPLOT procedure. Is **gender*age** significant? How about **age**? What are the linear regression equations for boys and girls?

If you chose the CS model, here are the program and output.

```
proc mixed data=sasuser.growthuni;
   class gender person;
   model growth = gender age gender*age / ddfm=kr outp=preddata s;
   repeated / type=cs subject=person ;
run;

proc gplot data=preddata;
   plot pred*age = gender;
   symbol1 v=circle c=red i=join l=1;
   symbol2 v=star c=blue i=join l=3;
   title 'Predicted Growth Curve';
run;
title;
quit;
```

Partial PROC MIXED Output

Solution for Fixed Effects

Effect	gender	Estimate	Standard Error	DF	t Value	Pr > |t|
Intercept		16.3406	0.9813	104	16.65	<.0001
gender	F	1.0321	1.5374	104	0.67	0.5035
gender	M	0	.	.	.	.
age		0.7844	0.07750	79	10.12	<.0001
age*gender	F	-0.3048	0.1214	79	-2.51	0.0141
age*gender	M	0	.	.	.	.

The linear regression models are

- for boys: **growth** = 16.3406 + 0.7844 * **age**
- for girls: **growth** = (16.3406 + 1.0321) + (0.7844 – 0.3048) * **age**
  = 17.3727 + 0.4796 * **age**.

Type 3 Tests of Fixed Effects

Effect	Num DF	Den DF	F Value	Pr > F
gender	1	104	0.45	0.5035
age	1	79	108.36	<.0001
age*gender	1	79	6.30	0.0141

The **age*gender** interaction is significant, which indicates the need of an unequal slope model. **age** is significant as well, which indicates that the overall slope is different from zero.

PROC GPLOT Output

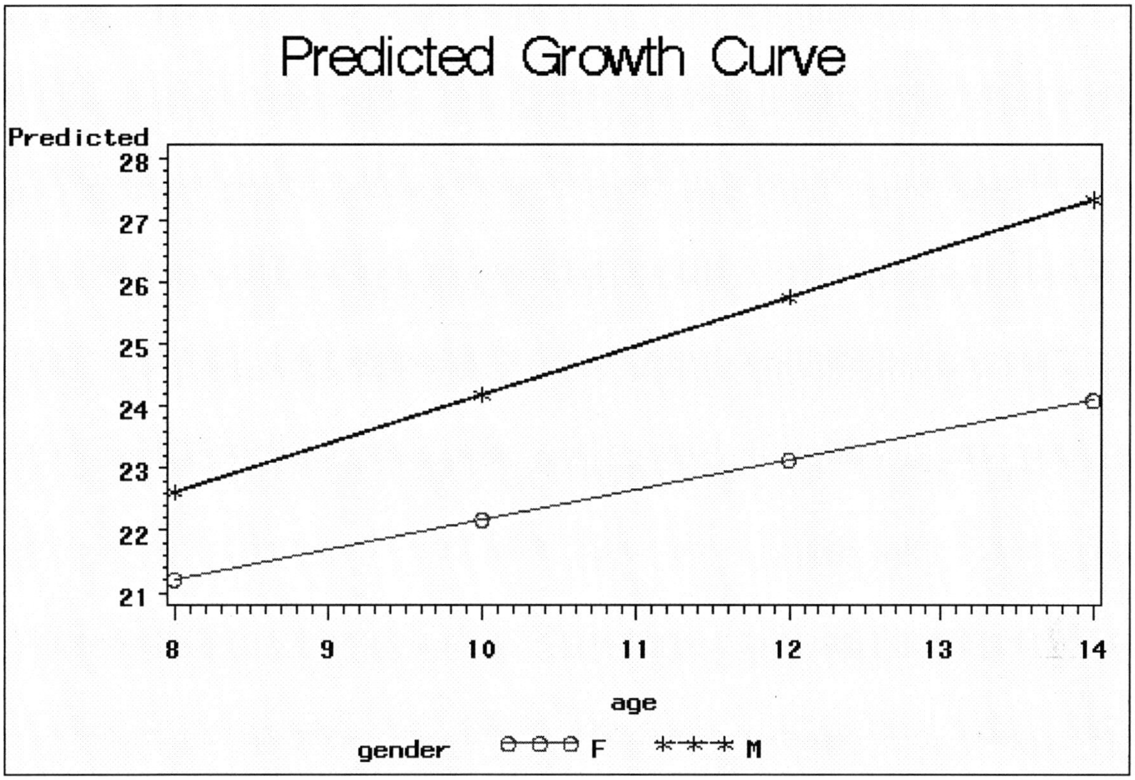

If you chose the TOEP model, here are the program and output.

```
proc mixed data=sasuser.growthuni;
   class gender person;
   model growth = gender age gender*age / ddfm=kr outp=preddata s;
   repeated / type=toep subject=person ;
run;

proc gplot data=preddata;
   plot pred*age = gender;
   symbol1 v=circle c=red i=join l=1;
   symbol2 v=star c=blue i=join l=3;
   title 'Predicted Growth Curve';
run;
title;
quit;
```

Partial PROC MIXED Output

Solution for Fixed Effects

Effect	gender	Estimate	Standard Error	DF	t Value	Pr > |t|
Intercept		16.2704	1.0723	41.2	15.17	<.0001
gender	F	1.1385	1.6799	41.2	0.68	0.5017
gender	M	0	.	.	.	.
age		0.7973	0.08674	28.1	9.19	<.0001
age*gender	F	-0.3214	0.1359	28.1	-2.37	0.0252
age*gender	M	0	.	.	.	.

The linear regression models are very similar to the CS model:

- for boys: **growth** = 16.2704 + 0.7973 * **age**
- for girls: **growth** = (16.2704 + 1.1385) + (0.7973 – 0.3214) * **age**
  = 17.4089 + 0.4759 * **age**.

Type 3 Tests of Fixed Effects

Effect	Num DF	Den DF	F Value	Pr > F
gender	1	41.2	0.46	0.5017
age	1	28.1	87.78	<.0001
age*gender	1	28.1	5.59	0.0252

The results are very similar to the CS model.

PROC GPLOT Output

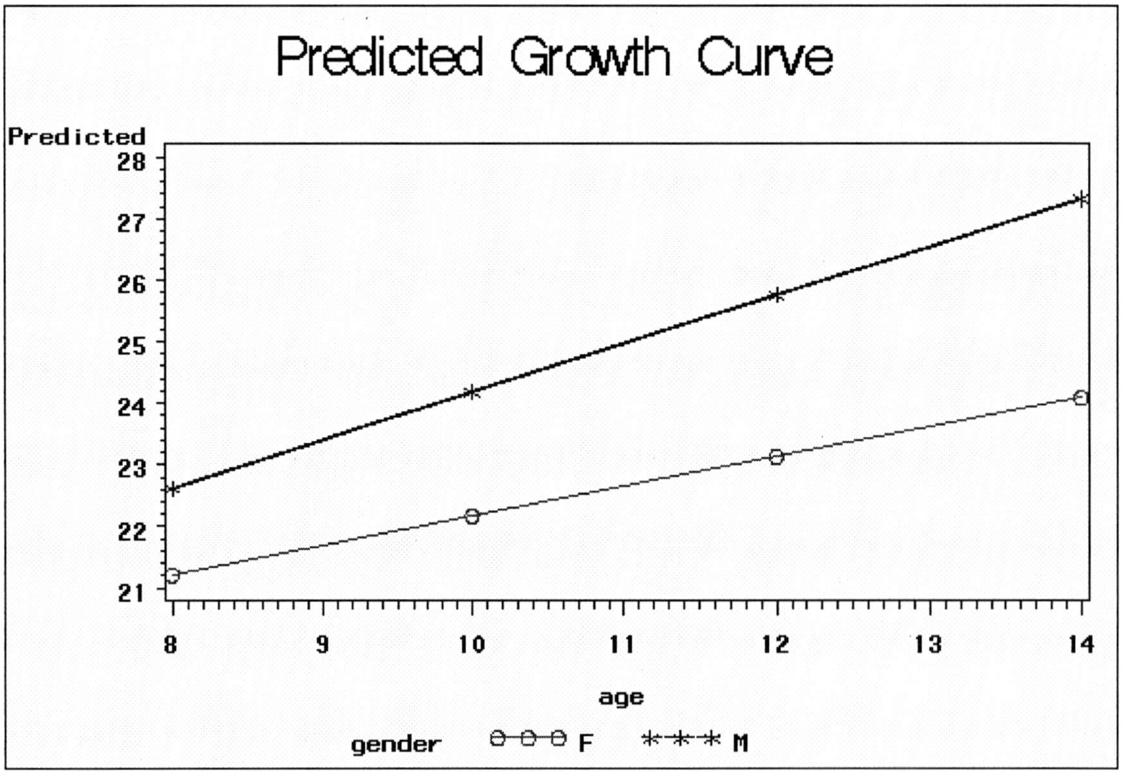

5. Adding the GROUP= Option

Add the GROUP=**gender** option to the TOEP model and the CS model. Does it seem to provide a better fit?

```
proc mixed data=sasuser.growthuni;
   class gender age person;
   model growth = gender age gender*age / ddfm=kr;
   repeated age / type=toep subject=person group=gender;
run;
```

Partial PROC MIXED Output

```
                         Fit Statistics

          -2 Res Log Likelihood          401.2
          AIC (smaller is better)        417.2
          AICC (smaller is better)       418.8
          BIC (smaller is better)        427.6
```

```
proc mixed data=sasuser.growthuni;
   class gender age person;
   model growth = gender age gender*age / ddfm=kr;
   repeated age / type=cs subject=person group=gender;
run;
```

Partial PROC MIXED Output

```
                         Fit Statistics

          -2 Res Log Likelihood          406.4
          AIC (smaller is better)        414.4
          AICC (smaller is better)       414.8
          BIC (smaller is better)        419.5
```

The best fitting model seems to be the CS with the group=**gender** option.

Redo the previous exercise with the better fitting model.

```
proc mixed data=sasuser.growthuni;
   class gender age person;
   model growth=gender age gender*age / ddfm=kr;
   repeated age / type=cs subject=person group=gender;
   lsmeans gender*age / slice=gender slice=age;
run;
```

Partial PROC MIXED Output

Covariance Parameter Estimates

Cov Parm	Subject	Group	Estimate
Variance	person	gender F	0.6470
CS	person	gender F	4.2689
Variance	person	gender M	2.8604
CS	person	gender M	2.6297

The Covariance Parameter Estimates table indicates that the variances of the repeated measures are fairly different for boys (2.86) and girls (0.65). The covariances between the repeated measures are fairly different as well, that is, 2.63 for boys and 4.27 for girls.

Type 3 Tests of Fixed Effects

Effect	Num DF	Den DF	F Value	Pr > F
gender	1	19.6	8.80	0.0077
age	3	68.4	45.08	<.0001
gender*age	3	68.4	3.01	0.0360

The **gender*age** interaction is significant (*p*-value=0.036), which suggests that the changes in the growth measurements over time are not the same for boys and girls.

Least Squares Means

Effect	gender	age	Estimate	Standard Error	DF	t Value	Pr > |t|
gender*age	F	8	21.1818	0.6685	12.3	31.69	<.0001
gender*age	F	10	22.2273	0.6685	12.3	33.25	<.0001
gender*age	F	12	23.0909	0.6685	12.3	34.54	<.0001
gender*age	F	14	24.0909	0.6685	12.3	36.04	<.0001
gender*age	M	8	22.8750	0.5858	35.5	39.05	<.0001
gender*age	M	10	23.8125	0.5858	35.5	40.65	<.0001
gender*age	M	12	25.7188	0.5858	35.5	43.91	<.0001
gender*age	M	14	27.4688	0.5858	35.5	46.89	<.0001

Tests of Effect Slices

Effect	gender	age	Num DF	Den DF	F Value	Pr > F
gender*age	F		3	30	26.10	<.0001
gender*age	M		3	45	23.37	<.0001
gender*age		8	1	31.8	3.63	0.0659
gender*age		10	1	31.8	3.18	0.0840
gender*age		12	1	31.8	8.74	0.0058
gender*age		14	1	31.8	14.44	0.0006

The output from the SLICE=**gender** option in the LSMEANS statement suggests that **age** is a significant factor for both boys and girls. The output from the SLICE=**age** option indicates that at ages 12 and 14, the growth measurements between boys and girls are significantly different (*p*-values are 0.0058 and 0.0006, respectively). At ages 8 and 10, the differences in growth measurements between boys and girls are marginally significant (*p*-values are 0.066 and 0.084, respectively).

Fit a growth curve model treating **age** as a continuous variable.

```
proc mixed data=sasuser.growthuni;
   class gender person;
   model growth=gender age gender*age / ddfm=kr outp=preddata s;
   repeated / type=cs subject=person group=gender;
run;
```

Partial PROC MIXED Output

Solution for Fixed Effects

Effect	gender	Estimate	Standard Error	DF	t Value	Pr > |t|
Intercept		16.3406	1.1287	60	14.48	<.0001
gender	F	1.0321	1.4183	86.5	0.73	0.4687
gender	M	0	.	.	.	.
age		0.7844	0.09382	47	8.36	<.0001
age*gender	F	-0.3048	0.1076	70.9	-2.83	0.0060
age*gender	M	0	.	.	.	.

The linear regression models are

- for boys: **growth** = 16.3406 + 0.7844 * **age**
- for girls: **growth** = (16.3406 + 1.0321) + (0.7844 – 0.3048) * **age**
  = 17.3727 + 0.4796 * **age**.

Type 3 Tests of Fixed Effects

Effect	Num DF	Den DF	F Value	Pr > F
gender	1	86.5	0.53	0.4687
age	1	70.9	138.11	<.0001
age*gender	1	70.9	8.03	0.0060

The Type 3 tests indicate that **age*gender** is a significant factor. The slopes for **age** are not the same between the boys and the girls.

Plot the predicted values by using PLOT **pred*age=gender** in PROC GPLOT.

```
proc gplot data=preddata;
   plot pred*age=gender;
   symbol1 v=circle c=red i=join l=1;
   symbol2 v=star c=blue i=join l=3;
   title 'Predicted Growth Curve';
run;
title;
quit;
```

PROC GPLOT Output

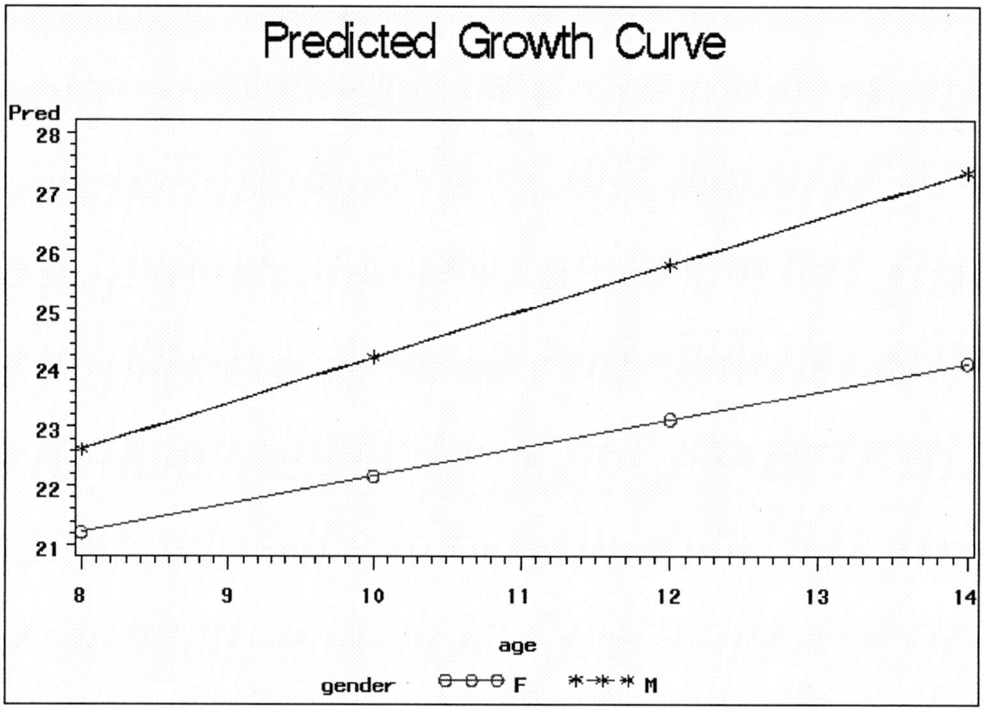

6. Fitting a Random Coefficient Model

Fit a random coefficient model to your data. Use the RANDOM statement (INT AGE / TYPE=UN SUBJECT=PERSON.) Use the S option in both MODEL and RANDOM statements. What is the predicted growth measurement for the first person at age 13? (Hint: Append the new observation for person 1 age 13 gender F to your data set and use PROC MIXED with the OUTP= option in the MODEL statement.)

```
proc mixed data=sasuser.growthuni;
   class gender person;
   model growth=gender age gender*age / s ddfm=kr;
   random int age / type=un subject=person s;
run;
```

Partial PROC MIXED Output

Covariance Parameter Estimates

Cov Parm	Subject	Estimate
UN(1,1)	person	5.7864
UN(2,1)	person	-0.2896
UN(2,2)	person	0.03252
Residual		1.7162

Fit Statistics

-2 Res Log Likelihood	432.6
AIC (smaller is better)	440.6
AICC (smaller is better)	441.0
BIC (smaller is better)	445.8

Solution for Fixed Effects

Effect	gender	Estimate	Standard Error	DF	t Value	Pr > |t|
Intercept		16.3406	1.0185	25	16.04	<.0001
gender	F	1.0321	1.5957	25	0.65	0.5237
gender	M	0	.	.	.	.
age		0.7844	0.08600	25	9.12	<.0001
age*gender	F	-0.3048	0.1347	25	-2.26	0.0326
age*gender	M	0	.	.	.	.

Solution for Random Effects

Effect	person	Estimate	Std Err Pred	DF	t Value	Pr > |t|
Intercept	1	-0.6413	2.3457	3.18	-0.27	0.8014
age	1	-0.04475	0.2043	2.58	-0.22	0.8428
Intercept	2	-0.6602	2.3457	3.18	-0.28	0.7957
age	2	0.09029	0.2043	2.58	0.44	0.6930
Intercept	3	-0.2489	2.3457	3.18	-0.11	0.9218
age	3	0.1136	0.2043	2.58	0.56	0.6230
Intercept	4	1.6611	2.3457	3.18	0.71	0.5273
age	4	0.02821	0.2043	2.58	0.14	0.9003
Intercept	5	0.5710	2.3457	3.18	0.24	0.8226
age	5	-0.05496	0.2043	2.58	-0.27	0.8080
Intercept	6	-0.8263	2.3457	3.18	-0.35	0.7467
age	6	-0.04806	0.2043	2.58	-0.24	0.8315
Intercept	7	0.05820	2.3457	3.18	0.02	0.9817
age	7	0.02348	0.2043	2.58	0.11	0.9169
Intercept	8	1.4133	2.3457	3.18	0.60	0.5871
age	8	-0.07178	0.2043	2.58	-0.35	0.7521
Intercept	9	-0.5389	2.3457	3.18	-0.23	0.8323
age	9	-0.07478	0.2043	2.58	-0.37	0.7423
Intercept	10	-2.9842	2.3457	3.18	-1.27	0.2884
age	10	-0.06270	0.2043	2.58	-0.31	0.7821
Intercept	11	2.1963	2.3457	3.18	0.94	0.4147
age	11	0.1015	0.2043	2.58	0.50	0.6587
Intercept	12	1.5820	2.3438	3.2	0.67	0.5453
age	12	0.08101	0.2051	2.64	0.40	0.7225
Intercept	13	-1.1523	2.3438	3.2	-0.49	0.6548
age	13	-0.02356	0.2051	2.64	-0.11	0.9167
Intercept	14	-0.4331	2.3438	3.2	-0.18	0.8645
age	14	-0.01868	0.2051	2.64	-0.09	0.9339
Intercept	15	2.9766	2.3438	3.2	1.27	0.2887
age	15	-0.1410	0.2051	2.64	-0.69	0.5472
...	...	...	...	...	...	...

You can use the solutions for the fixed effects and random effects to obtain regression equation for each person included in the study. For example, the equation for person 1 who is a girl is

growth = (16.3406 + 1.0321) + (0.7844 – 0.3048) * **age**
+ (–0.6413) + (–0.04475) * **age**
= 16.7314 + 0.4349 * **age**.

```
data new;
   input person gender $ age;
   datalines;
1 F 13
;
run;

data growth;
   set sasuser.growthuni new;
run;

proc mixed data=growth;
   class gender person;
   model growth=gender age gender*age / ddfm=kr outp=pred;
   random int age / type=un subject=person ;
run;

proc print data=pred;
   where age=13;
run;
```

PROC PRINT Output

```
                                                    StdErr
  Obs  person  gender  growth  age     Pred      Pred       DF     Alpha   Lower     Upper    Resid

  109     1       F       .     13   22.3837   0.77389   69.6779    0.05  20.8401   23.9273     .
```

The predicted growth measurement for person 1 at age 13 is 22.3837.

7. **(Self-Study) Fitting a Random Coefficient Model Plus an AR(1) Structure with GROUP=`gender` for the Residual Variances (the R Matrix)**

   Does this model fit your data better or worse compared with the previous random coefficient model with independent errors?

```
proc mixed data=sasuser.growthuni;
   class gender person;
   model growth = gender age gender*age / s ddfm=kr;
   random int age / type=un subject=person;
   repeated / type=ar(1) group=gender subject=person;
run;
```

Partial PROC MIXED Output

```
                 Covariance Parameter Estimates


         Cov Parm     Subject     Group        Estimate

         UN(1,1)      person                     5.4638
         UN(2,1)      person                    -0.2909
         UN(2,2)      person                    0.03737
         Variance     person      gender F       0.3870
         AR(1)        person      gender F      -0.1314
         Variance     person      gender M       2.2322
         AR(1)        person      gender M      -0.2555
```

Fit Statistics

-2 Res Log Likelihood	410.5
AIC (smaller is better)	424.5
AICC (smaller is better)	425.6
BIC (smaller is better)	433.6

Compared with the model you fit for the previous exercise, this model has smaller fit statistics. It seems to fit your data better.

Type 3 Tests of Fixed Effects

Effect	Num DF	Den DF	F Value	Pr > F
gender	1	24.7	0.73	0.3999
age	1	26.7	120.11	<.0001
age*gender	1	26.7	7.30	0.0118

The conclusions about fixed effects remain the same.

8. (Optional) Using the REPEATED Statement to Model Multivariate Responses

Recall the **sasuser.scores** data set you analyzed previously as an exercise in Chapter 3.

Fit a linear mixed model to this data considering the scales jointly. Use the LSMEANS statement with DIFF and CL options to compare the differences between the **social*scale** least squares means. What do you find?

Warning: Depending on the speed of your computer, this program can take a long time to run.

```
proc mixed data=sasuser.scores;
   class school social scale;
   model score=school social school*social scale
               school*scale social*scale / ddfm=kr;
   random scale / subject=teacher type=cs;
   repeated scale / subject=student type=un;
   lsmeans social*scale / diff cl;
run;
```

Partial PROC MIXED Output

Covariance Parameter Estimates

Cov Parm	Subject	Estimate
Variance	teacher	1.3474
CS	teacher	4.7482
UN(1,1)	student	132.87
UN(2,1)	student	22.7817
UN(2,2)	student	105.78

Type 3 Tests of Fixed Effects

Effect	Num DF	Den DF	F Value	Pr > F
school	13	43.2	1.75	0.0847
social	1	862	28.43	<.0001
school*social	13	850	1.51	0.1075
scale	1	39.7	55.98	<.0001
school*scale	13	34.8	2.24	0.0293
social*scale	1	872	4.26	0.0393

The Type 3 tests indicate that **social*scale** and **school*scale** interaction effects are significant. In other words, the effect of **social** on the exam scores depends on **scale** (qual or quan); the effect of **school** on the exam scores also depends on **scale** (qual or quan).

Least Squares Means

Effect	scale	social	Estimate	Standard Error	DF	t Value	Pr > |t|
social*scale	qual	0	35.9381	0.8339	228	43.10	<.0001
social*scale	quan	0	32.7867	0.7780	186	42.14	<.0001
social*scale	qual	1	42.1198	0.9259	327	45.49	<.0001
social*scale	quan	1	36.6968	0.8883	290	41.31	<.0001

Least Squares Means

Effect	scale	social	Alpha	Lower	Upper
social*scale	qual	0	0.05	34.2950	37.5812
social*scale	quan	0	0.05	31.2517	34.3216
social*scale	qual	1	0.05	40.2984	43.9413
social*scale	quan	1	0.05	34.9485	38.4450

The LSMEANS statement provides the estimates of exam scores for each **social*scale** combination. For the qualitative exam, the average **score** for **social**=0 is 35.94 and the average **score** for **social**=1 is 42.12. For the quantitative exam, the average **score** for **social**=0 is 32.79 and the average **score** for **social**=1 is 36.70, which is not as much a change as you see for the qualitative exam scores.

Differences of Least Squares Means

Effect	scale	social	_scale	_social	Estimate	Standard Error	DF
social*scale	qual	0	quan	0	3.1515	0.8423	165
social*scale	qual	0	qual	1	-6.1817	1.1327	1091
social*scale	qual	0	quan	1	-0.7587	1.1112	417
social*scale	quan	0	qual	1	-9.3332	1.1014	404
social*scale	quan	0	quan	1	-3.9101	1.0553	1016
social*scale	qual	1	quan	1	5.4231	0.7434	104

Differences of Least Squares Means

Effect	scale	social	_scale	_social	t Value	Pr > |t|	Alpha
social*scale	qual	0	quan	0	3.74	0.0003	0.05
social*scale	qual	0	qual	1	-5.46	<.0001	0.05
social*scale	qual	0	quan	1	-0.68	0.4951	0.05
social*scale	quan	0	qual	1	-8.47	<.0001	0.05
social*scale	quan	0	quan	1	-3.71	0.0002	0.05
social*scale	qual	1	quan	1	7.30	<.0001	0.05

Differences of Least Squares Means

Effect	scale	social	_scale	_social	Lower	Upper
social*scale	qual	0	quan	0	1.4883	4.8146
social*scale	qual	0	qual	1	-8.4043	-3.9592
social*scale	qual	0	quan	1	-2.9429	1.4256
social*scale	quan	0	qual	1	-11.4984	-7.1679
social*scale	quan	0	quan	1	-5.9810	-1.8392
social*scale	qual	1	quan	1	3.9490	6.8971

The pairwise comparisons suggest that regardless of the exam scales (`qual` or `quan`), **`social`** effects are significant (*p*-value<0.0001 for `qual`, *p*-value=0.0002 for `quan`). In addition, regardless of the social economic criterion (0 or 1), **`scale`** effects are significant (*p*-value=0.0003 for 0, *p*-value<0.0001 for 1).

Chapter 6 Exercises

1. **Conducting an Analysis of Covariance for an Unbalanced Data Set**

The data set **sasuser.multictr2** also contains a covariate **Flush0**. You will include this variable in your analysis. These variables are in the data set:

Clinic	the clinics where the clinical trial was carried out
Trt	the treatment, drug A or B
Patient	patient identification
Flush0	the flush measurements obtained prior to administration of the drugs
Flush	the flush measurement after the administration of the drugs.

a. Use the GPLOT procedure to plot **Flush** versus **Flush0** for each **Trt**. In the SYMBOL statement, use I=RL to request a linear regression line superimposed on the data points. Do linear models fit your data well?

b. Fit an ANCOVA model with random effects **Clinic** and **Clinic*Trt**. Specify **Trt Flush0 Trt*Flush0** in the MODEL statement with DDFM=KR and HTYPE=1, 2, 3 options. Are the three types of hypotheses the same? Are slopes equal to each other? Is the common slope equal to zero?

c. Based on the results from the above exercises, fit the appropriate model. Use the S option in the MODEL statement to obtain equations for the two treatments. Use the LSMEANS statement with AT=50 to compare treatment means for those patients with **Flush0** of 50. Use the ESTIMATE statement to compare treatment A and treatment B. What value of **Flush0** was used for the ESTIMATE statement calculations?

2. **Comparing the Results Using Satterthwaite's and KENWARDROGER Methods of Estimating the Denominator Degrees of Freedom**

Recall the **sasuser.scores** data set that you analyzed previously as exercises in Chapters 3, 4 and 5. These variables are included in the data set:

school	schools in a school district
teacher	teachers in each school
student	students taught by teachers
social	the socio-economic criterion (0 or 1) for a student
scale	the scales the test scores are for (qual or quan)
score	the test scores.

a. Create a data set **`quanscores`**, where only **`scale`**=`quan` is retained.

b. Fit the appropriate model to this data **`quanscores`** using the DDFM=SATTERTH option in the MODEL statement. Use the LSMEANS statement to compare the **`social`** effect. Fit the same model using the DDFM=KR option in the MODEL statement. Also use the LSMEANS statement to compare the **`social`** effect.

c. How does the choice of SATTERTH or KR method affect the tests of fixed effects? How does the choice affect the denominator degrees of freedom estimates? How about the LSMEANS estimates? How about the standard errors of the LSMEANS estimates?

Solutions to Chapter 6 Exercises

1. Conducting an Analysis of Covariance for an Unbalanced Data Set

a. Use the GPLOT procedure to plot **Flush** versus **Flush0** for each **Trt**. In the SYMBOL statement, use I=RL to request a linear regression line superimposed on the data points. Do linear models fit your data well?

```
proc gplot data=sasuser.multictr2;
   plot Flush*Flush0=Trt;
   symbol1 v=circle c=red i=rl l=1;
   symbol2 v=star c=blue i=rl l=3;
run;
quit;
```

PROC GPLOT Output

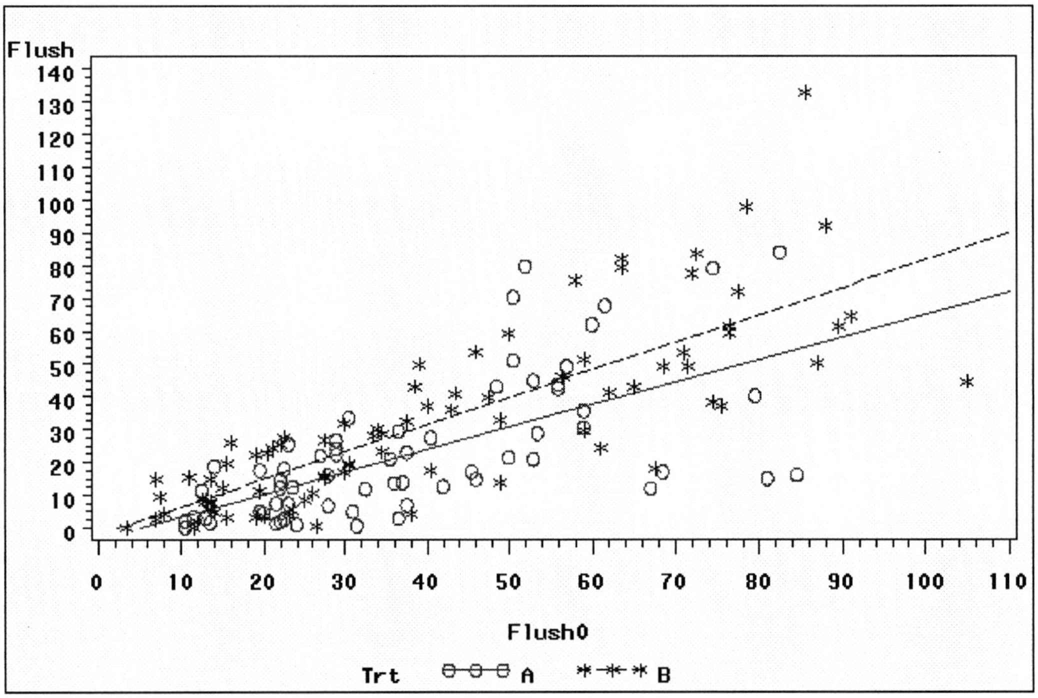

Linear models appear to fit your data well.

b. Fit an ANCOVA model with random effects **Clinic** and **Clinic*Trt**. Specify **Trt Flush0 Trt*Flush0** in the MODEL statement with DDFM=KR and HTYPE=1, 2, 3 options. Are the three types of hypotheses the same? Are slopes equal to each other? Is the common slope equal to zero?

```
proc mixed data=sasuser.multictr2;
   class Trt Clinic ;
   model Flush=Trt Flush0 Flush0*Trt / ddfm=kr htype=1,2,3;
   random Clinic Trt*Clinic;
run;
```

Partial PROC MIXED Output

Type 1 Tests of Fixed Effects

Effect	Num DF	Den DF	F Value	Pr > F
Trt	1	12	10.76	0.0066
Flush0	1	140	180.90	<.0001
Flush0*Trt	1	141	1.28	0.2602

Type 2 Tests of Fixed Effects

Effect	Num DF	Den DF	F Value	Pr > F
Trt	1	73.9	0.11	0.7434
Flush0	1	140	180.90	<.0001
Flush0*Trt	1	141	1.28	0.2602

Type 3 Tests of Fixed Effects

Effect	Num DF	Den DF	F Value	Pr > F
Trt	1	73.9	0.11	0.7434
Flush0	1	141	145.26	<.0001
Flush0*Trt	1	141	1.28	0.2602

The three types of tests are not identical. The Type I test indicates that the common slope is significantly different from zero (*p*-value < .0001). All types of tests indicate that slopes are not significantly different from each other (*p*-value=0.2602 for **Flush0*Trt**). Therefore, a common slope model may be appropriate.

c. Based on the results from the above exercises, fit the appropriate model. Use the S option in the MODEL statement to obtain equations for the two treatments. Use the LSMEANS statement with AT=50 to compare treatment means for those patients with **Flush0** of 50. Use the ESTIMATE statement to compare treatment A and treatment B. What value of **Flush0** was used for the ESTIMATE statement calculations?

```
proc mixed data=sasuser.multictr2;
   class Trt Clinic ;
   model Flush=Trt Flush0 / ddfm=kr htype=1,2,3 s;
   random Clinic Trt*Clinic;
   lsmeans Trt / at flush0=50 diff;
   estimate 'TrtA-TrtB' Trt 1 -1;
run;
```

Partial PROC MIXED Output

Solution for Fixed Effects

Effect	Trt	Estimate	Standard Error	DF	t Value	Pr > |t|
Intercept		0.1506	3.0830	45.8	0.05	0.9612
Trt	A	-7.6143	2.9525	13	-2.58	0.0229
Trt	B	0	.	.	.	.
Flush0		0.7841	0.05850	143	13.40	<.0001

The linear regression equations are

for treatment A: **Flush** = (0.1506 - 7.6143) + 0.7841***Flush0**
= -7.4637 + 0.7841***Flush0**.

for treatment B: **Flush** = 0.1506 + 0.7841***Flush0**.

Type 1 Tests of Fixed Effects

Effect	Num DF	Den DF	F Value	Pr > F
Trt	1	12.9	10.19	0.0071
Flush0	1	143	179.66	<.0001

Type 2 Tests of Fixed Effects

Effect	Num DF	Den DF	F Value	Pr > F
Trt	1	13	6.65	0.0229
Flush0	1	143	179.66	<.0001

Type 3 Tests of Fixed Effects

Effect	Num DF	Den DF	F Value	Pr > F
Trt	1	13	6.65	0.0229
Flush0	1	143	179.66	<.0001

The Type 1 test differs from the Type 2 and Type 3 tests. All tests indicate that the slope significantly differs from zero (*p*-value<0.0001 for **Flush0**) and the intercept significantly differs from zero as well.

Least Squares Means

Effect	Trt	Flush0	Estimate	Standard Error	DF	t Value	Pr > |t|
Trt	A	50.00	31.7408	2.2892	17.5	13.87	<.0001
Trt	B	50.00	39.3551	2.0506	12.6	19.19	<.0001

Differences of Least Squares Means

Effect	Trt	_Trt	Flush0	Estimate	Standard Error	DF	t Value	Pr > |t|
Trt	A	B	50.00	-7.6143	2.9525	13	-2.58	0.0229

At **Flush0**=50, treatment A resulted in an average **Flush** measurement of 7.6143 less than treatment B, and this difference is significant (*p*-value=0.0229).

Estimates

Label	Estimate	Standard Error	DF	t Value	Pr > |t|
TrtA-TrtB	-7.6143	2.9525	13	-2.58	0.0229

Treatment A resulted in an average **Flush** measurement of 7.6143 less than treatment B, and this difference is significant (*p*-value=0.0229). The comparison is made at the average **Flush0** value for the ESTIMATE statement. This result is identical to the result you obtained using the LSMEANS statement with the AT= option because you fit a common slope model.

2. **Comparing the Results Using Satterthwaite's and KENWARDROGER Methods of Estimating the Denominator Degrees of Freedom**

   a. Create a data set **quanscores**, where only **scale**=quan is retained.

```
data quanscores;
   set sasuser.scores;
   where scale='quan';
run;
```

   b. Fit the appropriate model to this data **quanscores** using the DDFM=SATTERTH option in the MODEL statement. Use the LSMEANS statement to compare the **social** effect. Fit the same model using the DDFM=KR option in the MODEL statement. Also use the LSMEANS statement to compare the **social** effect.

```
proc mixed data=quanscores;
   class school teacher social;
   model score=school social school*social/ddfm=satterth;
   random teacher;
   lsmeans social / diff cl;
   title 'Satterthwaite';
run;

proc mixed data=quanscores;
   class school teacher social;
   model score=school social school*social/ddfm=kr;
   random teacher;
   lsmeans social / diff cl;
   title 'KENWARDROGER';
run;
title;
```

Partial PROC MIXED Output

Satterthwaite

Type 3 Tests of Fixed Effects

Effect	Num DF	Den DF	F Value	Pr > F
school	13	42.6	1.78	0.0785
social	1	856	10.63	0.0012
school*social	13	849	0.97	0.4799

Least Squares Means

Effect	social	Estimate	Standard Error	DF	t Value	Pr > |t|	Alpha
social	0	32.7229	0.8374	126	39.08	<.0001	0.05
social	1	36.4840	1.0095	239	36.14	<.0001	0.05

Least Squares Means

Effect	social	Lower	Upper
social	0	31.0658	34.3800
social	1	34.4953	38.4728

Satterthwaite

Differences of Least Squares Means

Effect	social	_social	Estimate	Standard Error	DF	t Value	Pr > |t|
social	0	1	-3.7611	1.1536	856	-3.26	0.0012

Differences of Least Squares Means

Effect	social	_social	Alpha	Lower	Upper
social	0	1	0.05	-6.0253	-1.4970

KENWARDROGER

Type 3 Tests of Fixed Effects

Effect	Num DF	Den DF	F Value	Pr > F
school	13	43.6	1.78	0.0787
social	1	856	10.61	0.0012
school*social	13	850	0.97	0.4813

Least Squares Means

Effect	social	Estimate	Standard Error	DF	t Value	Pr > |t|	Alpha
social	0	32.7229	0.8384	126	39.03	<.0001	0.05
social	1	36.4840	1.0106	239	36.10	<.0001	0.05

Least Squares Means

Effect	social	Lower	Upper
social	0	31.0638	34.3820
social	1	34.4933	38.4748

Differences of Least Squares Means

Effect	social	_social	Estimate	Standard Error	DF	t Value	Pr > |t|
social	0	1	-3.7611	1.1549	856	-3.26	0.0012

Differences of Least Squares Means

Effect	social	_social	Alpha	Lower	Upper
social	0	1	0.05	-6.0279	-1.4944

The following observations can be made regarding Satterthwaite and KENWARDROGER methods:

- The denominator degrees of freedom for the fixed effects are similar but not identical.
- The *F* values for the tests of fixed effects are similar but not identical. The choice of SATTERTH or KR methods affects the *F*-tests results.
- The LSMEANS estimates are identical. In other words, the choice of SATTERTH or KR does not affect the LSMEANS estimates.
- The standard errors of the LSMEANS are similar but not identical. The choice of SATTERTH or KR does affect the standard errors of the LSMEANS estimates. It also affects the standard errors of the difference between the LSMEANS.

Chapter 7 Exercises

1. Fitting a Generalized Linear Mixed Model Using the GLIMMIX Procedure

Data was collected from newly minted Ph.D.'s who are clustered within universities. The sample consisted of 543 male biochemists who received their doctorates from 105 American universities in the late 1950s and early 1960s. One of the goals of the study was to investigate the relationship between whether or not the biochemists received any postdoctoral training (**pdoc**) and some explanatory variables. The data is stored in a data set named **sasuser.postdoc**. The variables in the data set include the following:

pdoc	whether biochemist got postdoctoral training (1) or not (0)
age	age in years at completion of the Ph.D.
marital	marital status (1 if married, 0 otherwise)
docrank	measure of the prestige of the doctoral institution in bioscience fields
under	measure of selectivity of the person's undergraduate institution
agdept	whether degree is from an agricultural department (1 if yes, 0 otherwise)
instituteid	ID number of the doctoral institution

This data set was created based on the data from Allison (1999).

a. Use the GLIMMIX procedure to fit a model to this data.

- Use the (event='1') option for the dependent variable in the MODEL statement to model the probability of obtaining postdoctoral training. Use the DIST=BINARY option in the MODEL statement.
- Include all the main effects plus **marital*agdept** and **under*agdept** interaction terms in the model. Specify **instituteid**, **marital**, and **agdept** as CLASS variables.
- Specify **instituteid** as the random effect. One common way of modeling clustered data is to treat the cluster variable as the random effect.

What is the variance component estimate for **instituteid**? Are there any significant interaction terms?

b. Use the LSMEANS statement to further investigate the significant interaction term **marital*agdept**. Use appropriate options to obtain the least squares means on the original (or inverse linked) scale, the difference of the least squares means and the odds ratios. Use the Tukey adjustment (adjust=tukey option). What are the odds ratios and how do you interpret them?

Solutions to Chapter 7 Exercises

1. Fitting a Generalized Linear Mixed Model Using the GLIMMIX Procedure

a.

```
proc glimmix data=sasuser.postdoc;
   class instituteid marital agdept;
   model pdoc(event='1')=age marital docrank agdept under
                      marital*agdept under*agdept
                      / dist=binary link=logit;
   random int / subject=instituteid;
run;
```

Partial PROC GLIMMIX Output

```
                        Response Profile

              Ordered                          Total
                Value     pdoc             Frequency

                    1     0                      279
                    2     1                      264

       The GLIMMIX procedure is modeling the probability that pdoc='1'.
```

```
                        Fit Statistics

           -2 Res Log Pseudo-Likelihood      2431.91
           Generalized Chi-Square             498.73
           Gener. Chi-Square / DF               0.93
```

```
                  Covariance Parameter Estimates

                                                      Standard
        Cov Parm      Subject           Estimate         Error

        Intercept     instituteid         0.4114        0.2102
```

The variance component for **instituteid** on the logit scale is 0.4114.

```
                  Type III Tests of Fixed Effects

                           Num       Den
      Effect                DF        DF     F Value     Pr > F

      age                    1       431       15.57     <.0001
      marital                1       431        8.75     0.0033
      docrank                1       431        6.02     0.0146
      agdept                 1       431        3.97     0.0470
      under                  1       431        5.92     0.0154
      marital*agdept         1       431        7.64     0.0060
      under*agdept           1       431        3.86     0.0501
```

marital*agdept is significant (*p*-value=0.006). **under*agdept** is almost significant (*p*-value=0.0501). In addition, the **age** and **docrank** main effects are significant as well.

b.

```
proc glimmix data=sasuser.postdoc;
   class instituteid marital agdept;
   model pdoc(event='1')=age marital docrank agdept under
                      marital*agdept under*agdept
                      / dist=binary link=logit;
   random int / subject=instituteid;
   lsmeans marital*agdept / diff ilink oddsratio adjust=tukey;
run;
```

Partial PROC GLIMMIX Output

marital*agdept Least Squares Means

marital	agdept	Estimate	Standard Error	DF	t Value	Pr > |t|	Mean	Standard Error Mean
0	0	0.4113	0.3045	431	1.35	0.1774	0.6014	0.07299
0	1	1.1309	0.5777	431	1.96	0.0509	0.7560	0.1066
1	0	0.3427	0.1512	431	2.27	0.0239	0.5849	0.03672
1	1	-0.7475	0.2430	431	-3.08	0.0022	0.3214	0.05300

The Estimate column has the least squares means for each **marital** and **agdept** combination. The Mean column has the least squares means on the inverse linked scale, or the original scale, for each combination. For example, the probability of obtaining post doctorate trainings for the Ph.D.'s who are married and come from the agricultural department is 0.32, whereas the probability of obtaining post doctorate trainings for those who are not married and also come from the agricultural department is 0.756.

Differences of marital*agdept Least Squares Means

marital	agdept	_marital	_agdept	Estimate	Standard Error	DF	t Value	Pr > |t|	Adj P
0	0	0	1	-0.7196	0.6408	431	-1.12	0.2621	0.6756
0	0	1	0	0.06859	0.3240	431	0.21	0.8325	0.9966
0	0	1	1	1.1589	0.3705	431	3.13	0.0019	0.0101
0	1	1	0	0.7882	0.5907	431	1.33	0.1828	0.5416
0	1	1	1	1.8784	0.5710	431	3.29	0.0011	0.0060
1	0	1	1	1.0903	0.2707	431	4.03	<.0001	0.0004

Differences of marital*agdept Least Squares Means

marital	agdept	_marital	_agdept	Odds Ratio
0	0	0	1	0.487
0	0	1	0	1.071
0	0	1	1	3.186
0	1	1	0	2.199
0	1	1	1	6.543
1	0	1	1	2.975

The odds ratios are listed under the Odds Ratio column. For example, the odds ratio for unmarried, non-agdept (**marital**=0 **agdept**=0) versus married agdept (**marital**=1 **agdept**=1) is 3.186. This means that the odds of obtaining post doctorate trainings for unmarried non-agricultural department Ph.D.'s are 3.186 times the odds for married agricultural department Ph.D.'s.

Appendix B Additional Resources

B.1 A Brief Introduction to Matrix Algebra

B.1.1 Introducing Matrices

A *matrix* is a rectangular or square array of values arranged in rows and columns. An $m \times n$ matrix **A** has m rows and n columns, and has a general form of

$$\mathbf{A}_{m\times n}=\begin{bmatrix} a_{11} & a_{12} & \cdots & a_{1n} \\ a_{21} & a_{22} & \cdots & a_{2n} \\ \cdots & \cdots & \cdots & \cdots \\ a_{m1} & a_{m2} & \cdots & a_{mn} \end{bmatrix}_{m\times n}$$

The element a_{ij} denotes the element in the ith row and the jth column in matrix **A**.

Example:

$$\mathbf{A}=\begin{bmatrix} 3 & 5 & 8 \\ 1 & 2 & 2 \end{bmatrix} \text{ is a 2×3 matrix; } \mathbf{B}=\begin{bmatrix} 1 & 0 \\ 3 & 6 \\ 7 & 2 \\ 2 & 9 \end{bmatrix} \text{ is a 4×2 matrix.}$$

A *vector* is a matrix with only one column (a *column vector*) or only one row (a *row vector*). For example,

$$\mathbf{x}=\begin{bmatrix} 3 \\ -2 \\ 1 \\ 5 \end{bmatrix} \text{ is a column vector,}$$

and $\mathbf{x}'=\begin{bmatrix} 3 & -2 & 1 & 5 \end{bmatrix}$ and $\mathbf{y}'=\begin{bmatrix} 4 & 7 & -5 \end{bmatrix}$ are row vectors.

A single number such as 2.4 or –6 is called a *scalar*. The elements of a matrix are usually scalars, although a matrix can be expressed as a matrix of smaller matrices.

B.1.2 Basic Operations

Transpose

The *transpose* of a matrix **A** is the matrix whose columns are rows of **A** (and therefore whose rows are columns of **A**), with order retained, from first to last. The transpose of **A** is denoted by **A′**.

Example:

$$\text{Let } \mathbf{A} = \begin{bmatrix} 3 & 2 & -6 \\ 7 & 1 & 2 \end{bmatrix}, \text{ then } \mathbf{A}' = \begin{bmatrix} 3 & 7 \\ 2 & 1 \\ -6 & 2 \end{bmatrix}.$$

You see that if **A** is 2×3, then **A′** is 3×2. In general if **A** is m×n, then **A′** is n×m, and $a'_{ij} = a_{ji}$.

The transpose of a row vector is a column vector.

Partitioned Matrices

The matrix **A** can be written as a matrix of matrices:

$$\mathbf{A} = \begin{bmatrix} \mathbf{A}_{11} & \mathbf{A}_{12} \\ \mathbf{A}_{21} & \mathbf{A}_{22} \end{bmatrix}$$

This specification of **A** is called a *partitioning* of **A**, and the matrices $\mathbf{A}_{11}$, $\mathbf{A}_{12}$, $\mathbf{A}_{21}$, $\mathbf{A}_{22}$ are said to be submatrices of **A**. **A** is called a *partitioned matrix.*

Example:

$$\text{Let } \mathbf{A} = \begin{bmatrix} 1 & 6 & 9 & 4 & 5 & 8 \\ 5 & 4 & 7 & 2 & 0 & 2 \\ 9 & 2 & 8 & 1 & 7 & 1 \\ 9 & 1 & 7 & 6 & 2 & 3 \\ 2 & 5 & 4 & 8 & 1 & 7 \end{bmatrix}$$

; each of the arrays of numbers in the four sections of **A** engendered by the dashed lines is a matrix:

$$\mathbf{A}_{11} = \begin{bmatrix} 1 & 6 & 9 & 4 \\ 5 & 4 & 7 & 2 \\ 9 & 2 & 8 & 1 \end{bmatrix} \qquad \mathbf{A}_{12} = \begin{bmatrix} 5 & 8 \\ 0 & 2 \\ 7 & 1 \end{bmatrix}$$

$$\mathbf{A}_{21} = \begin{bmatrix} 9 & 1 & 7 & 6 \\ 2 & 5 & 4 & 8 \end{bmatrix} \qquad \mathbf{A}_{22} = \begin{bmatrix} 2 & 3 \\ 1 & 7 \end{bmatrix}$$

Trace

The sum of the diagonal elements of a square matrix is called the *trace* of the matrix, that is, tr(**A**) = $a_{11} + a_{22} + \ldots + a_{nn} = \sum_{i=1}^{n} a_{ii}$.

Example:

Let $\mathbf{A} = \begin{bmatrix} 1 & 5 & 9 \\ -3 & 2 & 8 \\ 4 & 7 & 6 \end{bmatrix}$, then tr(**A**) = 1 + 2 + 6 = 9.

Addition and Subtraction

Matrices of the same size are added or subtracted by adding or subtracting corresponding elements.

Example:

Let $\mathbf{A} = \begin{bmatrix} 2 & 4 & 8 \\ 9 & -1 & 5 \end{bmatrix}$, and $\mathbf{B} = \begin{bmatrix} 1 & 5 & 3 \\ 2 & 3 & -7 \end{bmatrix}$, then

$$\mathbf{A} + \mathbf{B} = \begin{bmatrix} 2+1 & 4+5 & 8+3 \\ 9+2 & (-1)+3 & 5+(-7) \end{bmatrix} = \begin{bmatrix} 3 & 9 & 11 \\ 11 & 2 & -2 \end{bmatrix} \text{ and}$$

$$\mathbf{A} - \mathbf{B} = \begin{bmatrix} 2-1 & 4-5 & 8-3 \\ 9-2 & -1-3 & 5-(-7) \end{bmatrix} = \begin{bmatrix} 1 & -1 & 5 \\ 7 & -4 & 12 \end{bmatrix}.$$

Multiplication

The *inner product* of two vectors $\mathbf{a}' = [a_1 \ a_2 \ \ldots \ a_n]$ and $\mathbf{x} = \begin{bmatrix} x_1 \\ x_2 \\ \vdots \\ x_n \end{bmatrix}$ is defined as

$$\mathbf{a}'\mathbf{x} = a_1x_1 + a_2x_2 + \ldots + a_nx_n = \sum_{i=1}^{n} a_i x_i .$$

Example:

Let $\mathbf{a}' = [3 \ 1 \ 10]$ and $\mathbf{x} = \begin{bmatrix} 5 \\ 10 \\ 3 \end{bmatrix}$, then the inner product $\mathbf{a}'\mathbf{x} = 3(5) + 1(10) + 10(3) = 55$.

The product **AB** of two matrices **A** and **B** is defined and therefore exists only if the number of columns in **A** equals the number of rows in **B**. **AB** has the same number of rows as **A** and the same number of columns as **B**. The ij^{th} element of **AB** is the inner product of the ith row of **A** and j^{th} column of **B**.

Example:

Let $\mathbf{A} = \begin{bmatrix} 1 & 2 & 3 \\ -1 & 4 & 2 \end{bmatrix}$ and $\mathbf{B} = \begin{bmatrix} 0 & 6 & 1 & 5 \\ 2 & 1 & -2 & 3 \\ 4 & 1 & 2 & 5 \end{bmatrix}$, then

AB =

$$\begin{bmatrix} 1(0)+2(2)+3(4) & 1(6)+2(1)+3(1) & 1(1)+2(-2)+3(2) & 1(5)+2(3)+3(5) \\ -1(0)+4(2)+2(4) & -1(6)+4(1)+2(1) & -1(1)+4(-2)+2(2) & -1(5)+4(3)+2(5) \end{bmatrix} =$$

$$\begin{bmatrix} 16 & 11 & 3 & 26 \\ 16 & 0 & -5 & 17 \end{bmatrix}$$

Direct or Kronecker Product ⊗

Suppose **A** is $m \times n$ and **B** is $p \times q$. Then the *direct* or *Kronecker product* **A⊗B** is of size $mp \times nq$ and is most easily described as the partitioned matrix:

$$\mathbf{A}_{m\times n} \otimes \mathbf{B}_{p\times q} = \begin{bmatrix} a_{11}\mathbf{B} & a_{12}\mathbf{B} & \dots & a_{1n}\mathbf{B} \\ a_{21}\mathbf{B} & a_{22}\mathbf{B} & \dots & a_{2n}\mathbf{B} \\ \dots & \dots & \dots & \dots \\ a_{m1}\mathbf{B} & a_{m2}\mathbf{B} & \dots & a_{mn}\mathbf{B} \end{bmatrix}$$

Example:

Let $\mathbf{A} = \begin{bmatrix} 1 & 2 \\ -1 & 3 \end{bmatrix}$ and $\mathbf{B} = \begin{bmatrix} 1 & -1 & 1 & 2 \\ 3 & 2 & 0 & 1 \\ -1 & 0 & 2 & 3 \end{bmatrix}$, then

$$\mathbf{A} \otimes \mathbf{B} = \begin{bmatrix} 1 & -1 & 1 & 2 & 2 & -2 & 2 & 4 \\ 3 & 2 & 0 & 1 & 6 & 4 & 0 & 2 \\ -1 & 0 & 2 & 3 & -2 & 0 & 4 & 6 \\ -1 & 1 & -1 & -2 & 3 & -3 & 3 & 6 \\ -3 & -2 & 0 & -1 & 9 & 6 & 0 & 3 \\ 1 & 0 & -2 & -3 & -3 & 0 & 6 & 9 \end{bmatrix}$$

B.1.3 Some Special Matrices

A *square* matrix is a matrix whose number of columns equals the number of rows. The elements on the diagonal, a_{11}, a_{22}, …, a_{nn}, are referred to as the *diagonal elements* or *diagonal* of the matrix. Elements of a square matrix other than the diagonal elements are called *off-diagonal* or *nondiagonal* elements.

A *diagonal* matrix is a square matrix having zero for all its nondiagonal elements.

Example:

$$\mathbf{A} = \begin{bmatrix} 1 & 0 & 0 \\ 0 & 3 & 0 \\ 0 & 0 & 2 \end{bmatrix} \text{ is a diagonal matrix.}$$

A *triangular* matrix is a square matrix with all elements above (or below) the diagonal being zero.

Example:

$$\mathbf{A} = \begin{bmatrix} 1 & 4 & 6 \\ 0 & -2 & 9 \\ 0 & 0 & 7 \end{bmatrix} \text{ and } \mathbf{B} = \begin{bmatrix} 3 & 0 & 0 \\ -7 & 2 & 0 \\ 1 & -2 & 5 \end{bmatrix} \text{ are triangular matrices.}$$

A is an *upper triangular matrix* and **B** is a *lower triangular matrix.*

A diagonal matrix having all diagonal elements equal to unity is called an *identity* matrix, or sometimes a *unit* matrix. It is usually denoted by the letter **I**. For example,

$$\mathbf{I}_4 = \begin{bmatrix} 1 & 0 & 0 & 0 \\ 0 & 1 & 0 & 0 \\ 0 & 0 & 1 & 0 \\ 0 & 0 & 0 & 1 \end{bmatrix} \text{ is an identity matrix of order 4.}$$

For any matrix **A** of order $m \times n$, $\mathbf{I}_m\mathbf{A}_{m\times n} = \mathbf{A}_{m\times n}\mathbf{I}_n = \mathbf{A}_{m\times n}$.

A *symmetric* matrix is a square matrix when it equals its transpose.

Example:

$$\text{Let } \mathbf{A} = \begin{bmatrix} 1 & -2 & 3 \\ -2 & 4 & 5 \\ 3 & 5 & 6 \end{bmatrix}, \text{ then } \mathbf{A}' = \begin{bmatrix} 1 & -2 & 3 \\ -2 & 4 & 5 \\ 3 & 5 & 6 \end{bmatrix} = \mathbf{A}.$$

The matrix **A** is symmetric. In symmetric matrices, the area above the diagonal is a mirror image of the area below the diagonal.

Vectors whose every element is unity are called *summing vectors* because they can be used to express a sum of numbers in matrix notation as an inner product.

Example:

$\mathbf{1}' = [1\ \ 1\ \ 1\ \ 1]$ is a summing vector of order 4. For $\mathbf{x}' = [2\ \ 4\ \ -3\ \ 8]$,

$$\mathbf{1}'\mathbf{x} = [1\ \ 1\ \ 1\ \ 1]\begin{bmatrix} 2 \\ 4 \\ -3 \\ 8 \end{bmatrix} = 2 + 4 - 3 + 8 = 11 = \mathbf{x}'\mathbf{1}.$$

It follows that $\mathbf{1}'_n\mathbf{1}_n = \text{n}$ and $\mathbf{1}_m\mathbf{1}'_n = \mathbf{J}_{m \times n}$, a matrix having all elements unity.

A square $\mathbf{J}$ matrix is denoted by $\mathbf{J}_n$. $\mathbf{J}_n = \mathbf{1}_n\mathbf{1}'_n$ and $\mathbf{J}_n^{\,2} = n\mathbf{J}_n$. A useful variant of $\mathbf{J}_n$ is

$$\bar{\mathbf{J}}_n = \frac{1}{n}\mathbf{J}_n,\ \bar{\mathbf{J}}_n^2 = \bar{\mathbf{J}}_n.$$

Therefore, $\bar{\mathbf{J}}_n$ is an *idempotent* matrix which satisfies $\mathbf{K}^2 = \mathbf{K}$.

$\mathbf{C}_n = \mathbf{I} - \bar{\mathbf{J}}_n = \mathbf{I} - \dfrac{1}{n}\mathbf{J}_n$, is known as a *centering matrix*. It follows that

$\mathbf{C} = \mathbf{C}' = \mathbf{C}^2$, $\mathbf{C1} = 0$, and $\mathbf{CJ} = \mathbf{JC} = 0$.

An *orthogonal* matrix $\mathbf{A}$ is a matrix having the property $\mathbf{AA}' = \mathbf{I} = \mathbf{A}'\mathbf{A}$.

Example:

$$\text{Let } \mathbf{A} = \begin{bmatrix} 1/\sqrt{4} & 1/\sqrt{4} & 1/\sqrt{4} & 1/\sqrt{4} \\ 1/\sqrt{2} & -1/\sqrt{2} & 0 & 0 \\ 1/\sqrt{6} & 1/\sqrt{6} & -2/\sqrt{6} & 0 \\ 1/\sqrt{12} & 1/\sqrt{12} & 1/\sqrt{12} & -3/\sqrt{12} \end{bmatrix}$$

You can verify that $\mathbf{AA}' = \mathbf{I}$. Therefore, $\mathbf{A}$ is an orthogonal matrix. A matrix in the form shown above is called a *Helmert* matrix.

A *quadratic form* is the product of a row vector $\mathbf{x}'$, a matrix $\mathbf{A}$, and the column vector $\mathbf{x}$, that is, $\mathbf{x}'\mathbf{Ax}$. This is a quadratic function of the *x*s. Notice that to result in the same quadratic function of *x*s, you can use many different matrices. Each matrix has the same diagonal elements, and the sum of each pair of symmetrically placed off-diagonal elements a_{ij} and a_{ji} is the same.

For any particular quadratic form there is a unique *symmetric matrix* **A** for which the quadratic form can be expressed as $\mathbf{x}'\mathbf{A}\mathbf{x}$:

$$\mathbf{x}'\mathbf{A}\mathbf{x} = \sum_{i=1}^{n} x_i^2 a_{ii} + 2\sum_{j=i+1}^{n}\sum_{i=1}^{n} x_i x_j a_{ij}$$

Example:

$$\mathbf{x}'\mathbf{A}\mathbf{x} = \mathbf{x}'\begin{bmatrix} a_{11} & a_{12} & a_{13} \\ a_{21} & a_{22} & a_{23} \\ a_{31} & a_{32} & a_{33} \end{bmatrix}\mathbf{x}$$

$$= a_{11}x_1^2 + a_{22}x_2^2 + a_{33}x_3^2 + 2(a_{12}x_1x_2 + a_{13}x_1x_3 + a_{23}x_2x_3).$$

When $\mathbf{A} = \begin{bmatrix} 1 & 2 & 3 \\ 2 & 5 & 1 \\ 3 & 1 & 4 \end{bmatrix}$, then

$$\mathbf{x}'\mathbf{A}\mathbf{x} = [x_1 \; x_2 \; x_3]\begin{bmatrix} 1 & 2 & 3 \\ 2 & 5 & 1 \\ 3 & 1 & 4 \end{bmatrix}\begin{bmatrix} x_1 \\ x_2 \\ x_3 \end{bmatrix} = x_1^2 + 5x_2^2 + 4x_3^2 + 4x_1x_2 + 6x_2x_3 + 2x_2x_3$$

When $\mathbf{x}'\mathbf{A}\mathbf{x} > 0$ for all **x** other than $\mathbf{x} = 0$, then $\mathbf{x}'\mathbf{A}\mathbf{x}$ is a *positive definite* quadratic form, and $\mathbf{A} = \mathbf{A}'$ is correspondingly a *positive definite (p.d.) matrix.*

Example:

Let $\mathbf{A} = \begin{bmatrix} 2 & 2 & 1 \\ 2 & 5 & 1 \\ 1 & 1 & 2 \end{bmatrix}$, then

$$\mathbf{x}'\mathbf{A}\mathbf{x} = [x_1 \; x_2 \; x_3]\begin{bmatrix} 2 & 2 & 1 \\ 2 & 5 & 1 \\ 1 & 1 & 2 \end{bmatrix}\begin{bmatrix} x_1 \\ x_2 \\ x_3 \end{bmatrix}$$

$$= 2x_1^2 + 5x_2^2 + 2x_3^2 + 4x_1x_2 + 2x_2x_3 + 2x_2x_3$$

$$= (x_1 + 2x_2)^2 + (x_1 + x_3)^2 + (x_2 + x_3)^2 > 0 \text{ other than } \mathbf{x} = 0.$$

The matrix **A** is a positive definite matrix.

When $\mathbf{x}'\mathbf{A}\mathbf{x} \geq 0$ for all **x** and $\mathbf{x}'\mathbf{A}\mathbf{x} = 0$ for some $\mathbf{x} \neq 0$, then $\mathbf{x}'\mathbf{A}\mathbf{x}$ is a *positive semidefinite* quadratic form, and $\mathbf{A} = \mathbf{A}'$ is correspondingly a *positive semidefinite (p.s.d.) matrix*. The two classes of matrices taken together, positive definite and positive semidefinite, are called *nonnegative definite* (n.n.d.).

Example:

Let $\mathbf{A} = \begin{bmatrix} 37 & -2 & -24 \\ -2 & 13 & -3 \\ -24 & -3 & 17 \end{bmatrix}$, then

$$\mathbf{x}'\mathbf{A}\mathbf{x} = [x_1 \;\; x_2 \;\; x_3] \begin{bmatrix} 37 & -2 & -24 \\ -2 & 13 & -3 \\ -24 & -3 & 17 \end{bmatrix} \begin{bmatrix} x_1 \\ x_2 \\ x_3 \end{bmatrix}$$

$$= 37x_1^2 + 13x_2^2 + 17x_3^2 - 4x_1x_2 - 48x_2x_3 - 6x_2x_3$$

$$= (x_1 - 2x_2)^2 + (6x_1 - 4x_3)^2 + (3x_2 - x_3)^2$$

This is zero for $\mathbf{x}' = [2 \;\; 1 \;\; 3]$, and for any scalar multiple thereof, as well as for $\mathbf{x} = 0$. Then the matrix **A** is *positive semidefinite.*

Example:

$$\mathbf{x}'\mathbf{C}\mathbf{x} = \mathbf{x}'(\mathbf{I} - \bar{\mathbf{J}})\mathbf{x} = \sum_{i=1}^{n} (x_i - \bar{x})^2$$

is a positive semidefinite quadratic form because it is positive, except for being zero when all the x_is are equal. Its matrix, $\mathbf{I} - \bar{\mathbf{J}}$, which is idempotent, is also p.s.d., as are all symmetric idempotent matrices (except **I**, which is the only p.d. idempotent matrix).

B.1.4 Determinant

The *determinant* of a square matrix of order n, (that is, $\mathbf{A} = \{a_{ij}\}$, $i, j = 1, 2, \ldots, n$) is the sum of all possible products of n elements of $\mathbf{A}$ such that

1. each product has one and only one element from every row and column of $\mathbf{A}$,
2. the sign of a product being $(-1)^p$ for $p = \sum_{i=1}^{n} n_i$, where by writing
    a. the product with its i subscripts in natural order $a_{1j_1} a_{2j_2} \cdots a_{ij_i} \cdots a_{nj_n}$
    b. the j subscripts j_i, $i = 1, 2, \ldots, n$, being the first n integers in some order

n_i is defined as the number of js less than j_i that follow j_i in this order.

Therefore, the determinant of a matrix $\mathbf{A}$, denoted by $|\mathbf{A}|$, is a polynomial of the elements of a square matrix. It is a scalar. It is the sum of certain products of the elements of the matrix from which it is derived, each product being multiplied by +1 or –1 according to certain rules.

Example:

$$|\mathbf{A}| = \begin{vmatrix} 3 & 7 \\ 2 & 6 \end{vmatrix} = 3(6) - 7(2) = 4$$

$$|\mathbf{A}| = \begin{vmatrix} 1 & 2 & 3 \\ 4 & 5 & 6 \\ 7 & 8 & 10 \end{vmatrix} = 1(+1)\begin{vmatrix} 5 & 6 \\ 8 & 10 \end{vmatrix} + 2(-1)\begin{vmatrix} 4 & 6 \\ 7 & 10 \end{vmatrix} + 3(+1)\begin{vmatrix} 4 & 5 \\ 7 & 8 \end{vmatrix}$$

$$= 1(50 - 48) - 2(40 - 42) + 3(32 - 35) = -3$$

The determinant that multiplies each element of the chosen row (in this case, the first row) is the determinant derived from $|\mathbf{A}|$ by crossing out the row and column containing the element concerned. For example, the first element, 1, is multiplied by the determinant $\begin{vmatrix} 5 & 6 \\ 8 & 10 \end{vmatrix}$, which is obtained from $|\mathbf{A}|$ through crossing out the first row and column. Determinants obtained in this way are called *minors* of $|\mathbf{A}|$, that is, $\begin{vmatrix} 5 & 6 \\ 8 & 10 \end{vmatrix}$ is the minor of the element 1 in $|\mathbf{A}|$, and $\begin{vmatrix} 4 & 6 \\ 7 & 10 \end{vmatrix}$ is the minor of element 2.

The (+1) and (–1) factors in the expansion are decided on according to the following rule:

If $\mathbf{A}$ is written in the form $\mathbf{A} = \{a_{ij}\}$, the product of a_{ij} and its minor in the expansion of determinant $|\mathbf{A}|$ is multiplied by $(-1)^{i+j}$.

Therefore, because the element 1 in the example is the element a_{11}, its product with its minor is multiplied by $(-1)^{1+1} = +1$. For element 2, which is a_{12}, its product with its minor is multiplied by $(-1)^{1+2} = -1$.

Denote the minor of the element a_{ij} by $|\mathbf{M}_{ij}|$, where $\mathbf{M}_{ij}$ is a submatrix of $\mathbf{A}$ obtained by deleting the ith row and the jth column. The determinant of an n-order matrix is obtained by *expansion by the elements of a row* (*or column*), or *expansion by minors*:

$$|\mathbf{A}| = \sum_{j=1}^{n} a_{ij}(-1)^{i+j}\,|\mathbf{M}_{ij}| \text{ for any row } i \text{, or}$$

$$|\mathbf{A}| = \sum_{i=1}^{n} a_{ij}(-1)^{i+j}\,|\mathbf{M}_{ij}| \text{ for any column } j.$$

The signed minor $(-1)^{i+j}|\mathbf{M}_{ij}|$ is called a *cofactor*: $c_{ij} = (-1)^{i+j}|\mathbf{M}_{ij}|$.

This expansion is used recurrently when n is large, that is, each $|\mathbf{M}_{ij}|$ is expanded by the same procedure.

This method of evaluation requires lengthy computing for determinants of order exceeding 3 to 4. Fortunately, easier methods exist, but they are based on this expansion by minors method.

B.1.5 Inverse Matrices

The *inverse* of a square matrix **A** is a matrix whose product with **A** is the identity matrix **I**. The inverse matrix is denoted by $\mathbf{A}^{-1}$. The concept of "dividing" by **A** in matrix algebra is replaced by the concept of multiplying by the inverse matrix $\mathbf{A}^{-1}$.

An inverse matrix $\mathbf{A}^{-1}$ should have the following properties:

- $\mathbf{A}^{-1}\mathbf{A} = \mathbf{A}\mathbf{A}^{-1} = \mathbf{I}$
- $\mathbf{A}^{-1}$ unique for given **A**.

An *adjugate* (or *adjoint*) of matrix **A**, denoted by adj **A**, is obtained by replacing the elements in **A** by their cofactors and then transposing it.

The inverse of matrix **A**, $\mathbf{A}^{-1}$, can be described as the adjugate of **A** multiplied by the scalar 1/|**A**|:

$$\mathbf{A}^{-1} = \frac{1}{|\mathbf{A}|}\text{adj }\mathbf{A}$$

where adj **A** is the adjugate (or adjoint) matrix of **A**. Therefore,

$$\mathbf{A}^{-1} = \frac{1}{|\mathbf{A}|}\begin{bmatrix} \mathbf{A} \text{ with every element} \\ \text{replaced by its cofactor} \end{bmatrix}^{\text{transposed}}$$

Example:

Let $\mathbf{A} = \begin{bmatrix} 2 & 5 \\ 3 & 9 \end{bmatrix}$, the determinant of **A** is $|\mathbf{A}| = \begin{vmatrix} 2 & 5 \\ 3 & 9 \end{vmatrix} = 18 - 15 = 3$.

- The cofactor for $a_{11} = 2$ is $(-1)^{1+1}|9| = 9$.
- The cofactor for $a_{12} = 5$ is $(-1)^{1+2}|3| = -3$.
- The cofactor for $a_{21} = 3$ is $(-1)^{2+1}|5| = -5$.
- The cofactor for $a_{22} = 9$ is $(-1)^{2+2}|2| = 2$.

The adjugate matrix is $\begin{bmatrix} 9 & -5 \\ -3 & 2 \end{bmatrix}$, and so the inverse is

$$\mathbf{A}^{-1} = \frac{1}{3}\begin{bmatrix} 9 & -5 \\ -3 & 2 \end{bmatrix}$$

Conditions for existence of the inverse are

1. $\mathbf{A}^{-1}$ can exist only when **A** is square
2. $\mathbf{A}^{-1}$ does exist only if |**A**| is nonzero.

A square matrix is said to be *singular* when its determinant is zero and *nonsingular* when its determinant is nonzero.

Several computing procedures for inverting matrices are based on solving linear equations by successive elimination and backward substitution. The basic idea is as follows:

To solve the equations $\mathbf{Ax} = \mathbf{b}$, write the following matrix [**A** **I**], where **I** is the identity matrix of the same order as **A**. Perform row operations to this matrix to make the left submatrix become **I**, whereupon the right submatrix is $\mathbf{A}^{-1}$. Thus, starting with [**A** **I**], you now have [**I** $\mathbf{A}^{-1}$], providing $\mathbf{A}^{-1}$ exists.

Detailed information on row operations can be found in any matrix algebra textbook.

B.1.6 Linear Dependence and Rank

Define **X** as the matrix having columns $\mathbf{x}_1, \mathbf{x}_2, \ldots, \mathbf{x}_n$, and **a** as the vector of *a*s:

$\mathbf{X} = [\mathbf{x}_1\ \mathbf{x}_2\ \ldots\ \mathbf{x}_n]$ and $\mathbf{a}' = [a_1\ a_2\ \ldots\ a_n]$.

Then the *linear combination* of the set of *n* vectors is

$$a_1\mathbf{x}_1 + a_2\mathbf{x}_2 + \cdots + a_n\mathbf{x}_n = \sum_{i=1}^{n} a_i\mathbf{x}_i = \mathbf{Xa}$$

You see that

- **Xa** is a column vector, a linear combination of the columns of **X**.
- **b′X** is a row vector, a linear combination of the rows of **X**.
- **AB** is a matrix. Its rows are linear combinations of the rows of **B**, and its columns are linear combinations of the columns of **A**.

The vector **Xa** is sometimes called the *linear transformation* of the vector **a** to the vector **Xa**, with **X** being the matrix of the transformation.

Example:

Let $\mathbf{X} = \begin{bmatrix} 1 & -2 & 0 \\ 0 & 4 & 1 \\ -1 & 3 & 5 \\ 6 & 7 & 5 \end{bmatrix}$ and $\mathbf{a}' = \begin{bmatrix} a_1 & a_2 & a_3 \end{bmatrix}$, then

$$\mathbf{Xa} = \begin{bmatrix} \mathbf{x}_1 & \mathbf{x}_2 & \mathbf{x}_3 \end{bmatrix} \begin{bmatrix} a_1 \\ a_2 \\ a_3 \end{bmatrix} = \begin{bmatrix} 1 & -2 & 0 \\ 0 & 4 & 1 \\ -1 & 3 & 5 \\ 6 & 7 & 5 \end{bmatrix} \begin{bmatrix} a_1 \\ a_2 \\ a_3 \end{bmatrix} = \begin{bmatrix} a_1 - 2a_2 + 0a_3 \\ 0a_1 + 4a_2 + a_3 \\ -a_1 + 3a_2 + 5a_3 \\ 6a_1 + 7a_2 + 5a_3 \end{bmatrix}$$

is a vector for any scalar values a_1, a_2, and a_3.

If there exists a vector $\mathbf{a} \neq 0$, such that $a_1\mathbf{x}_1 + a_2\mathbf{x}_2 + \cdots + a_n\mathbf{x}_n = \mathbf{0}$, then provided none of $\mathbf{x}_1, \mathbf{x}_2, \ldots, \mathbf{x}_n$ is null, those vectors are said to be *linearly dependent vectors*.

An alternative statement of the definition is the following

If $\mathbf{Xa} = 0$ for some non-null **a**, then the columns of **X** are *linearly dependent vectors*, provided none is null.

If $\mathbf{a} = 0$ is the only vector for which $a_1\mathbf{x}_1 + a_2\mathbf{x}_2 + \cdots + a_n\mathbf{x}_n = \mathbf{0}$, then provided none of $\mathbf{x}_1, \mathbf{x}_2, \ldots, \mathbf{x}_n$ is null, those vectors (the columns of **X**) are said to be *linearly independent vectors*.

The *rank* of a matrix is the number of linearly independent rows (and columns) in the matrix. The rank of **A** is denoted by $r_{\mathbf{A}}$ or $r(\mathbf{A})$.

When $r(\mathbf{A}_{n\times n}) = n$, then **A** is *nonsingular*, that is, $\mathbf{A}^{-1}$ exists.

When $r(\mathbf{A}_{n\times n}) < n$, then **A** is *singular* and $\mathbf{A}^{-1}$ does not exist.

When $r(\mathbf{A}_{p\times q}) = p < q$, then **A** has *full row rank*, that is, its rank equals its number of rows.

When $r(\mathbf{A}_{p\times q}) = q < p$, then **A** has *full column rank*, that is, its rank equals its number of columns.

When $r(\mathbf{A}_{n\times n}) = n$, **A** has *full rank*, that is, its rank equals its order, it is nonsingular, its inverse exists, and it is called *invertible*.

Because it is easier to work with rank than determinants, you often determine the existence of $\mathbf{A}^{-1}$ by ascertaining whether $r(\mathbf{A}) < n$ or $r(\mathbf{A}) = n$ rather than by ascertaining whether $|\mathbf{A}|$ is zero or not.

Example:

Consider the following vectors:

$$\mathbf{x}_1 = \begin{bmatrix} 3 \\ -6 \\ 9 \end{bmatrix} \quad \mathbf{x}_2 = \begin{bmatrix} 0 \\ 5 \\ -5 \end{bmatrix} \quad \mathbf{x}_3 = \begin{bmatrix} 2 \\ 1 \\ 1 \end{bmatrix} \quad \mathbf{x}_4 = \begin{bmatrix} -6 \\ 12 \\ -18 \end{bmatrix} \quad \mathbf{x}_5 = \begin{bmatrix} 2 \\ -3 \\ 3 \end{bmatrix}$$

Because $2\mathbf{x}_1 + \mathbf{x}_4 = \begin{bmatrix} 6 \\ -12 \\ 18 \end{bmatrix} + \begin{bmatrix} -6 \\ 12 \\ -18 \end{bmatrix} = 0$, that is,

$$a_1\mathbf{x}_1 + a_2\mathbf{x}_4 = \mathbf{0} \text{ for } \begin{bmatrix} a_1 \\ a_2 \end{bmatrix} = \begin{bmatrix} 2 \\ 1 \end{bmatrix}, \text{ which is non-null,}$$

$\mathbf{x}_1$ and $\mathbf{x}_4$ are *linearly dependent* vectors. So are $\mathbf{x}_1$, $\mathbf{x}_2$, and $\mathbf{x}_3$ because

$$2\mathbf{x}_1 + 3\mathbf{x}_2 - 3\mathbf{x}_3 = \begin{bmatrix} 6 \\ -12 \\ 18 \end{bmatrix} + \begin{bmatrix} 0 \\ 15 \\ -15 \end{bmatrix} + \begin{bmatrix} -6 \\ -3 \\ -3 \end{bmatrix} = \begin{bmatrix} 0 \\ 0 \\ 0 \end{bmatrix} = \mathbf{0}$$

However, consider

$$a_1\mathbf{x}_1 + a_2\mathbf{x}_2 = \begin{bmatrix} 3a_1 \\ -6a_1 \\ 9a_1 \end{bmatrix} + \begin{bmatrix} 0 \\ 5a_2 \\ -5a_2 \end{bmatrix} = \begin{bmatrix} 3a_1 \\ -6a_1 + 5a_2 \\ 9a_1 - 5a_2 \end{bmatrix}$$

There are no values a_1 and a_2, which makes it a null vector other than $a_1 = 0 = a_2$. Therefore, $\mathbf{x}_1$ and $\mathbf{x}_2$ are *linearly independent* vectors.

The rank of the matrix $\mathbf{X} = \begin{bmatrix} \mathbf{x}_1 & \mathbf{x}_2 & \mathbf{x}_3 & \mathbf{x}_4 & \mathbf{x}_5 \end{bmatrix} = \begin{bmatrix} 3 & 0 & 2 & -6 & 2 \\ -6 & 5 & 1 & 12 & -3 \\ 9 & -5 & 1 & -18 & 3 \end{bmatrix}$

is 3.

The calculation of ranks can be performed by row operations, which is discussed in many matrix algebra textbooks.

✎ The linear dependence or linear independence of vectors is a characteristic pertaining to a set of vectors of the same order. It is not a characteristic of individual vectors.

Any non-null matrix **A** of rank r is equivalent to

$$\mathbf{PAQ} = \begin{bmatrix} \mathbf{I}_r & \mathbf{0} \\ \mathbf{0} & \mathbf{0} \end{bmatrix} = \mathbf{C}$$

where $\mathbf{I}_r$ is the identity matrix of order r, and the null submatrices are of appropriate order to make **C** the same order as **A**. For **A** of order $m \times n$, **P** and **Q** are nonsingular matrices of order m and n, respectively, being products of elementary operators.

The matrix **C** is called the *equivalent canonical form* or the *canonical form under equivalence*. It always exists and can be used to determine the rank of **A**.

B.1.7 Generalized Inverse

The generalized inverse plays an important role in understanding the solutions to linear equations $\mathbf{Ax} = \mathbf{y}$, when $\mathbf{A}$ has no inverse (but has generalized inverse).

A *generalized inverse* of a matrix $\mathbf{A}$ is any matrix $\mathbf{G}$ such that $\mathbf{AGA} = \mathbf{A}$. An alternative symbol for $\mathbf{G}$ is $\mathbf{A}^{-}$.

When $\mathbf{A}$ is not full rank, as occurs in many general linear models with $\mathbf{A} = \mathbf{X}'\mathbf{X}$, an infinite number of generalized inverses exist. Several ways of obtaining $\mathbf{G}$ exist. The approach to obtaining a generalized inverse used by SAS is to partition a singular matrix into several sets of matrices.

Example:

Consider an $\mathbf{X}'\mathbf{X}$ matrix of rank r that can be partitioned as

$$\mathbf{X}'\mathbf{X} = \begin{bmatrix} \mathbf{A}_{11} & \mathbf{A}_{12} \\ \mathbf{A}_{21} & \mathbf{A}_{22} \end{bmatrix}$$

where $\mathbf{A}_{11}$ is $r \times r$ and of rank r. Then $\mathbf{A}_{11}^{-1}$ exists, and a generalized inverse of $\mathbf{X}'\mathbf{X}$ is

$$(\mathbf{X}'\mathbf{X})^{-} = \begin{bmatrix} \mathbf{A}_{11}^{-1} & \mathbf{0} \\ \mathbf{0} & \mathbf{0} \end{bmatrix}$$

Because the generalized inverse is not unique, the solutions to normal equations in general linear models, $\mathbf{b} = (\mathbf{X}'\mathbf{X})^{-}\mathbf{X}'\mathbf{y}$, are not unique either. However, a class of linear functions ($\mathbf{Lb}$) called *estimable functions* exists, and $\mathbf{Lb}$ and its variance are invariant through all possible generalized inverses. In other words, the linear combination $\mathbf{Lb}$ is unique and is an unbiased estimate of $\mathbf{L\beta}$.

B.1.8 Eigenvalues and Eigenvectors

Consider equations

$$\mathbf{Ax} = \lambda\mathbf{x} \quad \text{or} \quad (\mathbf{A}-\lambda\mathbf{I})\mathbf{x} = 0$$

for $\mathbf{x}$ (a vector) and λ (a scalar), and solve for $\mathbf{x}$.

If the matrix $\mathbf{A}-\lambda\mathbf{I}$ is nonsingular, the unique solution to these equations is $\mathbf{x} = 0$. You only get a nontrivial solution when $|\mathbf{A}-\lambda\mathbf{I}| = 0$. If you expand this determinant, the condition becomes a polynomial equation in λ of degree p. This is called the *characteristic equation* of $\mathbf{A}$. Its p roots (which may be real or complex, simple or multiple) are called *eigenvalues* (or proper values, characteristic values, or latent roots) of $\mathbf{A}$. If λ is an eigenvalue, a nonzero vector $\mathbf{x}$ satisfying $\mathbf{Ax} = \lambda\mathbf{x}$ is called an *eigenvector* (or proper vector, characteristic vector, or latent vector) corresponding to λ. It is often convenient to normalize each eigenvector to have a squared length of 1.

Example:

The matrix $\mathbf{A} = \begin{bmatrix} 1 & 4 \\ 9 & 1 \end{bmatrix}$ has a characteristic equation:

$$\left|\begin{bmatrix} 1 & 4 \\ 9 & 1 \end{bmatrix} - \begin{bmatrix} \lambda & 0 \\ 0 & \lambda \end{bmatrix}\right| = 0; \text{ that is, } \begin{vmatrix} 1-\lambda & 4 \\ 9 & 1-\lambda \end{vmatrix} = 0.$$

$(1-\lambda)^2 - 36 = 0$, or $\lambda = -5$ or 7

It can be seen that

$$\begin{bmatrix} 1 & 4 \\ 9 & 1 \end{bmatrix}\begin{bmatrix} 2 \\ -3 \end{bmatrix} = -5\begin{bmatrix} 2 \\ -3 \end{bmatrix} \text{ and } \begin{bmatrix} 1 & 4 \\ 9 & 1 \end{bmatrix}\begin{bmatrix} 2 \\ 3 \end{bmatrix} = 7\begin{bmatrix} 2 \\ 3 \end{bmatrix}$$

therefore, $\begin{bmatrix} 2 \\ -3 \end{bmatrix}$ is an eigenvector corresponding to the eigenvalue –5,

and $\begin{bmatrix} 2 \\ 3 \end{bmatrix}$ is an eigenvector corresponding to the eigenvalue 7.

Some of the Basic Properties of Eigenvalues and Eigenvectors

For $\mathbf{Ax} = \lambda\mathbf{x}$,

1. $\mathbf{A}^k\mathbf{x} = \lambda^k\mathbf{x}$ and $\mathbf{A}^{-1}\mathbf{x} = \lambda^{-1}\mathbf{x}$, when $\mathbf{A}$ is nonsingular

2. $c\mathbf{Ax} = c\lambda\mathbf{x}$ for any scalar c

3. $f(\mathbf{A})\mathbf{x} = f(\lambda)\mathbf{x}$ for any polynomial function $f(\mathbf{A})$

4. $\sum_{i=1}^{n} \lambda_i = \mathrm{tr}(\mathbf{A})$ and $\prod_{i=1}^{n} \lambda_i = |\mathbf{A}|$, that is, the sum of eigenvalues of a matrix equals its trace, and their product equals its determinant

5. If $\mathbf{A}$ is symmetric, then
   - eigenvalues of matrix $\mathbf{A}$ are all real
   - $\mathbf{A}$ is diagonable
   - eigenvectors are orthogonal to each other
   - the rank of $\mathbf{A}$ equals the number of nonzero eigenvalues
   - positive definite matrices have eigenvalues all greater than zero and vice versa.

The matrix $\mathbf{A}$ is *diagonable* when a nonsingular matrix $\mathbf{X}$ exists, and consists of the n eigenvectors, that is, $\mathbf{X} = [\mathbf{x}_1 \quad \mathbf{x}_2 \quad \cdots \quad \mathbf{x}_n]$, where all n eigenvectors are linearly independent, such that

$$\mathbf{X}^{-1}\mathbf{AX} = \mathbf{D} = \mathrm{diag}\{\lambda_1, \lambda_2, \ldots, \lambda_n\}$$

For symmetric matrix $\mathbf{A}$, because the eigenvectors are orthogonal to each other, the above equation becomes

$$\mathbf{X}'\mathbf{AX} = \mathbf{D} = \mathrm{diag}\{\lambda_1, \lambda_2, \ldots, \lambda_n\}$$

It follows that $\mathbf{A}$ can be written as $\mathbf{XDX}'$, or

$$\mathbf{A} = \lambda_1\mathbf{x}_1\mathbf{x}_1' + \lambda_2\mathbf{x}_2\mathbf{x}_2' + \ldots + \lambda_n\mathbf{x}_n\mathbf{x}_n'$$

This is called the *spectral decomposition* of the matrix $\mathbf{A}$.

When $\mathbf{A}$ is nonsingular, the spectral decomposition of $\mathbf{A}^{-1}$ is

$$\mathbf{A}^{-1} = \lambda_1^{-1}\mathbf{x}_1\mathbf{x}_1' + \lambda_2^{-1}\mathbf{x}_2\mathbf{x}_2' + \ldots + \lambda_n^{-1}\mathbf{x}_n\mathbf{x}_n'$$

When $\mathbf{A}$ is singular, a generalized inverse of $\mathbf{A}$ can be obtained from its spectral decomposition in exactly the same way, by omitting the terms for which $\lambda_i = 0$.

B.1.9 Cholesky Root

If **A** is positive definite of size $n \times n$, you can find an upper triangular matrix **U** such that **A** = **U′U**, so that **U** is sort of a square root of **A**, also referred to as the *Cholesky root* of the matrix **A**.

The rule for the construction of **U** is simply

(column i of **U**) × (column j of **U**) = a_{ij},

that is,

$$\begin{aligned} u_{11}^2 &= a_{11}, \\ u_{11}u_{12} &= a_{12}, \\ u_{11}u_{13} &= a_{13}, \\ &\ldots \\ u_{12}^2 + u_{22}^2 &= a_{22}, \\ u_{12}u_{13} + u_{22}u_{23} &= a_{23}, \\ &\ldots \\ u_{13}^2 + u_{23}^2 + u_{33}^2 &= a_{33}, \end{aligned}$$

and so on.

The procedure for forming **U** (called the *square-root* or *Cholesky* procedure) provides a basis for an excellent numerical method for solving simultaneous linear equations and inverting matrices. This procedure can also be applied when **A** is only positive semidefinite. If, when a zero u_{ii} occurs, you set all subsequent elements in the same row of **U** to zero, the relation **A** = **U′U** remains and the matrix $\mathbf{U}^{-}(\mathbf{U}')^{-}$ is a generalized inverse of **A**.

B.2 Univariate and Multivariate ANOVA for Repeated Measures Data

The model for the univariate ANOVA for repeated measures data is

$$y_{ijk} = \mu + \alpha_i + b_{j(i)} + \gamma_k + (\alpha\gamma)_{ik} + e_{ijk}$$

where

y_{ijk}	the **fev1** measurement at the kth hour on the jth patient assigned to the ith drug
$\mu + \alpha_i + \gamma_k + (\alpha\gamma)_{ik}$	the mean **fev1** for drug i at hour k, containing effects for drug α_i, hour γ_k, and drug*hour interaction $(\alpha\gamma)_{ik}$.
$b_{j(i)}$	the random effect associated with the jth patient assigned to drug i, $b_{j(i)} \sim \text{i.i.d. } N(0, \sigma_b^2)$
e_{ijk}	the random error associated with the jth patient assigned to the ith drug at hour k, $e_{ijk} \sim \text{i.i.d. } N(0, \sigma^2)$.

Assume $b_{j(i)}$ and e_{ijk} are independent random variables that follow a normal distribution with mean of zero and variances of σ_b^2 and σ^2, respectively.

- $E(y_{ijk}) = \mu + \alpha_i + \gamma_k + (\alpha\gamma)_{ik}$ is the mean **fev1** for drug i at hour k.
- $Var(y_{ijk}) = Var(b_{j(i)} + e_{ijk}) = Var(b_{j(i)}) + Var(e_{ijk}) = \sigma_b^2 + \sigma^2$ is the variance for an observation.
- $Cov(y_{ijk}, y_{ijl}) = Cov(b_{j(i)} + e_{ijk}, b_{j(i)} + e_{ijl}) = Var(b_{j(i)}) = \sigma_b^2$ for $k \neq l$ is the covariance between two measurements taken at different hours from the same subject.

As you can see, measurements at each time have equal variances and are the sum of the between- (σ_b^2) and the within-subject (σ^2) variance components; the covariance between two observations taken at different hours from the same subject is the same for all pairs of observations (σ_b^2), regardless of their proximity in time. These assumptions are often not realistic. When the assumptions hold, the univariate ANOVA method is valid for repeated measures data.

The following program conducts a univariate ANOVA using the GLM procedure.

```
proc glm data=sasuser.fev1uni;
   class drug patient hour;
   model fev1=drug patient(drug) hour drug*hour;
   random patient(drug)/test;
run;                                 ***B02d1.sas;
```

As discussed earlier, the patient assigned to a drug is a random effect. This was specified by the RANDOM **patient(drug)** statement in PROC GLM. The TEST option in the RANDOM statement performs hypothesis tests for each effect specified in the model, using appropriate error terms as determined by the expected mean squares.

Partial PROC GLM Output

```
                              The GLM Procedure

                           Class Level Information

Class        Levels  Values

drug              3  a c p

patient          24  201 202 203 204 205 206 207 208 209 210 211 212 214 215
                     216 217 218 219 220 221 222 223 224 232

hour              8  1 2 3 4 5 6 7 8


                      Number of Observations Read         576
                      Number of Observations Used         576
```

```
Dependent Variable: fev1

                                        Sum of
 Source                      DF        Squares    Mean Square   F Value   Pr > F

 Model                       92    296.6455233      3.2244079     51.08   <.0001

 Error                      483     30.4902594      0.0631268

 Corrected Total            575    327.1357826


           R-Square     Coeff Var      Root MSE     fev1 Mean

           0.906796      8.138859      0.251251      3.087049
```

The overall *F*-test is significant, which indicates that the model is significant.

Source	DF	Type I SS	Mean Square	F Value	Pr > F
drug	2	25.7825670	12.8912835	204.21	<.0001
patient(drug)	69	247.4124906	3.5856883	56.80	<.0001
hour	7	17.1703993	2.4529142	38.86	<.0001
drug*hour	14	6.2800663	0.4485762	7.11	<.0001

Source	DF	Type III SS	Mean Square	F Value	Pr > F
drug	2	25.7825670	12.8912835	204.21	<.0001
patient(drug)	69	247.4124906	3.5856883	56.80	<.0001
hour	7	17.1703993	2.4529142	38.86	<.0001
drug*hour	14	6.2800663	0.4485762	7.11	<.0001

PROC GLM treats **`patient(drug)`** effect as fixed even though you specified it as random. As a result, some of the tests for each source of variation are valid and some are not. In particular, the *F*-test for **`drug`** is **not** appropriate because it does not use the correct denominator as a measure of error term.

Source	Type III Expected Mean Square
drug	Var(Error) + 8 Var(patient(drug)) + Q(drug,drug*hour)
patient(drug)	Var(Error) + 8 Var(patient(drug))
hour	Var(Error) + Q(hour,drug*hour)
drug*hour	Var(Error) + Q(drug*hour)

The Type III expected mean squares for each source of variation are produced by the RANDOM statement. This information can be used to construct the correct *F*-test for each effect.

```
                          The GLM Procedure
         Tests of Hypotheses for Mixed Model Analysis of Variance

Dependent Variable: fev1

   Source                    DF    Type III SS   Mean Square  F Value  Pr > F

*  drug                       2      25.782567     12.891284     3.60  0.0327

   Error                     69     247.412491      3.585688
Error: MS(patient(drug))
* This test assumes one or more other fixed effects are zero.


   Source                    DF    Type III SS   Mean Square  F Value  Pr > F

   patient(drug)             69     247.412491      3.585688    56.80  <.0001
*  hour                       7      17.170399      2.452914    38.86  <.0001
   drug*hour                 14       6.280066      0.448576     7.11  <.0001

   Error: MS(Error)         483      30.490259      0.063127
* This test assumes one or more other fixed effects are zero.
```

The TEST option gives the valid F-tests provided the model assumptions are correct. Notice that the appropriate test for **drug** uses MS(**patient(drug)**) as the denominator of the F statistic, with a p-value of 0.0327. The appropriate tests for **hour** and **drug*hour** use MS(Error) in the denominator. You can verify these denominator terms by examining the Type III Expected Mean Square table shown previously.

Care must be taken in using LSMEANS, CONTRAST, and ESTIMATE statements, because by default MS(Error) is used in the denominator of the F statistic, which may not always be valid. It can be shown that the correct error term for the standard errors and comparisons of the means for **drug** is MS(**patient(drug)**). Therefore, you can submit the following program to compute and compare the LSMEANS for **drug**:

```
   lsmeans drug / pdiff=all stderr e=patient(drug);
run;                                      ***B02d2.sas;
```

Selected LSMEANS statement option:

E= specifies an effect in the model to use as an error term.

Output from the LSMEANS Statement

```
                          Least Squares Means
               Adjustment for Multiple Comparisons: Tukey


 Standard Errors and Probabilities Calculated Using the Type III MS for
                      patient(drug) as an Error Term

                                   Standard                    LSMEAN
      drug       fev1 LSMEAN          Error    Pr > |t|        Number

      a           3.12276042     0.13665819      <.0001             1
      c           3.32645833     0.13665819      <.0001             2
      p           2.81192708     0.13665819      <.0001             3


                   Least Squares Means for effect drug
                   Pr > |t| for H0: LSMean(i)=LSMean(j)

                        Dependent Variable: fev1

            i/j              1              2              3

              1                        0.5457         0.2490
              2         0.5457                        0.0258
              3         0.2490         0.0258
```

The statistically significant difference in the mean **fev1** measurements was found to be between drug c (new drug) and drug p (placebo).

When you write a CONTRAST statement, the RANDOM statement in PROC GLM produces the expected mean squares for the contrast, which helps you determine the appropriate tests.

```
   contrast 'a-c overall' drug 1 -1 0;
   contrast 'a-c at hour 1' drug 1 -1 0
                           drug*hour 1 0 0 0 0 0 0 0
                                    -1 0 0 0 0 0 0 0;
   random patient(drug);
run;                                    ***B02d3.sas;
```

The expected mean squares for the effects in the model and the contrasts are shown as follows:

```
Source                Type III Expected Mean Square

drug                  Var(Error) + 8 Var(patient(drug)) + Q(drug,drug*hour)

patient(drug)         Var(Error) + 8 Var(patient(drug))

hour                  Var(Error) + Q(hour,drug*hour)

drug*hour             Var(Error) + Q(drug*hour)


Contrast              Contrast Expected Mean Square

a-c overall           Var(Error) + 8 Var(patient(drug)) + Q(drug,drug*hour)

a-c at hour 1         Var(Error) + Var(patient(drug)) + Q(drug,drug*hour)
```

From this Type III Expected Mean Square table and the Contrast Expected Mean Square table, you can see that the appropriate error term for comparing drugs a and c averaged over hours (`a-c overall`) is MS(**`patient(drug)`**), but there is no available mean squares appropriate for comparing drugs a and c at a particular hour (`a-c at hour 1`). By default, PROC GLM uses MS(Error) as the denominator for the *F* statistics for the two CONTRAST statements, which is clearly invalid.

```
Dependent Variable: fev1

 Contrast                 DF    Contrast SS    Mean Square   F Value   Pr > F

 a-c overall               1     3.98331276     3.98331276     63.10   <.0001
 a-c at hour 1             1     0.46216875     0.46216875      7.32   0.0071
```

The results indicate a significant difference between drug a and drug c averaged over hours, with a *p*-value < 0.0001 for `a-c overall` contrast, and a significant difference between drug a and drug c at the first hour, with a *p*-value of 0.0071 for `a-c at hour 1` contrast. Again, due to the invalid error terms used in the *F*-tests, the results are **not** valid.

You can use the E= option in the CONTRAST statement to specify the correct error term. You can only do this for the first CONTRAST statement, because no single mean square is appropriate for use as the error term for the second CONTRAST statement. You can submit the following program to obtain the appropriate test:

```
   contrast 'a-c overall' drug 1 -1 0 / e=patient(drug);
run;
quit;                                    ***B02d4.sas;
```

Output from the CONTRAST Statement

```
Dependent Variable: fev1

                  Tests of Hypotheses Using the Type III
                   MS for patient(drug) as an Error Term

 Contrast                 DF   Contrast SS    Mean Square  F Value  Pr > F

 a-c overall               1    3.98331276     3.98331276     1.11  0.2956
```

The *p*-value for comparing drugs a and c averaged over hours is 0.2956. You conclude that there is not enough evidence to say the drugs a and c are different averaged over hours. Notice that if you omit the E= option in the CONTRAST statement and therefore use the MS(Error) as the error term, you would erroneously conclude a significant difference between drug a and drug c averaged over hours.

The SAS data set **sasuser.fev1mult** can be used to perform the multivariate analysis of the asthma data. The REPEATED statement in the GLM procedure allows you to examine trends over time.

```
proc glm data=sasuser.fev1mult;
   class drug;
   model fev11h fev12h fev13h fev14h fev15h fev16h fev17h fev18h=drug;
   repeated hour / printe summary;
run;
quit;                                                  ***B02d5.sas;
```

The MODEL statement alone computes ANOVA tables for each hour, **fev11h** through **fev18h**. You can use the NOUNI option to suppress the display of these univariate ANOVA tables. The REPEATED statement is followed by the word `hour`, which is not a variable name in the SAS data set **sasuser.fev1mult**, but simply a word used to associate with the eight response variables, **fev11h** through **fev18h**.

Selected REPEATED statement options:

PRINTE displays the **E** matrix for each combination of within-subject factors, as well as partial correlation matrices for both the original dependent variables and the variables defined by the transformations specified in the REPEATED statement. In addition, the PRINTE option provides sphericity tests for each set of transformed variables. If the requested transformations are not orthogonal, the PRINTE option also provides a sphericity test for a set of orthogonal contrasts.

SUMMARY produces analysis-of-variance tables for each contrast defined by the within-subject factors. Along with tests for the effects of the independent variables specified in the MODEL statement, a term labeled MEAN tests the hypothesis that the overall mean of the contrast is zero.

The transformations specified in the REPEATED statement define a variety of single degree-of-freedom contrasts. Transformations include CONTRAST (default), HELMERT, MEAN, POLYNOMIAL, and PROFILE. Detailed information on these transformations can be found in the SAS online documentation.

The sphericity test produced by the PRINTE option basically tests whether the H-F condition is met, or in other words, whether the univariate ANOVA is valid.

Selected PROC GLM Output

```
Dependent Variable: fev11h

                                          Sum of
 Source                       DF         Squares    Mean Square  F Value  Pr > F

 Model                         2      9.99482500     4.99741250    11.00  <.0001

 Error                        69     31.33466250     0.45412554

 Corrected Total              71     41.32948750


           R-Square     Coeff Var      Root MSE    fev11h Mean

           0.241833      20.23942      0.673888       3.329583
                                          ....
                                          ....

Dependent Variable: fev18h

Source                        DF         Squares    Mean Square  F Value  Pr > F

 Model                         2      0.96811944     0.48405972     0.96  0.3871

 Error                        69     34.71461250     0.50311033

 Corrected Total              71     35.68273194


           R-Square     Coeff Var      Root MSE    fev18h Mean

           0.027131      24.74911      0.709303       2.865972
```

The univariate ANOVA for each response variable, **fev11h** through **fev18h**, indicates that the

- mean squares errors are essentially the same (~ 0.5) across all eight hours. This implies that the variances may be constant over time.
- drug effect seems to be significant at hours 1 through 5, but not at hours 6, 7, and 8.

```
Partial Correlation Coefficients from the Error SSCP Matrix / Prob > |r|

   DF = 69          fev11h         fev12h         fev13h         fev14h

   fev11h         1.000000       0.947354       0.939327       0.877290
                                   <.0001         <.0001         <.0001

   fev12h         0.947354       1.000000       0.953603       0.928445
                    <.0001                        <.0001         <.0001

   fev13h         0.939327       0.953603       1.000000       0.950646
                    <.0001         <.0001                        <.0001

   fev14h         0.877290       0.928445       0.950646       1.000000
                    <.0001         <.0001         <.0001

   DF = 69          fev15h         fev16h         fev17h         fev18h

   fev11h         0.849003       0.833356       0.747934       0.803328
                    <.0001         <.0001         <.0001         <.0001

   fev12h         0.904953       0.845329       0.786126       0.835204
                    <.0001         <.0001         <.0001         <.0001

   fev13h         0.907989       0.867392       0.810935       0.855238
                    <.0001         <.0001         <.0001         <.0001

   fev14h         0.905495       0.848955       0.810209       0.852875
                    <.0001         <.0001         <.0001         <.0001

   DF = 69          fev11h         fev12h         fev13h         fev14h
   fev15h         0.849003       0.904953       0.907989       0.905495
                    <.0001         <.0001         <.0001         <.0001

   fev16h         0.833356       0.845329       0.867392       0.848955
                    <.0001         <.0001         <.0001         <.0001

   fev17h         0.747934       0.786126       0.810935       0.810209
                    <.0001         <.0001         <.0001         <.0001

   fev18h         0.803328       0.835204       0.855238       0.852875
                    <.0001         <.0001         <.0001         <.0001

   DF = 69          fev15h         fev16h         fev17h         fev18h

   fev15h         1.000000       0.928608       0.864207       0.918064
                                   <.0001         <.0001         <.0001

   fev16h         0.928608       1.000000       0.899701       0.932298
                    <.0001                        <.0001         <.0001

   fev17h         0.864207       0.899701       1.000000       0.896999
                    <.0001         <.0001                        <.0001

   fev18h         0.918064       0.932298       0.896999       1.000000
                    <.0001         <.0001         <.0001
```

The correlation coefficients based on the sum of squares and cross products are shown above. You can see that the correlation between **fev11h** and **fev12h** through **fev18h** generally decreases from 0.95 to 0.80. This is a common phenomenon of repeated measure data; that is, measures closer in time are more highly correlated than measures farther apart in time. It usually means that the H-F condition (for example, equal correlation) of the covariance structure is not met and therefore the univariate ANOVA performed in the previous section is flawed.

E = Error SSCP Matrix

hour_N represents the contrast between the nth level of hour and the last

	hour_1	hour_2	hour_3	hour_4
hour_1	13.0596	10.5003	9.4969	7.5530
hour_2	10.5003	11.5963	9.1475	8.3580
hour_3	9.4969	9.1475	9.9463	8.3554
hour_4	7.5530	8.3580	8.3554	10.1226
hour_5	4.0731	5.2938	4.6063	4.6017
hour_6	3.4016	2.7393	2.7998	2.2550
hour_7	1.7724	1.8626	2.0664	2.1203

	hour_5	hour_6	hour_7
hour_1	4.0731	3.4016	1.7724
hour_2	5.2938	2.7393	1.8626
hour_3	4.6063	2.7998	2.0664
hour_4	4.6017	2.2550	2.1203
hour_5	6.2759	2.7152	1.5681
hour_6	2.7152	4.6472	2.4593
hour_7	1.5681	2.4593	7.1255

The PRINTE option in the REPEATED statement also produces the elements of the error matrix, also called the *Error Sum of Squares and Crossproducts matrix*, for the contrasts between the nth level of hour and the last, denoted by hour_N.

Partial Correlation Coefficients from the Error SSCP Matrix of the Variables Defined by the Specified Transformation / Prob > |r|

DF = 69	hour_1	hour_2	hour_3	hour_4
hour_1	1.000000	0.853251 <.0001	0.833269 <.0001	0.656917 <.0001
hour_2	0.853251 <.0001	1.000000	0.851746 <.0001	0.771424 <.0001
hour_3	0.833269 <.0001	0.851746 <.0001	1.000000	0.832701 <.0001

DF = 69	hour_5	hour_6	hour_7
hour_1	0.449908 <.0001	0.436636 0.0002	0.183738 0.1279
hour_2	0.620540 <.0001	0.373144 0.0015	0.204904 0.0888
hour_3	0.583020 <.0001	0.411816 0.0004	0.245453 0.0406

Partial Correlation Coefficients from the Error SSCP Matrix of the Variables Defined by the Specified Transformation / Prob > |r|

DF = 69	hour_1	hour_2	hour_3	hour_4
hour_4	0.656917 <.0001	0.771424 <.0001	0.832701 <.0001	1.000000
hour_5	0.449908 <.0001	0.620540 <.0001	0.583020 <.0001	0.577341 <.0001
hour_6	0.436636 0.0002	0.373144 0.0015	0.411816 0.0004	0.328781 0.0055
hour_7	0.183738 0.1279	0.204904 0.0888	0.245453 0.0406	0.249661 0.0371

DF = 69	hour_5	hour_6	hour_7
hour_4	0.577341 <.0001	0.328781 0.0055	0.249661 0.0371
hour_5	1.000000	0.502774 <.0001	0.234492 0.0507
hour_6	0.502774 <.0001	1.000000	0.427373 0.0002
hour_7	0.234492 0.0507	0.427373 0.0002	1.000000

The PRINTE option in the REPEATED statement also displays the partial correlation matrix associated with the E matrix, for the contrasts between the nth level of hour and the last, denoted by hour_N (the default CONTRAST transformation).

```
                              Sphericity Tests

                                    Mauchly's
Variables                     DF    Criterion     Chi-Square    Pr > ChiSq

Transformed Variates          27    0.0033417      378.86425        <.0001
Orthogonal Components         27    0.0654899      181.13982        <.0001
```

The sphericity tests produced by the PRINTE option include a test for sphericity applied to the default CONTRAST transformation and a test for sphericity applied to a set of orthogonal components. The latter one is appropriate to use to test the hypothesis whether the H-F conditions are satisfied under which the univariate ANOVA is valid. This is a likelihood ratio test, and the test statistics (181.13982) based on the Mauchly's criterion follow a chi-square distribution. The highly significant p-value (<0.0001) indicates that the H-F conditions are not satisfied by the data. Thus the univariate ANOVA tests in the previous section are suspect.

```
                Manova Test Criteria and Exact F Statistics
                    for the Hypothesis of no hour Effect
                     H = Type III SSCP Matrix for hour
                           E = Error SSCP Matrix

                          S=1     M=2.5     N=30.5

Statistic                        Value    F Value    Num DF    Den DF    Pr > F

Wilks' Lambda               0.41804056      12.53         7        63    <.0001
Pillai's Trace              0.58195944      12.53         7        63    <.0001
Hotelling-Lawley Trace      1.39211241      12.53         7        63    <.0001
Roy's Greatest Root         1.39211241      12.53         7        63    <.0001


                  Manova Test Criteria and F Approximations
                  for the Hypothesis of no hour*drug Effect
                   H = Type III SSCP Matrix for hour*drug
                           E = Error SSCP Matrix

                           S=2     M=2     N=30.5

Statistic                        Value    F Value    Num DF    Den DF    Pr > F

Wilks' Lambda               0.51191319       3.58        14       126    <.0001
Pillai's Trace              0.55490980       3.51        14       128    <.0001
Hotelling-Lawley Trace      0.82292043       3.66        14    97.495    <.0001
Roy's Greatest Root         0.60834527       5.56         7        64    <.0001

        NOTE: F Statistic for Roy's Greatest Root is an upper bound.
               NOTE: F Statistic for Wilks' Lambda is exact.
```

The output above contains the results of multivariate tests applied to differences between the repeated measures (hour_N). As you can see, the effects of **hour** and **hour*drug** are highly significant. This implies that the changes over time are highly pronounced, and the changes are not the same for all drugs.

The four multivariate tests are based on an unstructured within-subject variance-covariance matrix, which wastes the information inherent in the repeated measures and often results in less powerful tests for the within-subject effects. If the Huynh-Feldt condition is met, the univariate ANOVA tests are usually more powerful; that is, you would have a greater probability of detecting significant effects using the univariate tests.

The four multivariate tests can yield different p-values. In general, the order of preference in terms of power is Pillai's Trace, Wilk's Lambda, Hotelling-Lawley Trace, and Roy's Greatest Root. However, Wilk's Lambda is the most commonly used test.

```
              Tests of Hypotheses for Between Subjects Effects

Source                  DF    Type III SS    Mean Square   F Value   Pr > F

drug                     2     25.7825670     12.8912835      3.60   0.0327
Error                   69    247.4124906      3.5856883

          Univariate Tests of Hypotheses for Within Subject Effects

Source                  DF    Type III SS    Mean Square   F Value   Pr > F

hour                     7    17.17039931     2.45291419     38.86   <.0001
hour*drug               14     6.28006632     0.44857617      7.11   <.0001
Error(hour)            483    30.49025937     0.06312683

                                           Adj Pr > F
                 Source                   G - G     H - F

                 hour                    <.0001    <.0001
                 hour*drug               <.0001    <.0001
                 Error(hour)


                  Greenhouse-Geisser Epsilon     0.4971
                  Huynh-Feldt Epsilon            0.5419
```

The test for the between-subject effect, **drug**, is consistent with the one produced by using the TEST option in the RANDOM statement in the previous section. The significant p-value (0.0327) indicates that drug has a significant effect on **fev1** measures. Notice that the validity of this test does not depend on the covariance structure of repeated measures because it is based on means for each subject averaged over the repeated measures.

The univariate tests of within-subject effects, **hour** and **hour*drug**, are also consistent with the univariate tests produced in the previous section. Notice that the validity of these tests depends on the covariance structure. Specifically, the covariance structure must obey the Huynh-Feldt condition in order to make the F-tests for **hour** and **hour*drug** valid. But the sphericity test showed that the H-F condition is not met. Therefore, the univariate ANOVA F-tests are suspect. In this case, the adjusted tests labeled G-G and H-F are the valid ones to use.

The Greenhouse-Geisser (G-G) and Huynh-Feldt (H-F) adjusted p-values are obtained by referring the F values to distributions with reduced degrees of freedom. The reduced degrees of freedom (both numerator and denominator) are equal to the ordinary degrees of freedom multiplied by epsilon, given at the bottom of the output. The adjusted p-values still indicate significant **hour** and **hour*drug** effects (<0.0001 for both). This may not be the case in other situations.

Analysis of Variance of Contrast Variables

hour_N represents the contrast between the nth level of hour and the last

Contrast Variable: hour_1

Source	DF	Type III SS	Mean Square	F Value	Pr > F
Mean	1	15.47533889	15.47533889	81.76	<.0001
drug	2	4.95388611	2.47694306	13.09	<.0001
Error	69	13.05957500	0.18926920		

Contrast Variable: hour_2

Source	DF	Type III SS	Mean Square	F Value	Pr > F
Mean	1	13.84256806	13.84256806	82.37	<.0001
drug	2	2.85541111	1.42770556	8.50	0.0005
Error	69	11.59632083	0.16806262		

Contrast Variable: hour_3

Source	DF	Type III SS	Mean Square	F Value	Pr > F
Mean	1	8.96761250	8.96761250	62.21	<.0001
drug	2	1.95842500	0.97921250	6.79	0.0020
Error	69	9.94626250	0.14414873		

Contrast Variable: hour_4

Source	DF	Type III SS	Mean Square	F Value	Pr > F
Mean	1	4.63093889	4.63093889	31.57	<.0001
drug	2	1.19181111	0.59590556	4.06	0.0215
Error	69	10.12265000	0.14670507		

Contrast Variable: hour_5

Source	DF	Type III SS	Mean Square	F Value	Pr > F
Mean	1	1.77347222	1.77347222	19.50	<.0001
drug	2	0.54738611	0.27369306	3.01	0.0559
Error	69	6.27594167	0.09095568		

Contrast Variable: hour_6

Source	DF	Type III SS	Mean Square	F Value	Pr > F
Mean	1	0.62533472	0.62533472	9.28	0.0033
drug	2	0.02916944	0.01458472	0.22	0.8058
Error	69	4.64719583	0.06735066		

```
Contrast Variable: hour_7

 Source                  DF    Type III SS    Mean Square  F Value  Pr > F

 Mean                     1     0.00700139     0.00700139     0.07  0.7953
 drug                     2     0.08841944     0.04420972     0.43  0.6535
 Error                   69     7.12547917     0.10326781
```

These univariate ANOVA results of contrast variables are produced by the SUMMARY option in the REPEATED statement. The contrasts are the differences between each hour and hour 8. So, **hour_1** is the difference between hour 1 and hour 8, **hour_2** is the difference between hour 2 and hour 8, and so forth. For each contrast variable, tests labeled **Mean** and **Drug** are produced. These are univariate tests and their validity does not depend on the covariance structure.

You must be careful in interpreting the test results. Consider the variable **hour_1**. The test for **Mean** is a test of whether the average value of **hour_1** over the three drugs differs from zero. Because the variable **hour_1** is the difference between hour 1 and hour 8, the test for **Mean** is really a test for whether the average difference between hour 1 and hour 8 is zero across all three drugs, in other words, whether there is a significant change from hour 1 to hour 8 averaged across all three drugs. The significant *p*-value (<0.0001) indicates that hour 1 is different from hour 8 averaged across all drugs. The test for **drug** is a test of whether the average values of **hour_1** are different for the three drugs. It tests whether the change from hour 1 to hour 8 differs between the drugs. Thus the test for **drug** is a test for interaction between drugs and the contrast hour 1 minus hour 8. The significant *p*-value (<0.0001) indicates that the change from hour 1 to hour 8 is different among all three drugs.

B.3 Additional SAS Programs

Testing the Carry-Over Effect in a Crossover Design

The following program and output illustrate the testing for the carry-over effect in a crossover design. The data set **sasuser.heart** is discussed in Chapter 2.

To account for carry-over effects in the model, it may be easiest to create covariates explicitly that reflect the residual of the previous treatment. They are named **co_a**, **co_c**, and **co_p** in the program shown below.

The values of the residual effects are 0 for the first visit because there is no period prior to the first period to contribute a carry-over effect. The values for visits 2 and 3 are 0 or 1 depending on the level of drug in the previous visit. For visits 2 and 3, if the previous treatment is drug a, then the value of **co_a** = 1 and the others = 0. If the previous treatment is drug c, then the value of **co_c** = 1 and the others = 0. If the previous treatment is p (placebo), then the value for **co_p** = 1 and for the others = 0.

This coding method, known as *GLM coding* or *reference level coding*, provides estimates of carry-over effects compared to a reference level. In this case, the reference level will be the placebo. This means that the carry-over effect of drug a δ_a is actually the carryover of drug a compared to the carryover of the placebo, *p*. This is consistent with the way that PROC MIXED parameterizes class variables and the estimates produced in the Solution table.

By creating three dummy variables, you can choose which drug to use as the reference level to evaluate the carry-over effect. In this example, the placebo carryover will be treated as the reference level for the carryover due to **drug** a and **drug** c, and, therefore, the parameter estimate for the carry-over effect of placebo will be set to 0. All of the carry-over effects, when combined with visit, can be represented with only two dummy variables, so **co_p** is not used in the model.

```
/* carry-over effect indicators */
data sasuser.heart_co;
   set sasuser.heart;
   by patient;
   x = lag(drug);
   if first.patient then do;
      co_a = 0;
      co_c = 0;
      co_p = 0;
   end;
   else if x = 'p' then do;
      co_a = 0;
      co_c = 0;
      co_p = 1;
   end;
   else if x = 'c' then do;
      co_a = 0;
      co_c = 1;
      co_p = 0;
   end;
   else if x = 'a' then do;
      co_a = 1;
      co_c = 0;
      co_p = 0;
   end;
run;

proc print;
run;                                ***carryover.sas;
```

The dummy-coded data set is shown below (partial output):

Obs	patient	sequence	visit	basehr	basefev1	hr1h	fev11h	drug	cop	cob	coa	changehr	x	co_a	co_c	co_p
1	201	B	2	92	2.14	84	2.36	p	0	0	0	-8		0	0	0
2	201	B	3	92	2.30	104	3.41	c	1	0	0	12	p	0	0	1
3	201	B	4	68	2.46	72	2.68	a	0	1	0	4	c	0	1	0
4	202	E	2	54	2.91	64	3.92	c	0	0	0	10	a	0	0	0
5	202	E	3	64	3.37	54	3.03	p	0	1	0	-10	c	0	1	0
6	202	E	4	80	3.50	72	3.95	a	1	0	0	-8	p	0	0	1
7	203	F	2	84	1.88	82	1.99	p	0	0	0	-2	a	0	0	0
8	203	F	3	84	2.08	74	2.52	a	1	0	0	-10	p	0	0	1
9	203	F	4	88	1.96	84	2.28	c	0	0	0	-4	a	1	0	0
10	204	D	2	72	3.44	72	4.08	a	0	0	1	0	c	0	0	0
11	204	D	3	78	3.02	98	4.43	c	0	0	1	20	a	1	0	0
12	204	D	4	96	3.10	80	3.24	p	0	1	0	-16	c	0	1	0
13	205	C	2	80	3.26	72	4.55	c	0	0	0	-8	p	0	0	0
14	205	C	3	96	2.80	64	4.09	a	0	1	0	-32	c	0	1	0
15	205	C	4	72	2.91	60	3.35	p	0	0	1	-12	a	1	0	0
16	206	B	2	68	2.29	62	3.04	p	0	0	0	-6	p	0	0	0
17	206	B	3	80	2.29	88	4.25	c	1	0	0	8	p	0	0	1
18	206	B	4	64	2.36	78	3.79	a	0	1	0	14	c	0	1	0
19	207	A	2	100	1.77	68	3.82	a	0	0	0	-32	a	0	0	0
20	207	A	3	78	2.20	80	2.46	p	0	0	1	2	a	1	0	0
21	207	A	4	106	1.96	100	3.00	c	1	0	0	-6	p	0	0	1

The first level of **visit** (**visit** = 2) is always coded as 0 for all three dummies, because there is no carryover to estimate for the first measurement on a patient. The dummy codes for visits 3 and 4 reflect the level of drug administered at the visit immediately preceding.

```
proc mixed data=sasuser.heart_co;
   title 'Carry-over Effects';
   class patient sequence visit drug;
   model changehr = sequence visit drug co_a co_c / ddfm=kr solution;
   random patient(sequence);
run;
title;                         *** carryover.sas;
```

Partial PROC MIXED Output

Covariance Parameter Estimates

Cov Parm	Estimate
patient(sequence)	1.8534
Residual	94.4028

The model with carry-over effects is different than the model without carry-over effects, and so the variance component estimates have changed slightly. The variance component estimate for patient σ_p^2 = 1.8534 and the residual variance component estimate σ^2 =94.4028.

Solution for Fixed Effects

Effect	sequence	drug	visit	Estimate	Standard Error	DF	t Value	Pr > |t|
Intercept				-7.6042	4.7008	58.4	-1.62	0.1111
sequence	A			1.8333	4.0817	18	0.45	0.6587
sequence	B			6.7917	4.3159	22.4	1.57	0.1296
sequence	C			-0.3125	4.3159	22.4	-0.07	0.9429
sequence	D			4.8542	4.3159	22.4	1.12	0.2726
sequence	E			3.4583	4.3159	22.4	0.80	0.4314
sequence	F			0	.	.	.	.
visit			2	-4.4167	3.7104	42	-1.19	0.2406
visit			3	-1.5833	2.8048	42	-0.56	0.5754
visit			4	0	.	.	.	.
drug		a		0.5208	3.1359	42	0.17	0.8689
drug		c		3.9792	3.1359	42	1.27	0.2115
drug		p		0	.	.	.	.
co_a				0.8125	4.2072	42	0.19	0.8478
co_c				-1.0625	4.2072	42	-0.25	0.8019

The carry-over effects of drugs a and c, compared to the placebo, are

Drug a: 0.8125

Drug c: -1.0625

These are the carry-over effects of the drugs, relative to the carry-over effect of the placebo. These estimates result from the GLM-style coding for the carry-over dummy variables. You could also specify sum-to-zero coding to obtain the direct carry-over effects of each drug, although the interpretation in the presence of a reference level may not be as useful.

Algebraically, obtaining the direct carry-over effects for all three **drugs** is a trivial task using the solution table:

Drug a: 0.8958 = 0.8125 – (1/3)(0.8125 -1.0625 + 0.0000)

Drug c: -0.9792 = -1.0625 – (1/3)(0.8125 -1.0625 + 0.0000)

Drug p: 0.0833 = 0.0000 - (1/3)(0.8125 -1.0625 + 0.0000)

Type 3 Tests of Fixed Effects

Effect	Num DF	Den DF	F Value	Pr > F
sequence	5	20.9	0.85	0.5289
visit	2	42	0.72	0.4945
drug	2	42	0.95	0.3944
co_a	1	42	0.04	0.8478
co_c	1	42	0.06	0.8019

The inferences for **sequence**, **visit** and **drug** are essentially the same with the carry-over effects in the model as they are without them. In this case, carry-over effects are negligible, as indicated by the nonsignificant **co_a** and **co_c** values.

Cubic Regression Model Programs

The following program and output show the cubic regression model you could have fit to the data set **sasuser.fev1uni** that was analyzed in Chapter 5.

```
data fev1;
   set sasuser.fev1uni;
   hc=hour-4.5;
   hc2=hc*hc;
   hc3=hc2*hc;
run;

proc mixed data=fev1;
   class drug patient hour;
   model fev1=basefev1 drug hc*drug hc2*drug hc3*drug
         / noint ddfm=kr solution htype=1,3;
   repeated hour / type=TOEP subject=patient(drug);
run;

proc mixed data=fev1;
   class drug patient;
   model fev1=basefev1 drug hc*drug hc2*drug hc3*drug
             / noint ddfm=kr solution htype=1,3 ;
   random int hc hc2 hc3 / type=un subject=patient(drug);
   title 'Random Coefficient Model';
run;
title;                                          ***B03d1.sas;
```

The variable **hc** in the data set **fev1** is a centered continuous variable for **hour**, and it is used as one of the predictor variables in the regression model. Recall that in polynomial regression you want to center the predictor variable(s) to reduce the collinearity. The terms **hc*drug**, **hc2*drug**, and **hc3*drug** with the NOINT option are used to fit a separate linear, quadratic, and cubic term for each drug, respectively. The SOLUTION option is used to obtain the regression coefficients. The HTYPE= option indicates the types of hypothesis test to perform on the fixed effects. Types 1 and 3 are used. Refer to the Mixed Models with Covariates section in the course for discussions of this specification of the model. Alternatively, you could use the following MODEL statement to specify the same model using different parameterizations:

```
model fev1=basefev1 drug hc hc*drug hc2 hc2*drug
           hc3 hc3*drug / ddfm=kr solution htype=1,3 ;
```

Partial PROC MIXED Output

Covariance Parameter Estimates

Cov Parm	Subject	Estimate
TOEP(2)	patient(drug)	0.2284
TOEP(3)	patient(drug)	0.2156
TOEP(4)	patient(drug)	0.2070
TOEP(5)	patient(drug)	0.1908
TOEP(6)	patient(drug)	0.1821
TOEP(7)	patient(drug)	0.1690
TOEP(8)	patient(drug)	0.1582
Residual		0.2664

Fit Statistics

-2 Res Log Likelihood	236.4
AIC (smaller is better)	252.4
AICC (smaller is better)	252.6
BIC (smaller is better)	270.6

Solution for Fixed Effects

Effect	drug	Estimate	Standard Error	DF	t Value	Pr > |t|
basefev1		0.8869	0.1019	67.8	8.70	<.0001
drug	a	0.7081	0.2896	70	2.45	0.0170
drug	c	0.9763	0.2873	70.1	3.40	0.0011
drug	p	0.5008	0.2865	70.1	1.75	0.0848
hc*drug	a	-0.08610	0.02289	194	-3.76	0.0002
hc*drug	c	-0.1734	0.02289	194	-7.57	<.0001
hc*drug	p	-0.03725	0.02289	194	-1.63	0.1053
hc2*drug	a	0.009160	0.004039	59.8	2.27	0.0270
hc2*drug	c	0.001001	0.004039	59.8	0.25	0.8051
hc2*drug	p	-0.00504	0.004039	59.8	-1.25	0.2168
hc3*drug	a	-0.00044	0.001786	111	-0.25	0.8058
hc3*drug	c	0.006283	0.001786	111	3.52	0.0006
hc3*drug	p	0.002080	0.001786	111	1.17	0.2465

The models are

- drug a: **fev1** = 0.7081 – 0.0861***hc** + 0.00916***hc2** – 0.00044***hc3** + 0.8869***basefev1**
- drug c: **fev1** = 0.9763 – 0.1734***hc** + 0.001***hc2** + 0.006283***hc3** + 0.8869***basefev1**
- drug p: **fev1** = 0.5008 – 0.03725***hc** – 0.00504***hc2** + 0.00208***hc3** + 0.8869***basefev1**.

You see that the cubic coefficient for drug c is significant (*p*-value = 0.0006). None of the linear, quadratic, or cubic coefficients for drug p is significant, which is consistent with the plot.

This model is useful for making inferences or predictions for patients with known values of **basefev1**. For the purpose of making inferences or predictions for any patients, you can substitute the average **basefev1** value, 2.6493, into the above set of equations and obtain the following models:

- drug a: **fev1** = 3.0578 – 0.0861***hc** + 0.00916***hc2** – 0.00044***hc3**
- drug c: **fev1** = 3.3260 – 0.1734***hc** + 0.001***hc2** + 0.006283***hc3**
- drug p: **fev1** = 2.8505 – 0.03725***hc** – 0.00504***hc2** + 0.00208***hc3**.

Type 1 Tests of Fixed Effects

Effect	Num DF	Den DF	F Value	Pr > F
basefev1	1	71.1	3299.57	<.0001
drug	3	70.2	7.20	0.0003
hc*drug	3	75.2	40.66	<.0001
hc2*drug	3	59.8	2.25	0.0913
hc3*drug	3	111	4.60	0.0045

Type 3 Tests of Fixed Effects

Effect	Num DF	Den DF	F Value	Pr > F
basefev1	1	67.8	75.75	<.0001
drug	3	80.9	6.11	0.0008
hc*drug	3	194	24.72	<.0001
hc2*drug	3	59.8	2.25	0.0913
hc3*drug	3	111	4.60	0.0045

The **hc3*drug** effect is significant (*p*-value=0.0045), which means the third order coefficient is significantly different from zero for at least one of the three drugs. The quadratic term **hc2*drug** is marginally significant (*p*-value=0.0913). You want to keep this term in your model to preserve the hierarchy.

The second PROC MIXED program fits a random coefficient model. The selected output is shown below.

Covariance Parameter Estimates

Cov Parm	Subject	Estimate
UN(1,1)	patient(drug)	0.2285
UN(2,1)	patient(drug)	-0.00927
UN(2,2)	patient(drug)	0.01053
UN(3,1)	patient(drug)	-0.00202
UN(3,2)	patient(drug)	0.000275
UN(3,3)	patient(drug)	0.000070
UN(4,1)	patient(drug)	0.001225
UN(4,2)	patient(drug)	-0.00046
UN(4,3)	patient(drug)	-0.00003
UN(4,4)	patient(drug)	0.000020
Residual		0.03707

Fit Statistics

-2 Res Log Likelihood	225.1
AIC (smaller is better)	247.1
AICC (smaller is better)	247.6
BIC (smaller is better)	272.1

Compared with the previous regression model you fit using the REPEATED statement, this random coefficient model has a smaller AICC value but a slightly bigger BIC value. Random coefficient models are useful for the purpose of obtaining EBLUPs for each subject, for example, the predicted response (**fev1**) for patient 201 (a) at hours 2.5, 4.5, and 9.

Type 1 Tests of Fixed Effects

Effect	Num DF	Den DF	F Value	Pr > F
basefev1	1	68.8	3289.25	<.0001
drug	3	70.4	6.76	0.0005
hc*drug	3	69	37.23	<.0001
hc2*drug	3	69	3.04	0.0348
hc3*drug	3	69	4.29	0.0078

Type 3 Tests of Fixed Effects

Effect	Num DF	Den DF	F Value	Pr > F
basefev1	1	68	82.77	<.0001
drug	3	72.4	5.79	0.0013
hc*drug	3	69	18.44	<.0001
hc2*drug	3	69	3.04	0.0348
hc3*drug	3	69	4.29	0.0078

You can also use the OUTP= option in the MODEL statement to obtain EBLUPs for each patient, and then construct the predicted profile plot for each patient. To obtain predictions at hours other than those included in the data set (for example, hour 4.5), append a new data set containing values for every variable included in your model except the dependent variable (**fev1** would have missing values in this new data set) to the original data set. The OUTP= option will produce desired predictions.

```
data new;
   input basefev1 drug $ hour patient;
   datalines;
   2.46 a 2.5 201
   2.46 a 4.5 201
   2.46 a 9 201
;
run;

data fev1new;
   set sasuser.fev1uni new;
   hc=hour-4.5;
   hc2=hc*hc;
   hc3=hc2*hc;
run;

proc mixed data=fev1new;
   class drug patient;
   model fev1=basefev1 drug hc*drug hc2*drug hc3*drug
            / noint ddfm=residual htype=1,3 outp=eblups;
   random int hc hc2 hc3 / type=un subject=patient(drug);
run;

proc print data=eblups;
   var patient drug basefev1 hour hc fev1 pred;
run;

proc sort data=eblups;
   by drug;
run;

proc gplot data=eblups;
   by drug;
   symbol v=none i=join l=1 c=blue r=24;
   plot pred*hour=patient / nolegend;
run;
quit;                                        ***B03d2.sas;
```

Partial PROC PRINT Output

Obs	patient	drug	basefev1	hour	hc	fev1	Pred
1	201	a	2.46	1	-3.5	2.68	2.84640
2	201	a	2.46	2	-2.5	2.76	2.60151
3	201	a	2.46	3	-1.5	2.50	2.45671
4	201	a	2.46	4	-0.5	2.30	2.38196
5	201	a	2.46	5	0.5	2.14	2.34721
6	201	a	2.46	6	1.5	2.40	2.32241
7	201	a	2.46	7	2.5	2.33	2.27752
8	201	a	2.46	8	3.5	2.20	2.18249
9	202	a	3.50	1	-3.5	3.95	3.69254
10	202	a	3.50	2	-2.5	3.65	3.39288
11	202	a	3.50	3	-1.5	2.93	3.18846
12	202	a	3.50	4	-0.5	2.53	3.06175
13	202	a	3.50	5	0.5	3.04	2.99519
14	202	a	3.50	6	1.5	3.37	2.97126
15	202	a	3.50	7	2.5	3.14	2.97242
16	202	a	3.50	8	3.5	2.62	2.98112
...	...	...	...	...	...	...	...
577	201	a	2.46	2.5	-2.0	.	2.51848
578	201	a	2.46	4.5	0.0	.	2.36146
579	201	a	2.46	9.0	4.5	.	2.00728

PROC GPLOT Output

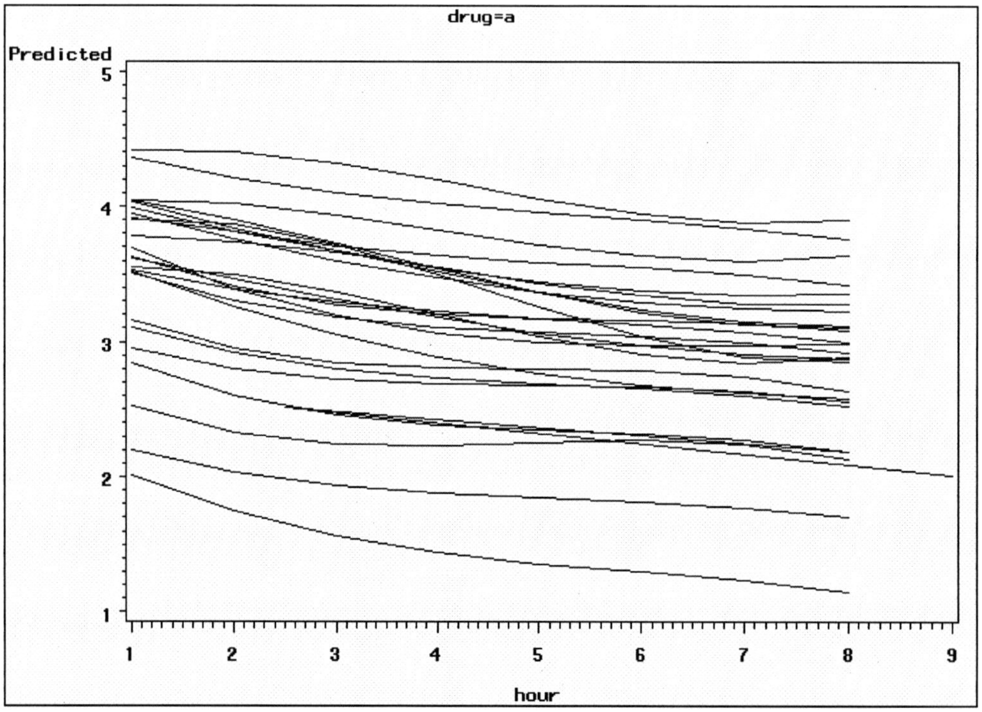

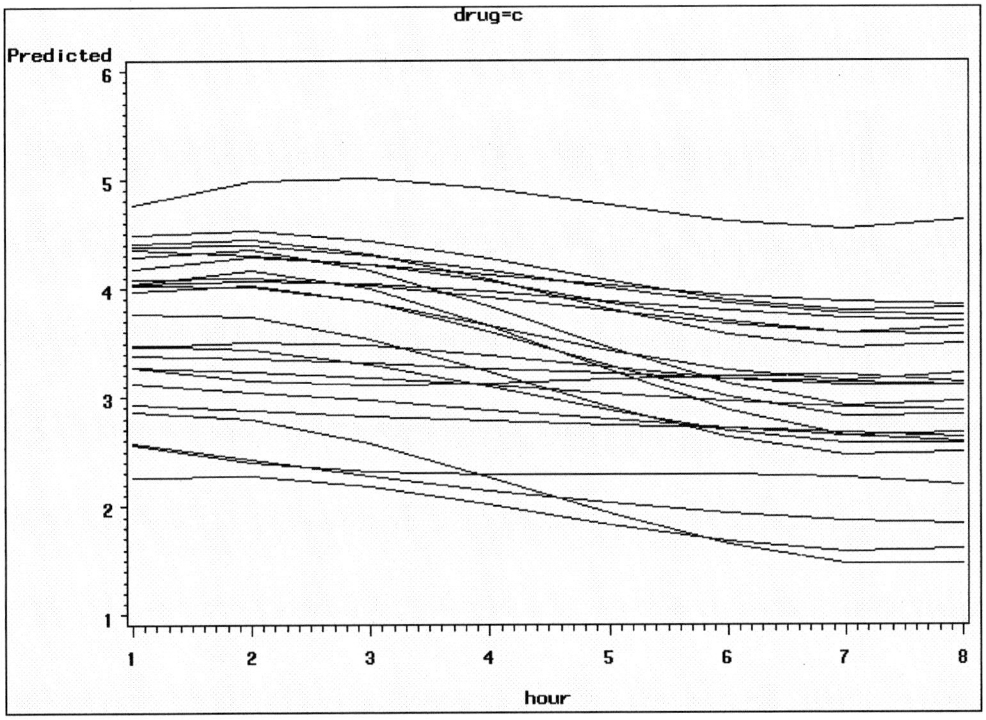

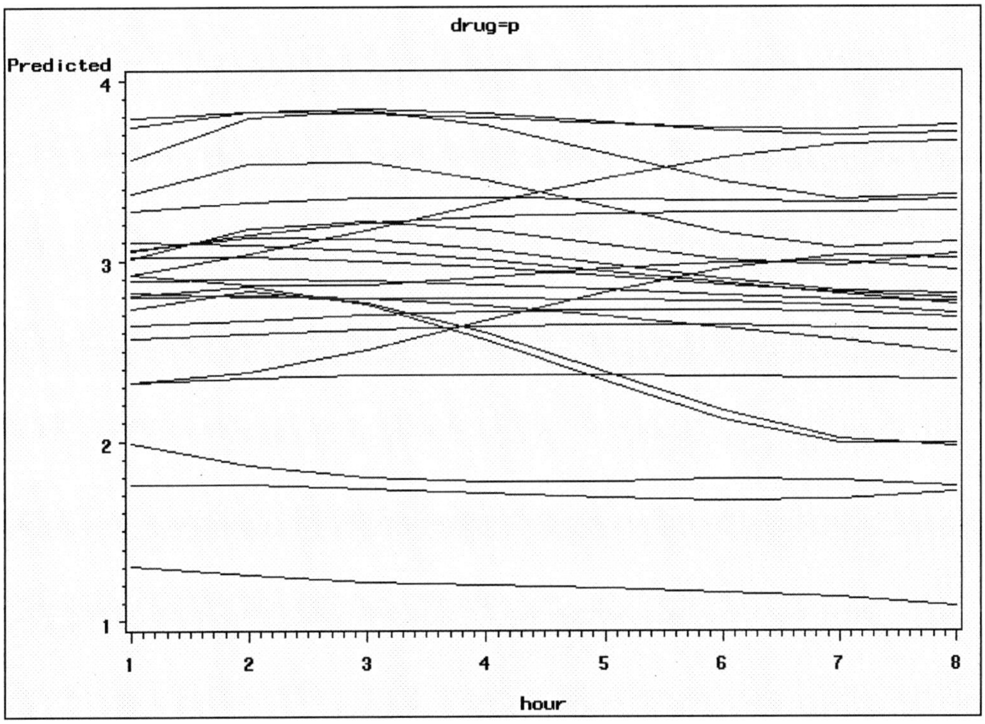

The predicted values for patients taking drugs c and p tend to level off at hours 7 and 8. Some drug a patients are still on a slightly declining trend at hour 8. The predicted value for patient 201 (a) at hour 9 is shown on the first graph. This can be easily changed to obtain predictions for any other patients at other hours. Investigators can identify several interesting patients based on certain criteria and conduct further examinations on these patients.

Fitting a Generalized Linear Mixed Model Using %GLIMMIX or PROC NLMIXED

Because the GLIMMIX procedure is currently only available on the Windows platform, you may need to use alternative tools for generalized linear mixed models. The following programs provide some examples of using %GLIMMIX or PROC NLMIXED to analyze the **sasuser.favorable** data set you analyzed before.

Using %GLIMMIX:

```
/** turn the data sasuser.favorable from the binomial outcome to
    the binary outcome to avoid convergence problems  **/
data zeroone (drop=i);
   set sasuser.favorable;
   do i=1 to fav;
      y=1;
      output;
   end;
   do i=1 to unfav;
      y=0;
      output;
   end;
run;

%include 'glimmix.sas' ;  /** may add the path of glimmix.sas
                              here **/
run;

%glimmix (data=zeroone,
          procopt=method=reml,
          stmts=%str(
                class clinic trt;
                model y=trt / ddfm=kr;
                random clinic clinic*trt;
                lsmeans trt / diff cl;),
                error=binomial,
                link=logit);
run;                                    ***B03d3.sas;
```

Partial %GLIMMIX Output

```
                     Covariance Parameter
                          Estimates

                    Cov Parm        Estimate

                    clinic            2.0332
                    clinic*trt       0.08133
                    Residual          0.9311
```

Solution for Fixed Effects

Effect	trt	Estimate	Standard Error	DF	t Value	Pr > |t|
Intercept		-0.4182	0.5675	7.67	-0.74	0.4831
trt	0	-0.7597	0.3647	4.62	-2.08	0.0962
trt	1	0	.	.	.	.

Type 3 Tests of Fixed Effects

Effect	Num DF	Den DF	F Value	Pr > F
trt	1	4.62	4.34	0.0962

Least Squares Means

Effect	trt	Estimate	Standard Error	DF	t Value	Pr > |t|	Alpha	Lower	Upper
trt	0	-1.1779	0.5757	7.89	-2.05	0.0755	0.05	-2.5088	0.1530
trt	1	-0.4182	0.5675	7.67	-0.74	0.4831	0.05	-1.7369	0.9004

Differences of Least Squares Means

Effect	trt	_trt	Estimate	Standard Error	DF	t Value	Pr > |t|	Alpha	Lower	Upper
trt	0	1	-0.7597	0.3647	4.62	-2.08	0.0962	0.05	-1.7204	0.2011

Using PROC NLMIXED:

```
/** obtain starting values for the parameters **/
data favorable;
   set sasuser.favorable;
   phat=fav/n;
   if fav=0 then phat=0.1/n;
   y=log(phat/(1-phat));
run;

proc logistic data=favorable;
   model fav/n = trt;
run;

proc mixed data=favorable;
   class trt clinic;
   model y = trt ;
   random clinic;
run;

/** fitting a model with only one random effect clinic
    using PROC NLMIXED  **/
proc sort data=sasuser.favorable;
   by clinic;
run;

proc nlmixed data=sasuser.favorable;
   parms b0=-0.7 b1=0.4 s2c=2.5;
   logit=b0+b1*trt+c;
   explogit=exp(logit);
   p = explogit / (1+explogit);
   model fav ~ binomial(n, p);
   random c ~ normal(0, s2c) subject=clinic;
   estimate 'odds ratio' exp(b1);
   predict p out=predp(rename=(pred=p));
run;

proc print data=predp;
run;                                         ***B03d4.sas;
```

Partial PROC NLMIXED Output

```
                         Fit Statistics

         -2 Log Likelihood                  74.0
         AIC (smaller is better)            80.0
         AICC (smaller is better)           82.0
         BIC (smaller is better)            80.3
```

Parameter Estimates

Parameter	Estimate	Standard Error	DF	t Value	Pr > |t|	Alpha	Lower	Upper	Gradient
b0	-1.1976	0.5564	7	-2.15	0.0684	0.05	-2.5134	0.1181	-2.37E-6
b1	0.7385	0.3004	7	2.46	0.0436	0.05	0.02807	1.4488	-0.00012
s2c	1.9620	1.1933	7	1.64	0.1441	0.05	-0.8596	4.7836	-3.8E-6

Additional Estimates

Label	Estimate	Standard Error	DF	t Value	Pr > |t|	Alpha	Lower	Upper
odds ratio	2.0927	0.6287	7	3.33	0.0126	0.05	0.6061	3.5793

Obs	clinic	trt	fav	unfav	n	p	StdErr Pred	DF	tValue	Probt	Alpha	Lower	Upper
1	1	1	11	25	36	0.36401	0.06679	7	5.4503	0.00096	0.05	0.20608	0.52193
2	1	0	10	27	37	0.21476	0.05227	7	4.1084	0.00452	0.05	0.09115	0.33837
3	2	1	16	4	20	0.80074	0.05946	7	13.4674	0.00000	0.05	0.66015	0.94134
4	2	0	22	10	32	0.65757	0.07228	7	9.0977	0.00004	0.05	0.48666	0.82848
5	3	1	14	5	19	0.63002	0.08404	7	7.4966	0.00014	0.05	0.43130	0.82875
6	3	0	7	12	19	0.44865	0.08781	7	5.1090	0.00139	0.05	0.24100	0.65629
7	4	1	2	14	16	0.14757	0.06868	7	2.1486	0.06875	0.05	-0.01484	0.30997
8	4	0	1	16	17	0.07640	0.04020	7	1.9003	0.09916	0.05	-0.01867	0.17147
9	5	1	6	11	17	0.26563	0.08734	7	3.0413	0.01881	0.05	0.05910	0.47217
10	5	0	0	12	12	0.14737	0.06071	7	2.4273	0.04560	0.05	0.00381	0.29094
11	6	1	1	10	11	0.11297	0.07402	7	1.5261	0.17081	0.05	-0.06207	0.28801
12	6	0	0	10	10	0.05737	0.04130	7	1.3889	0.20746	0.05	-0.04030	0.15503
13	7	1	1	4	5	0.23802	0.12227	7	1.9466	0.09263	0.05	-0.05111	0.52715
14	7	0	1	8	9	0.12988	0.07637	7	1.7006	0.13280	0.05	-0.05071	0.31047
15	8	1	4	2	6	0.78211	0.10606	7	7.3743	0.00015	0.05	0.53132	1.03290
16	8	0	6	1	7	0.63171	0.13991	7	4.5152	0.00275	0.05	0.30088	0.96254

B.4 New Experimental Features

New Experimental Features

- ODS graphics
- Residual and influence diagnostics in PROC MIXED

1

ODS Graphics (Experimental)

ODS statistical graphics are

- an experimental feature that is subject to change in a future release
- an extension to the ODS that enables procedures to create statistical graphics automatically
- incorporated in many procedures such as GENMOD, GLM, LIFETEST, LOGISTIC, MIXED, REG, and so on.

More information can be found in the SAS/STAT User's Guides or SAS online documentation.

2

ODS statistical graphics are experimental, meaning that both the graphical results and the syntax for specifying them are subject to change in a future release. They should never be used in production jobs.

A number of procedures in SAS/STAT and SAS/ETS software are using ODS graphics, an experimental extension to the Output Delivery System (ODS) that enables them to create statistical graphics as automatically as tables by default or by some options in the procedures. These procedures in SAS/STAT include ANOVA, CORRESP, GAM, GENMOD, GLM, KDE, LIFETEST, LOESS, LOGISTIC, MI, MIXED, PHREG, PLS, PRINCOMP, PRINQUAL, REG, ROBUSTREG, and TPSLINE.

Mixed Model Diagnostics (Experimental)

- Experimental RESIDUAL option of the MODEL statement in PROC MIXED computes raw residuals, Pearson residuals, and studentized residuals. The VCIRY option computes the scaled residuals.
- Experimental INFLUENCE option of the MODEL statement in PROC MIXED computes influence statistics by noniterative or iterative methods.
- Experimental ODS graphics can be used to display the results for both options.
- More information can be found in the SAS/STAT User's Guides or SAS online documentation.

3

Detailed information about different types of residuals can be found in the SAS/STAT user's guides or SAS online documentation. Examples of different types of residuals are summarized below.

Type of Residuals	**Marginal**	**Conditional**
Raw	$r_{mi} = Y_i - \mathbf{x}'_i \hat{\beta}$	$r_{ci} = r_{mi} - z'_i \hat{\gamma}$
Studentized	$r_{mi}^{student} = \frac{r_{mi}}{\sqrt{\hat{\text{var}}(r_{mi})}}$	$r_{ci}^{student} = \frac{r_{ci}}{\sqrt{\hat{\text{var}}(r_{ci})}}$
Pearson	$r_{mi}^{Pearson} = \frac{r_{mi}}{\sqrt{\hat{\text{var}}(Y_i)}}$	$r_{ci}^{Pearson} = \frac{r_{ci}}{\sqrt{\hat{\text{var}}(Y_i \mid \gamma)}}$
Scaled	$\hat{\mathbf{C}}^{-1} r_m$ where $\hat{\mathbf{C}}\hat{\mathbf{C}}' = \mathbf{V}(\hat{\theta})$	

Residuals

- OUTP= option of the MODEL statement computes the raw conditional residuals $r_{ci} = y_i - \mathbf{x}_i'\hat{\beta} - \mathbf{z}_i'\hat{\gamma}$
- OUTPM= option of the MODEL statement computes the raw marginal residuals $r_{mi} = y_i - \mathbf{x}_i'\hat{\beta}$
- The experimental RESIDUAL option of the MODEL statement requests the Pearson residuals and studentized residuals be added to OUTP= and OUTPM= data sets.
- The experimental RESIDUAL option has no effect unless the OUTP= or OUTPM= option is specified or you request the experimental ODS graphics.

4

Example of Residual Plots

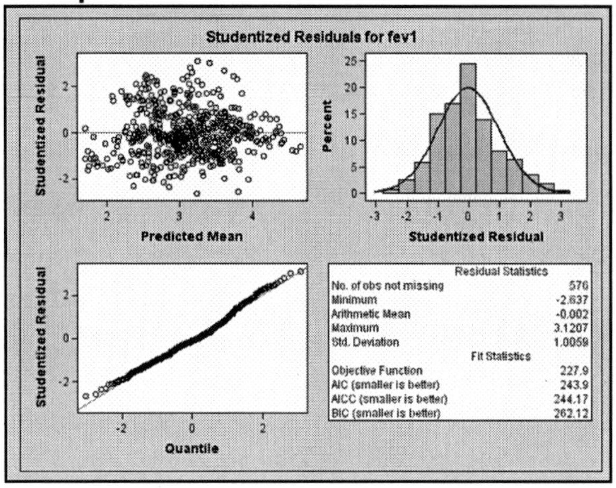

5

Influence Diagnostics

1. Fit the model to the data and obtain estimates of all parameters.
2. Remove one or more data points from the analysis and compute updated estimates of model parameters.
3. Based on full- and reduced-data estimates, contrast quantities of interest to determine how the absence of the observations changes the analysis.

6

The Nature of the Influence

The influential points can affect

- the overall objective function—likelihood distance
- the estimates of fixed effects—Cook's D or multivariate DFFITS
- the estimates of the precision of the fixed effects—COVTRACE or COVRATIO
- the estimates of the covariance parameters—Cook's D or Multivariate DFFITS
- the estimates of the precision of the covariance parameters—COVTRACE or COVRATIO
- fitted and predicted values—DFFITS and PRESS residuals.

7

Detailed information about these influential statistics can be found in the SAS/STAT user's guides or SAS online documentation.

Iterative and Noniterative Influence Analysis (Experimental)

Iterative influence analysis

- refits the model and iteratively re-estimates the covariance parameters when the observations in questions are removed
- has some merits but is computationally intensive.

Noniterative influence analysis

- relies on closed-form update formulas for the fixed effects without updating the (unprofiled) covariance parameters
- is computationally efficient and is the default analysis.

8

Example of Influence Diagnostics

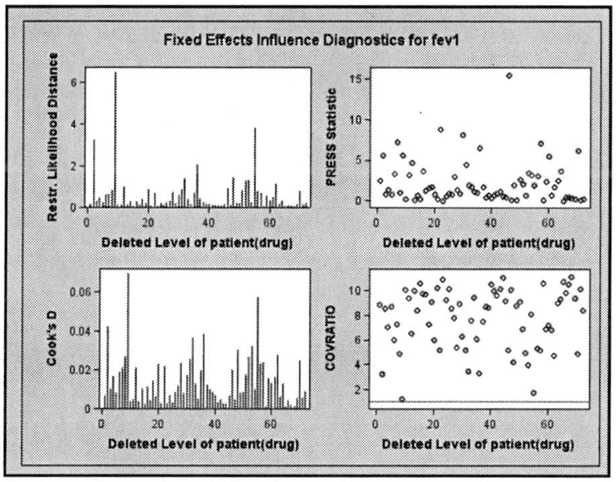

9

Example of Influence Diagonostics

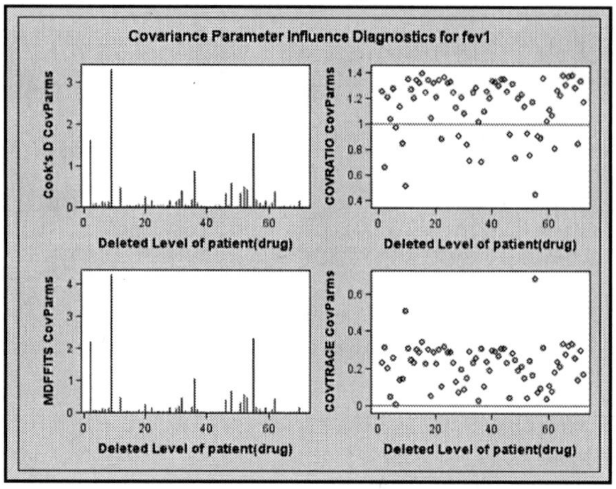

10

B.5 References

Agresti, A. (1990), *Categorical Data Analysis*, New York: John Wiley & Sons, Inc.

Akaike, H. (1974), "A New Look at the Statistical Model Identification," *IEEE Transaction on Automatic Control*, AC-19, 716-723.

Beckman, R.J., Nachtsheim, C.J., and Cook, R.D. (1987), "Diagnostics for Mixed-Model Analysis of Variance," *Technometrics*, 29(4), 413-426.

Box, G.E.P. and Tiao, G.C. (1973), *Bayesian Inference in Statistical Analysis*, Wiley Classics Library Edition Published 1992, New York: John Wiley & Sons, Inc.

Breslow, N.E. and Clayton, D.G. (1993), "Approximate Inference in Generalized Linear Mixed Models," *Journal of American Statistical Association*, 88, 9-25.

Breslow, N.E. and Lin, X. (1995), "Bias Correction in Generalized Linear Mixed Models with a Single Component of Dispersion," *Biometrika*, 82, 1, 81-91.

Brown, H. and Prescott, R. (1999), *Applied Mixed Models in Medicine*, Chichester, England: John Wiley & Sons, Inc.

Bryk, A.S. and Raudenbush, S.W. (1992), *Hierarchical Linear Models: Applications and Data Analysis Methods*, Newbury Park, CA: SAGE Publications, Inc.

Burnham, K.P. and Anderson, D.R. (1998), *Model Selection and Inference: A Practical Information-Theoretic Approach*, New York: Springer-Verlag.

Cochran, W.G. and Cox, G.M. (1957), *Experimental Designs*, New York: John Wiley & Sons, Inc.

Cressie, N.A.C. (1993), *Statistics for Spatial Data*, New York: John Wiley & Sons, Inc.

Diggle, P.J., Liang, K.Y., and Zeger, S.L. (1994), *Analysis of Longitudinal Data*, Clarendon Press, Oxford.

Goldstein, H. and Rasbash, J. (1996), "Improved Approximations for Multilevel Models with Binary Responses," *Journal of Royal Statistical Society*, A, 159, 505-513.

Guerin, L. and Stroup, W.W. (2000), "A Simulation Study to Evaluate PROC MIXED Analysis of Repeated Measures Data," *Proceedings of the 2000 Conference on Applied Statistics in Agriculture*, Manhattan, KS: Kansas State University.

Harville, D.A. and Jeske, D.R. (1992), "Mean Squared Error of Estimation of Prediction Under a General Linear Model," *Journal of the American Statistical Association*, 87, 724-731.

Healy M.J.R. (1995), *Matrices for Statistics*, Clarendon Press, Oxford.

Hocking, R.R. (1984), *The Analysis of Linear Models*, Monterey, CA: Brooks-Cole Publishing Co.

John, P.W.M. (1971), *Statistical Design and Analysis of Experiments*, New York: The Macmillan Company.

Kackar, R.N. and Harville, D.A. (1984), "Approximations for Standard Errors of Estimators of Fixed and Random Effects in Mixed Linear Models," *Journal of the American Statistical Association*, 79, 853-862.

Kenward, M.G. and Roger, J.H. (1997), "Small Sample Inference for Fixed Effects from Restricted Maximum Likelihood," *Biometrics*, 53, 983-997.

Liang, K.Y. and Zeger, S.L. (1986), "Longitudinal Data Analysis using Generalized Linear Models," *Biometrika*, 73, 13-22.

Lin, X. and Breslow, N.E. (1996), "Bias Correction in Generalized Linear Mixed Models with Multiple Components of Dispersion," *Journal of American Statistical Association*, Vol. 91, No. 435, 1007-1016.

Littell, R.C., Milliken, G.A., Stroup, W.W., and Wolfinger, R.D. (1996), *SAS® System for Mixed Models*, Cary, NC: SAS Institute Inc.

Littell, R.C., Milliken, G.A., Stroup, W.W., Wolfinger, R.D., and O. Schabenberger (2006), *SAS® for Mixed Models, Second Edition*. Cary, NC: SAS Institute Inc.

Littell, R.C., Pendergast, J., and Natajan, R. (2000), "Modeling Covariance Structure in the Analysis of Repeated Measures Data," *Statistics in Medicine*, 19, 1793-1819.

Littell, R.C., Stroup, W.W., and Freund, R.J. (2002) *SAS® System for Linear Models*, Cary, NC: SAS Institute Inc.

Little, R.J.A. and Rubin, D.B. (1987), *Statistical Analysis with Missing Data*, New York: John Wiley & Sons, Inc.

McCullagh, P. (1983), "Quasi-Likelihood Functions," *Annals of Statistics*, 11, 59-67.

McCullagh, P. and Nelder, J.A. (1989), *Generalized Linear Models*, Second Edition, London: Chapman and Hall.

McCulloch, C.E. and Searle, S.R. (2001), *Generalized, Linear, and Mixed Models*, New York: John Wiley & Sons, Inc.

Milliken, G.A. and Johnson, D.E. (1992), *Analysis of Messy Data, Volume 1: Designed Experiments*, New York: Chapman & Hall.

Montgomery, D.C. (1997), *Design and Analysis of Experiments, Fourth Edition*, New York: John Wiley & Sons, Inc.

Nelder, J.A. and Wedderburn, R.W.M. (1972), "Generalized Linear Models," *Journal of the Royal Statistical Society A*, 135, 370-384.

Pinheiro, J.C. and Bates, D.M. (1995), "Approximation to the Log-likelihood Function in the Nonlinear Mixed-effects Model," *Journal of Computational and Graphical Statistics*, 4, 12-35.

Prasad, N.G.N. and Rao, J.N.K. (1990), "The Estimation of Mean Squared Error of Small-Area Estimators," *Journal of the American Statistical Association*, 85, 163-171.

Rodriguez, G. and Goldman, N. (1995), "An Assessment of Estimation Procedures for Multilevel Models with Binary Responses," *Journal of Royal Statistical Society*, A, 158, 73-90.

SAS Institute Inc. (1996), *SAS/STAT® Technical Report: Spatial Prediction Using the SAS® System*, Cary, NC: SAS Institute Inc.

SAS Institute Inc. (1999), *SAS/GRAPH® Software: Reference, Version 8, Volume 1*, Cary, NC: SAS Institute Inc.

SAS Institute Inc. (1999), *SAS/STAT® User's Guide, Version 8*, Cary, NC: SAS Institute Inc.

Schabenberger, O. and Pierce, F.J. (2002), *Contemporary Statistical Models for the Plant and Soil Sciences*, Boca Raton, FL: CRC Press LLC.

Schaalje, G.B., McBride, J.B., and Fellingham, G.W. (2001) "Approximation to Distributions of Test Statistics in Complex Mixed Linear Models Using SAS PROC MIXED", *SAS Users Group International (SUGI26)l*, Cary, NC: SAS Institute Inc.

Schwarz, G. (1978), "Estimating the Dimension of a Model," *Annals of Statistics*, 6, 461-464.

Searle, S.R. (1982), *Matrix Algebra Useful for Statistics*, New York: John Wiley & Sons, Inc.

Searle, S.R. (1987), *Linear Models for Unbalanced Data*, New York: John Wiley & Sons, Inc.

Searle, S.R., Casella, G., and McCulloch, C.E. (1992), *Variance Components*, New York: John Wiley & Sons, Inc.

Singer, J.D. (1998), "Using SAS PROC MIXED to Fit Multilevel Models, Hierarchical Models, and Individual Growth Models," *Journal of Educational and Behavioral Statistics*, Vol. 24, No. 4, 323-355.

Swallow, W.H. and Monahan, J.F. (1984), "Monte Carlo Comparison of ANOVA, MIVQUE, REML and ML Estimators of Variance Components," *Technometrics*, 28, 47-57.

Verbeke, G. and Molenberghs, G. (1997), *Linear Mixed Models in Practice: A SAS-Oriented Approach*, New York: Springer-Verlag.

Verbeke, G. and Molenberghs, G. (2000), *Linear Mixed Models for Longitudinal Data*, New York: Springer-Verlag.

Wedderburn, R.W.M. (1974), "Quasilikelihood Methods, Generalized Linear Models, and the Gauss-Newton Method," *Biometrika*, 61, 439-447.

Wolfinger, R.D. (1998), "Towards Practical Application of Generalized Linear Mixed Models," *Proceedings of the 13th International Workshop on Statistical Modeling*, 388-395.

Wolfinger, R.D. and Kass, R.E. (2000), "Nonconjugate Bayesian Analysis of Variance Component Models," *Biometrics*, 56, 768-774.

Wolfinger, R. and O'Connell, M. (1993), "Generalized Linear Mixed Models: A Pseudo-Likelihood Approach," *Journal of Statistical Computation and Simulation*, 48, 233-243.

Appendix C Index